Bonnard

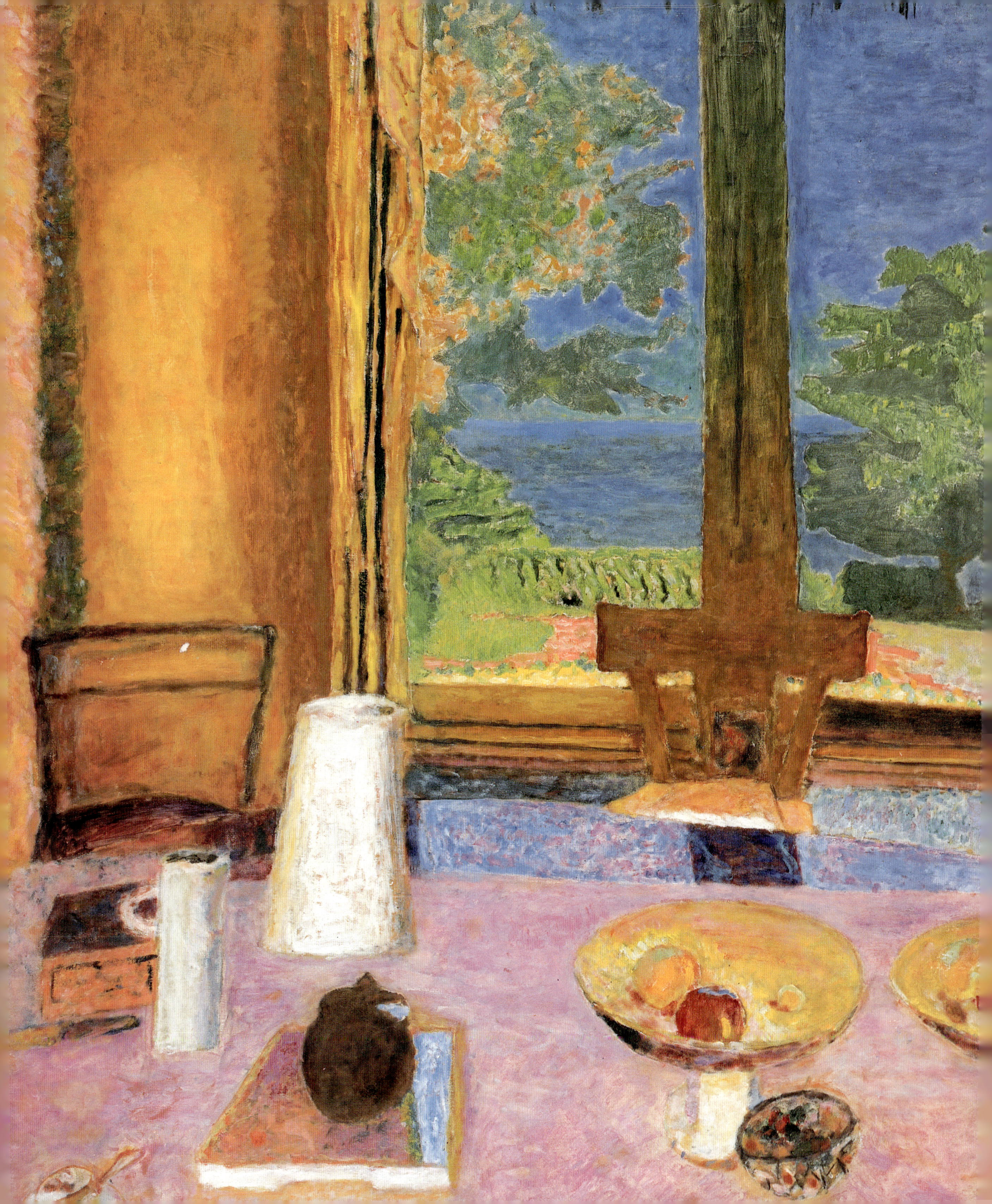

Bonnard

Nicholas Watkins

BCA
LONDON NEW YORK SYDNEY TORONTO

For Natalia and Anna

This edition published 1994
by BCA by arrangement with
Phaidon Press Limited

CN 9453

Printed in Hong Kong

Frontispiece : detail of Plate 135

Contents

Acknowledgements

I am deeply grateful to all those who made this book possible. Numerous museums, galleries, private collectors, dealers and auction houses enabled me to study works by Bonnard and provided photographs. Among those individuals and organizations who helped me in my work I would especially like to thank M. Guy Wildenstein and Mr Joseph Baillio of Wildenstein & Co., Mr Christian Neffe of JPL Fine Arts, Paul and Ellen Josefowitz, M. Marc Benady, M. et Mme Leteurte, Mr William R. Acquavella and Mr Duncan MacGuigan of Acquavella Galleries, Miss Valerie Beston of Marlborough Fine Art Ltd., Mme Sophie Fourny-Dargère, Mrs Jacqueline Cartwright of Messrs Alex Reid and Lefevre Ltd., Mr John Lumley of Christie's, Colta Ives of the Metropolitan Museum of Art, Mr Simon Matthews of Arthur Tooth & Sons, Mr William Darby of Browse & Darby, Belinda Thomson, the staffs of the libraries at the University of Leicester and Coventry University. In my research I was greatly helped by MM. Antoine and Michel Terrasse, who offered unique insights into their great-uncle's art and kindly answered my numerous questions. I owe a great debt to earlier studies of Bonnard's art and to the more recent publications listed in the notes and bibliography. I benefited enormously from discussions with Sargy Mann and Edmund Fairfax-Lucy and from the contributions of my students over the years, notably Valerie Swales. Any errors or misguided opinions that have crept into the book are due to the author alone.

My task was greatly facilitated by my head of department, Dr Alison Yarrington, by the suggestions and encouragement of my colleagues, and by two grants from our faculty research fund. The staff of the Phaidon Press did everything possible to ensure the successful production of the book. Above all, I would like to thank my wife, Nadia, and two daughters, Natalia and Anna, for sustaining me with considerable tolerance throughout a prolonged period of near total distraction.

Nicholas Watkins
Department of the History of art
University of Leicester

Preface

Pierre Bonnard (1867-1947)

Pierre Bonnard was extremely precocious. In his early twenties he made his initial contribution to the history of modern art as a founder member of the Nabis group, whose first exhibition opened in Paris in December 1891. Inspired by Gauguin, Symbolism and Japanese prints, he evolved a highly decorative style based on the direct observation of nature which has come to be seen as a new departure, conveniently filling the gap between the end of Impressionism and the advent in 1905 of Fauvism, the first movement of twentieth-century modernism. Yet he went on to develop an art that has been taken to have much in common with Impressionism; so much so, in fact, that the catalogues of successive retrospective exhibitions of his work have characterized him as the last of the Impressionists.

Bonnard made his breakthrough as a graphic artist rather than as a painter. In March 1891 his famous poster advertising France-Champagne (Plate 22) appeared on the streets of Paris, establishing a frenetically cheerful image of a liberated woman which has come to symbolize the mood of the 1890s. He went on to execute the poster for the avant-garde magazine *La Revue Blanche* (Plate 23) and a lithographic screen, *La Promenade* (Plate 31). He knew everybody who was anybody in the Parisian avant-garde of the 1890s. Everything seems to have been going for him when, towards the end of 1900, he started leaving Paris for long periods each year to work like an Impressionist in the countryside.

Bonnard's withdrawal from Paris and his subsequent reversion to the Impressionism of the 1880s, with its struggles to find a compromise between realism, light, heightened colour and the enduring qualities of classical art, posed the same problems for his contemporaries as for us today. It was as though, like Proust, he had put the shutters down on novel experiences and was going to spend the rest of his life coming to terms with, and developing, the influences that had shaped his life and art until then. The clock was stopped. Marthe, his beloved companion and later wife, stayed as an eternally youthful nymph, often a water nymph caught at her bath, while his domestic milieu of the 1890s, like his subjects drawn from a classical Golden Age, appeared to represent a legendary era of happiness which he could only cut back to in his memory through art.

Paradoxically, however, the seemingly retrogressive features of Bonnard's art are inseparably bound up with the qualities that command our attention. By picking up on issues pioneered by others, and by concentrating on familiar subjects over a long period, he was able to experiment with new ways of expressing them with greater immediacy and feeling, so as to re-create on canvas the palpitating, living presence of the visible world. There is absolutely nothing derivative about Bonnard's art: a Bonnard is always quite unmistakably a Bonnard. His contract of faith with his audience was to take as a starting point an apparently conventional glimpse of the exterior world; his originality was to express it in a highly unconventional way.

Bonnard's extraordinary ability to see things afresh came through his practice of basing a painting on the memory of a particular visual experience, which was often captured in a specific drawing. He was reluctant to paint in front of the motif as the Impressionists had done, but like his contemporary and close friend Matisse (1869–1954), he accepted the robust empiricism and freedom from systems that came with Impressionism, although he rejected their dependence on superficial sensations and their lack of compositional structure. He went on to combine the objectivity of Impressionism with the Symbolist assertion of the primacy of cultural memory and feeling. He was able to preserve through drawing the experience of the first glance – 'all one sees on first entering a room' – and then, through the contemplation of the evolving relationships between forms and colours in the studio, to infuse the canvas with feeling and to achieve a dream-like, light-filled vision of an earthly paradise, whose origins go back to the Rococo, to Watteau and the eighteenth century.

He explored this vision literally in his mythological decorations. The more immediate nudes and interiors, on the other hand, resulted in some of the most glorious paintings in the history of art. Colouristically and spatially they are extremely complex. Forms merge in a surface pattern of reflected colour. A nude, rather than a window, acts as the principal light source, while a window opens on to colour rather than a view. Objects crop up as islands in a sea of colour. Above all, these paintings are about the transforming power of light to absorb all form and colour in the expressive atmosphere of a vision. Bonnard told a young painter, 'Our God is light. A day will come when you will understand what that means.'

This book does not set out to reconcile the graphic inventiveness of Bonnard's early work with his mature explorations of colour, composition and light, but to show how the very complexity of his art was in part the product of a culture dominated by antitheses on many levels. The decade of the 1890s, Bonnard's formative years, was a period both of experimentation in the arts and of nostalgia as the century came to an end. Realism competed with idealism, the transient with the permanent, in Bonnard's construction of a decorative art form derived from nature. Stylistic solutions and themes that he developed in this period persisted throughout his career, making his art at times notoriously difficult to date. So rather than impose a rigidly chronological structure, I have followed Bonnard's method, chopping backwards and forwards in time as his themes evolved and developed. Chapters one and two deal with themes arising out of the analysis of his art in the first two decades of his career, from *c.*1889 to *c.*1899 and from *c.*1900 to *c.*1910, while chapters three and four concentrate in particular on his evolution of two themes from *c.*1911 to 1939: the dialogue between the north and the south in his treatment of landscape, and the transformation of the domestic interior into an internal paradise. Chapter five covers Bonnard's final years from 1940 to 1947.

A central argument is that Bonnard was not a sentimental survivor of Impressionism but a highly demanding formal artist responding to challenges in the evolving culture of painting. He successfully involves us in the formal problems posed in a painting to the point where we see everyday subjects in a completely new way. It is not surprising, therefore, that artists, alert to questions of form and colour shaped in relation to subject-matter, rather than critics, have been largely responsible for the serious reassessment of Bonnard's art.

Chapter One

The early years

Pierre Bonnard emerges from the literary sources and photographs as an endearing loner, sheltering behind metal-rimmed glasses and the floppy brim of a crumpled summer hat, the last link with the gentler values of nineteenth-century French culture and a fitting antidote to the extravagances of modernism and the subsequent manic quest for international stardom. With the slightly shambolic gait, overlarge limbs and the unexpected enthusiasms of a protracted adolescence, he could be both entertaining and disconcerting. The critic Pierre Courthion described him as having the 'stupified expression of a dog leaving water'.[1] His modesty, alert intelligence and playful sense of humour were accompanied by a stubborn, melancholic, sometimes sardonic side to his personality. His natural self-defensiveness could, according to his early supporter, the critic Claude Roger-Marx, border on distrust.[2] He avoided theories and was notoriously reluctant to accept anything without persuasive evidence. His restlessness later found an easy outlet in a passion for motoring. As he grew older he became increasingly cut off from even his closest friends by an antisocial wife, although, in fairness to her, this enforced isolation may have created the necessary conditions for his art.

While Bonnard never gave anything away in his diary, beyond constant references to the weather, his self-portraits, by contrast, which for the most part remained in his possession to his death, provide an intensely personal record of his life: the buttoned-up prodigy in his early twenties, self-consciously including the tools of his adopted profession (Plate 2); the gangly, naked lover in his thirties retrieving his clothes from behind a screen (Plate 3); the middle-aged artist caught glancing back with the look of a mature satyr fired up by the contemplation of his nymphs (Plate 4); the puny boxer in his sixties, face pulped red, defiantly struggling on (Plate 5); the introverted recluse in his seventies, devoured by light in the silence of his home (Plate 6); and finally the aged, monk-like figure nearing death, completely resigned to his fate, staring with blank eyes through the mask of his face (Plate 7). To show himself literally stripped naked, baring both his body and his soul, goes against a common perception of his art and is strikingly at odds with the mood of his work as a whole. But as Bonnard himself remarked in his diary entry of 17 January 1944: 'Celui qui chante n'est pas toujours heureux' – 'He who sings is not always happy.'

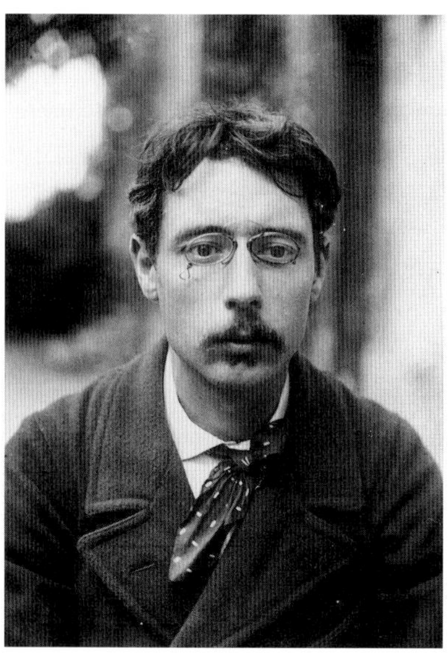

1
Pierre Bonnard, *c.*1890.
Photograph by Alfred Natanson

Pierre Bonnard belonged to the same generation as Toulouse-Lautrec (1864–1901) and Henri Matisse (1869–1954). He was born on 3 October 1867 at Fontenay-aux-Roses, a suburb of Paris, the second child of Eugène Bonnard, a successful career civil servant who had worked himself up the hierarchy to be *Chef de Bureau* at the Ministry of

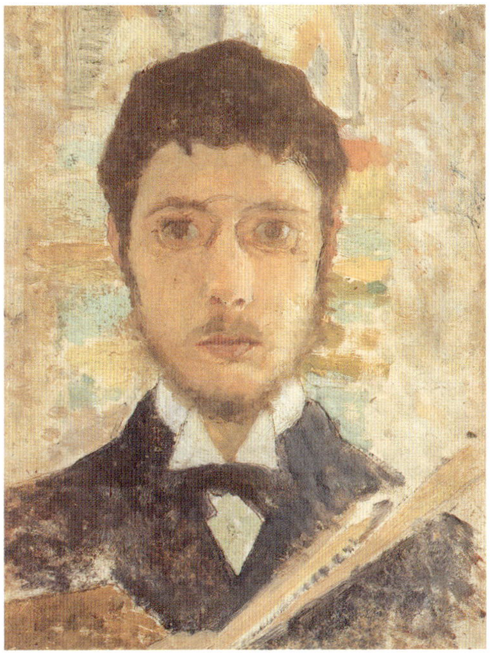

2
*Portrait de l'artiste par lui-même. c.*1889.
Tempera on board, 21.5×15.8cm.
Private collection, Fontainebleau

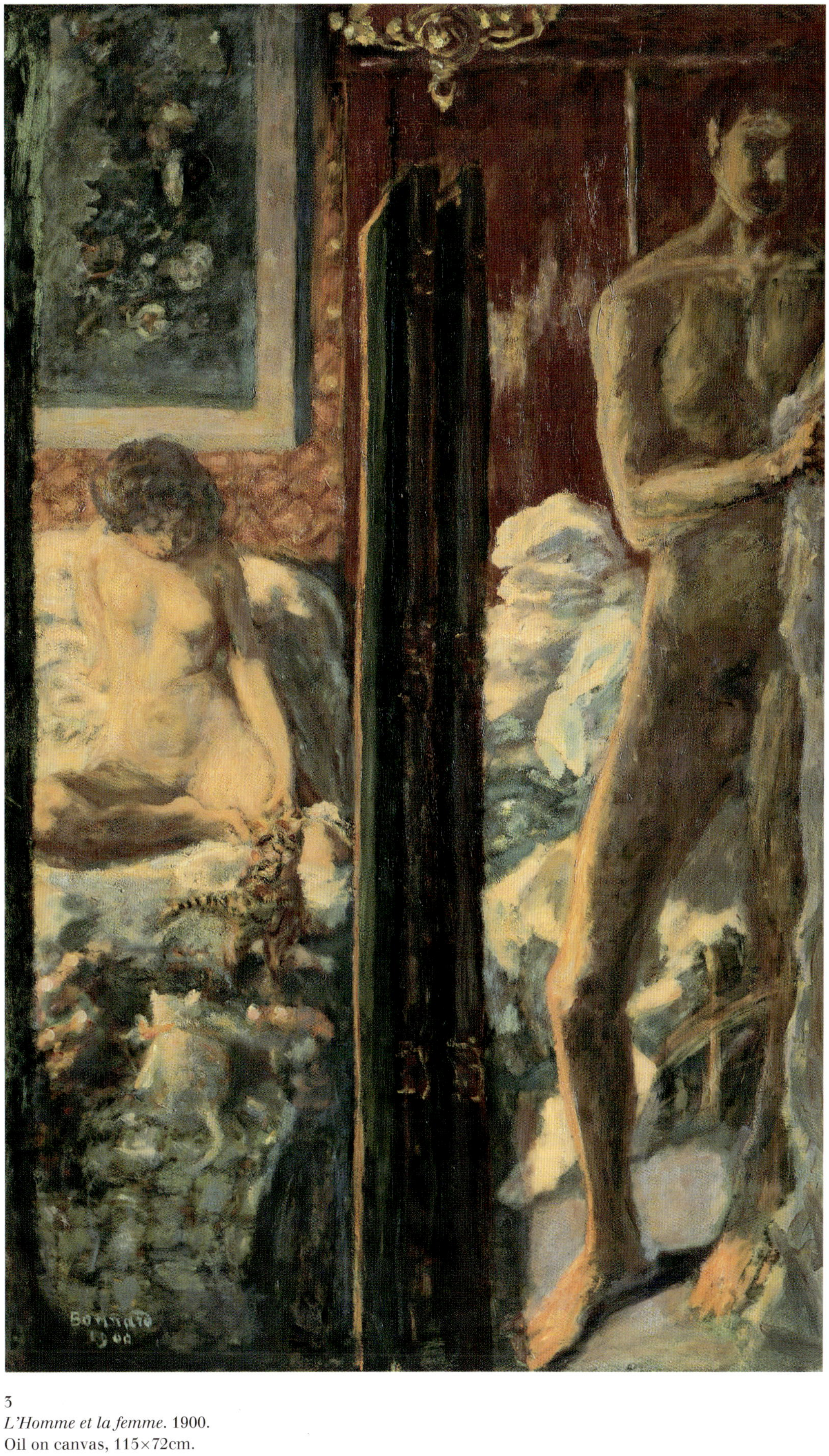

3
L'Homme et la femme. 1900.
Oil on canvas, 115×72cm.
Musée d'Orsay, Paris

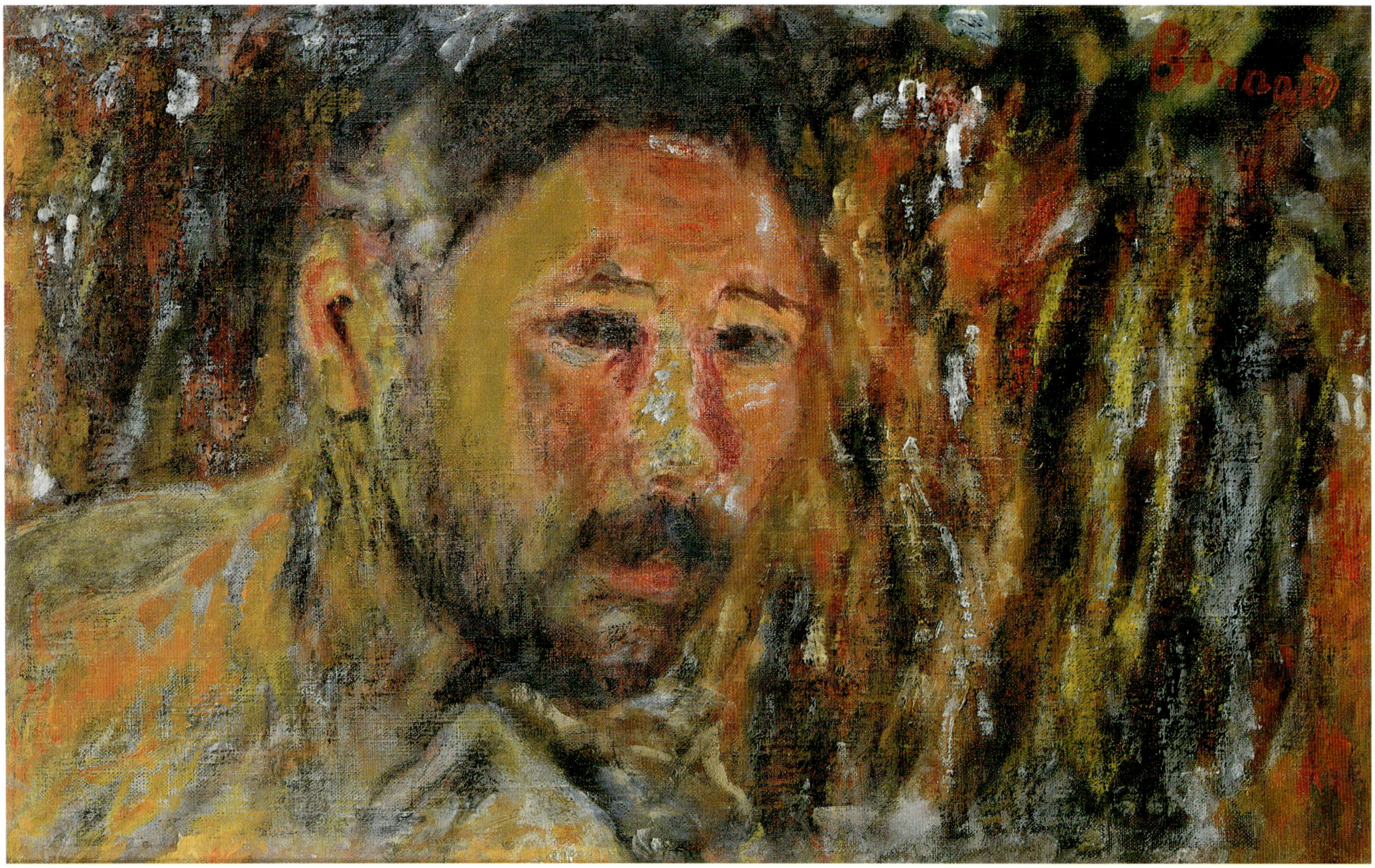

4
Autoportrait à la barbe. *c.* 1920.
Oil on canvas mounted on board, 28×44.5cm.
Private collection, London

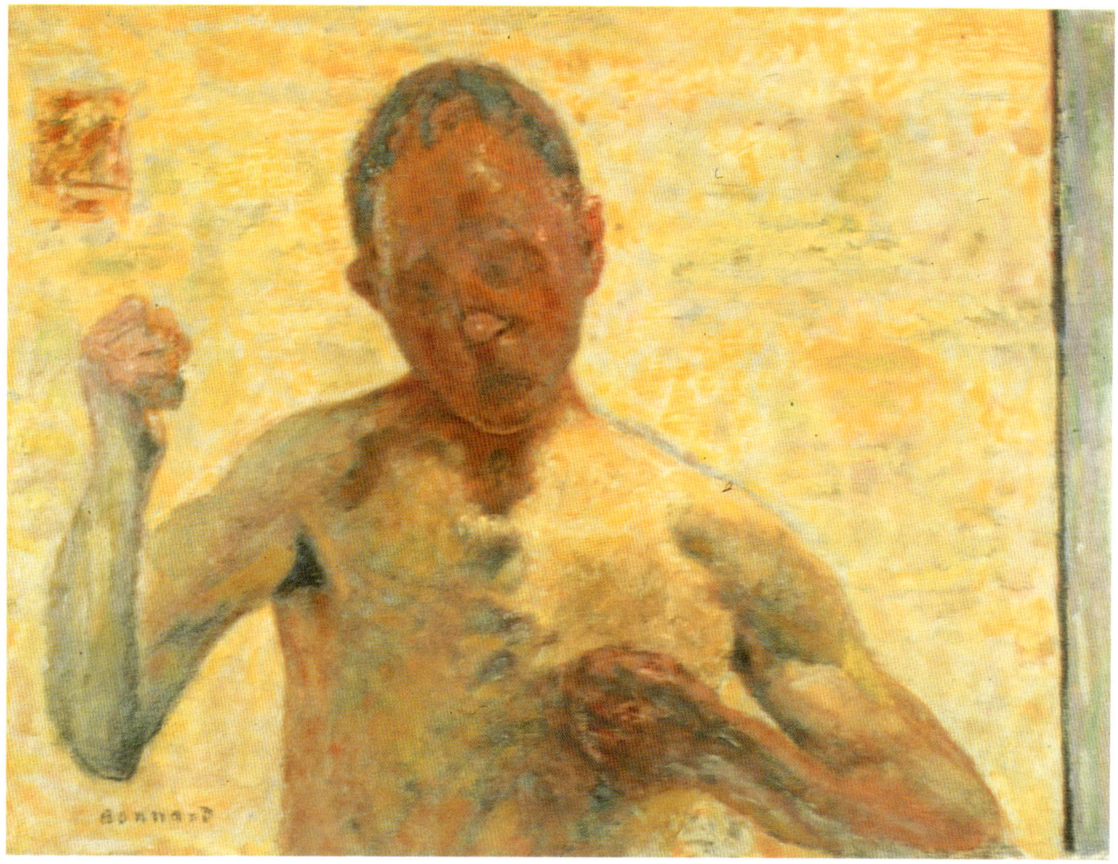

5
Le Boxeur. 1931.
Oil on canvas, 54×74cm.
Private collection, Switzerland

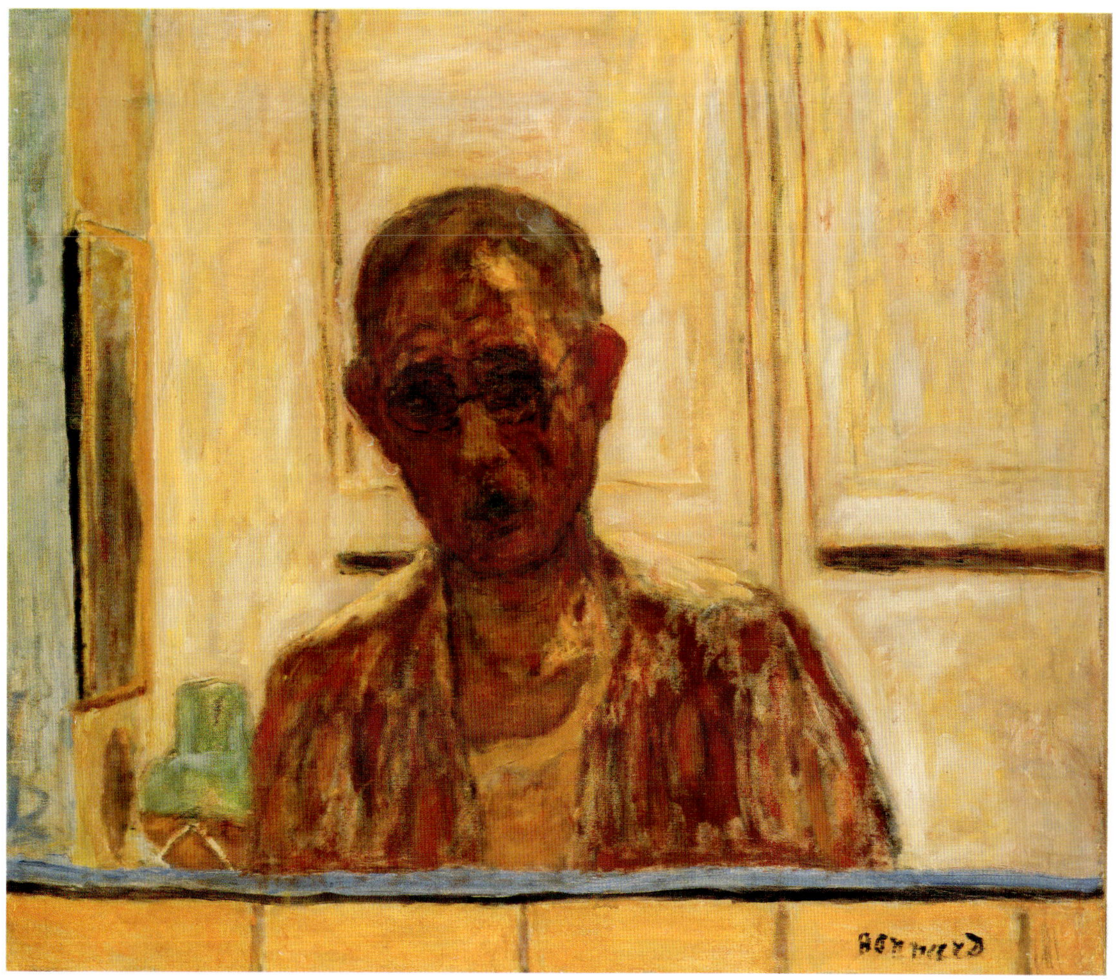

6
Autoportrait dans la glace. 1939.
Oil on canvas, 56×68.5cm.
Private collection, USA

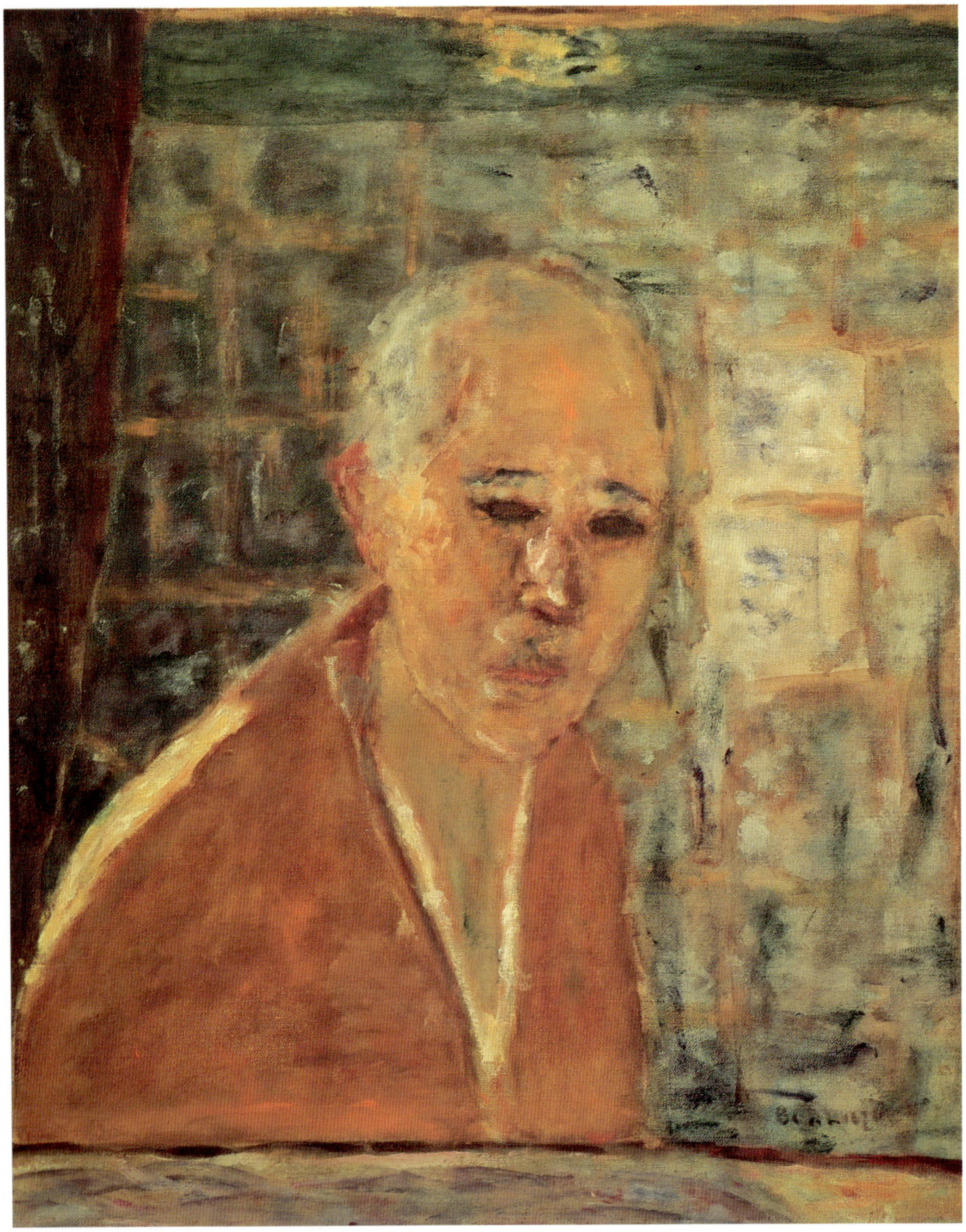

7
Portrait du peintre par lui-même. 1945.
Oil on canvas, 56×46cm.
Private collection, USA

War, and his wife Élisabeth, née Mertzdorff, who came from an Alsatian family that had apparently lost most of its money. His elder brother Charles was born in 1864 and his sister Andrée in 1872. The immediate family circle was completed by his maternal grandmother, Mme Frédéric Mertzdorff. Eugène Bonnard's roots lay in the country, and he retained his family home, Le Clos, in Le Grand-Lemps, a village tucked away in the Dauphiné (now Isère) between Lyons and Grenoble near the French Alps, where his father had been a farmer and grain merchant.[3]

Like most boys from his background, Pierre was dispatched to boarding school at the age of ten to be moulded into membership of the upper-middle class, the *bonne bourgeoisie*, make potentially useful contacts and pass the baccalaureate. After attending the lycée at Vanves, he was moved to and fro between two prestigious lycées in Paris, the lycée Louis-le-Grand and the lycée Charlemagne, where he passed the baccalaureate.[4] He was a quiet but extremely able student who won school prizes and developed what was to become a lifelong passion for classical literature and philosophy, and for such authors as La Fontaine.[5] He certainly drew and painted while still at school in Paris, and on leaving attended part-time a private art school, the Académie Julian, to prepare for his entrance into the École des Beaux-Arts in March 1887. However, any wish that he might have expressed of becoming an artist was temporarily thwarted by his father, who steered him towards the law, with a view to his following in his own footsteps into the civil service. He was enrolled in the Faculté de Droit in 1886, passed his bar exams in 1888, but failed the civil service exam. The obvious explanation for this failure by a bright student is that he was by now determined to study art full time and only going through the motions to oblige his father.

Bonnard evidently detested both boarding school and the law and sought release in two abiding passions: art and the countryside. Like Matisse who similarly obtained his father's reluctant permission to abandon the law, he took up art more as a quest for personal freedom than as the adoption of an alternative career. He later explained in an interview with Raymond Cogniat: 'I think that what attracted me then was less art itself than the artistic life, with all that I thought it meant in terms of free expression of imagination and freedom to live as one pleased. Of course I had been attracted by painting and drawing for a long time, without this becoming an irresistible passion; at any cost, however, I wanted to escape from a monotonous existence.'[6]

Pierre Bonnard's formative years were extraordinarily important for his future art. Few artists drew so extensively on their family circle for subject-matter. Much can be made of his reaction against an authoritarian father and a repressive school system, and – conversely – the support and encouragement he received from his mother and grandmother. Upright to the point of being severe, Eugène Bonnard probably behaved no differently from many a father in his position. He was himself interested in art, especially Delacroix, loved gardens, and even tried woodcarving in retirement. In the first major painting of the family, *La Partie de croquet*, 1892 (Plate 14), the father, wearing a shapeless hat, is placed above the bush in the left-hand corner without in any way dominating the proceedings. In fact his father, who died on 22 November 1895, and mother, who was embarrassed at posing, appeared rarely in Bonnard's early work. Featured instead were his cousin and first love Berthe Schaedlin, his grandmother, an ever-available model, and his sister Andrée and her husband, the composer Claude Terrasse (1867–1923; they were married at Le Grand-Lemps on 25 September 1890), and their children. The Terrasses became Bonnard's surrogate family, his closest friends and promoters.

Coming after the confinement of boarding school, Bonnard's annual holidays at Le Clos were for him a return to an earthly paradise, a place of childhood innocence, and he continued to go there each year until the house was sold in 1928. His early memories of the house merged with memories of the Terrasse children holidaying there in the 1890s, to provide recurring subjects in his art. He subsequently mythologized his childhood, and in old age published his reminiscences in the form of a series of letters, focusing on little vignettes which could well act as descriptions of some of his paintings in the 1890s: the dining room at Le Clos with the dog at his feet and the two cats on the table, the inquisitive cow sticking its head through the window, picking fruit in the orchard, and a boiling hot summer with the Terrasse children cooling off in the ornamental pond by the house.[7]

Although Bonnard began drawing while still at the lycée, his earliest datable paintings are little landscapes executed, possibly *en plein air*, in the neighbourhood of Le Grand-Lemps in 1887 and 1888, when he was already a part-time art student at the Académie Julian. Given his later reputation for informal, slightly loose compositions, they show by contrast a decided concern for geometric structure. For instance, *Petit paysage du Dauphiné*, *c.*1888 (Plate 8), is composed in horizontal tonal bands, going from the dark foreground strip to the line of grey hills, caught by pink patches of light, rising up behind the central accent of the red farm roofs in the background. This predilection for naturalistic observation within a tight geometric structure has quite justifiably given rise to a comparison with Corot's landscape studies, rather than with the work of any of Bonnard's teachers at the time.

Bonnard seems to have owed remarkably little to his art school education at the Académie Julian and the École des Beaux-Arts, and there is no mention of him ever copying in the Louvre while at the École des Beaux-Arts. He was only in the system from 1886 to mid-1889, some of that part-time, and even then his attendance was intermittent.[8] He thus finished when Matisse was only just beginning a decade-long apprenticeship. Instruction at the Académie Julian revolved round the gradual mastery of the human figure. Although Bonnard appreciated the wider curriculum of the École des Beaux-Arts, he preferred the freedom of the Académie Julian, where he could come and go as he pleased without having his work corrected by the master, and he returned there while at the École. He also got on well with Paul Sérusier (1864–1927), *massier* or student-treasurer at the Académie Julian, who was to play a key role in the formation of the Nabis. Nevertheless, while at the École he entered – unsuccessfully – for the Prix

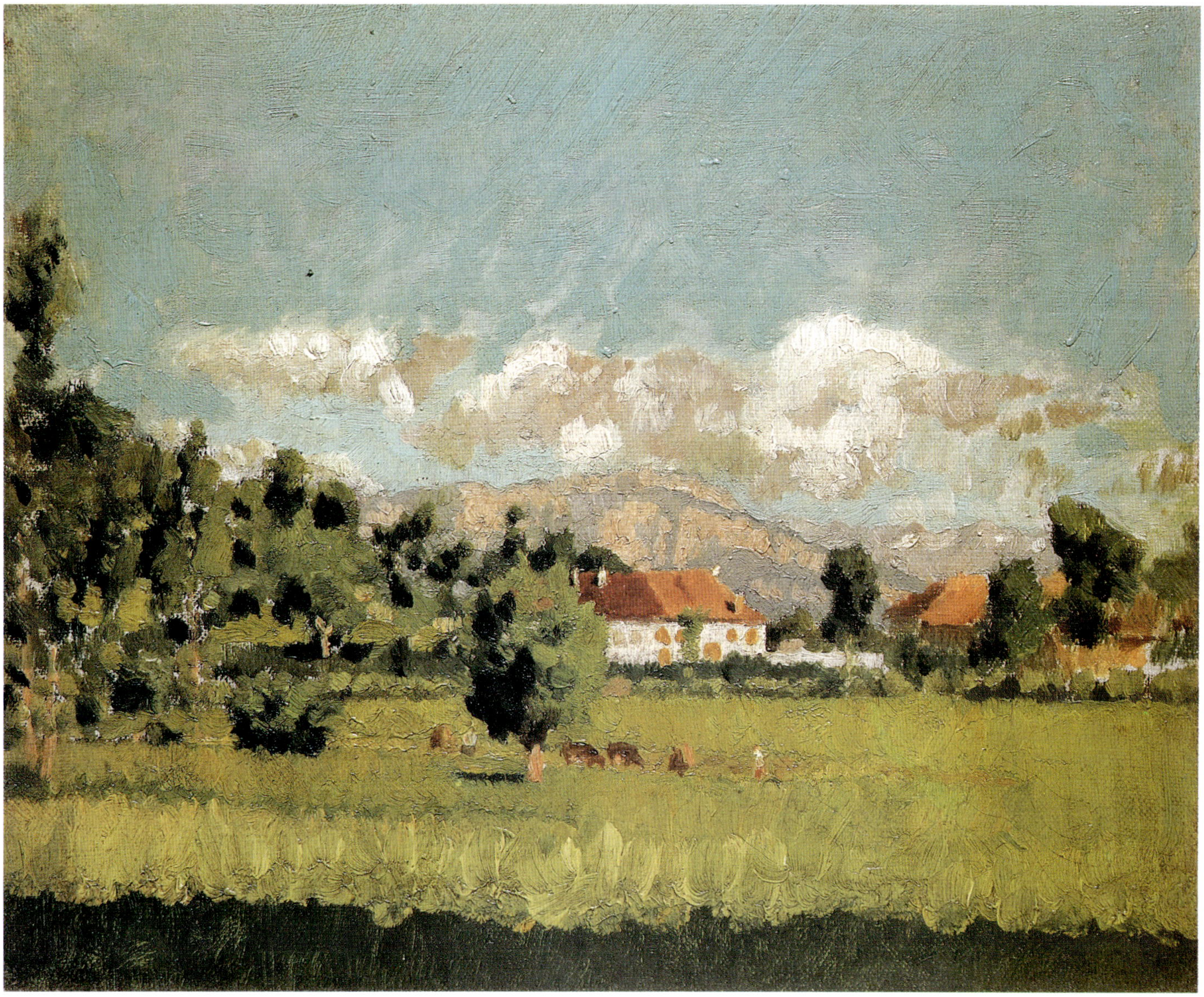

8
*Petit paysage du Dauphiné. c.*1888.
Oil on canvas, 21×26cm.
Private collection, Fontainebleau

de Rome, the ultimate objective of a student bent on official recognition, with the unlikely subject of the Triumph of Mordecai; unless of course it was done as a ruse to avoid military service. In retrospect, though, one could argue that Bonnard's lifelong belief in the primacy of drawing and in the female nude as subject-matter, two central tenets of the classical tradition, was a direct outcome of his brief spell of academic instruction.

If Bonnard got little from his teachers, he certainly owed a considerable debt to his contemporaries.[9] Paul Sérusier visited Gauguin in Brittany in October 1888, and under his guidance painted in the Bois d'Amour near Pont-Aven a little landscape on a cigar-box lid, known as *The Talisman* (Plate 10), which he took back to Paris and first showed to his friends and fellow students at the Académie Julian, Maurice Denis (1870–1943), Paul Ranson (1861–1909), Henri-Gabriel Ibels (1867–1936) and Bonnard. They were unaware of Impressionism, let alone Post-Impressionism, at the time, and the painting came to them as a complete revelation. Gauguin's very words to Sérusier were set down by Denis: 'What colour do you see that tree? Is it green? Then use green, the finest green on your palette. And that shadow? It's blue, if anything? Don't be afraid to paint it as blue as you possibly can.'[10] Central to the thinking behind the painting was the notion that a work of art was a decorative entity in its own right and that enhanced colours – in addition to representing the subject – could in themselves convey feeling and thought. Denis summoned up this approach in his famous 'Définition du néotraditionnisme', published in the review *Art et critique* in 1890: 'Remember that a picture, before being a war horse, a nude woman or some anecdote, is essentially a flat surface covered with colours and assembled in a certain order.' To pursue these ideas further, the Nabis was formed by the five friends early in 1889.

The initial grouping was soon expanded to include Édouard Vuillard (1868–1940), Ker-Xavier Roussel (1967–1944), René Piot (1866–1934) and, a little later, the Dutchman Jan Verkade (1868–1946), the Dane Francesco Mögens Ballin (1871–1914), the Swiss Félix Vallotton (1865–1925), the sculptor Georges Lacombe (1868–1916) and the Hungarian Jozsef Rippl-Ronaï (1861–1927). Finally, in 1895, just when it was losing momentum, Aristide Maillol (1861–1944) became associated with the group. There is something of the nature of a religious experience about the Nabis' formation; the very name was taken from the Hebrew word for a prophet. The members behaved rather self-consciously as a mystical brotherhood, gave each other nicknames (Bonnard was the 'Nabis japonard' because of his love of Japanese prints), adopted oriental costumes at monthly dinners, and attended weekly meetings at Ranson's studio, christened The Temple, with Madame Ranson presiding as 'the light of the Temple'. How seriously they took all this is difficult to say.

The Nabis were part of the wider Symbolist movement, with which they shared a general distaste for science and material progress. The Symbolists' quest for a new artistic language went hand-in-hand with a reassertion of traditional values and practices. Underlying their various ideas was the perception that contemporary society had

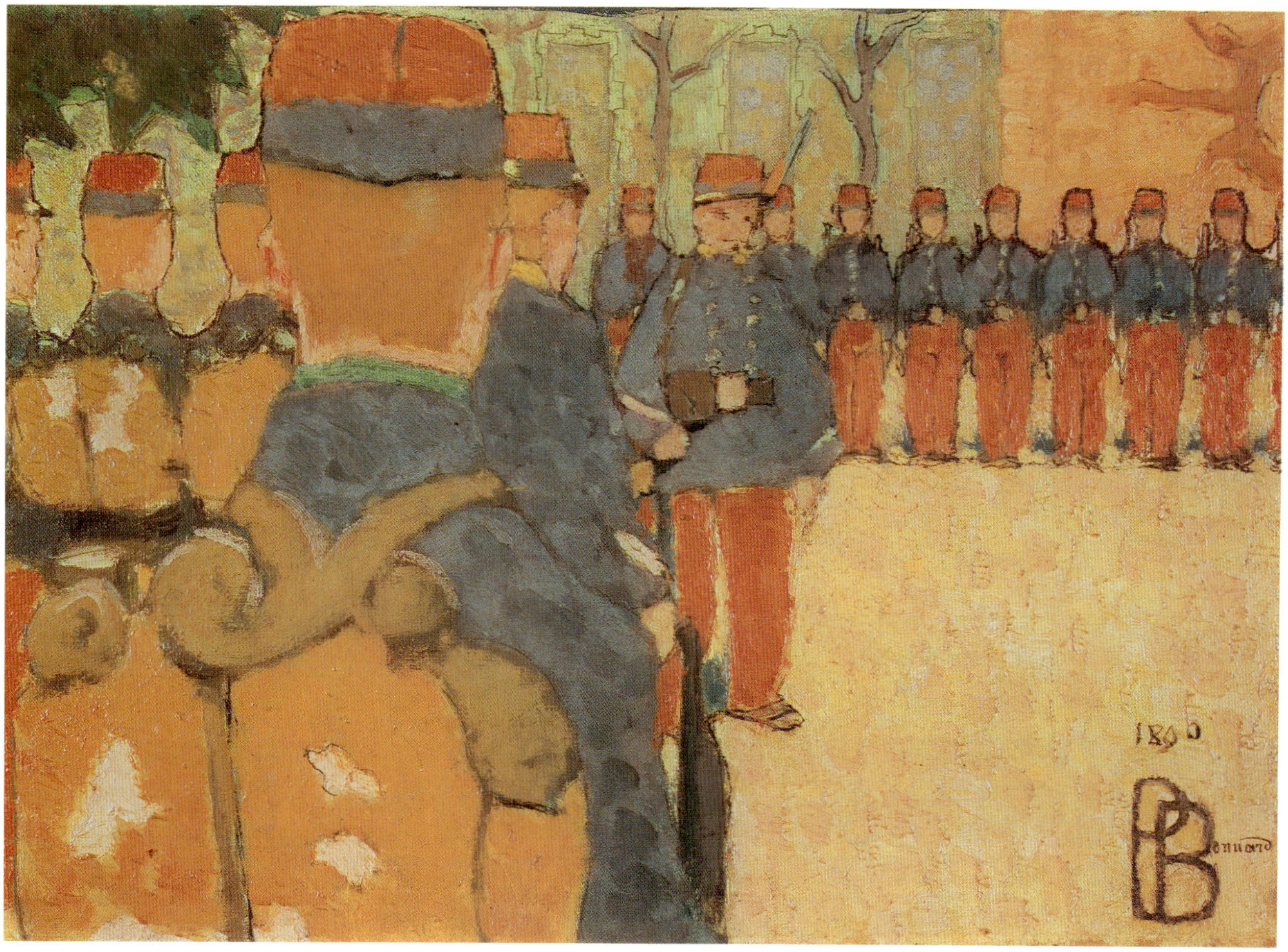

9
L'Exercise. 1890.
Oil on canvas, 23×31cm.
Private collection, Paris

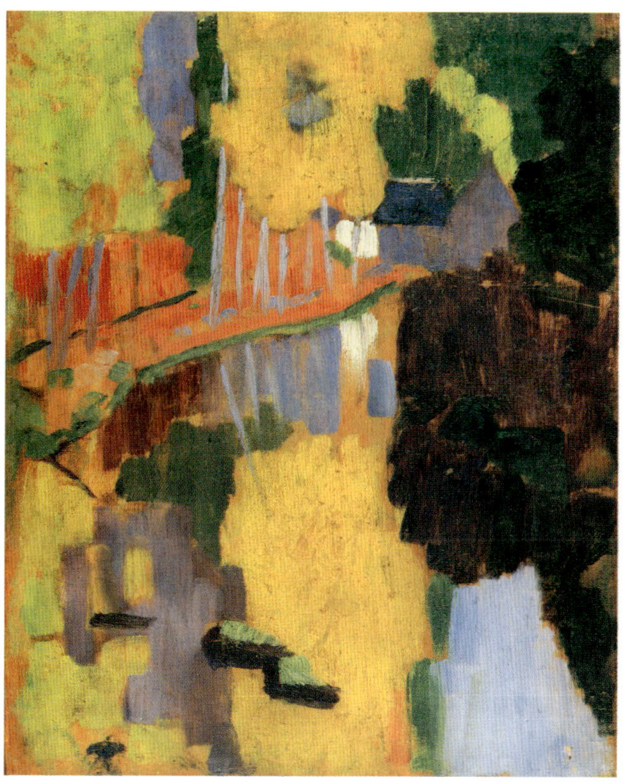

10
Paul Sérusier
The Talisman. 1888.
Oil on panel, 27×22cm.
Musée d'Orsay, Paris

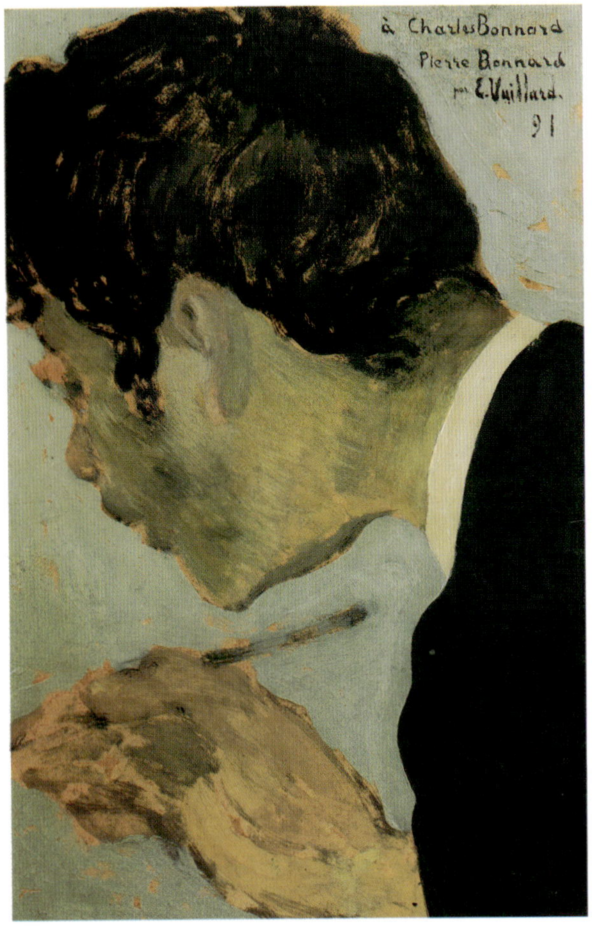

11
Édouard Vuillard
Portrait de Pierre Bonnard. 1891.
Oil on board, 24.6×12.8cm.
Private collection, Fontainebleau

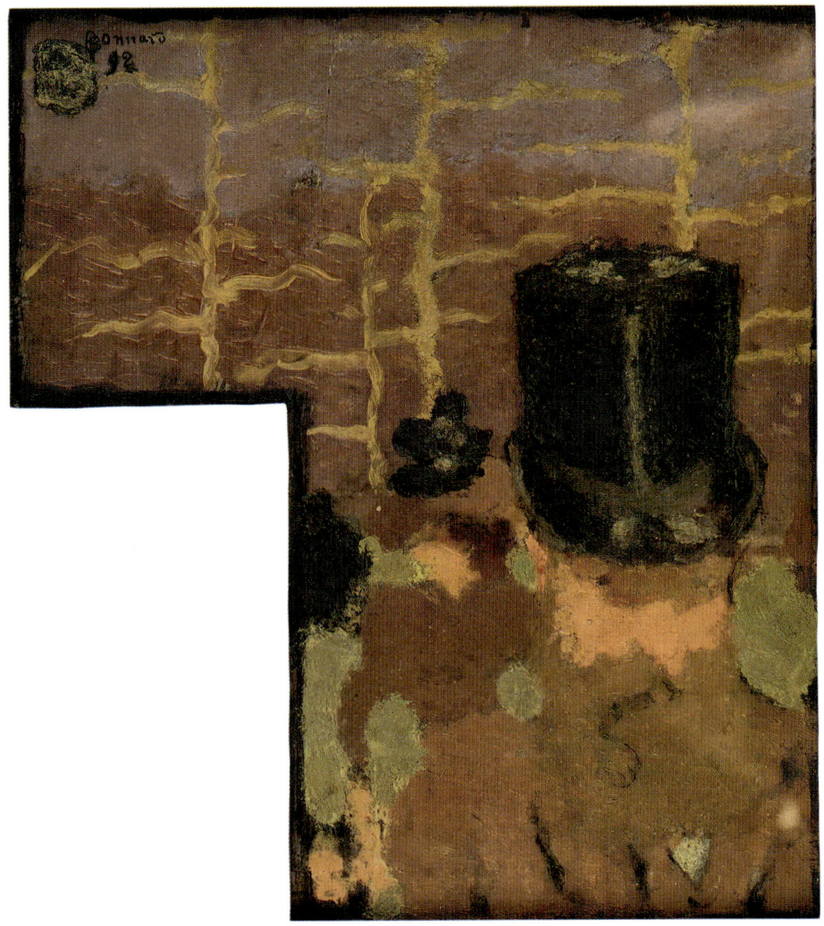

12
Portrait de Vuillard. 1892.
Oil on panel, 10.8×24.2 and 14.5×21.8cm.
Musée d'Orsay, Paris

lost its roots. The continuous drift from country to city had cut people off from the land, just as the belief in materialism had cut them off from religion and cultural memory, alienating feeling from thought and action. They equated naturalism with materialism, and regarded it as a superficial view of reality bound up with the representation of surface appearances. Art, they felt, was a form of knowledge whose spiritual task was to express the mysterious aspects of existence.

The Symbolist movement as a whole embraced a wide variety of individual views, and likewise the ideological positions of the Nabis were as diverse as the backgrounds of the members themselves. Maurice Denis, a devout Roman Catholic, wanted to restore tradition and religion to art.[11] Ballin and Verkade converted to Catholicism, the latter becoming a monk at Beuron. By contrast, Lacombe and Ranson shared the republican anticlerical obsession, while Ranson believed in theosophy and the occult. Sérusier was both a theosophist and a Catholic. Roussel, Ibbels and Vallotton were anarchists.[12] Although Bonnard and Vuillard shared a studio with Denis in 1891 there is no evidence that they subscribed to his beliefs. If anything they stood apart from the others in their distrust of theory and in their adherence to the study of nature as the basis of art. However, themes and issues common to the Nabis run through Bonnard's work. Bonnard and Vuillard were extremely close. They saw each other almost daily and for a time lived together and shared a studio. They had many friends and patrons in common. They even went on holiday together. Vuillard painted Bonnard in 1891 (Plate 11), myopically poring over his work. They addressed each other formally, and Bonnard painted Vuillard in 1892 (Plate 12), formally attired in a top hat.

Two major influences shaped Bonnard's early style: Gauguin and Japanese art. He saw some sixty-four paintings by Gauguin and his followers, seventeen by Gauguin alone, at the exhibition of the 'Impressionist and Synthetist Group', organized by Gauguin at the Café Volpini in June 1889 to coincide with the Universal Exhibition. Symbolism, like Surrealism later, began as a literary movement, and Gauguin was the first artist to make a concerted attempt to find within the vocabulary of painting – colour, line and composition – an equivalent for the Symbolist poets' use of language to evoke, rather than just describe, a subject. His solution was to evolve a simplified style of flat colour interacting with line in the definition of form. Something of Gauguin's influence can be seen in the flat style of Bonnard's *L'Exercise* (Plate 9), painted as an emotional response to the brutishness and mindless boredom of his military service from the end of 1889 to the spring of 1890. There is no escaping the over-disciplined arrangement of the composition in successive lines, from the bull-necked automaton filling the foreground on the left to the stilted line of men ordered like toy soldiers across the background on the right. A comparison between Gauguin's celebrated *Vision after the Sermon*, 1888 (Plate 13) and Bonnard's *La Partie de croquet* (Plate 14) shows Bonnard adapting Gauguin's style and compositional methods to his own ends, and choosing subjects drawn from his own experience rather than from the Pont-Aven group. Bonnard's great-nephew Antoine Terrasse has pointed out the clever transcription of the figure of Jacob wrestling with the angel in the background of *Vision after the Sermon* into the ecstatic ring of dancing women in *La Partie de croquet*.[13] The juxtaposition of foreground and background, literally of two levels of reality, is clearly evident in both.

Gauguin's influence on Bonnard was soon superseded by that of Japanese art, *ukiyo-e* woodblock prints, textiles, kimonos and other decorative artefacts. *Japonisme* had become a fashion in the mid-1870s, but each generation adapted it to its own ends. Bonnard had every opportunity to see and collect woodblock prints. Siegfried Bing (1838–1905) was instrumental in promoting Japanese art, through both his shop in the rue Chauchat and the monthly publication *Le Japon artistique* (1888–91), and he was largely responsible for the enormous exhibition of some 725 woodblock prints and 421 illustrated books, held at the École des Beaux-Arts in April and May 1890, which marked the zenith of *Japonisme*'s popularity.[14]

Bonnard discovered in Japanese woodblock prints a way of avoiding the nostalgic element in Gauguin's art, as he explained to Gaston Diehl in 1943: 'I covered the walls of my room with this naïve and gaudy imagery. To me, Gauguin and Sérusier alluded to the past. But what I had in front of me was something tremendously alive and extremely clever.'[15] Furthermore, it suggested to him novel ways of structuring highly decorative compositions in interlocking patterns and sinuous arabesques, while retaining the freshness and immediacy of the direct experience of nature. *Le Peignoir*, *c.*1890 (Plate 15), for instance, is overtly Japanese in its format, subject and style.[16] The graceful figure is seen from the back to exploit the curving line of her flowing form. Floral patterns unite foreground and background in an overall rhythm, and actual silk is glued to the canvas to emphasize the physicality of the painting as a decorative object.

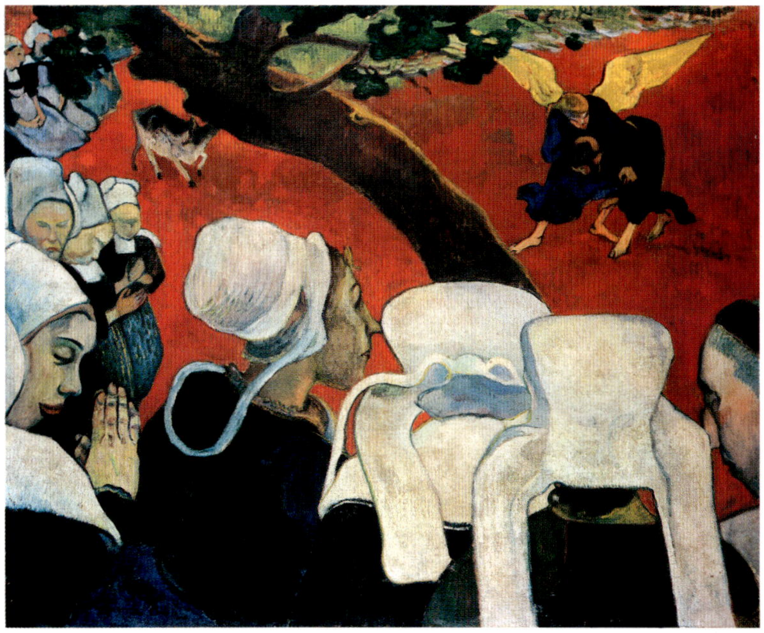

13
Paul Gauguin
Vision after the Sermon. 1888.
Oil on canvas, 73×92cm.
National Gallery of Scotland, Edinburgh

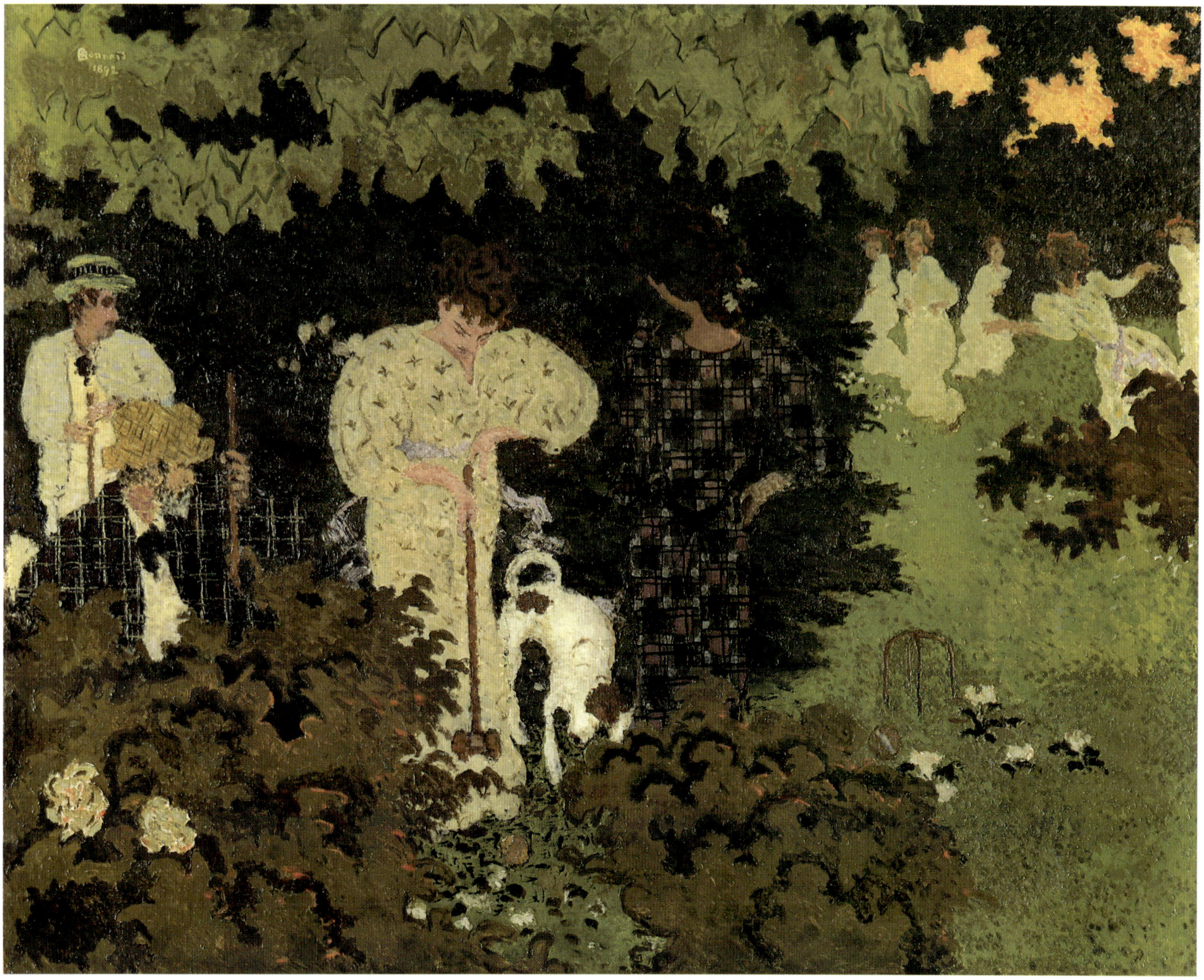

14
La Partie de croquet. 1892.
Oil on canvas, 130×162cm.
Musée d'Orsay, Paris

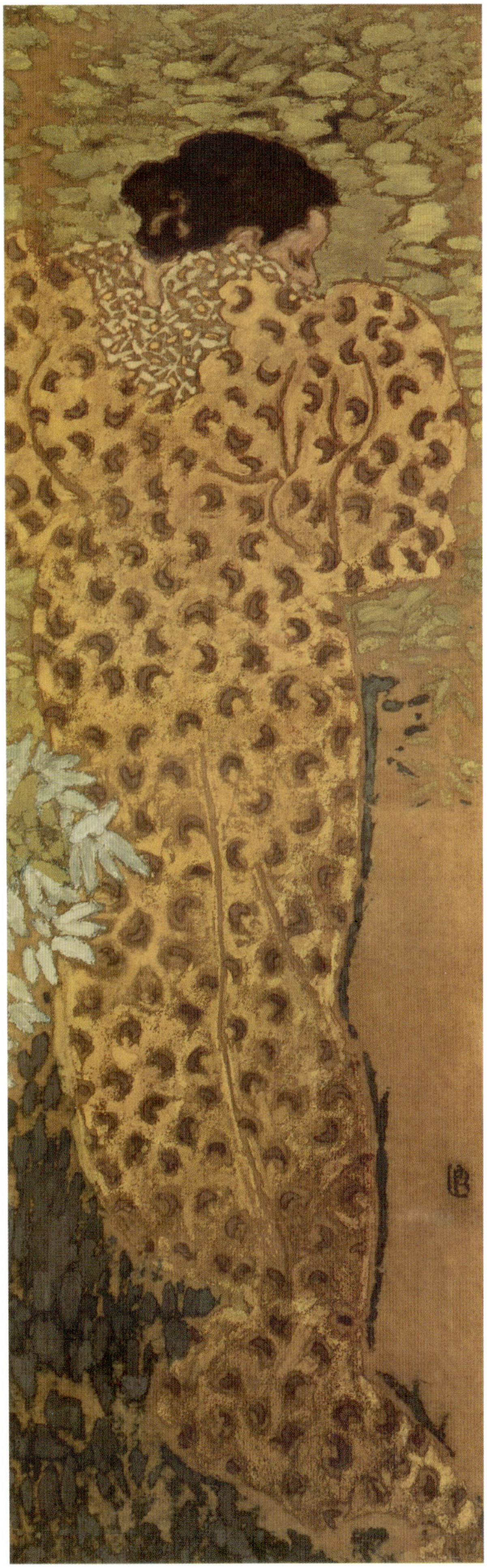

15
Le Peignoir. *c*.1890.
Oil on silk mounted on canvas, 154×54cm.
Musée d'Orsay, Paris

In *Femmes au chien*, 1891 (Plate 16), Bonnard employed the Japanese compositional method of banking the two women and the dog up behind each other to suggest the intimacy of their relationship, and then creating depth through the abrupt change in scale to the three men in the top left-hand corner. The dog, which looks as though it is knitted, seems to act as a surrogate for Bonnard himself. The still life *Les Boules de neige*, 1891 (Plate 18), with eight flowers, their leaves and a hovering butterfly all pressed in a pattern against the picture plane, takes up a subject common in Japanese prints. The butterfly conjured up the idea of a beautiful young woman, while the flowers suggested a display of her beauty. Bonnard pursued this analogy in his seductive *Portrait de Berthe Schaedlin*, 1892 (Plate 19), with her hair writhing in ringlets like Medusa's snakes and framed by a painted floral border.

Above all, Japanese prints awakened in Bonnard the emotive power of pure colour as an expressive and constructional entity, as he later recalled: 'I realized that colour could express everything, as it did in this exhibition, with no need for relief or texture. I understood that it was possible to translate light, shapes and character by colour alone, without the need for values.'[17] This can be seen in the way he constructed his sister Andrée's red dress in *Le Corsage à carreaux*, 1892 (Plate 17) out of what looks like a mosaic of brightly coloured tesserae. The play between surface pattern and illusionistic space became one of Bonnard's abiding interests.

The Nabis' emphasis on the autonomy of the work of art as a decorative object in its own right led to their breaking down the barrier between the fine and decorative arts and to the belief that they could take part with all the other arts – poetry, music and theatre – in a total art work, a *Gesamtkunstwerk*. According to Bonnard, 'Our generation always sought to link art with life. At that time I personally envisaged a popular art that was of everyday application: engravings, fans, furniture, screens, etc.'[18] Japanese art again served as his primary source of inspiration. He designed a desk, since lost, for Thadée Natanson, and in October 1891 entered a competition, organized by the Union Centrale des Arts Décoratifs, to design within a limited budget and without plagiarism furniture for a dining room. Bonnard's scheme was rejected by the jury, but he went on to develop his design for the bottom right-hand door of the cabinet into the decorative painting *Deux chiens jouant*, 1891 (Plate 20). Although the treatment of the dogs is stylized, they derive from studies of an actual dog, perhaps Ravageau, who features in a number of paintings of that year. He also designed fans in the Japanese style, ceramics and stained glass. None of these could exactly be described as popular art forms readily available to a mass market. It was more a moral stance to affirm the collaborative ideal of artists working together like anonymous medieval craftsmen on common projects.

The experimental theatre was the only area where this ideal became in any way a reality. In 1890 Bonnard contributed two projects to the Théâtre Libre, founded by André Antoine in 1887 to bring theatre closer to life through more naturalistic productions. In 1891 Sérusier, Bonnard and Vuillard, who was especially interested in theatre,

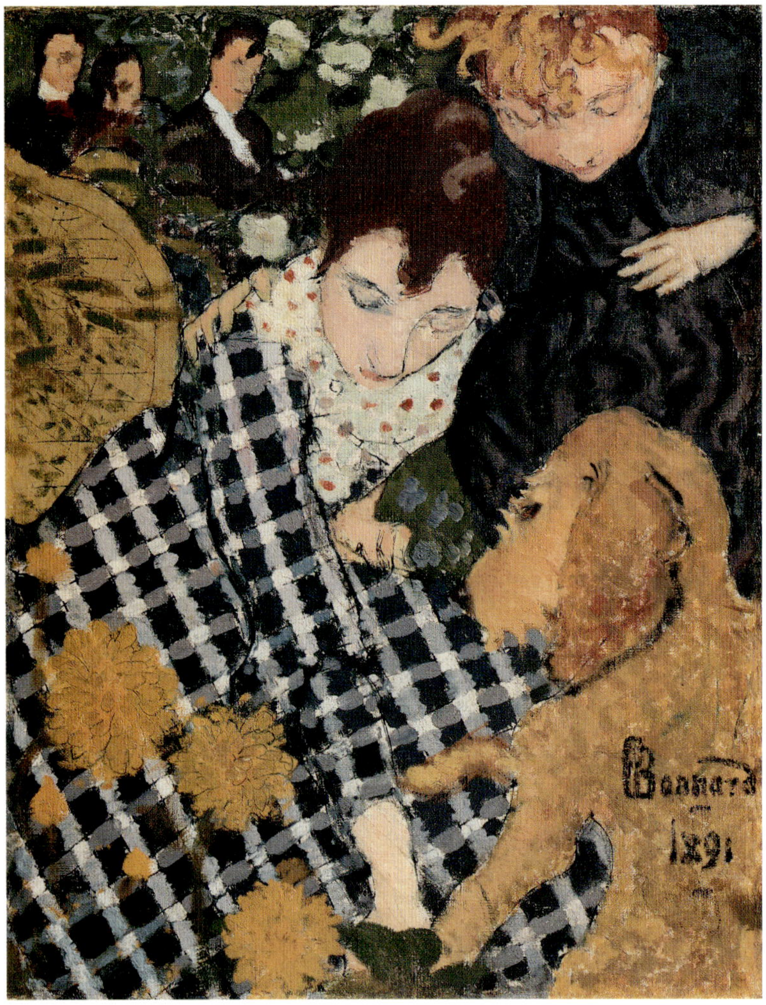

16
Femmes au chien. 1891.
Oil on canvas, 40.6×32.4cm.
Sterling and Francine Clark Art Institute, Williamstown

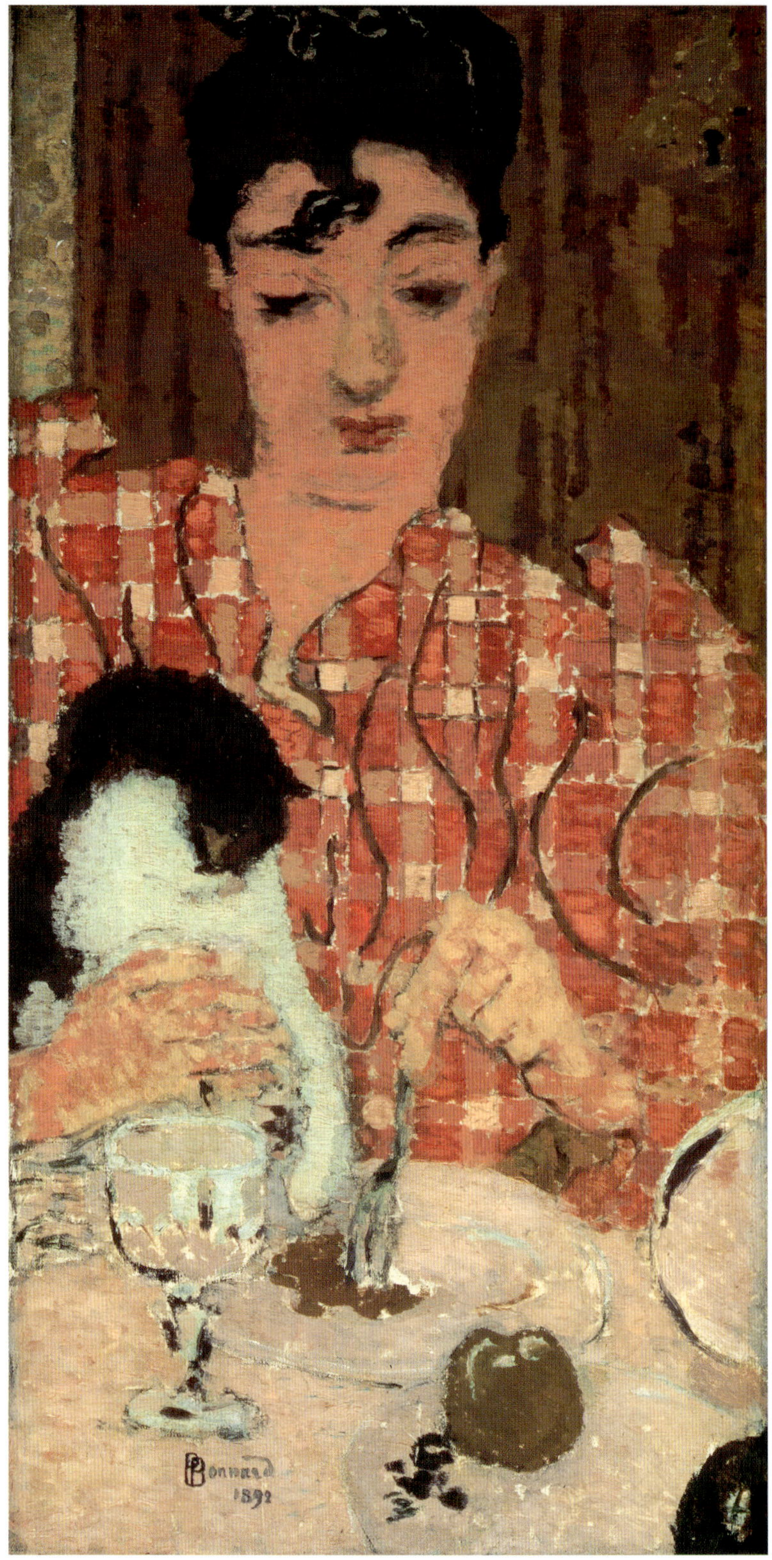

17
Le Corsage à carreaux. 1892.
Oil on canvas, 61×33cm.
Musée d'Orsay, Paris

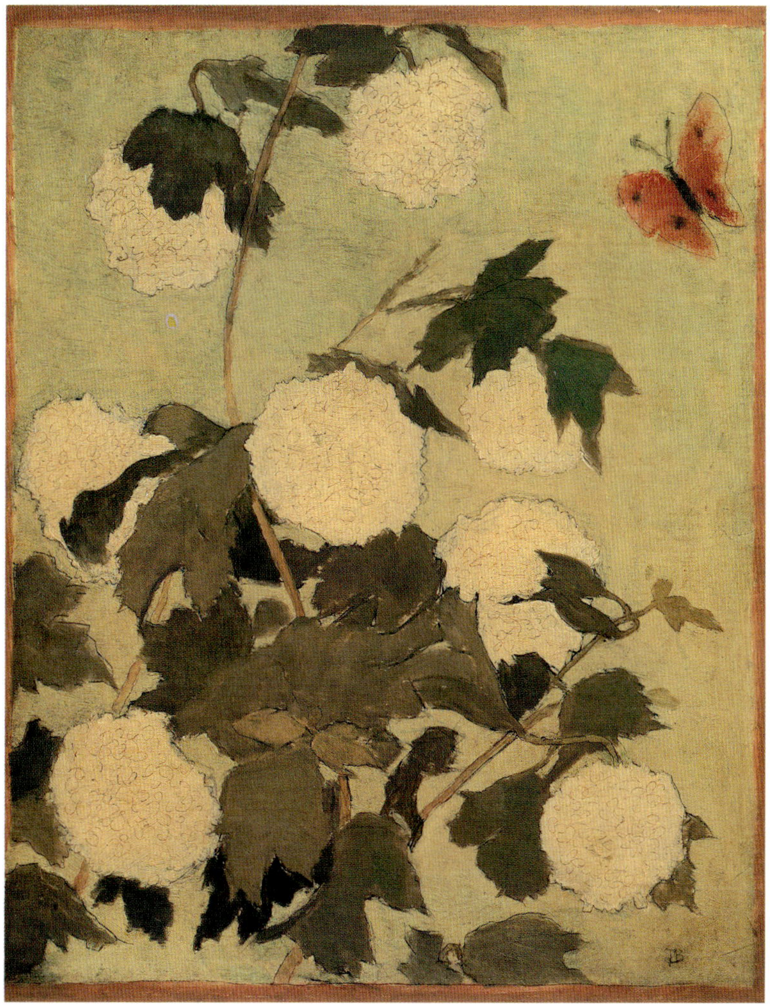

18
Les Boules de neige. 1891.
Oil on canvas, 40.6×32.4cm.
Private collection

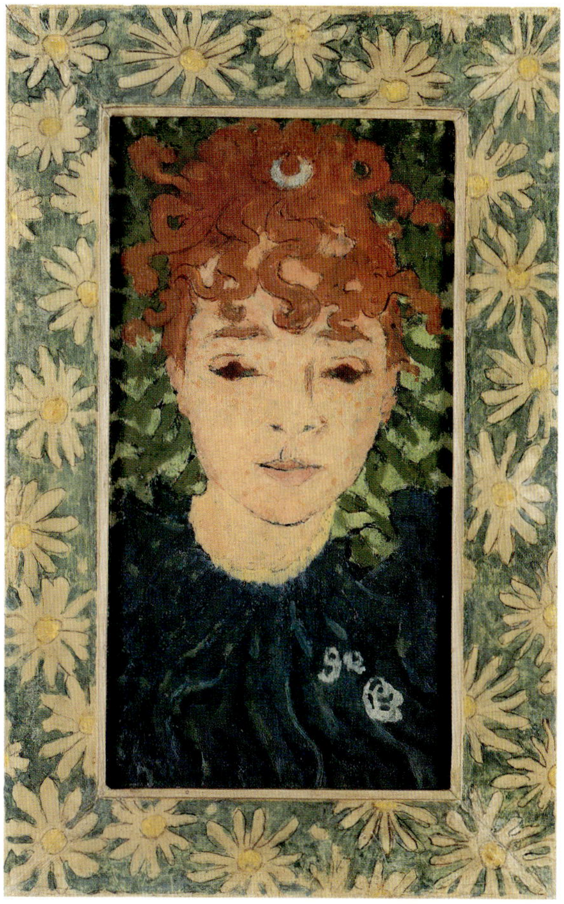

19
Portrait de Berthe Schaedlin. 1892.
Oil on panel, 31×16.5cm.
Private collection

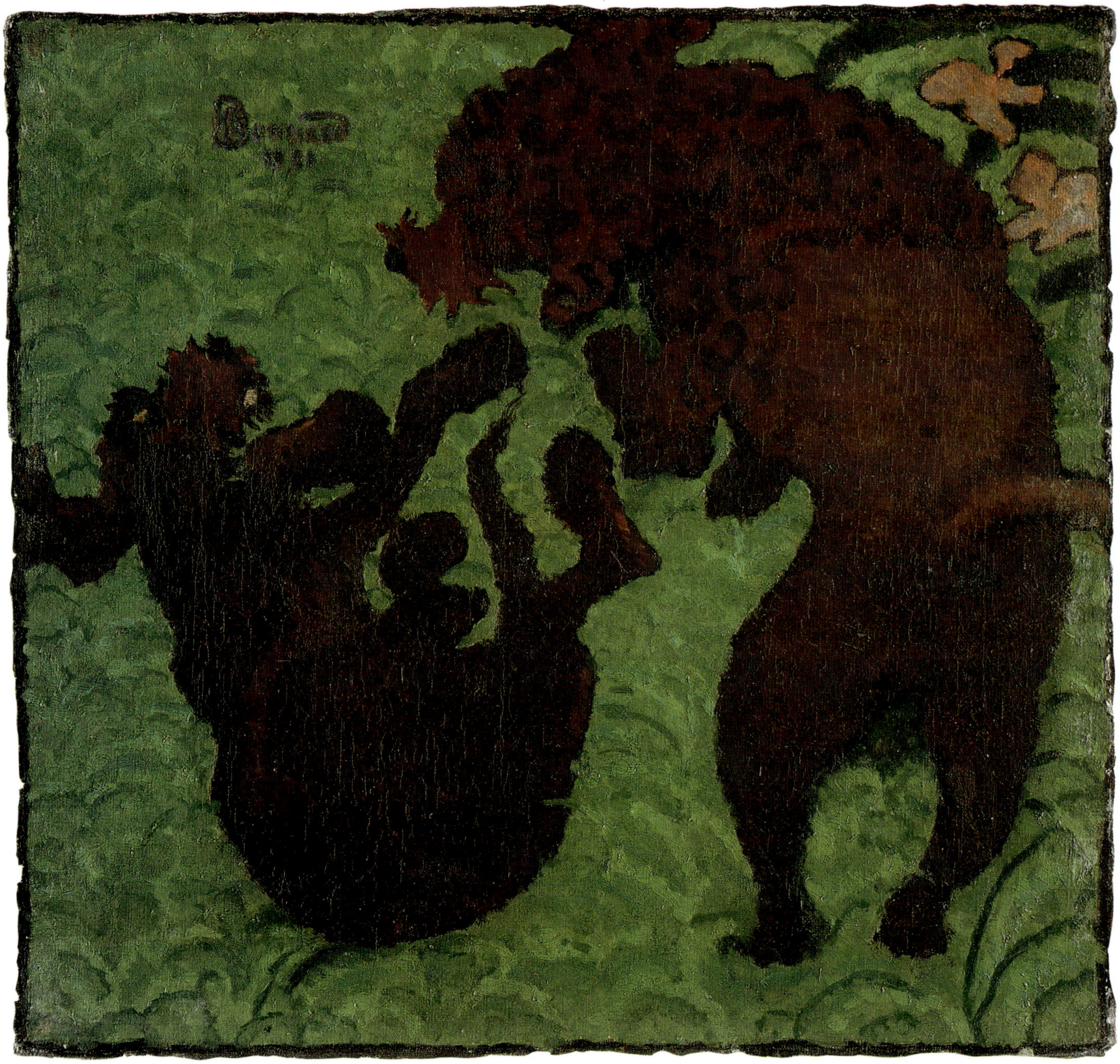

20
Deux chiens jouant. 1891.
Oil on canvas, 36.3×39.7cm.
Southampton City Art Gallery

executed the décors for *Geste du roi*, three medieval pieces, at Paul Fort's short-lived Théâtre de l'Art (1890–2), which promoted Symbolist ideas and used sets in non-naturalistic ways to generate atmosphere.[19] The Nabis were most closely associated with Lugné-Poe, who worked for the Théâtre Libre before founding his own Théâtre de l'Oeuvre in 1893. Lugné was a student at the lycée Condorcet with Denis, Vuillard and Roussel, and the experience of sharing the studio at 28 rue Pigalle with Bonnard, Denis and Vuillard pushed him, as he later acknowledged, towards experimentation with a Symbolist theatre.[20] Bonnard also contributed to the puppet theatre in Ranson's studio and later to the Théâtre des Pantins, founded by his brother-in-law Claude Terrasse, Franc-Nohain and Alfred Jarry in 1898. Although the Nabis' sets have not survived, Bonnard's involvement with theatre may well have proved crucial in his development of the intimist interior and in his conception of pictorial space as a stage around which the attention of the spectator had to be moved as the subject unfolded.

Both Bonnard and Vuillard were imbued with the aspirations of the Symbolist poets and playwrights to loosen the connection between word and image, and to discover within language itself evocative relationships which conjured up the mysterious nature of human experience. Mallarmé became their exemplar. His programme was set out in an interview in 1891: '... to suggest [an object], there's the dream. It is the perfect usage of this mystery that constitutes the symbol: to evoke an object little by little so as to show a state of soul or, inversely, to choose an object and disengage from it a state of soul, for a series of decipherings.'[21] The revelation of Ibsen and the discovery of the Belgian Symbolist poet Maurice Maeterlinck (1862–1949) were two of the literary events of 1890.[22] In the summer of 1894 Lugné-Poe accompanied Thadée and Misia Natanson on a pilgrimage to meet Ibsen in Norway. While there is little of the melodramatic in Bonnard's art, which on one level continued the realist tradition established by Chardin, nevertheless Ibsen's 'drames d'intérieur' and Maeterlinck's plays contributed to a general expansion in the consciousness of rooms as potential subject-matter.

Bonnard was more extensively involved in those areas of the decorative arts that were closely linked to painting and drawing: screens and the graphic arts, particularly posters and illustrations. Screens, functioning on the border between painting and decoration in an art form designed literally to shape domestic space, ideally suited the Nabis' ambition to bring art into life. Bonnard originally conceived *Femmes au jardin*, 1891 (Plate 21) as a Japanese-inspired screen, but shortly before it was exhibited at the Salon des Indépendants of 1891, his first exhibition, he felt that it was overloaded, too much like a painting, and therefore hung the four panels separately as *Decorative Panel 1, 2, 3, and 4*.[23] His sister Andrée and cousin Berthe Schaedlin were probably the models for the women in the panels, which, it has been suggested, take up the popular Japanese subject of the four seasons.[24] The golden and russet red colour scheme of the panel with the woman seen from the rear protectively ensconced in a cape could well represent autumn, but the other three appear to be surrounded by summer foliage. The women are boldly silhouetted and a wide variety of marks are employed in the patterns

overleaf
21
Femmes au jardin. 1891.
Oil on paper mounted on canvas, 4 panels, 160×48cm each.
Musée d'Orsay, Paris

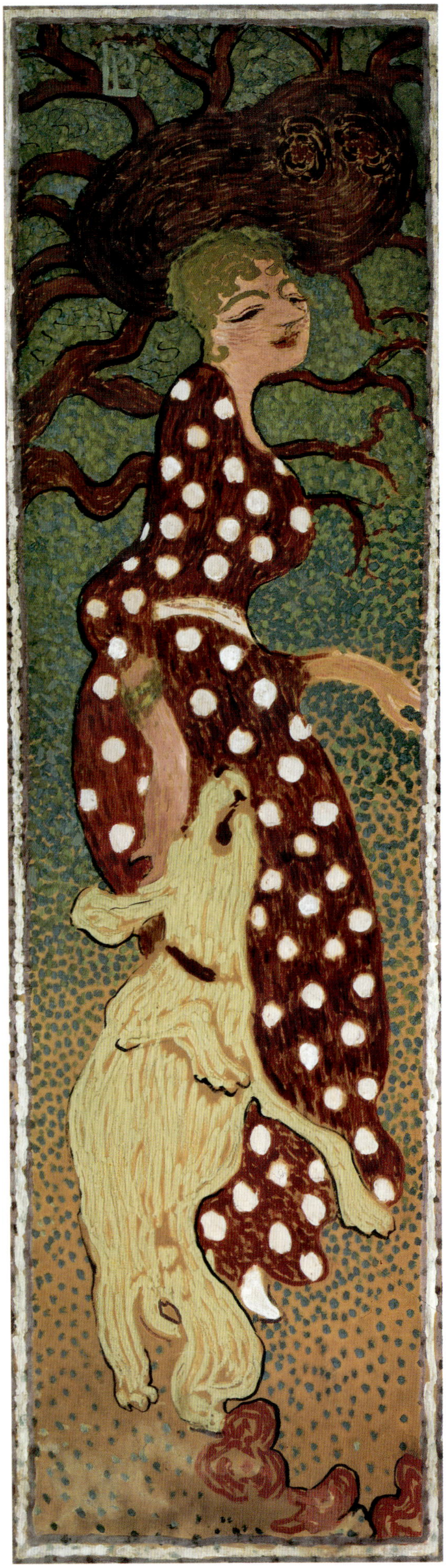

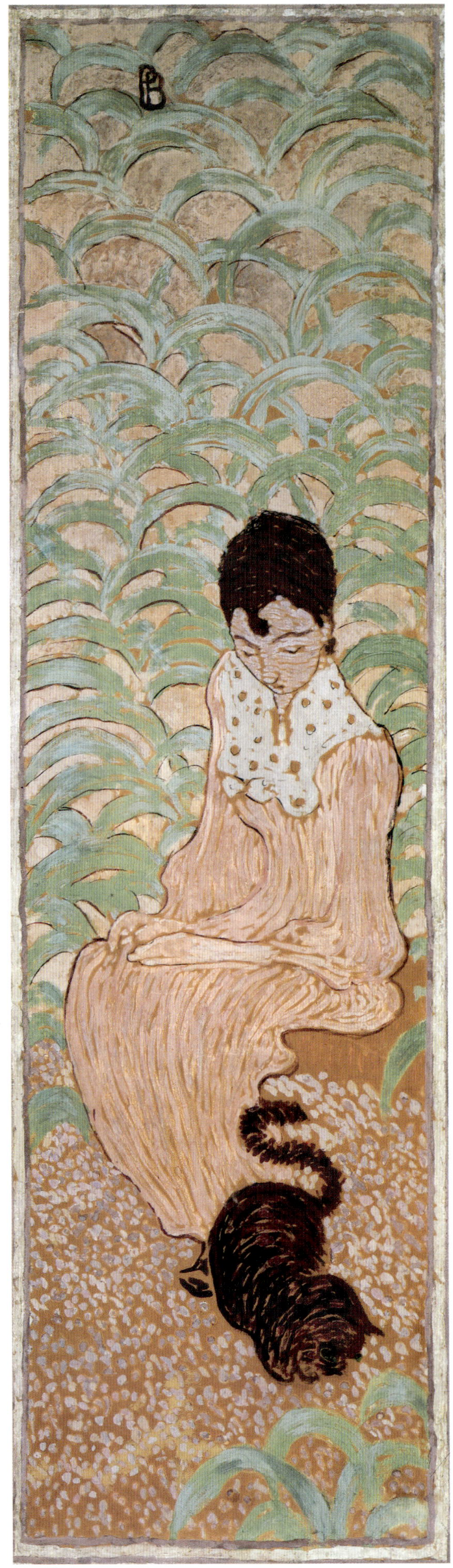

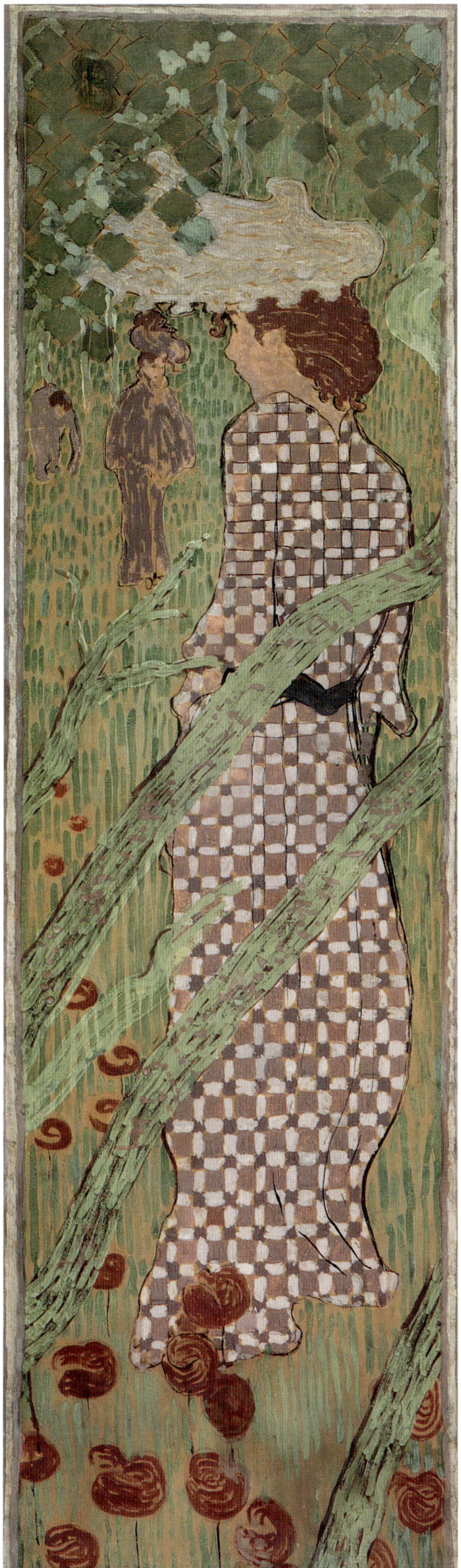

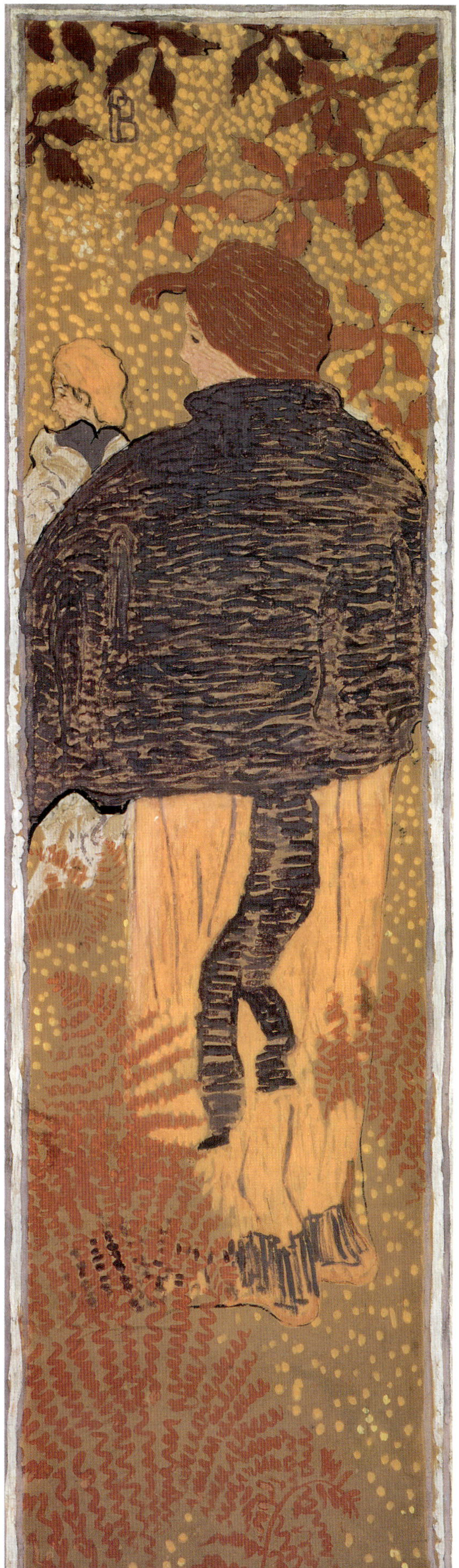

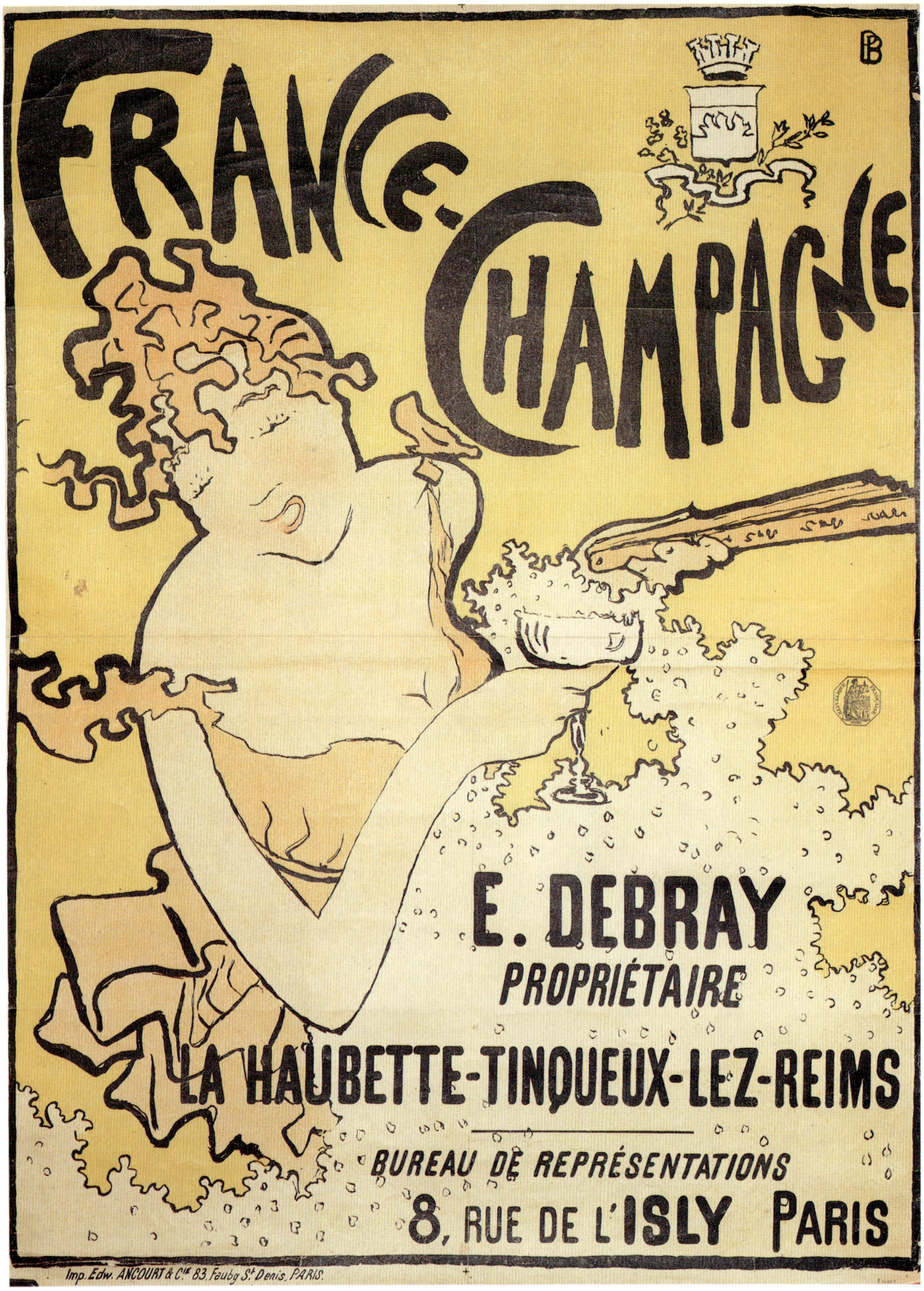

22
France-Champagne. 1891.
Lithograph in 3 colours, 78×50cm

both to describe form and to assert a changing rhythm across the surface. The dots in two of them are a decorative translation of the divisionist technique of Seurat, who had a large exhibition at the Salon des Indépendants the following year. In an interview in *L'Echo de Paris* of 28 December 1891, Bonnard claimed with the confidence of youth: 'Painting must above all be decorative. Talent will reveal itself in the way lines are arranged. I do not belong to any school. I am only trying to do something personal.' He was just twenty-four.

Bonnard first made his reputation – and his money – as a graphic artist, and graphic art was central to his artistic production in the 1890s. He executed over 250 lithographs between 1889 and 1902. Jules Chéret had popularized colour lithography, a medium previously despised by serious artists and collectors, and in late March 1891 Bonnard's famous poster advertising *France-Champagne* (Plate 22) appeared on the streets of Paris. *France-Champagne* employs a heady mixture of word and image to evoke, rather than describe, the atmosphere generated by the product on a festive occasion. The hostess tips towards the spectator trailing a cloud of bubbles from her glass. Forms and the letters 'France-Champagne' are galvanized in the intoxicating rhythm of her movements across the surface. Berthe Schaedlin was probably the model. His poster tapped the energy of the cabaret performer and the cartoons of the small circulation satirical magazines that grew up with the relaxation of censorship during the Third Republic. In it Bonnard transformed Chéret's athletic heroine, dubbed the Cherette, into something dynamic and strikingly new which inspired Toulouse-Lautrec to produce coloured lithographs in a similar style. Japanese woodcut prints were again the most likely source for the graphic notation of swirling movement.

The perceptive Symbolist critic and dandy, Félix Fénéon, who led a double life as conscientious civil servant and committed anarchist, first drew attention to *France-Champagne* and Bonnard's invention of the 'arabesque' of the agile modern woman.[25] The arabesque in Symbolist terminology was much more than a sexy art-nouveau curve liberating the image of the modern woman, for it provided the imaginative means of uniting the different elements in a composition, so that the relationships between objects and the picture surface as a whole took precedence over the description of the objects themselves. Imagination did not mean escapist fantasy; it was understood as something approaching divine insight into the hidden relationships behind surface appearances, which allowed the creation of a work of art through analogy and metaphor. Fénéon became editor of the magazine *La Revue Blanche* in 1896, and later Bonnard's dealer at the Bernheim-Jeune gallery. Ironically, Fénéon commented unfavourably on the yellow background of *France-Champagne*, a colour that became a characteristic feature of Bonnard's mature style.

Bonnard went on to design nine more posters, including the poster for *La Revue Blanche*, 1894 (Plate 23). If it were not for the street-wise urchin jerking a thumb towards the magazine, it would at first be difficult to see what the poster is advertising. The fashionably dressed woman, eyes staring out alluringly from the depths of her cape, casually proffers the title-page like a menu discreetly listing her services. The extraordinarily witty interplay between word and image, figure and ground, owed a considerable debt to Japanese woodblock prints, but Bonnard made it very much his own. The 'l' of '*la*' hangs down from the woman's arm like an umbrella, while the 'a' curls round defining the form of her leg. The bold use of the silhouette may reflect Bonnard's interest in the revival of shadow plays at the Chat Noir cabaret. [26]

La Revue Blanche, founded in Liège in 1889, moved to Paris the following year under the direction of Bonnard's friends and patrons the Natanson brothers, Alexandre (1866–1936) and Thadée (1868–1951). Until its closure in April 1903 the magazine acted as a forum for the leading members of the avant-garde.[27] Thadée, who commissioned the poster (for which his wife Misia served as the model), became especially close to Bonnard, eventually publishing a monograph on the artist in 1951.

Bonnard was not the only one to be attracted by Misia. Painted by amongst others Vuillard, Toulouse-Lautrec and Renoir, written about by Proust and Cocteau, and courted by Diaghilev and Coco Chanel, she was the patron and muse who captivated and entertained many of the leading figures of her day. She had an unerring eye for young talent, went through three marriages and ended up in old age as a semi-blind drug addict.[28] After a terrible childhood – her mother died giving birth to her on 30 March 1872 in St Petersburg and her father, the flamboyant Polish sculptor Cyprien Godebski, went off with another woman, leaving Misia, christened Marie Godebska, to be brought up by her grandmother in Belgium – she eventually married Thadée Natanson on 25 April 1893. Thadée opened up a new world to her. Absorbed by art and literature (he loved the poetry of Mallarmé and Verlaine), his money and position as joint owner of *La Revue Blanche* made him and Misia popular hosts in Paris and at their country house, La Grangette at Valvins near Fontainebleau. Bonnard and Vuillard practically took up residence there for long periods, and Toulouse-Lautrec was a frequent visitor. Mallarmé had his summer house nearby. When La Grangette became too small to accommodate them all, Thadée and Misia moved to a house called Le Relais at Villeneuve-sur-Yvonne, which features in Vuillard's two decorative panels of 1898 (Plate 58). Through the Natanson circle Bonnard established the beginnings of a support network that provided him with the necessary basis for a successful career. It was the type of companionable, intelligent and monied patronage of which artists dream but which carried with it the danger for those less committed and more social than Bonnard of diverting them from their purpose, suffocating their art or destroying them if it suddenly ceased.

In 1893 Bonnard had become involved with a woman who was everything that Misia was not. She hated society with the intensity of someone rejected by it. Nobody seemed to know her proper name, her age or where she came from. She posed as a sixteen-year-old with the unlikely name of Marthe de Méligny, though she prefered to be called simply Marthe. In fact her real name, it transpired, was Maria Boursin, and she was twenty-four. She was then working as an assistant in a shop making artificial flowers for funerals, and they met when Bonnard helped her cross the busy boulevard Haussmann;

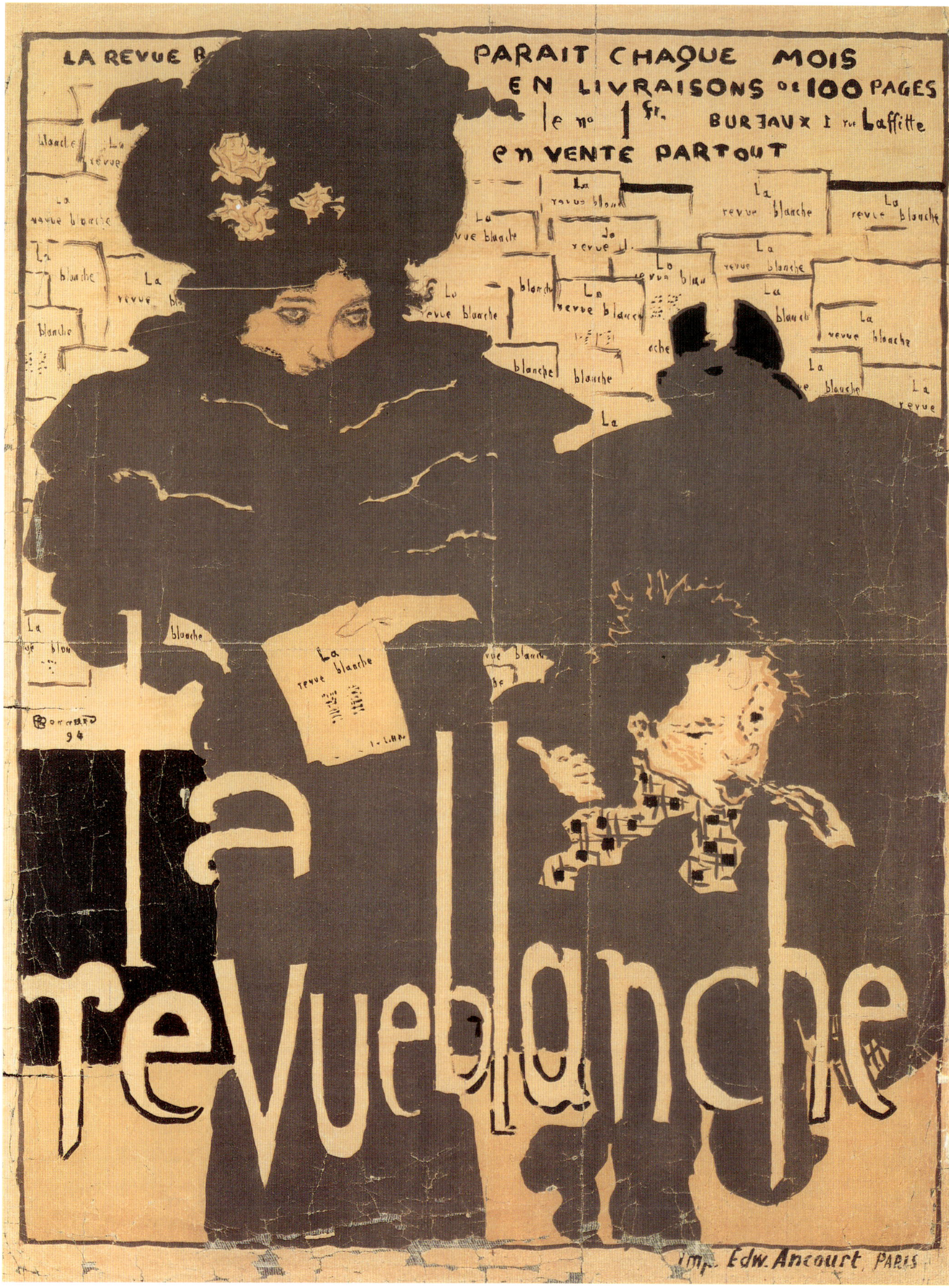

23
La Revue Blanche. 1894.
Lithograph in 4 colours, 80×62cm

but even this charming story is probably untrue.[29] On the face of it she was an unlikely partner for Bonnard. She came from a different class, which was difficult for Bonnard's family to accept, put off his friends, and made his life a misery with her constant complaints about poor health. Bonnard had affairs with other women and yet remained devoted to her, eventually marrying her in 1925, and he was devastated by her death on 26 January 1942. The trouble did not stop with her death; unbeknownst to Bonnard, she had relations who turned up to claim half his estate.

Marthe became one of Bonnard's principal subjects. She provided the companionship and feminine presence necessary for his art and ensured the protective silence that he needed to get on with it. In company or alone in a room he usually portrayed her with averted gaze, head bowed, often hovering on the periphery of vision. She seems to pervade the atmosphere of his interiors even when not there. But it was not always like that. At the turn of the century, fired by the commission to illustrate Verlaine's *Parallèlement*, he produced some of the most erotic paintings in the history of Western art. Bonnard preserved her youthful body and invented a neo-Mannerist tapering anatomy to describe it. Her obsessive, near-pathological need to wash and wash provided him with a subject which he turned to his advantage in what many critics regard as his greatest paintings, the bather series.

With the arrival of Marthe on the scene, Berthe Schaedlin dropped out of his art. Freed from the conventions of representing a woman from his own background, behaving with appropriate decorum, and working within the Bohemian ambience of Montmartre, Bonnard began to experiment with the subject of the nude. Although the political leadership asserted the values of discipline and work, conservative critics felt that the Third Republic, formed in the aftermath of the defeat in the Franco-Prussian war and the disaster of the Commune massacre, had resulted in decadence and the moral decline of the nation. The Bohemian artists and writers of Montmartre, with their headquarters in café and cabaret, had acquired a reputation for licentious behaviour; but their places of entertainment, which consciously rejected bourgeois standards of behaviour, soon ended up by being patronized by the bourgeoisie themselves. By the late 1880s the Chat Noir had become a tourist attraction, visited by the rich and famous and even listed in foreign guides, and by the late 1890s the whole quarter was dedicated to the marketing of pleasure.[30]

Bonnard's treatment of the nude varied between the real and the idealized. In *La Baignade*, 1893 (Plate 24), Marthe acts the part of a nymph leaning over a pool in a drama by Maeterlinck, who had become extremely popular with the Nabis. The sinuous outline and graceful curve of her long back reflect the influence of Japanese woodblock prints, notably the work of Utamaro (1753–1806). The technique of the painting shows that it was conceived in terms of line; in places such as the back of her left hand the contour is virtually incized into the surface of the panel. The transformation of Marthe into a nymph in a landscape setting in *La Baignade* anticipates the subject-matter of Bonnard's illustrations to *Daphnis et Chloé*, published in 1902.

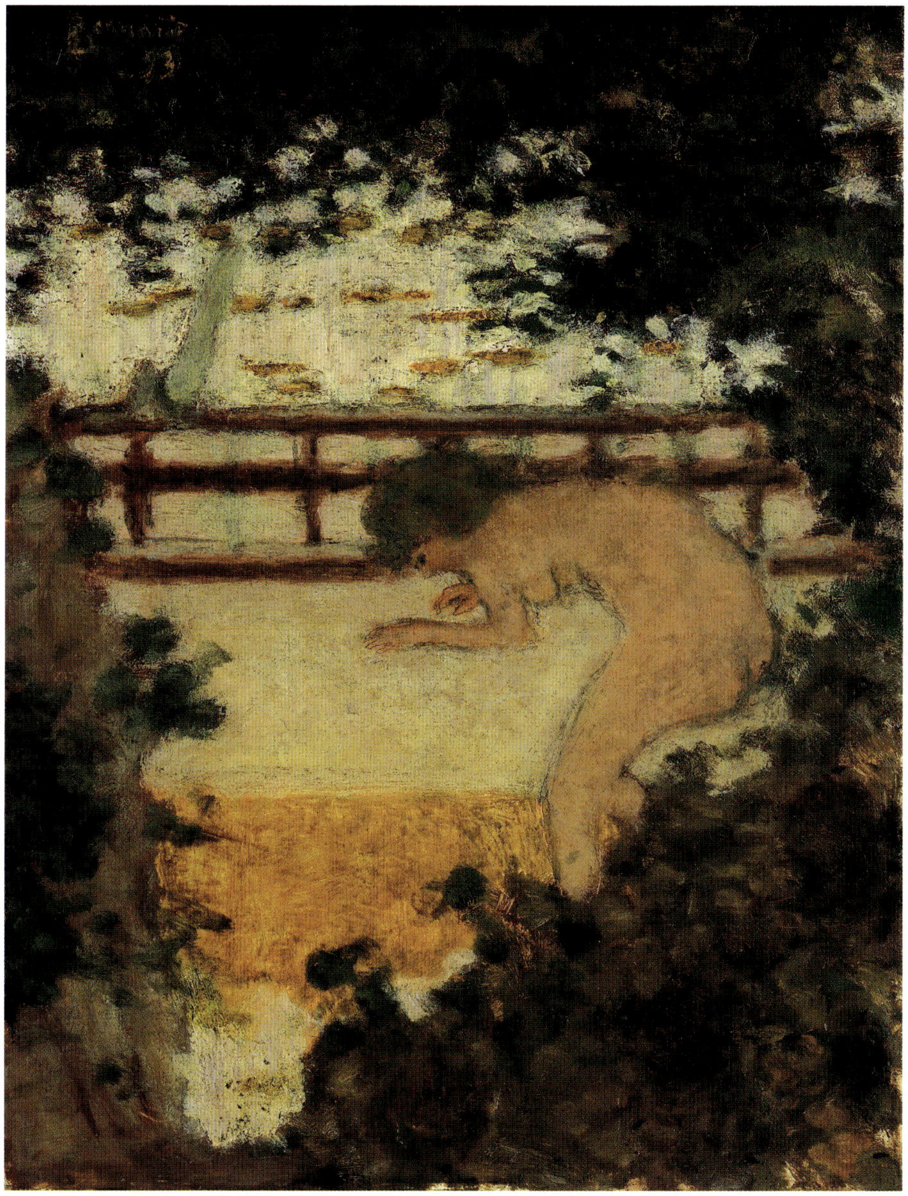

24
La Baignade. 1893.
Oil on panel, 34.9×26.7cm.
Private collection

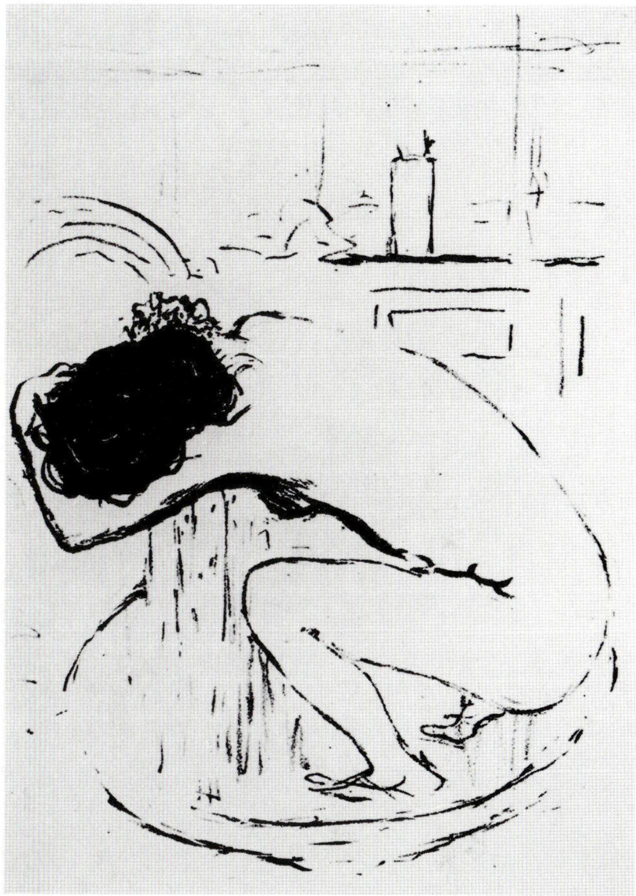

25
Le Tub. 1894.
Lithograph in black, 18×13cm

When dealing with sexual subjects, Bonnard employed the well-established iconography of sexual pleasure – black-stockinged legs and crumpled sheets – as part of a homely routine enacted in a domestic interior, painted tentatively on small panels. Degas had pioneered the naturalistic treatment of the posed nude by portraying women engaged in everyday tasks such as washing. Bonnard was too young to have seen the first major exhibition of Degas's bathers at the eighth Impressionist exhibition in 1886, but his depiction of Marthe in the nude in the lithograph *Le Tub*, 1894 (Plate 25), shows that he had been looking at Degas prior to his avowed discovery of Impressionism at the end of the decade.[31] Marthe was again the model in Bonnard's illustrations for the novel *Marie* by Peter Nansen, published in 1898, which so impressed Renoir and confirmed Bonnard's growing reputation as a gently erotic illustrator of the nude in a charming style.

Bonnard was not a straightforward observer faithfully recording anything and everything that caught his eye. He was deeply attached to the women in his life, whom he cast in roles associated with specific human conditions and emotional states. If Marthe signified for him erotic passion and sex, his sister Andrée took the role of mother and tender carer, the very image of instinctual warmth and feeling that informs his two lithographs of 1892 and 1893, titled *Scène de famille* (Plate 27). Andrée is no longer centre stage. Her place and personality have been subsumed by the expansive form of a large baby, her son Jean, who was born on 6 May 1892, and she is flattened into an enveloping protective presence in the top right-hand corner, leaving the bottom corners free for the adoration by her father in the first lithograph and by Bonnard himself in the second. The subject was probably suggested by Utamaro, who had inspired Mary Cassatt's coloured etchings of motherhood, exhibited at the Durand-Ruel gallery in 1891.[32] Andrée went on to have five more children, Charles (1893–1982),

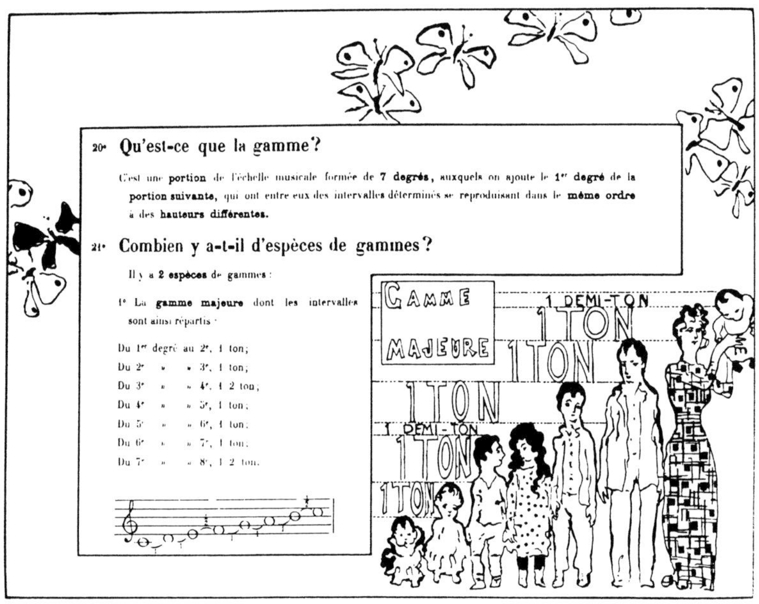

26
Gamme majeure.
Page 8 of *Petit solfège illustrée.* 1893.
Lithograph in black, 21.3×28.3cm

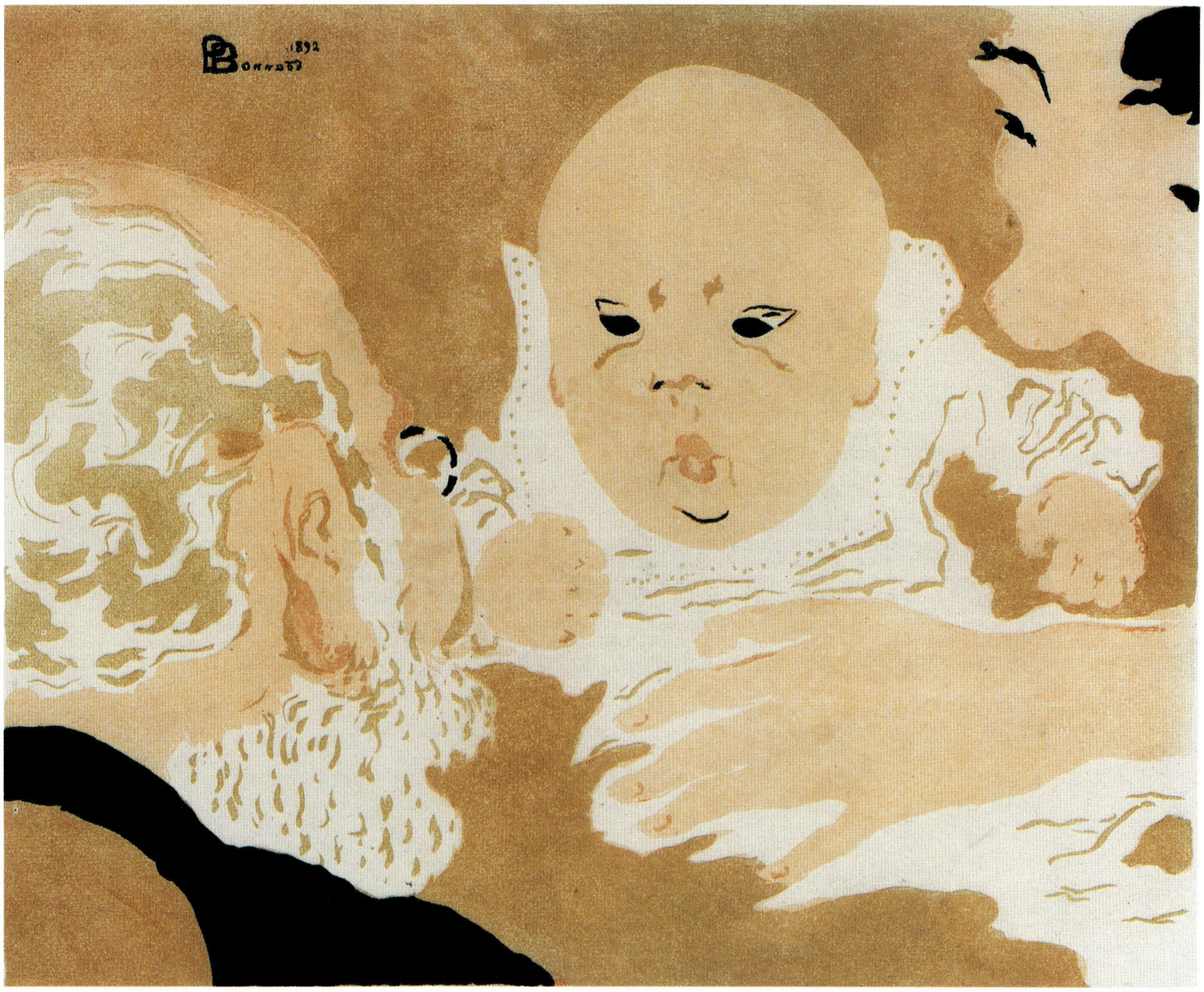

27
Scène de famille. 1893.
Lithograph in 4 colours, 18×31cm

Renée (1894–1985), Robert (1896–1966), Marcel (1897–8) and Eugénie, known as Vivette (1899).

The Terrasse children opened up a range of new subjects for Bonnard. Affectionate, amusing and informal, he felt close to them and often depicted them in close-up, cut off by the framing edge. Much of his time was taken up with the illustration of a musical grammar for children written by his brother-in-law Claude Terrasse, *Petit solfège illustré*, published in 1893. He also worked on *Un Alphabet sentimental* which – apart from a few studies – never got off the ground, and a family album of piano music, *Petites scènes familières*, which finally came out in 1895. Bonnard took enormous trouble with Petit Solfège illustré. In despair he wrote to Vuillard on 13 April 1891, 'I have to think of the decorators of ancient missals, or of the art that the Japanese put into the decoration of encyclopedic dictionaries to give myself some courage ...'[33] In contrast to Claude Terrasse's difficult text, Bonnard tried to make his illustrations accessible to children by picturing musical grammar in familiar terms. For instance, a baby held up by the mother is the top note in the major scale (Plate 26), acted out by a family of seven. *Prestissimo* is illustrated by race-horses galloping flat out across the page. He explained his thinking behind *Un Alphabet sentimental* in a letter to his mother of 11 February 1893: 'For each letter there will be a word beginning with that letter and representing an emotion or a mood, which I will render by little everyday scenes with babies, animals, views of the country, etc. The idea is to make things and beings speak.'[34] In a similar way his illustrations for *Petites scènes familières* included such subjects as the family with a baby, the blackness of sadness, melancholy at the departure of friends, hope in prayer, the reverie of a dreaming woman, the ecstasy of dance and the forced, upright mood of Sunday morning.

Bonnard's early reputation was partly based on his ability to convey an attractive dynamic image of modern life. In his review of the Salon des Indépendants of 1893, Claude Roger-Marx noted his talent 'for picking out and rapidly capturing the picturesque in every spectacle'.[35] At the root of his art lay the impetus to isolate and give significance to the passing incidents of everyday existence. Life itself became his spectacle – and it was free. In his autobiography the dealer Ambroise Vollard, who played an important part in Bonnard's print production, described the only affordable amusement at the outset of his career in the mid-1890s as a Sunday visit 'to watch the procession of smart carriages from under the trees lining the avenue des Champs Elysées'.[36] This kind of observation was a sophisticated city habit cultivated by the *flâneur*, a connoisseur of daily life, as opposed to the *badaud* who gawped at the obvious, such as the activity of a building site or a man having a tooth yanked out on a pavement.[37]

Bonnard's subjects were those of a *flâneur*. A waif-like young woman in *Boulevard des Batignolles*, 1893 (Plate 28), hitches up her skirt to cross the rain-soaked street, her feet reflected in the puddles. The painting could commemorate his first meeting with Marthe, but it was more likely to have been one of those chance glimpses of an attractive face that he caught in a croquis, a quick sketch, on one of his ritual morning walks

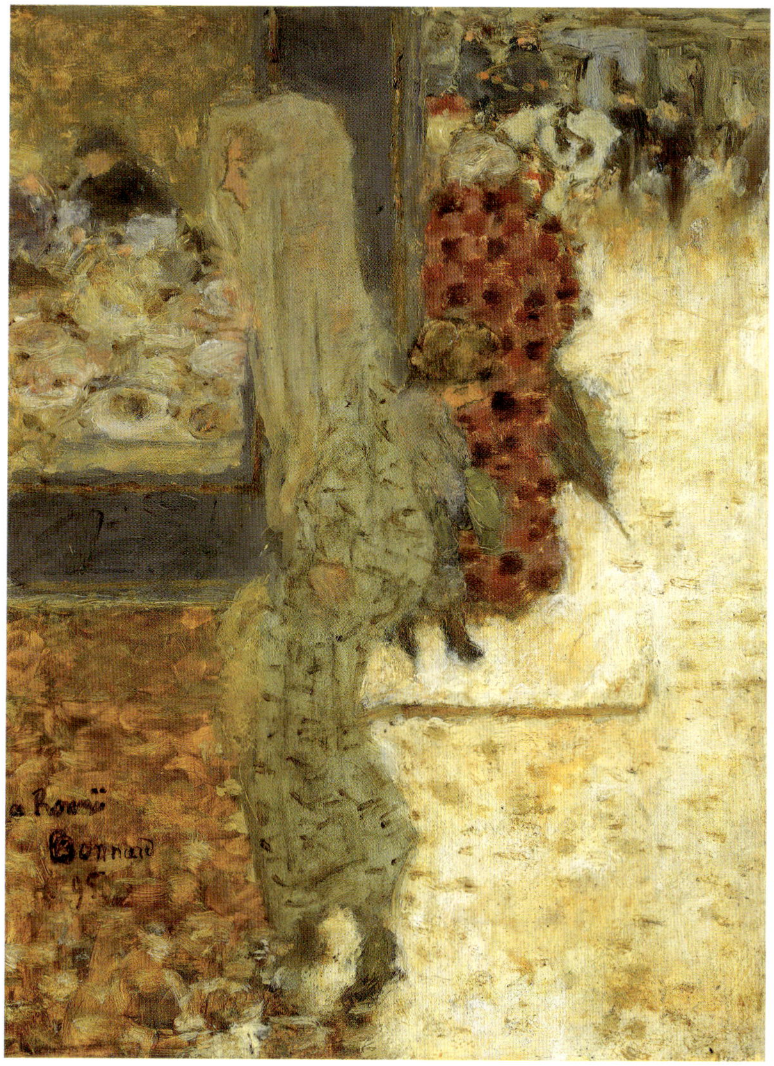

28
Boulevard des Batignolles. 1895.
Oil on panel, 33.5×27cm.
Private collection

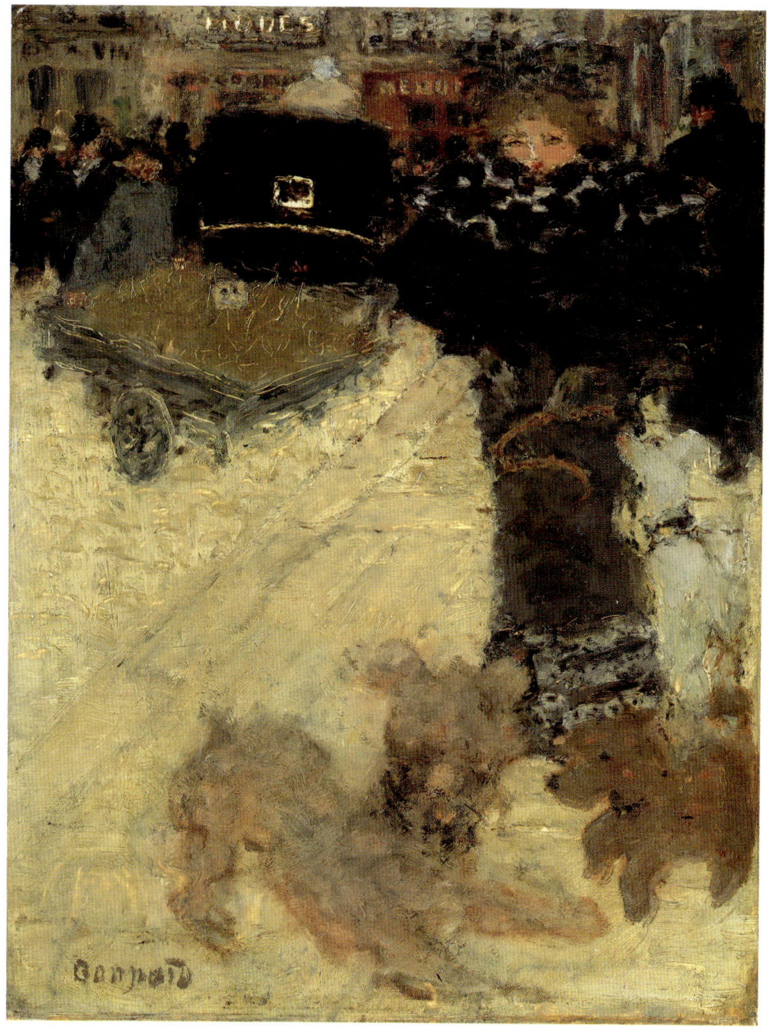

29
Scène dans la rue or *La Place Clichy*. *c*.1895.
Oil on board, 35.3×27cm.
Metropolitan Museum of Art, New York, The Jacques and Natasha Gelman Collection

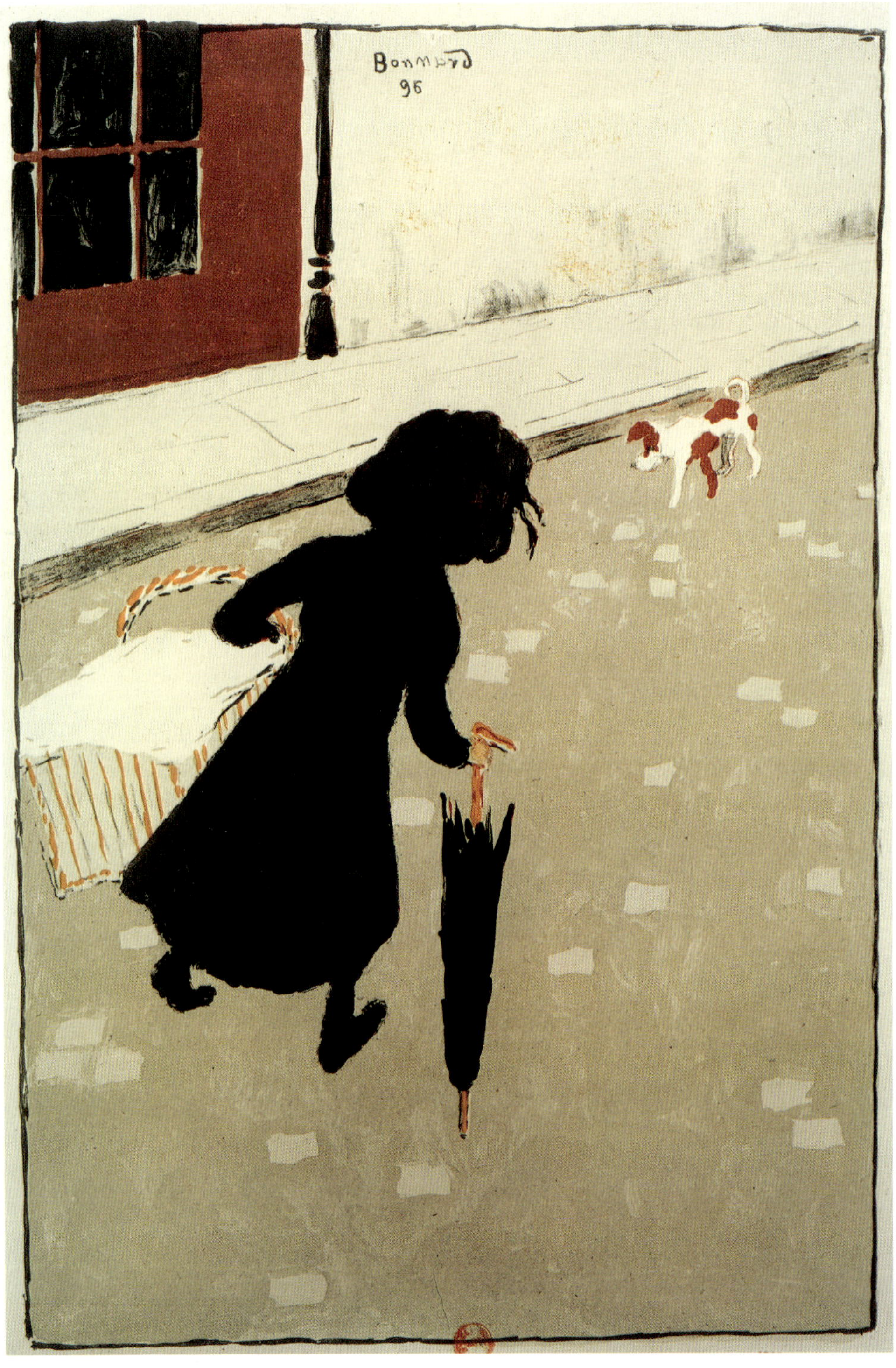

30
La Petite Blanchisseuse. 1896.
Lithograph in 5 colours, 30×19cm

and later painted. *La Petite Blanchisseuse*, 1896 (Plate 30), a colour lithograph commissioned by Vollard, captures the quaintly stilted silhouette of a girl delivering washing, one of the daily sights of Paris where an estimated quarter of the population were occupied in the laundry business.[38] His subjects included incidents from both high and low life; the stiff and formal were juxtaposed with the informality of children and dogs. In *Scène dans la rue* or *La Place Clichy*, *c.*1895 (Plate 29), a fashionable lady, like Misia in the *Revue Blanche* poster, walks down the pavement escorted by her engagingly shaggy, gambolling dogs. In *Les Grands Boulevards*, *c.*1898 (Plate 32), a gaggle of children bustling back from school first caught his eye.

From as early as 1889 Bonnard had become fascinated by the changing patterns formed by people passing along the streets of Paris in the neighbourhood of his successive studios near the Place Clichy by Montmartre, a modern-life subject opened up by the Impressionists. In his treatment of the streets he explored a number of formal options which he rephrased from painting to painting. He would change his viewpoints like seats in a theatre, in some looking down as though from a box, in others peering out between spectators as though from the stalls below. The streets either rush away in steep perspective or are cut back in successive horizontal bands as in a relief. Precedents for both are readily found in Japanese wood-block prints and in the work of Degas.

Ideas from little paintings would be synthesized in a large-scale decoration, which in turn would generate further paintings and prints. The genesis of *Les Grands Boulevards*, for instance, was inseparably linked with the painted screen in four panels, *La Promenade des nourrices, frise de fiacres*, *c.*1895–7, exhibited at Bonnard's first one-man exhibition at the Durand-Ruel gallery in January 1896, and its lithographed version (Plate 31). The masterpiece of his city subjects, the lithograph shows three fashionably dressed children pushing hoops across the wide expanse of the Place de la Concorde, accompanied by the same stylish lady, and with a frieze of carriages lined along the top of the composition. *Les Grands Boulevards* focuses on the spatial relationship in the two right-hand panels between the three children and the cart, instead of a carriage, and the setting changes to a tree-lined boulevard which he had established in a number of relief-type compositions, culminating in the lithograph, *Boulevard*, *c.*1896 (Plate 33), from the suite of city subjects, *Quelques aspects de la vie de Paris*, commissioned by Vollard and finally published in 1899. The muted, predominantly grey colour scheme became a hallmark of his city views.

A recurring problem faced by Bonnard was how to preserve the freshness and informality of the first glance while at the same time reconciling it with the highly decorative art form favoured by the Nabis. The linear style that he evolved under the influence of Gauguin and Japanese art was particularly effective when the subject itself was either highly stylized, as in the fashionably dressed women and children, or lent itself to stylization, such as the vegetation filling the three panels of his screen *Ensemble champêtre*, *c.*1894 (Plate 34). The fourth panel, *L'Enfant au seau* (Plate 35), showing one of his

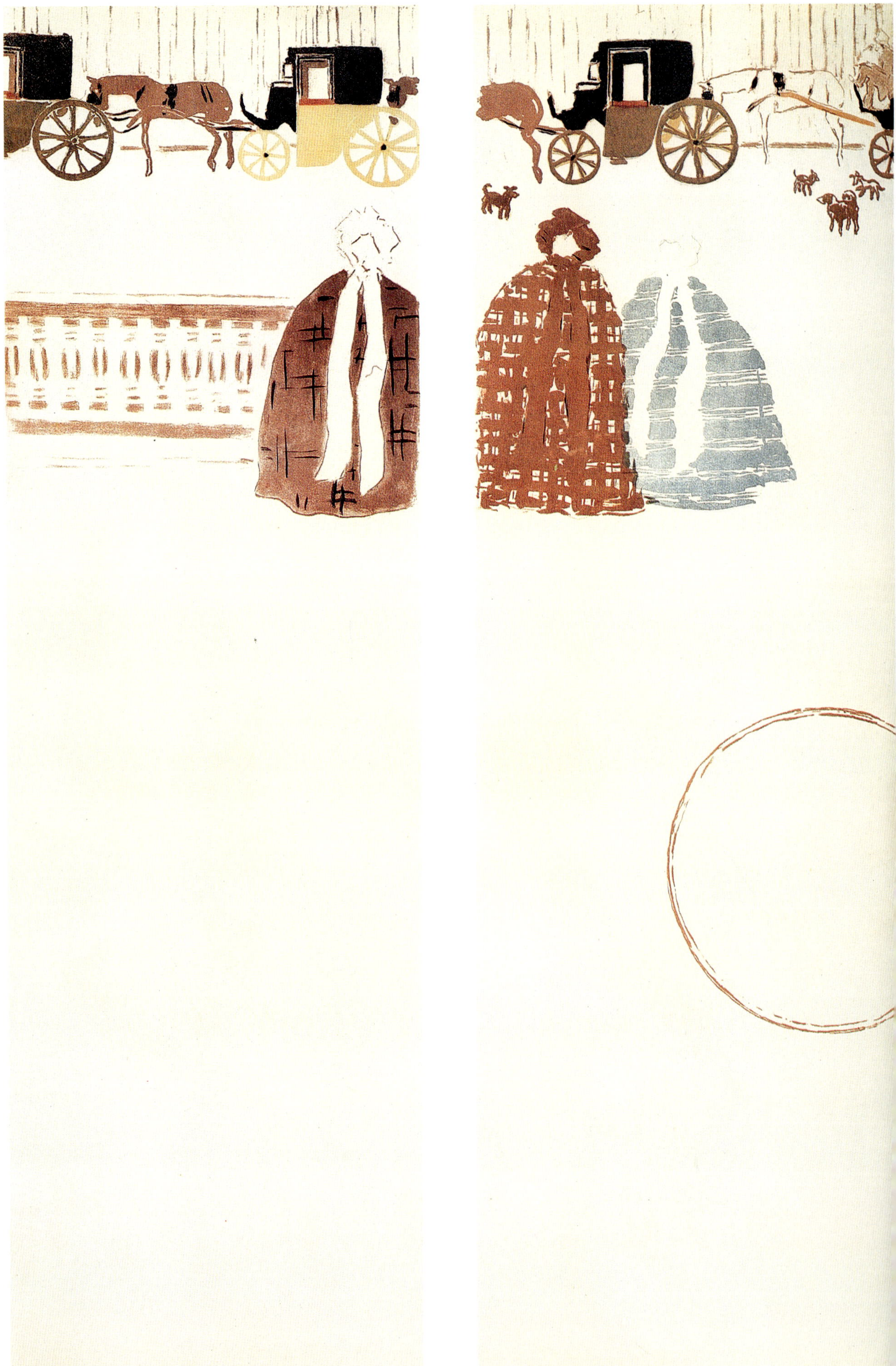

31
La Promenade des nourrices,
frise de fiacres c.1895–7.
Folding screen.
Lithograph, in 5 colours, 4 panels,
150×200cm

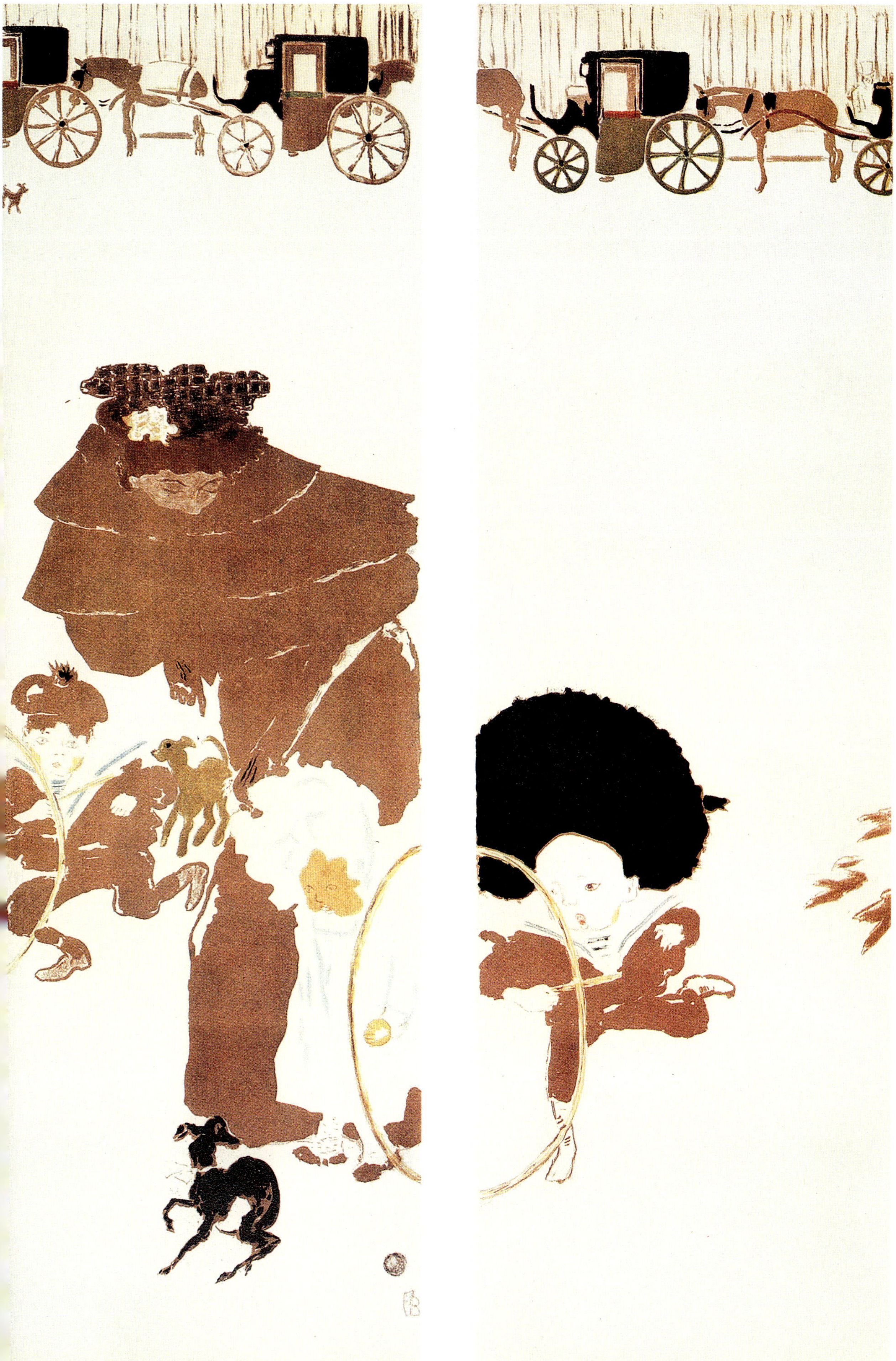

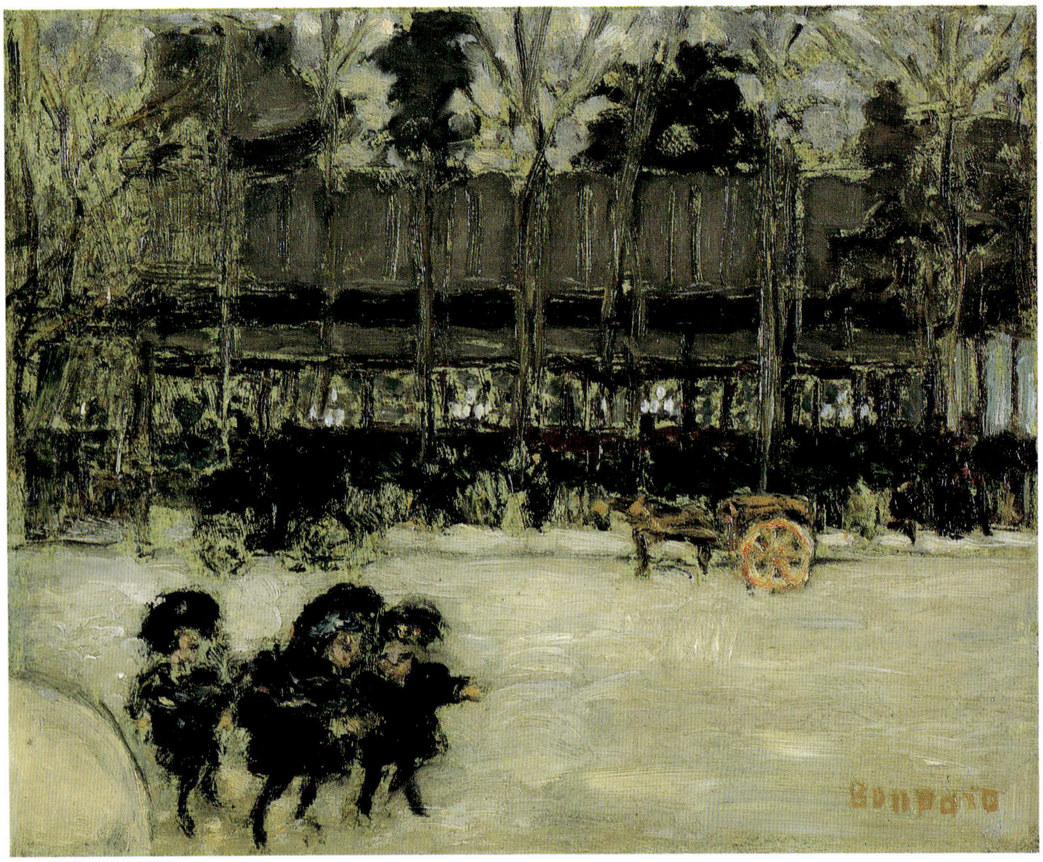

32
Les Grands Boulevards. *c*.1898.
Oil on canvas, 27×33.6cm.
Sir Robert and Lady Sainsbury

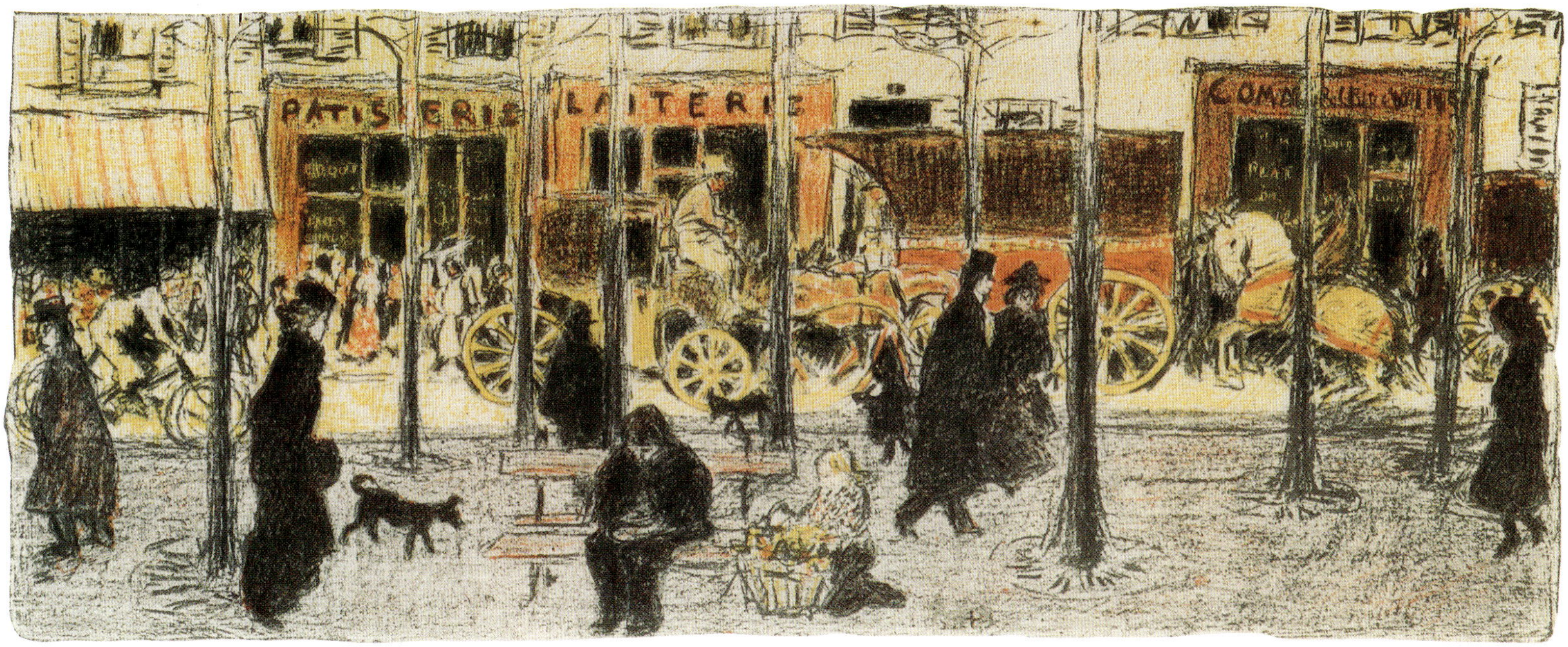

33
Boulevard. 1899.
Lithograph in 4 colours, 17×43cm

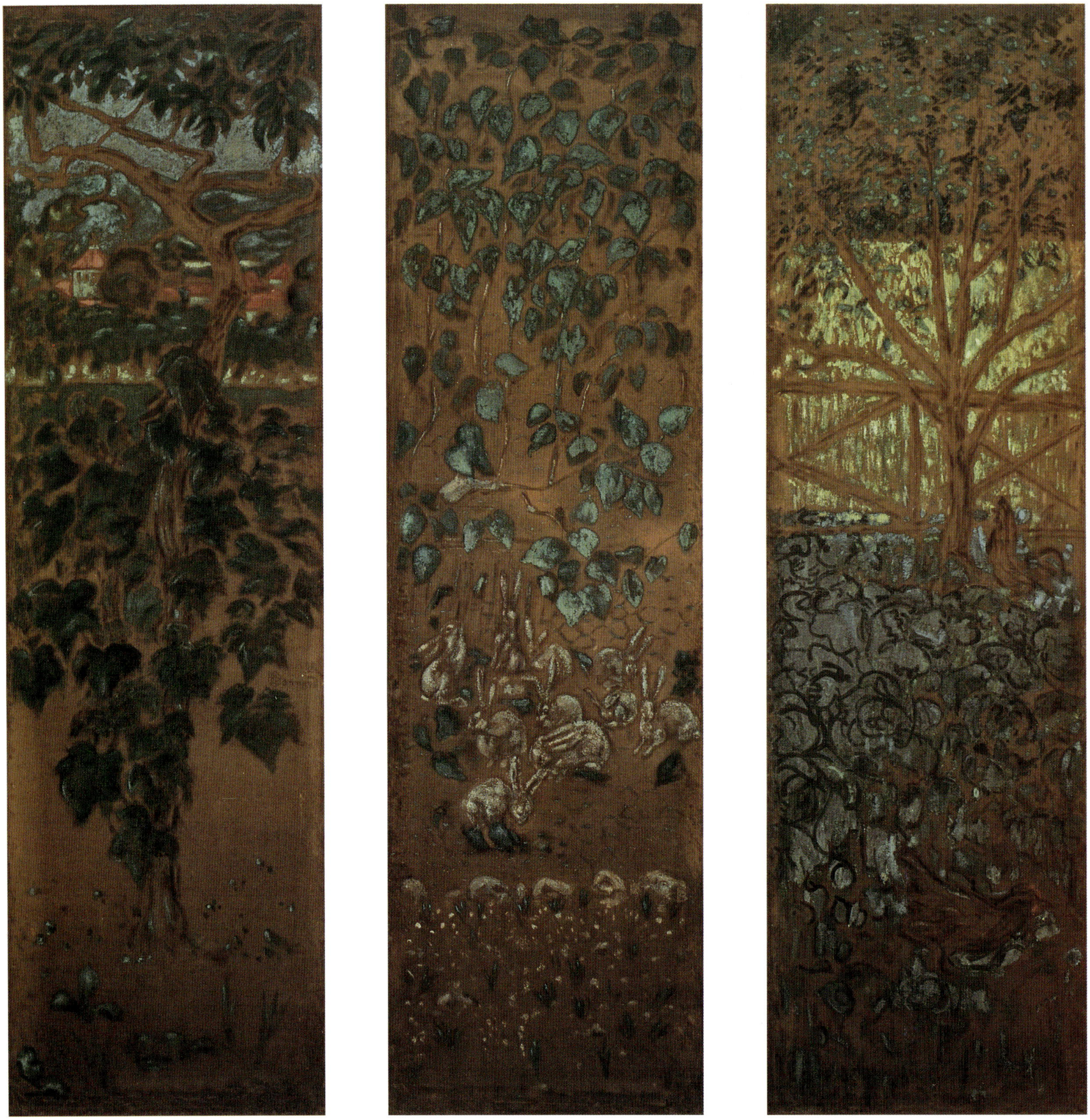

34
Ensemble champêtre. c.1894.
Oil on canvas, 3 panels, 167×50.8cm each.
Museum of Modern Art, New York,
gift of Mr and Mrs Allan D. Emil

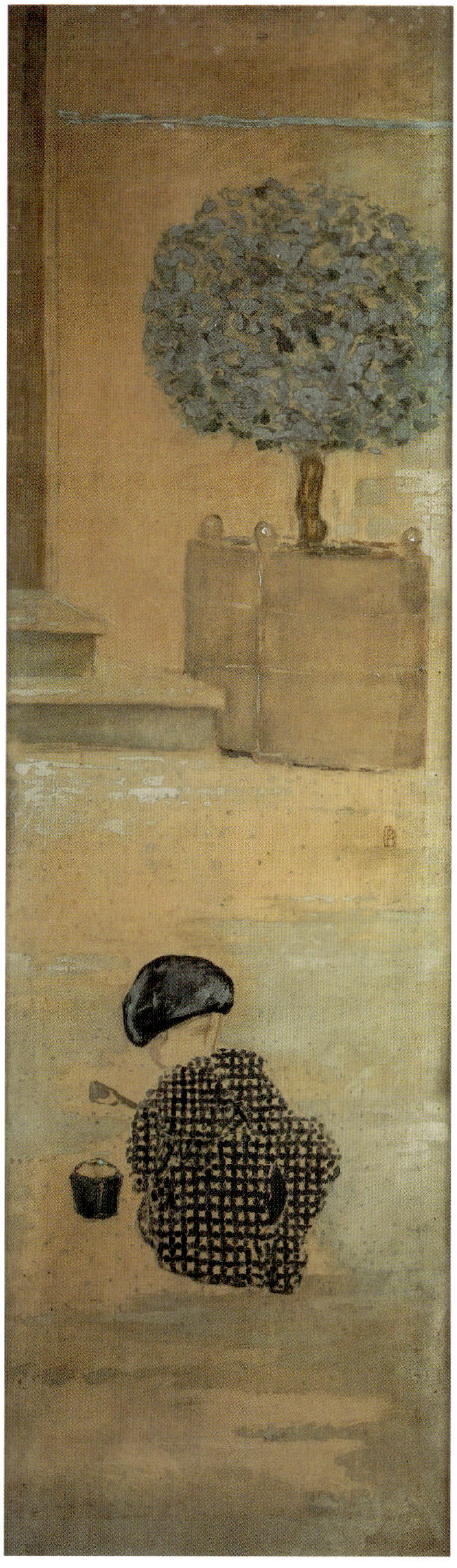

35
*L'Enfant au seau. c.*1894.
Distemper on canvas, 167×50cm
Musée d'Orsay, Paris

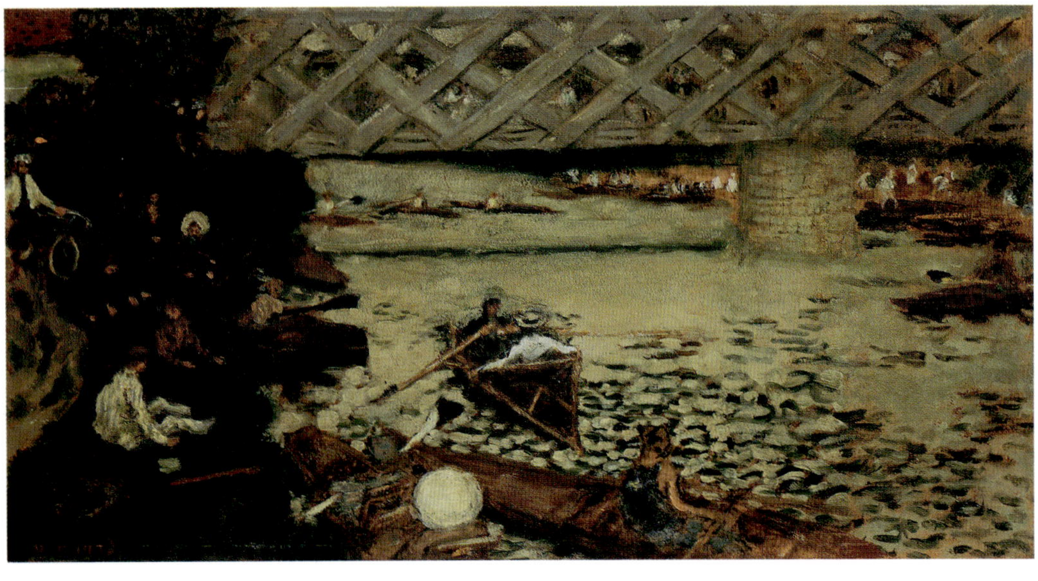

36
Le Canotage sur la Seine, le pont à Chatou. 1896.
Oil on panel, 31.7×59.5cm.
Private collection

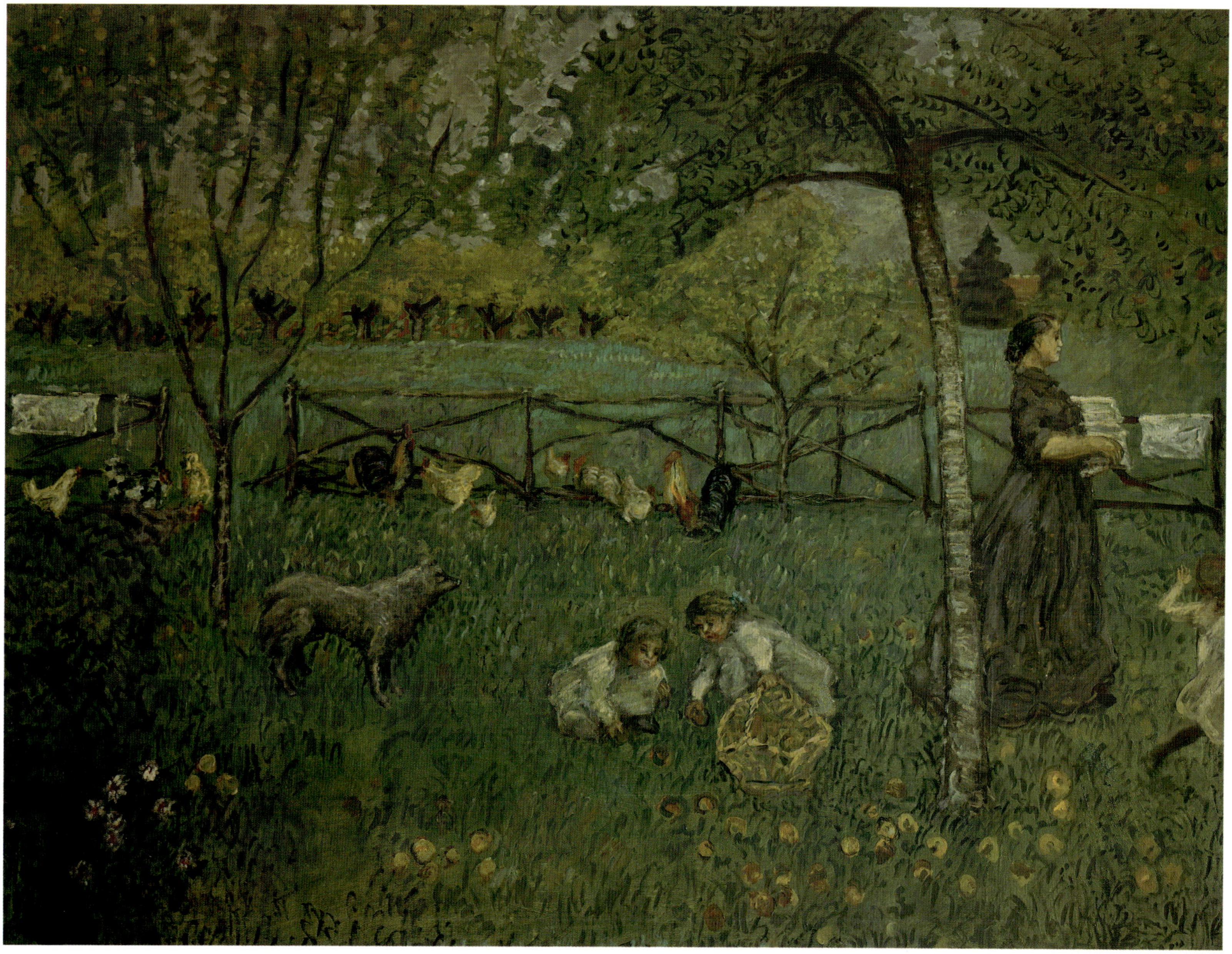

37
Le Grand Jardin. 1895–6.
Oil on canvas, 167.5×220cm.
Musée d'Orsay, Paris

nephews playing in front of Le Clos, a subject he later photographed, was detached by Bonnard sometime after it was photographed in his studio in 1905; presumably because it is in a softer style, like a Japanese painting on silk, with the pale brown ground colour of the canvas describing both the sand and wall behind. He combined three such country incidents from daily life at le Clos – chickens feeding in the orchard, his nephews gathering fruit, and a maid putting out the washing – in a major decorative panel, *Le Grand Jardin*, 1895–6 (Plate 37), which is slightly stiff and awkward in the way that it is composed in rigid horizontal bands, as in one of his city street scenes.

The irony was that although Bonnard preferred country life the linear style that made his name did not suit his perception of rural subjects. By the second half of the 1890s a crisis was developing in his art which led him to loosen up his style in terms of the broken brushwork and more informal compositional methods pioneered by the Impressionists. *Canotage sur la Seine, le pont à Chatou*, 1896 (Plate 36) is Impressionist in both style and subject matter. Impressionism had achieved official recognition when 38 out of the 67 Impressionist paintings bequeathed by Gustave Caillebotte, including all seven by Degas, eight by Monet, seven by Pissarro and two by Cézanne, were finally accepted by the Luxembourg, the museum of contemporary art in Paris, and went on show early in 1897. Bonnard later told Raymond Cogniat: 'I remember very well that at that time I knew nothing about Impressionism, and we admired Gauguin's work for itself and not in its context. Besides, when we discovered Impressionism a little later, it came as a new enthusiasm, a sense of revelation and liberation, because Gauguin is a classic, almost a traditionalist, and Impressionism brought us freedom.' [39]

The freedom that Impressionism brought was to suggest a method of breaking away from a dependence on the object. Whereas Bonnard's early reputation had been founded on his ability to create striking images, he now went to the opposite extreme in his intimist interiors, slowing the pace down, taking attention away from the figures and making them part of the overall atmosphere of a room. His aim was to draw the spectator into a painting on a contemplative journey, in which familiar objects are encountered as though for the first time, forming unexpected relationships and assuming new meanings, and generating in the process a consciousness of the complexity of the experience that constitutes awareness on entering a room.

Bonnard had begun painting intimist interiors as early as 1889, but it was Vuillard who subsequently developed the subject and made it his own, while the former was concentrating on city scenes. Vuillard introduced a new spatial complexity to the intimist interior that had a profound influence on Bonnard. Their work was also at times so close that in the case of *Jeune femme à la lampe*, *c.*1900 (Plate 38), there is some confusion as to which of them actually painted it.

Rooms became analogues of human experience. They contained memories and told stories about their inhabitants' lives and status. They were places of refuge where different generations met at table or under the secure warm glow of a lamp. The objects in a room – like household pets – had their own functions and existence as they inter-

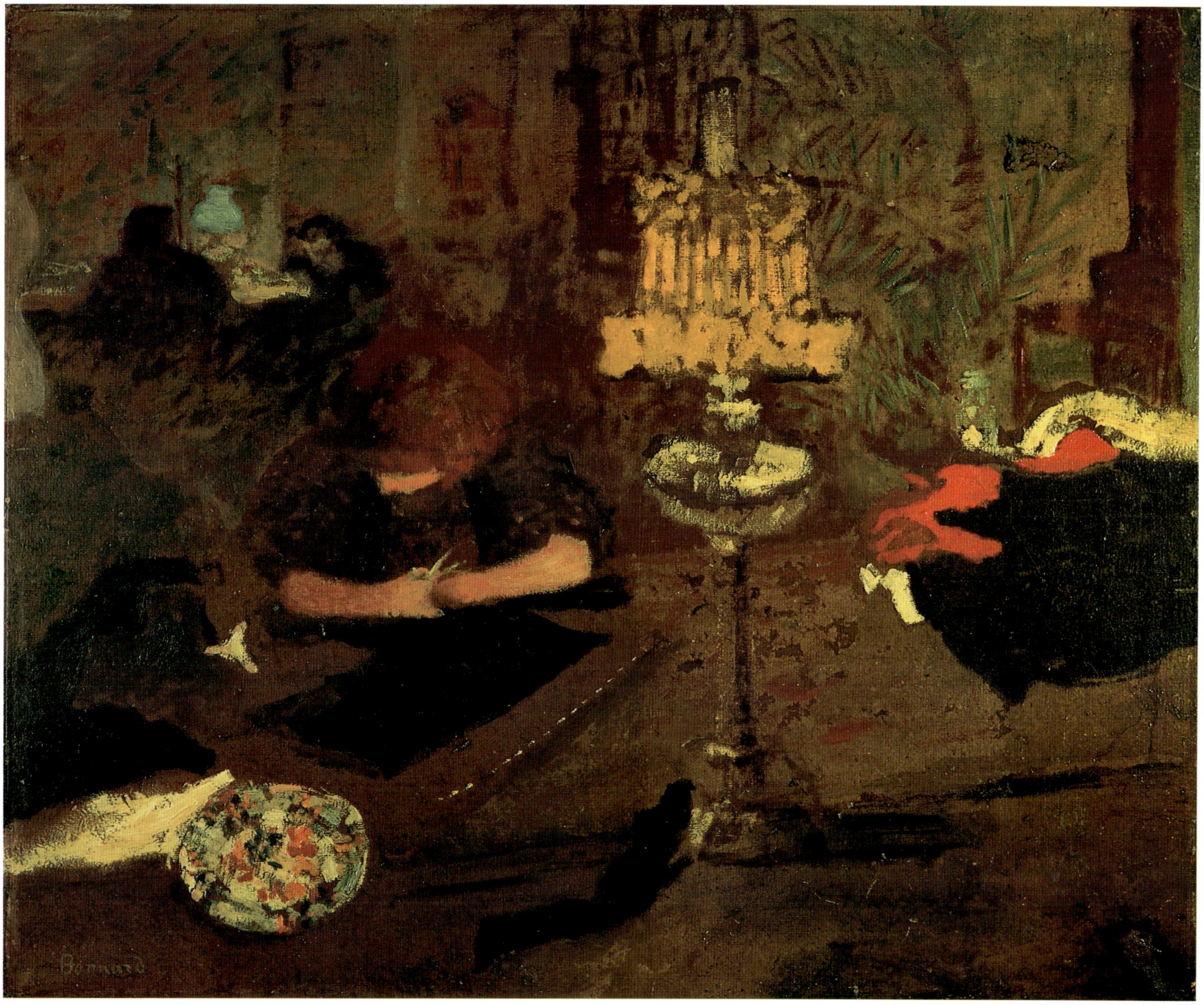

38
*Jeune femme à la lampe. c.*1900.
Oil on canvas, 61.5×75cm.
Musée des Beaux-Arts, Berne

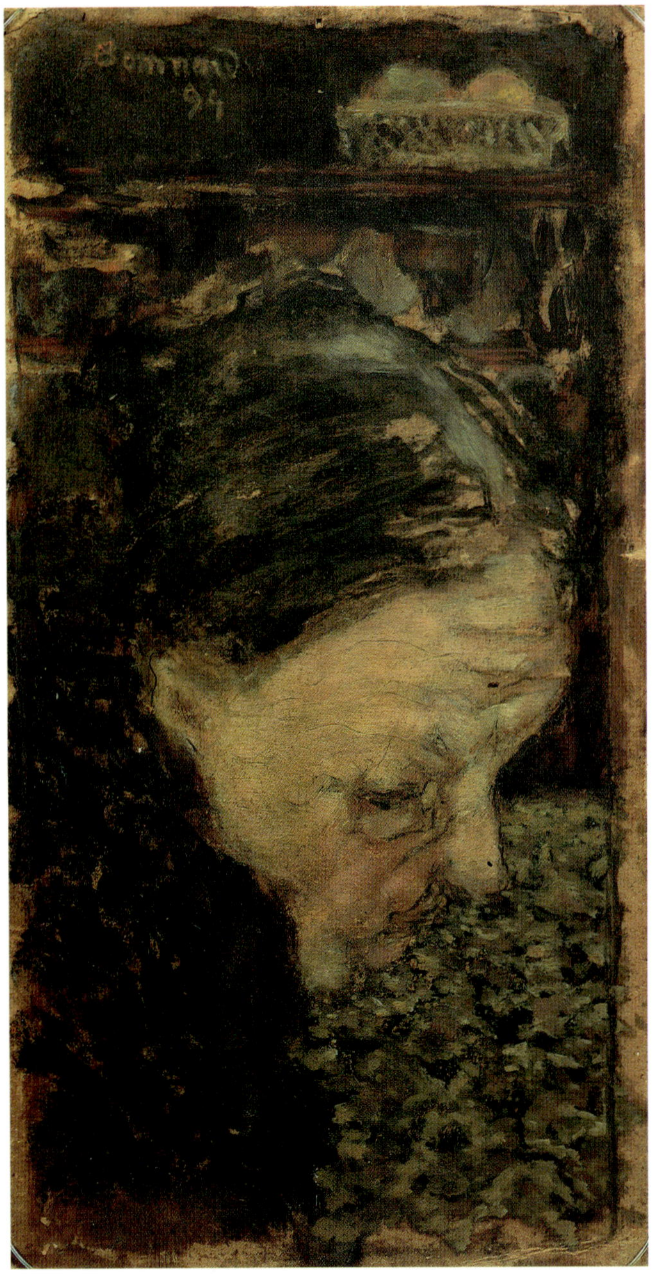

39
Ma Grand-mère. 1894.
Oil on board, 35.6×18.6cm.
Musée départemental du Prieuré,
Saint-Germain-en-Laye

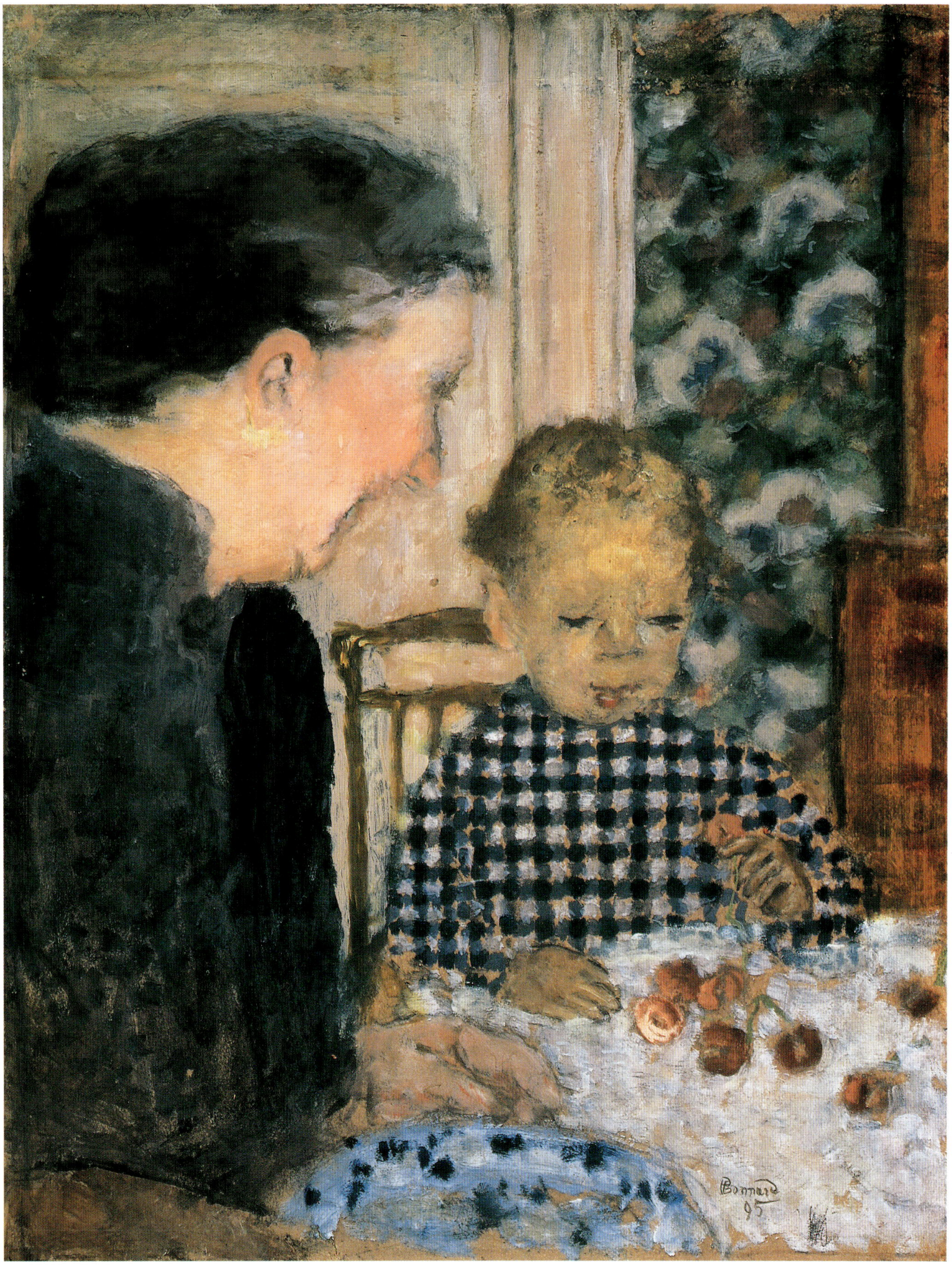

40
Enfant mangeant des cerises. 1895.
Oil on board, 52×41cm.
National Gallery of Ireland, Dublin

acted with human life. A chair could be arch and unwelcoming – one to be avoided; a table ungenerous in its proportions, bringing acquaintances too close together for comfort. There was a language in the control of tonal values that in the transition between light and dark could reveal form, create mood and dictate the way a spectator reads a work (because the eye moves from dark to light). Verlaine in his poetry stressed the shade and the nuance at the expense of colour. A slit in a curtain could let through the first calming gleam of morning light to relieve the anxiety of a sleepless night. Darkness could be both protective and disturbing; it could signify the encroachment of death. The atmosphere of silence in a room could represent anything from a pregnant pause, a gentle feeling of unspoken acquiescence, to an awful premonition of disaster. Maeterlinck's play *Intérieur*, performed at the Théâtre de l'Oeuvre in 1895, employed silence as a metaphor for non-communication where the important went unsaid. Surrounding space could be a spiritual void, a sense of hopelessness, a total black-out.

The rooms that Bonnard selected to paint in the 1890s were for the most part those at Le Clos, where he was returning to the atmosphere of his childhood.[40] His grandmother, Mme Frédéric Mertzdorff (1812–1900), the repository of family memory, was the presiding spirit in these rooms, merging with and forming part of the atmosphere of the background (Plate 39). She was evidently intimately involved in the lives of her great-grandchildren. In *Enfant mangeant des cerises*, 1895 (Plate 40), she looks on indulgently while Jean demolishes a plateful of cherries that she has just brought him. The charm of this delightful painting artfully conceals the skill with which Bonnard has combined in an understated way several familiar themes: intimism with decoration, the closely observed with geometric structure, tone with colour, and youth with old age.

Bonnard concentrated on familiar motifs in order to transcend and imbue with feeling subjects which the Impressionists had treated in a seemingly too objective way. His paintings of the dining room at Le Clos are not about changes in light so much as atmosphere, incidents and relationships that caught his eye. In *La Collation*, 1899 (Plate 41), Bonnard's niece, Renée Terrasse, who was to look after her uncle following the death of Marthe in 1942, faces her great-grandmother without really communicating. The atmosphere is one of silence. Mme Mertzdorff sits detached, as absorbed in thought as she is in the shadow. She was to die the following year. In *Le Déjeuner*, 1899 (Plate 42), Renée is joined by her mother, Bonnard's sister Andrée, and two brothers. In both paintings the real action takes place on the table, tilted up like a stage, a theatre in the round with the spectator joining the family as the audience. The background is darkened to concentrate attention on the white tablecloth, where a sequence of relationships between the still-life elements unfolds. The transformation of a table into a stage was to prove one of Bonnard's most important formal innovations.[41]

Like Proust, Bonnard was fascinated by the way memory shaped his perception of the world. He described a work of art as 'a stopping of time'.[42] A painting could both freeze a momentary action, making it eternal, and condense time. Memory held the

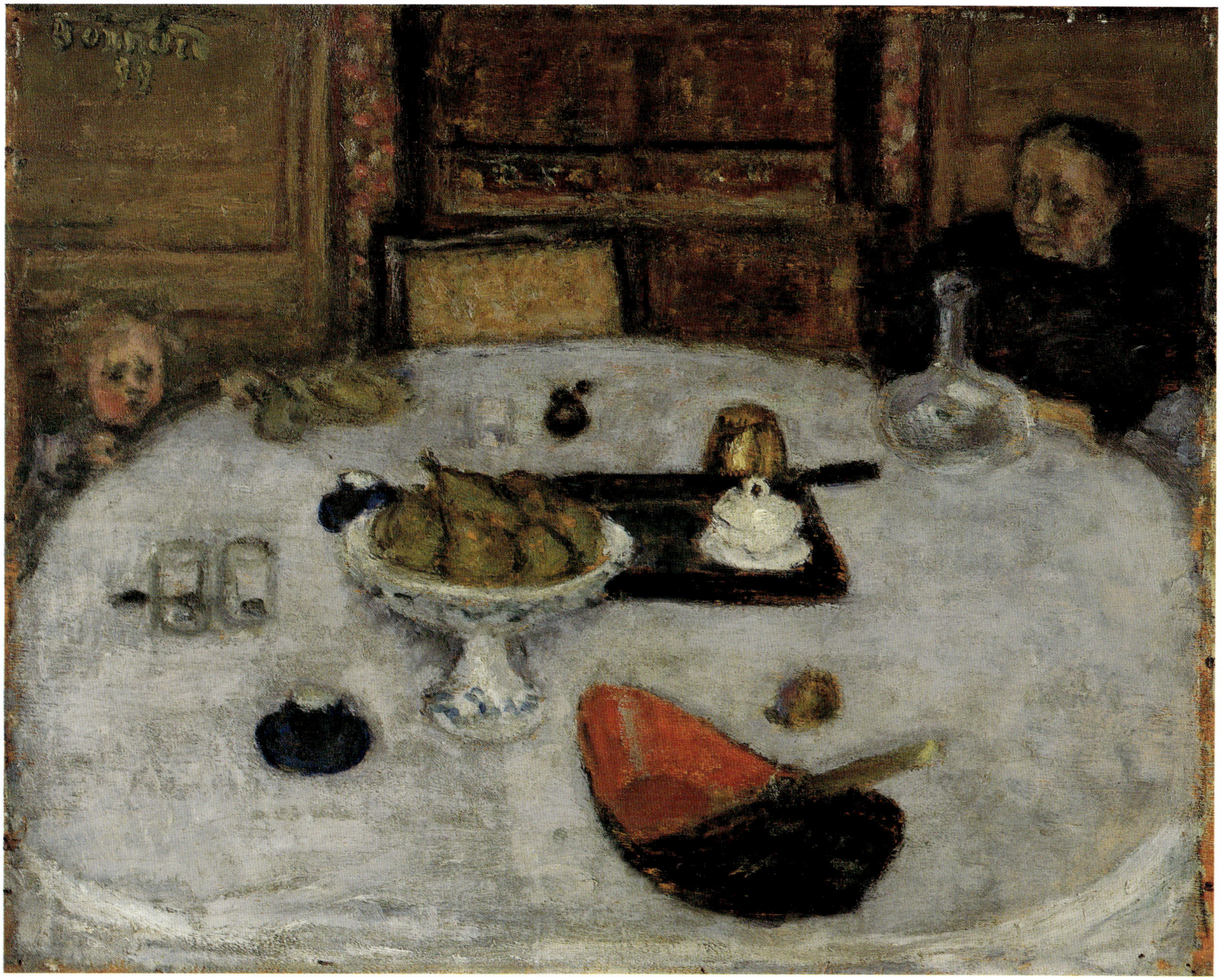

41
La Collation. 1899.
Oil on panel, 30.5×38.7cm.
Private collection

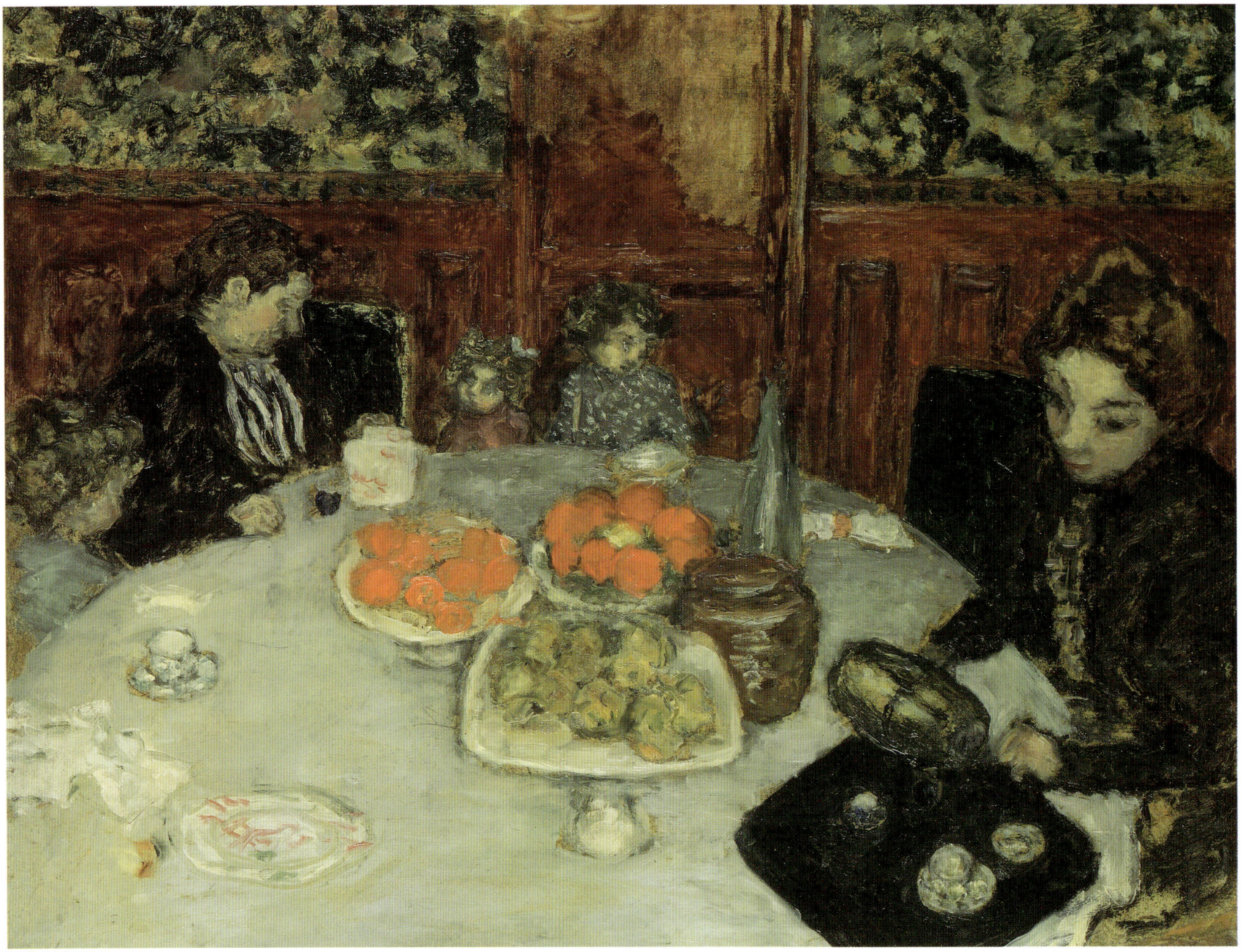

42
Le Déjeuner. 1899.
Oil on board, 55×70cm.
Stiftung Sammlung E.G. Buhrle, Zürich

key to his creative process. It enabled him to distil and come to terms with experience, without being dominated by the motif, and to preserve his first, crucial idea for a painting. This initial idea could be something as simple as a ray of light catching a face in a darkened interior. During the process of painting, his memory of this particular experience would become enriched and transformed into a decorative whole.

It is no exaggeration to say that there was enough going on in the intimist interior to keep Bonnard busy for a life-time. Shortly before his death, he wrote to the critic Georges Besson: 'I float between intimism and decoration, one does not reformulate oneself.'[45]

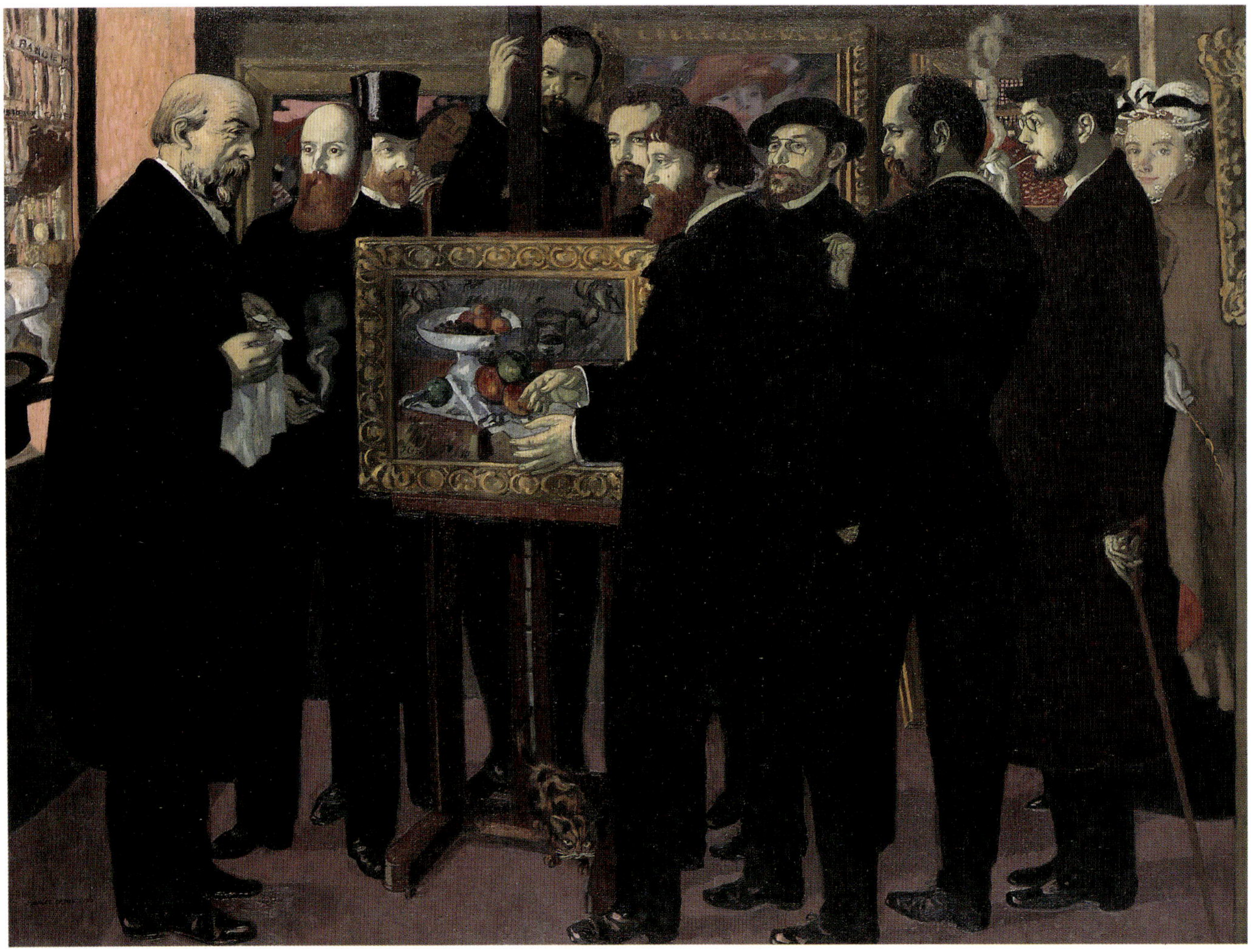

43
Maurice Denis.
Homage to Cézanne. 1900.
Oil on canvas, 180×240cm.
Musée d'Orsay, Paris

Chapter 2

A time of experiment: between city and country

The end of the 1890s marked more than the turn of the century. It was the end of an era. Many of those who had pioneered the advance of modernism in the early 1890s lost their way and ended up either destroying themselves or being left as living reminders of a former age. Gauguin, who had inspired the formation of the Nabis, attempted suicide in 1898 and finally died on 8 May 1903 in the Marquesas. Toulouse-Lautrec's intense production began to decline after 1896. By 1900 he had given up the will to live – let alone work – and he died the following year aged 36. Even the Nabis by 1895 were moving toward the naturalism they had initially rejected. The literary drive behind Symbolism had similarly declined. Félix Fénéon, one of the most observant spokesmen of his generation, stopped writing after 1893. Lugné-Poe's Théâtre de l'Oeuvre petered out in public indifference. The *Revue Blanche* closed its doors in 1903. Feeling that the achievements of the 1890s were being allowed to ebb away, André Mellerio organized a group exhibition, in homage to Redon, of Symbolists, Neo-Impressionists and Nabis at the Durand-Ruel gallery in March 1899. Neither the exhibition, nor Maurice Denis's *Homage to Cézanne*, 1900 (Plate 43), showing the Nabis with Redon on the extreme left, could disguise the fact that the precocious young artists had grown up and gone their separate ways. Bonnard stands on the right of the main group, a little detached, drawing ruminatively on his pipe.

This cultural shift accentuated the developing tension in Bonnard's art between his growing interest in Impressionism and the achievements in the Nabis style which had made his name. His gradual rapprochement with Impressionism had not been easy. Camille Pissarro, the father-figure of Impressionism, dismissed his first one-man exhibition at the Durand-Ruel gallery in 1896 as 'another Symbolist fiasco!'[1] Bonnard was supported in his move away from Symbolism by Vuillard and to a lesser extent Roussel, his two companions on a trip to Venice in 1899, documented in a delightful series of photographs. They firmly equated Impressionism with a transient form of naturalism. Looking back on this period in 1937, Bonnard told an interviewer: 'When my friends and I decided to pick up the research of the Impressionists and try to take it further, we wanted to outshine them in their naturalistic impressions of colour. Art is not Nature. We were stricter in composition. There was a lot more to be got out of colour as a means of expression.'[2] The concern for composition drew Bonnard to Renoir, Cézanne and especially Degas, rather than to Sisley, Pissarro and Monet.

Like many of the Impressionists, Bonnard had evolved a seasonal routine, working in the spring in the Seine valley and then at his family home at Le Grand-Lemps in the summer and early autumn, returning to Paris for the winter. He also repeatedly visited the Normandy coast, the birthplace of Impressionism. In going back to Impressionism he was as it were returning to the origins of modern art in landscape painting. Also by leaving Paris for long periods each year, he was escaping the competitive pressures of the contemporary art scene and giving himself the opportunity to find his own feet through contact with nature. In addition he made numerous short trips abroad, apart from Venice visiting London, Spain in 1901 with Vuillard and Emmanuel Bibesco, Holland in 1902 with the Hessels, Vuillard and Roussel, Berlin in 1905 to paint the wife of the painter Curt Herrmann, Belgium and Holland again in 1905 and 1906 aboard Misia Edwards's yacht Aimée, and Algeria and Tunisia in 1908. *Le Yacht*, *c.*1906 (Plate 44), shows the *Aimée*, whose name was a phonetic transcription of E for Edwards and M for Misia, with Misia on the extreme left of the bridge reading. Bonnard recorded his trips on the yacht in two sketch books and in a series of photographs.

Bonnard's journeys pose a fascinating problem. On a superficial level they can be seen as a sign of his restlessness. Certainly – with rare exceptions such as the trips on the *Aimée* – there is little correlation between where he went and what he produced.

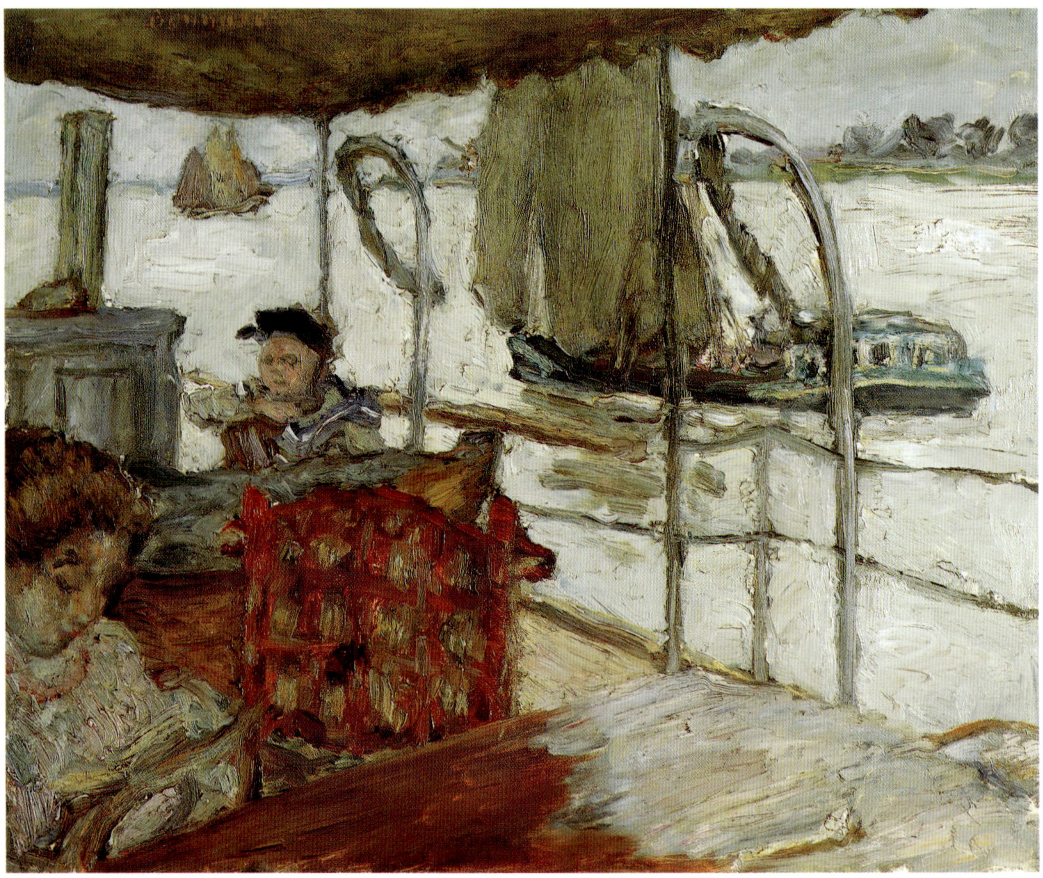

44
Le Yacht. *c.*1906.
Oil on canvas, 43.2×48.3cm.
The Duke of Roxburghe, Floors Castle, Kelso

He first went down to the south of France in 1906, but there was no conversion to southern light until his second, longer stay in 1909. They were not painting trips, or constant quests for fresh motifs. Unlike an archetypal Impressionist, he did not leave us for instance with a series of Venetian views. He still concentrated on familiar subjects over a long period of time. Yet in a curious way these journeys opened up the conflict between realism and decoration in his early Nabis work into a series of dialogues in which he was engaged for the rest of his life: between northern realism and southern idealism, between the transient light of the north and the permanence of atmosphere of the south, and by extension between the subdued palette of the north and the high-keyed colour of the south.

Although undeniably dependent on sensations drawn from nature, Bonnard would persistently pick up on ideas and issues that had passed out of fashion. For many an artist this would have been a recipe for oblivion (not that Bonnard did not suffer from periods of critical neglect), but this disregard for fashion became a feature of his style. His acceptance of the commissions by Vollard to illustrate Verlaine's *Parallèlement* and Longus's *Daphnis et Chloé* are cases in point. The books brought to a conclusion his Paris period of the 1890s, and at the same time firmly established two very important subjects on his artistic agenda, the nude and the pastoral.

Parallèlement in itself proved to be out of touch with contemporary taste when it was published in 1900. The very freedom of the illustrations spilling across the pages, just as Verlaine's verses overflow the lines, went against the fashion for crisply defined woodcut images. The book comprises 109 lithographs and nine woodcuts after drawings by Bonnard. Bonnard said that he chose rose-sanguine for the lithographs 'to convey more of the poetic atmosphere of Verlaine'.[3] Vollard probably selected Verlaine because his funeral in Paris in 1896 was a major public event, widely reported in the press and attended by many of the leading members of the avant-garde. The poems in *Parallèlement* are often highly erotic. The first part contains six lesbian sonnets of 1867, the second features prostitutes in a brothel, the third poems from prison and the fourth sexual inversion. It was only passed by the public censor because it was thought to be a book on geometry.[4]

If the selection of Verlaine by Vollard was casual the same cannot be said of Bonnard's involvement in the project, which took him two years to complete. The parallels between Bonnard and Verlaine are surprisingly close. Both were against theorizing and refused to be pinned down by labels. When asked in 1891 what he thought about Symbolism, Verlaine protested that he did not know what it meant. Both believed that a work should result from direct experience, while at the same time recognizing that it was the product of a complex series of often contradictory aspirations rooted in the human psyche: thought competed with action, the mystic with a ravening carnality.[5] Verlaine christened them 'parallels', because parallels can never meet.

The outwardly mild-mannered Bonnard was attracted to outrageous characters such as Alfred Jarry, who defied social convention and carried their behaviour to excess.

Verlaine was another case in point, although Bonnard did not necessarily know much about his life. He was a totally irresponsible, lying alcoholic who battered his wife and had a protracted affair with another man, the poet Rimbaud. He was unkind to his mother and yet craved maternal warmth to the end of his life, with the memory of his childhood in Metz becoming a refuge, an earthly paradise. In his work he cultivated an aura of detachment, partly as a protection against the violence of his own temperament, advocated an art for art's sake, independent of morality, discovering in eighteenth-century art, especially Watteau, a way of dealing with sensuous experience in a classical style.[6] The brutality of raw experience was refined in lyric poems of great beauty which gently savour the remembered atmosphere of bodies brought together in passionate embrace. The wistful melody of his poetry has come to be regarded as perhaps his genuinely original note.[7]

Bonnard's illustrations capture the dualism and the mood of Verlaine's poems. On the one hand they evoke a classical era seen through eighteenth-century eyes. A faun and nymph recline in the shade of a tree above the poem 'Allégorie' (Plate 47), while on the opposite page the hill is topped with a classical temple. On the other hand they deal with the erotic physicality of the female figure. For Bonnard Marthe meant sex, and in a remarkable series of preparatory sketches, begun in the spring of 1897, he transferred her from the domesticity of his illustrations for Peter Nansen's *Marie* into the passionate situations in *Parallèlement*. It is her body that is splayed across the pages of *Parallèlement* in a variety of recumbent poses. In the second illustration for the poem 'Été' (Plate 46) she is seen from the back, in 'Séguidille' (Plate 49) tossed back over the poem in a state of complete abandon, and in 'Auburn' (Plate 48) relaxing on her front.

Bonnard is now known to have had Marthe photographed in the nude to sort out the poses. In some cases the correspondence between the photographs and the illustrations is extremely close. For instance, the photograph of Marthe seen from the back sitting on the bed (Plate 45) must have provided the source for the illustration of 'Été'. Bonnard's own photographs were for the most part informal 'snaps' of family and friends, taken in the open air with a Kodak pocket-model which came on to the

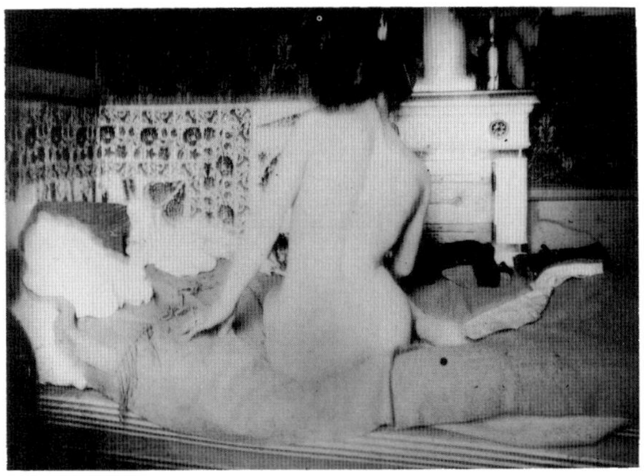

45
Marthe sitting on a bed. 1899–1900.
Photograph.
Musée d'Orsay, Paris

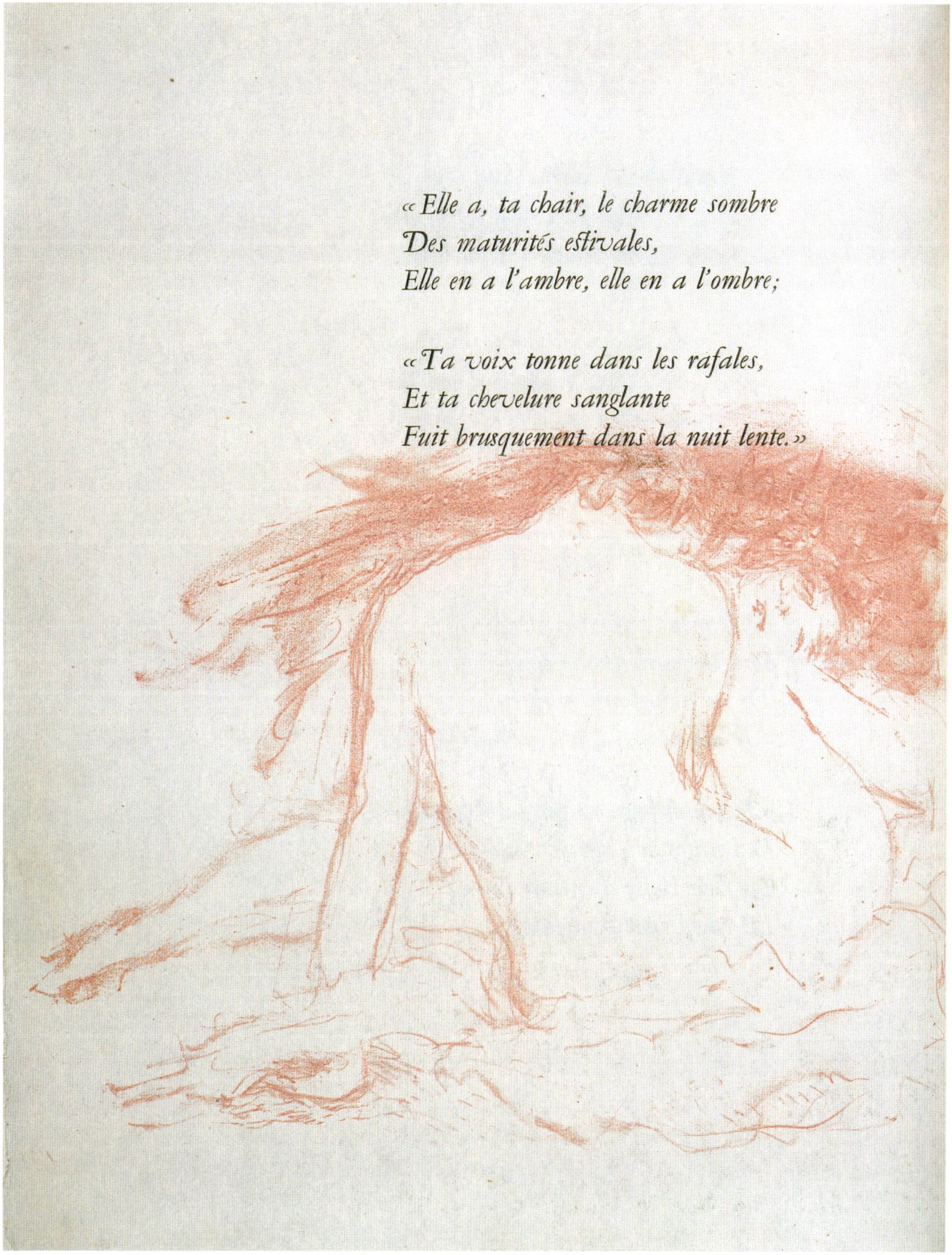

46
L'Été.
Page 18 from Paul Verlaine, *Parallèlement*, 1900.
Colur lithograph in pink sanguine, 30.5×25cm

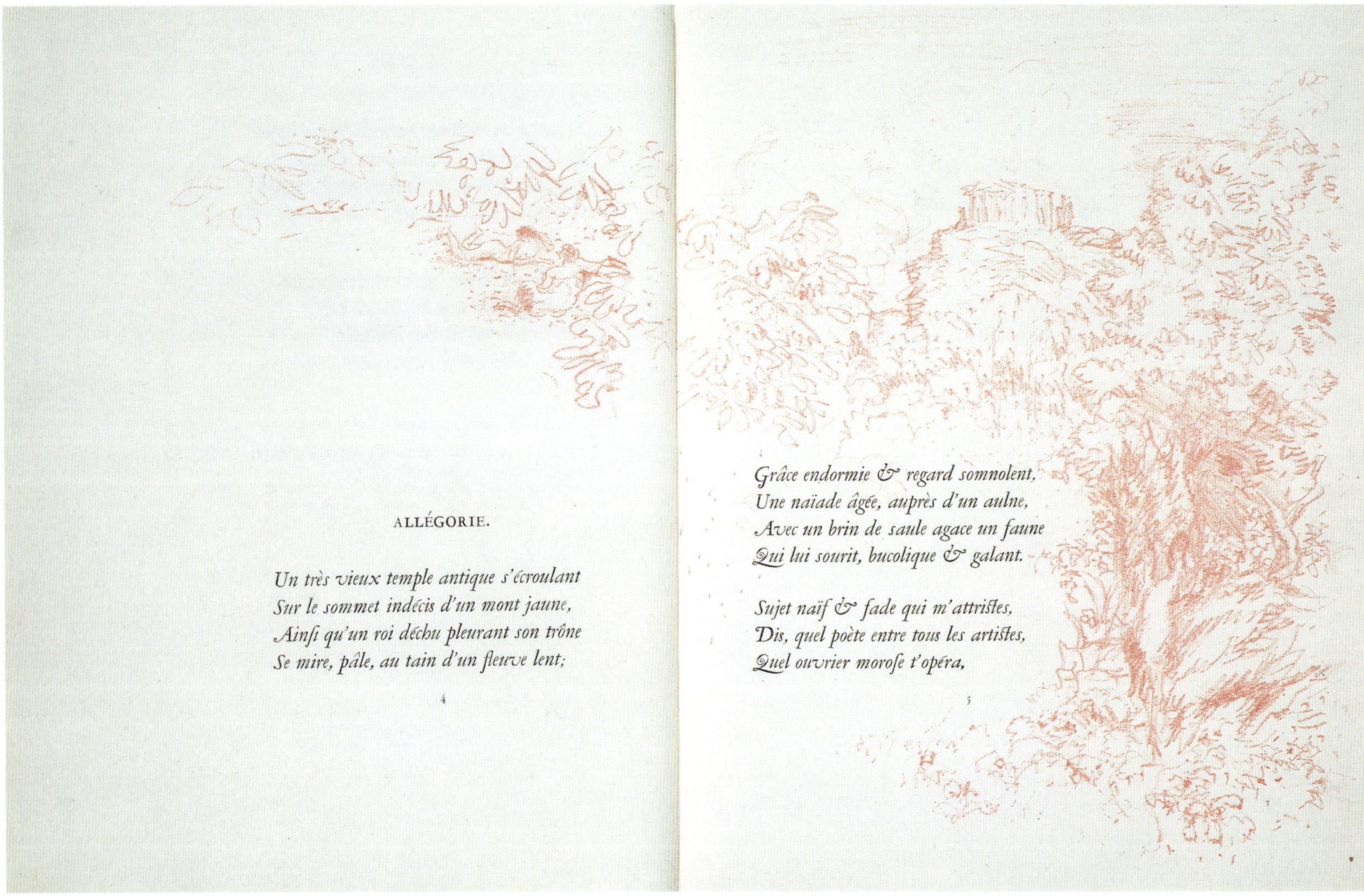

ALLÉGORIE.

Un très vieux temple antique s'écroulant
Sur le sommet indécis d'un mont jaune,
Ainſi qu'un roi déchu pleurant son trône
Se mire, pâle, au tain d'un fleuve lent;

4

Grâce endormie & regard somnolent,
Une naïade âgée, auprès d'un aulne,
Avec un brin de saule agace un faune
Qui lui sourit, bucolique & galant.

Sujet naïf & fade qui m'attriſtes,
Dis, quel poète entre tous les artiſtes,
Quel ouvrier moroſe t'opéra,

5

47
Allégorie.
Pages 4 and 5 from Paul Verlaine, *Parallèlement*, 1900.
Colour lithograph in pink sanguine, 30.5×50cm

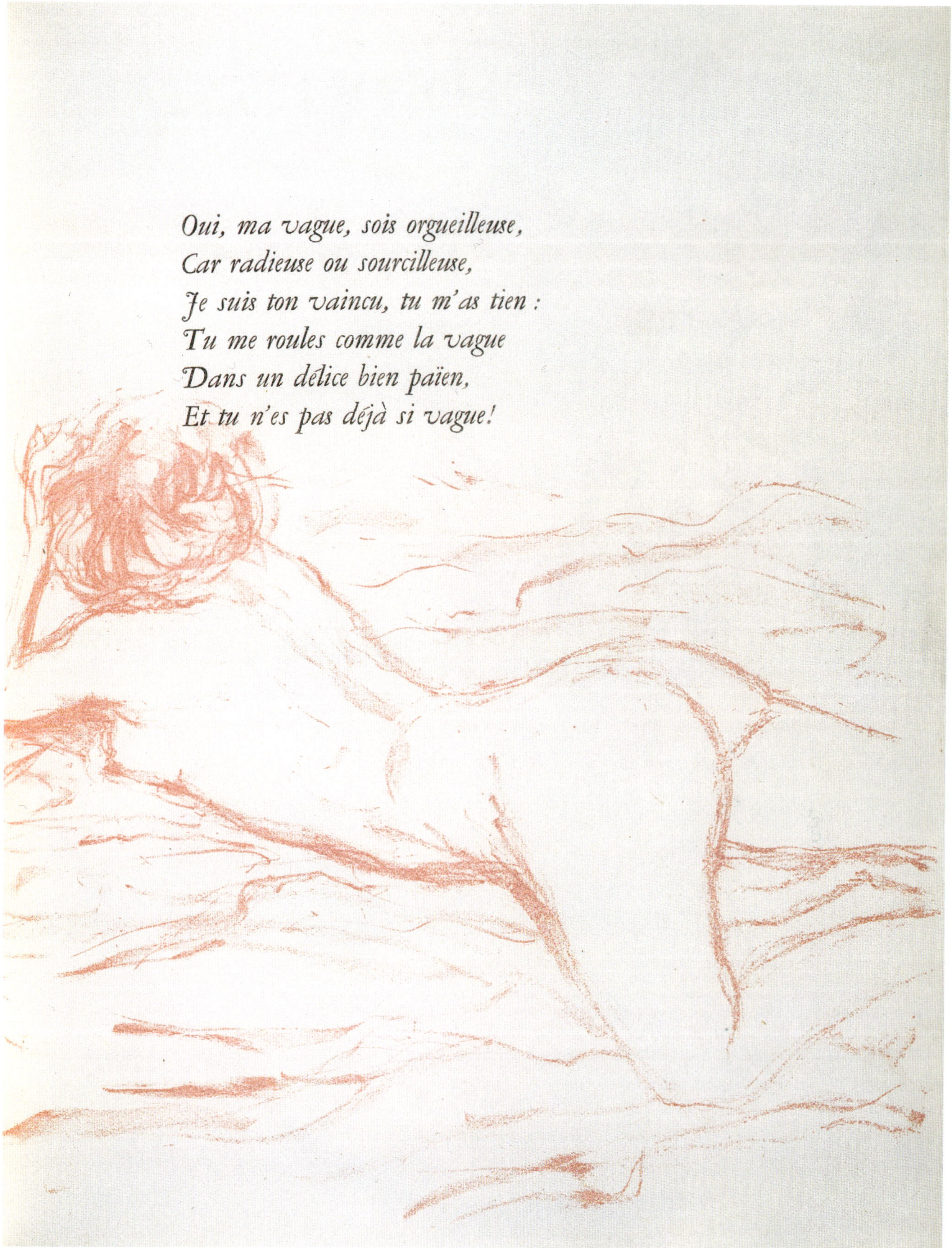

48
Auburn.
Page 36 from Paul Verlaine, *Parallèlement*, 1900.
Colour lithograph in pink sanguine, 30.5×25cm

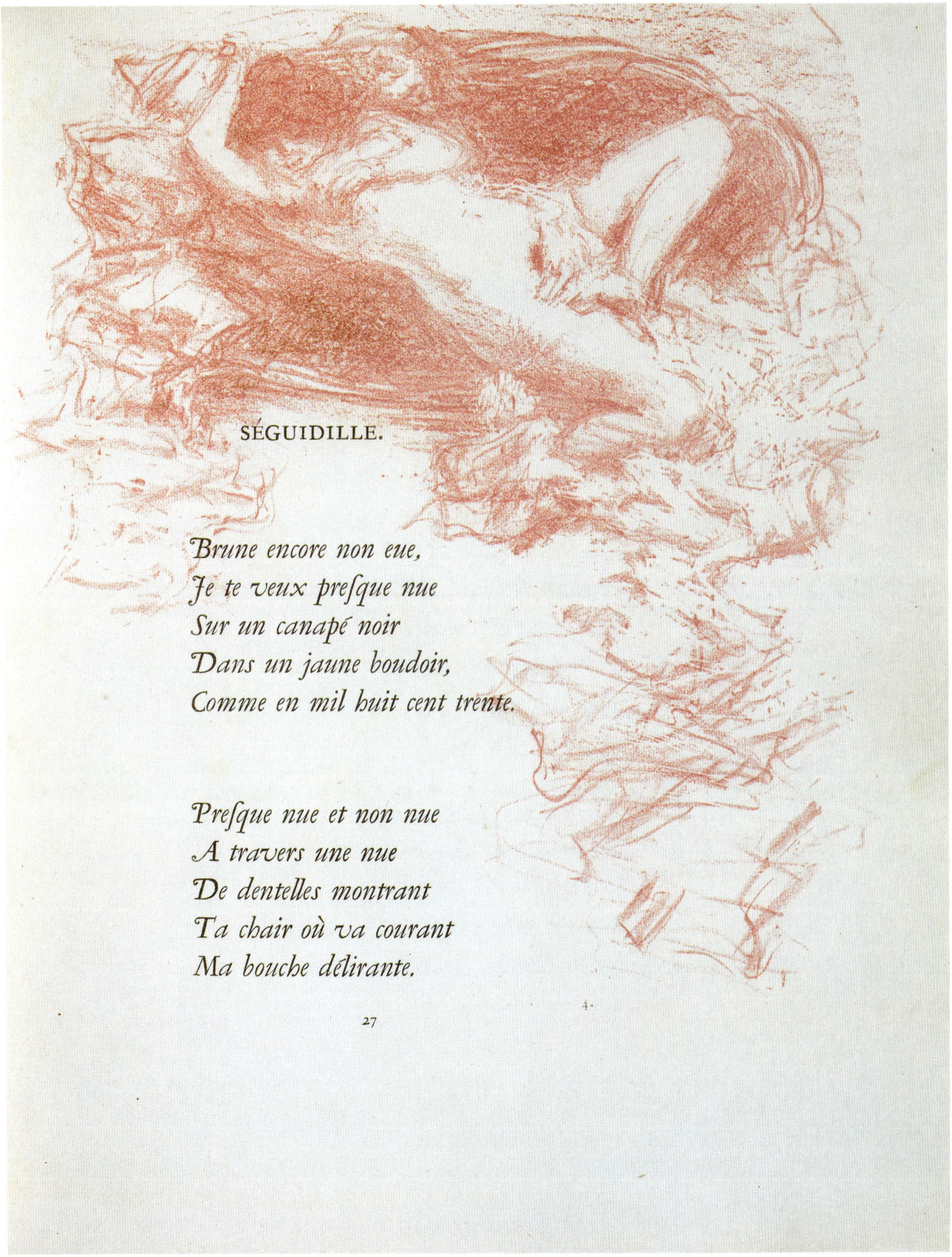
SÉGUIDILLE.

Brune encore non eue,
Je te veux presque nue
Sur un canapé noir
Dans un jaune boudoir,
Comme en mil huit cent trente.

Presque nue et non nue
A travers une nue
De dentelles montrant
Ta chair où va courant
Ma bouche délirante.

27

49
Séguidille.
Page 27 from Paul Verlaine, *Parallèlement*, 1900.
Colour lithograph in pink sanguine, 30.5×25cm

market in 1888.[8] While he had no pretensions as a photographer, these photographs nevertheless played an important part in the development of his 'informal' vision and – although not necessarily planned as such – served, like working drawings, as the starting point for paintings and prints. The photographs of Marthe in the nude, however, are formally posed on the bed in his Paris apartment, like Degas's photographs, which suggests that Bonnard had them taken specifically for the job in hand.

In Bonnard's creative process photography was but one source in an exploration of poses that moved between drawing, painting and prints. His obsessive interest in female sexuality, stimulated by *Parallèlement*, in turn led on to a series of major paintings on the theme. In the unique case of the illustration to the poem 'Séguidille', the pose, perhaps suggested by the figure of Dawn from Michelangelo's Medici tombs, went through this entire sequence of media and achieved its ultimate formulation in the great painting *L'Indolente*, *c.*1899 (Plate 50). Whereas the illustrations to *Parallèlement* are filtered through an essentially gentle Rococo vision of nudes softly outlined in red chalk, the paintings are quite exceptional in Bonnard's art in their depiction of the female nude as powerfully erotic. This is partly due to the fact that many of the illustrations deal with lesbian love, something of a chic diversion at the time.[9] By contrast, the subject-matter of the paintings was both highly autobiographical and provocative.

The content of these paintings is varied. *Nu aux bas noirs*, *c.*1900 (Plate 52), for instance, suggests a life study, catching the model placed in an intimist interior and in the act of pulling the rest of her clothes over her head. Bonnard was evidently fascinated by the juxtaposition of lamp-lit flesh tones and black stockings. His employment of the antique sculpture *The Sleeping Hermaphrodite* for the pose of *La Sieste*, 1900 (Plate 51), continues the theme of sexual ambiguity running through *Parallèlement*. *L'Indolente* and *L'Homme et la femme*, 1900 (Plate 3) are clearly autobiographical. Marthe is so positioned in *L'indolente* as to imply that Bonnard had just left her. In *L'Homme et la femme* he is seen retrieving his clothes from behind the screen. Sex as the primal connection between man and woman is over and the screen indicates that a barrier has come down between them. The Norwegian artist Edvard Munch, who was well known in Nabis circles, had given the subject of sex a new impetus; but by contrast with Munch's nudes, Marthe is depicted without guilt, having enjoyed sex with all the naturalness of an animal act.[10] As if to emphasize the animal side of her nature, she is seen playing with two kittens on the bed.

Undeterred by the hostile reaction to *Parallèlement*, Vollard commissioned Bonnard to illustrate Longus's *Daphnis et Chloé*, which was published in 1902. In choosing *Daphnis et Chloé* Vollard was on safer ground. Written towards the end of the second or early third century BC, the book had long since proved a popular subject for illustration. The link between literature and art is firmly established in the prologue with the author's discovery in a wood of a painting of lovers, which he decides to emulate in words 'as an offering to Love and the Nymphs and Pan, and as a source of pleasure for the human race – something to heal the sick and comfort the afflicted, to refresh the

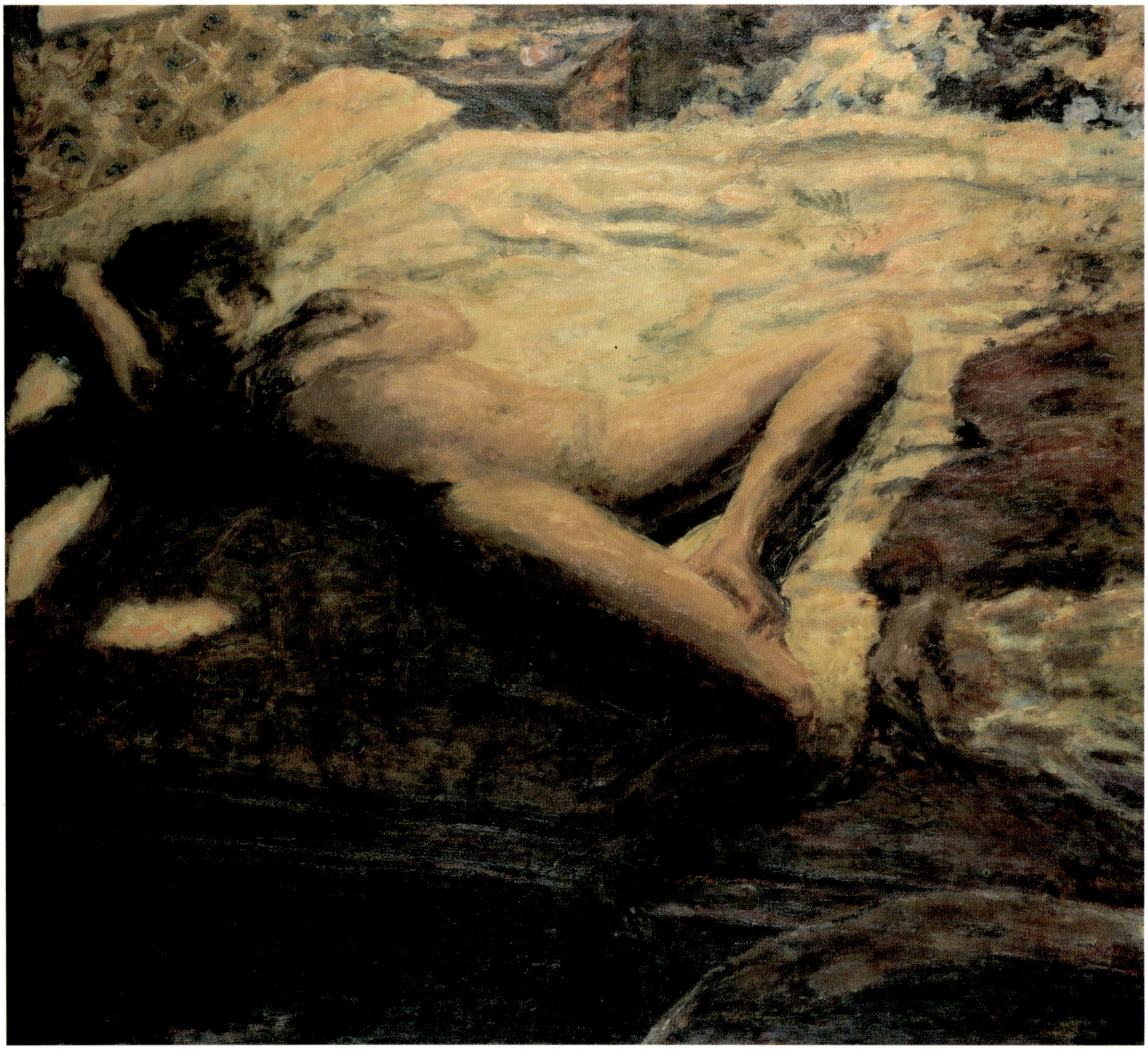

50
L'Indolente (preliminary version). *c.* 1899.
Oil on canvas, 92×108cm.
Josefowitz Collection

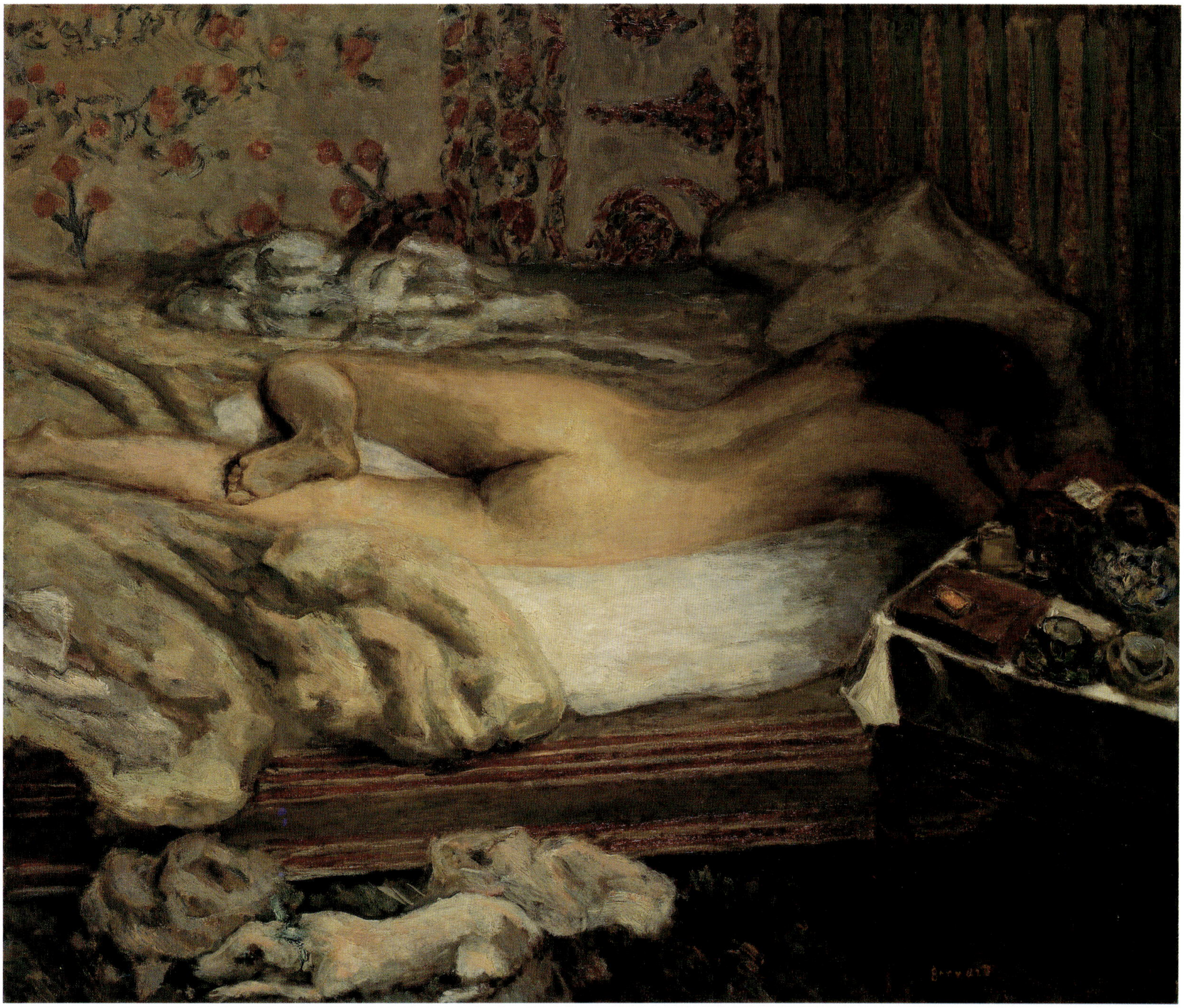

51
La Sieste. 1900.
Oil on canvas, 109×132cm.
National Gallery of Victoria, Melbourne

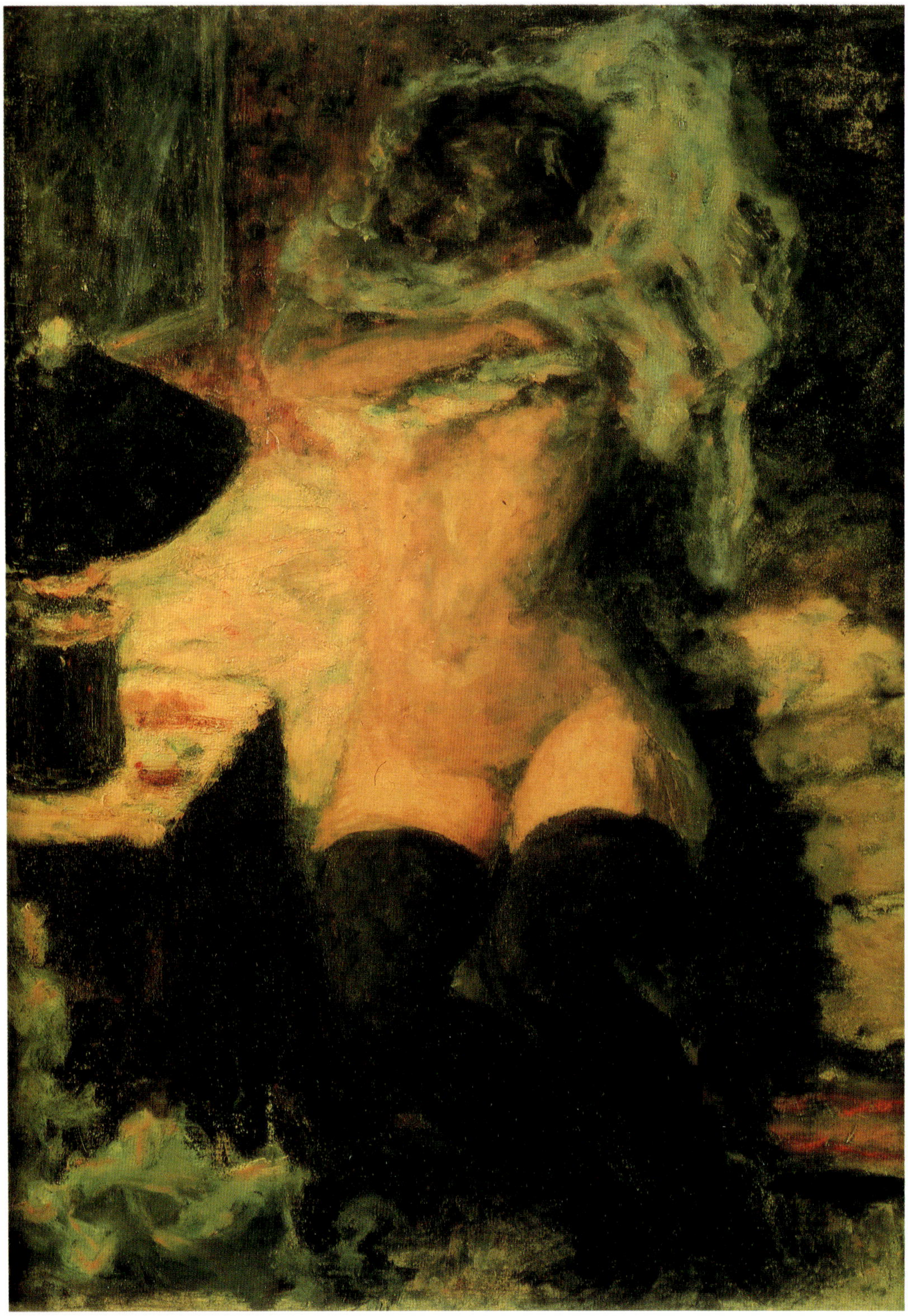

52
Nu aux bas noirs. *c*.1900.
Oil on panel, 59×43cm.
Private collection, on loan to
City of Sheffield Art Galleries

memory of those who have been in love and educate those who have not'.[11] The story tells of the meeting and subsequent love affair between Daphnis and Chloë, both abandoned by their respective parents and brought up by simple country folk in an idyllic pastoral world controlled by the seasons. For a pair brought up in the country, looking after animals, they prove astonishingly ignorant of sexual matters, and their education is drawn out slowly and enjoyably across the four books. After numerous adventures, they are reunited with their true parents, marry and choose to remain faithful to their upbringing by continuing to live the pastoral life.

Bonnard evidently took the commission very much to heart, as he later recalled: 'On every page I evoked the shepherd of Lesbos with a sort of frenzied happiness that carried me along in spite of myself.'[12] In a sense the overt passion of *Parallèlement* and the ensuing paintings went against the grain of his art, whereas *Daphnis et Chloé* gave him the opportunity to take stock and to discover in the pastoral ways of dealing with reality in a more complex form, blending the past with the present, contemporary experience with classical myth. His 156 lithographed illustrations, set uniformly in the centre of a five-lined page, follow the text closely, but instead of portraying this idyllic pastoral world as a classical landscape, under a cloudless sky, he relocated the whole story in settings that he knew well. The landscapes of the Île-de-France and the Dauphiné became his Lesbos. There was nothing particularly original about this move. After all Monet and his fellow Impressionists had discovered in the rivers and water-meadows of the Île-de-France the classical qualities of warmth, peace and plenty hitherto associated with the Roman Campagna, and his fellow Nabis and close friend Roussel had taken the next step in 1899 when he settled in the village of L'Étang-de-Ville and began populating the landscape round his home with fauns and nymphs from the pages of Virgil and Lucretius.[13] Bonnard then followed Roussel when he rented a house in the nearby village of Montval.

But there is a clear distinction to be made between Bonnard's uses of the two settings. Whereas his photographs of the Terrasse children playing in the garden at Le Clos (Plate 54), in combination with his own childhood memories, provided the source for such scenes of unaffected innocence as the young Daphnis wandering about naked with bunches of wildflowers in each hand (Plate 55) or sitting by a fountain (Plate 53), he employed the landscape of the Île-de-France for something much more immediately erotic. He and Marthe abandoned the bed in the Paris apartment for the garden of the house at Montval, where they stripped naked and photographed each other in the roles of Daphnis and Chloë (Plate 56).[14] Quite why he should have gone to such lengths is difficult to determine. Apart from the obvious need to base his art on reality, he seems to have been following the objective in the prologue 'to refresh the memory of those who have been in love' rather literally. For Bonnard the recovery of the past was only possible in terms of an equivalent discovered in the present. It was almost as though he were putting the clock back to their first meeting in 1893 and re-creating their initial affair in the pastoral conditions he would ideally have chosen. To register

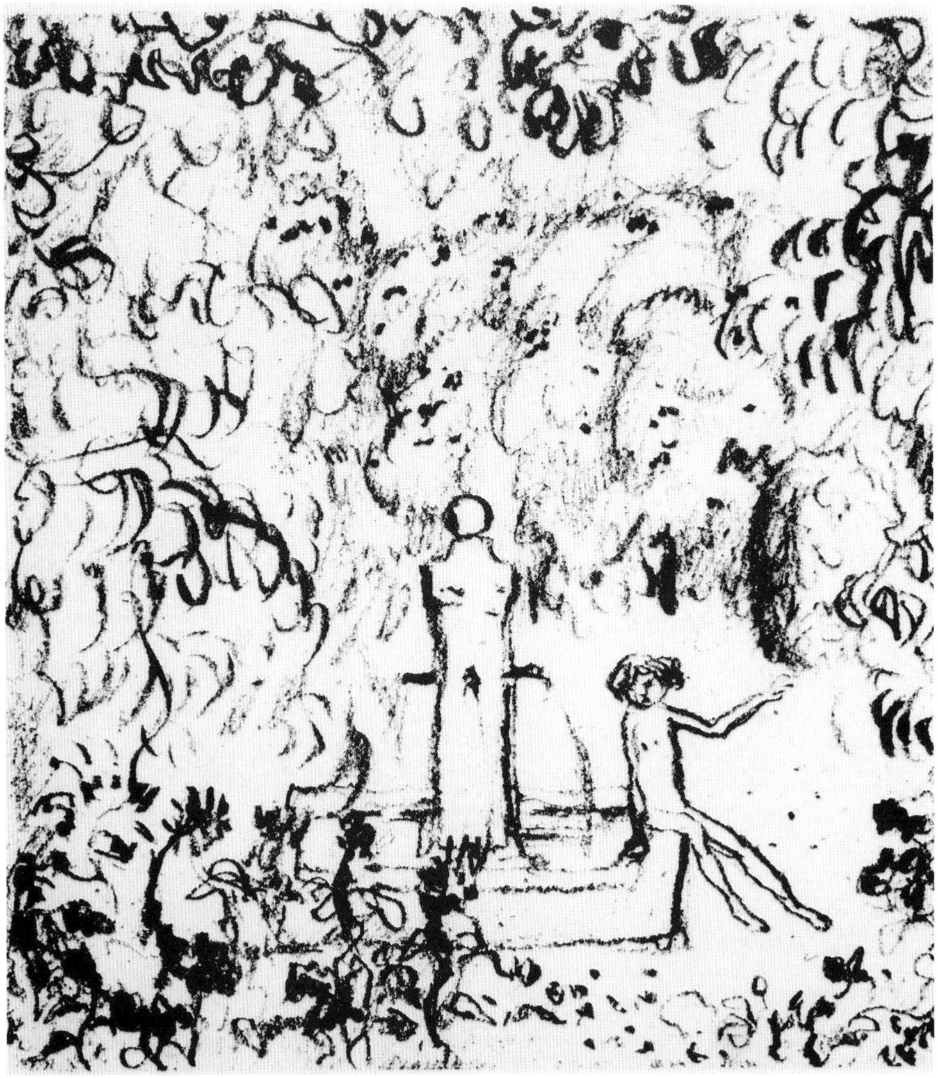

53
At the fountain.
From Longus,
Daphnis et Chloé, 1902.
Lithograph in black, 15.3×14cm

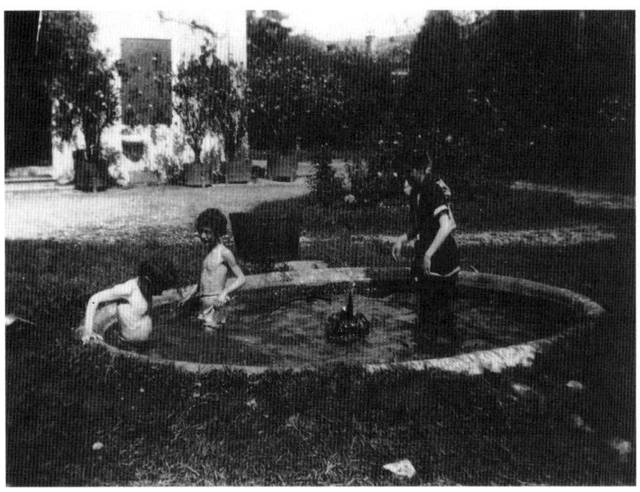

54
Andrée, Charles and
Jean Terrasse. 1889.
Photograph.
Musée d'Orsay, Paris

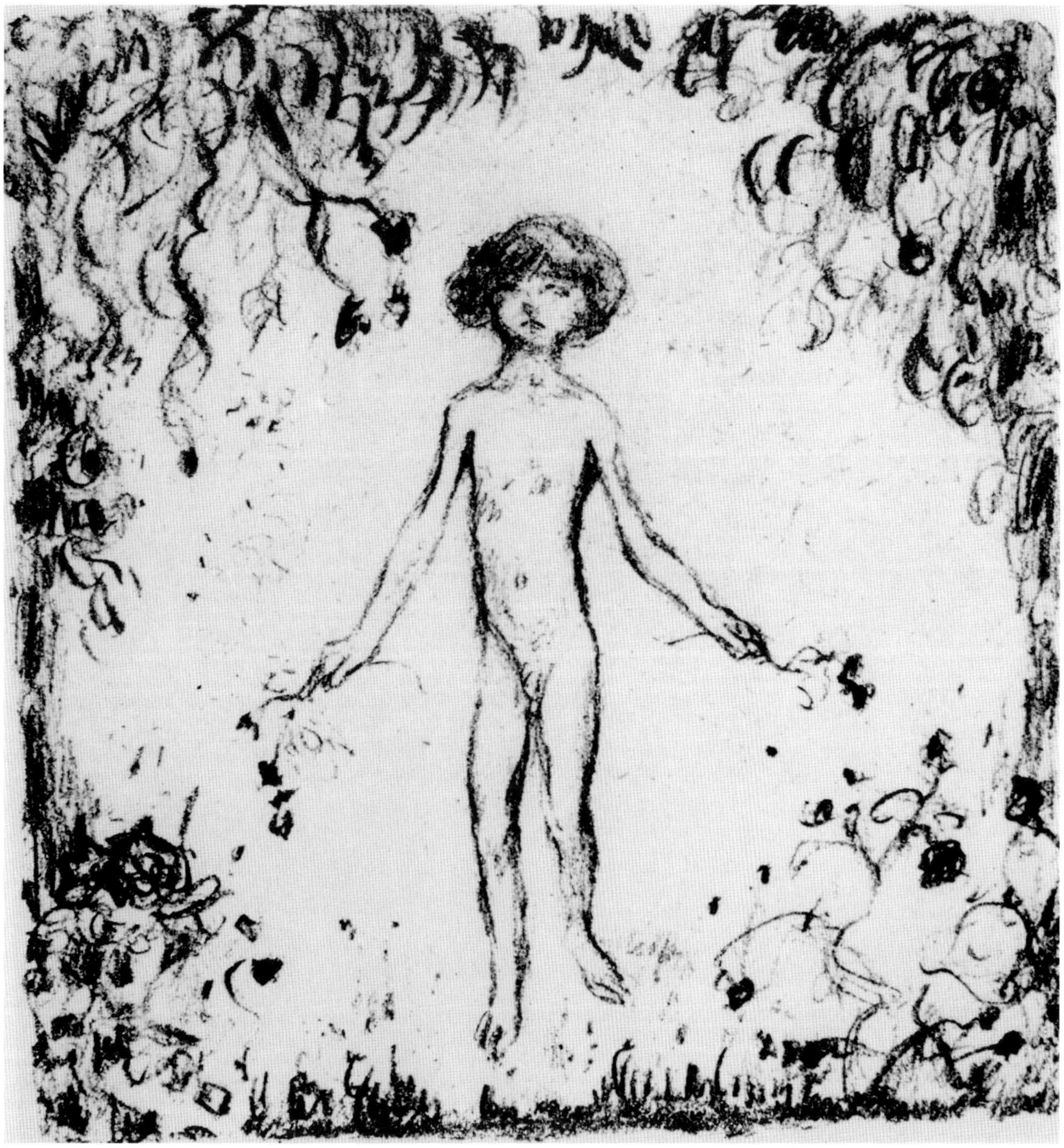

55
Daphnis.
From Longus,
Daphnis et Chloé, 1902.
Lithograph in black, 15.3 x 14cm

his tenuous grasp of this fleeting reality, as well as the delicacy and essential vulnerablity of the lovers' predicament, Bonnard employed an Impressionist, sketch-like technique, for which he was criticized, rather than a firm, classical style of crisp linear contours. The tremulous nature of the sketch-like style was peculiarly effective in scenes where Daphnis and Chloë feel their fingers pulsate at the touch of each other's bodies (Plate 57).

Behind the pastoral vision lies the archetype of the primeval paradise. Bonnard shared Proust's stated belief that 'the true paradises are the paradises we have lost.'[15] An ever-present feeling of loss pervades his vision of the pastoral, and nostalgia became his means of connecting the past with the present. The viewer is absorbed in a nostalgia for the sensuous perfection of lost worlds. The landscape around Le Clos became a lost world of childhood innocence, a demi-Eden before the Fall, briefly revived each summer by the Terrasse children holidaying there. The garden at Montval became a place of passion remembered. Even the classical tradition that he had been brought up to believe in as a specifically French inheritance appeared to be a lost culture, facing ultimate destruction by material progress and by the ever-present power of Germany. That such a programme had been initiated by *Daphnis et Chloé* was entirely apt, for it too came at the end of a culture in decline and has come to be regarded as the last great creation of pagan literature. It is no surprise to find that translations have often coincided with times of stress when people sought security in a comforting picture of an earthly paradise.[16]

Bonnard's illustrations for *Daphnis et Chloé* initiated a series of large-scale decorative paintings. In *L'Après-midi bourgeoise* (Plate 59), exhibited at the Salon des Indépendants of 1900, the notion of the family as a metonym for mental peace and security conflicts with the tensions in the relationships between the figures. The painting shows the Terrasse family and a visiting couple, the Prudhommes, sitting in front of Le Clos. The women really run the show, and the men seem content to sit back and let it all happen. The voluminous figure of Mme Prudhomme, chatting to her godson Charles Terrasse, occupies the centre of the composition, with a basket of fruit and two bottles to sustain her. Claude Terrasse reclines on the left, while her husband, safely hidden

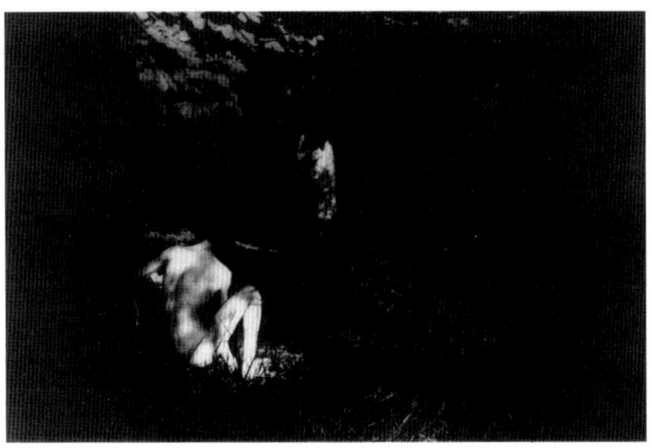

56
Pierre Bonnard sitting on the grass. 1900–1.
Photograph taken by Marthe.
Musée d'Orsay, Paris

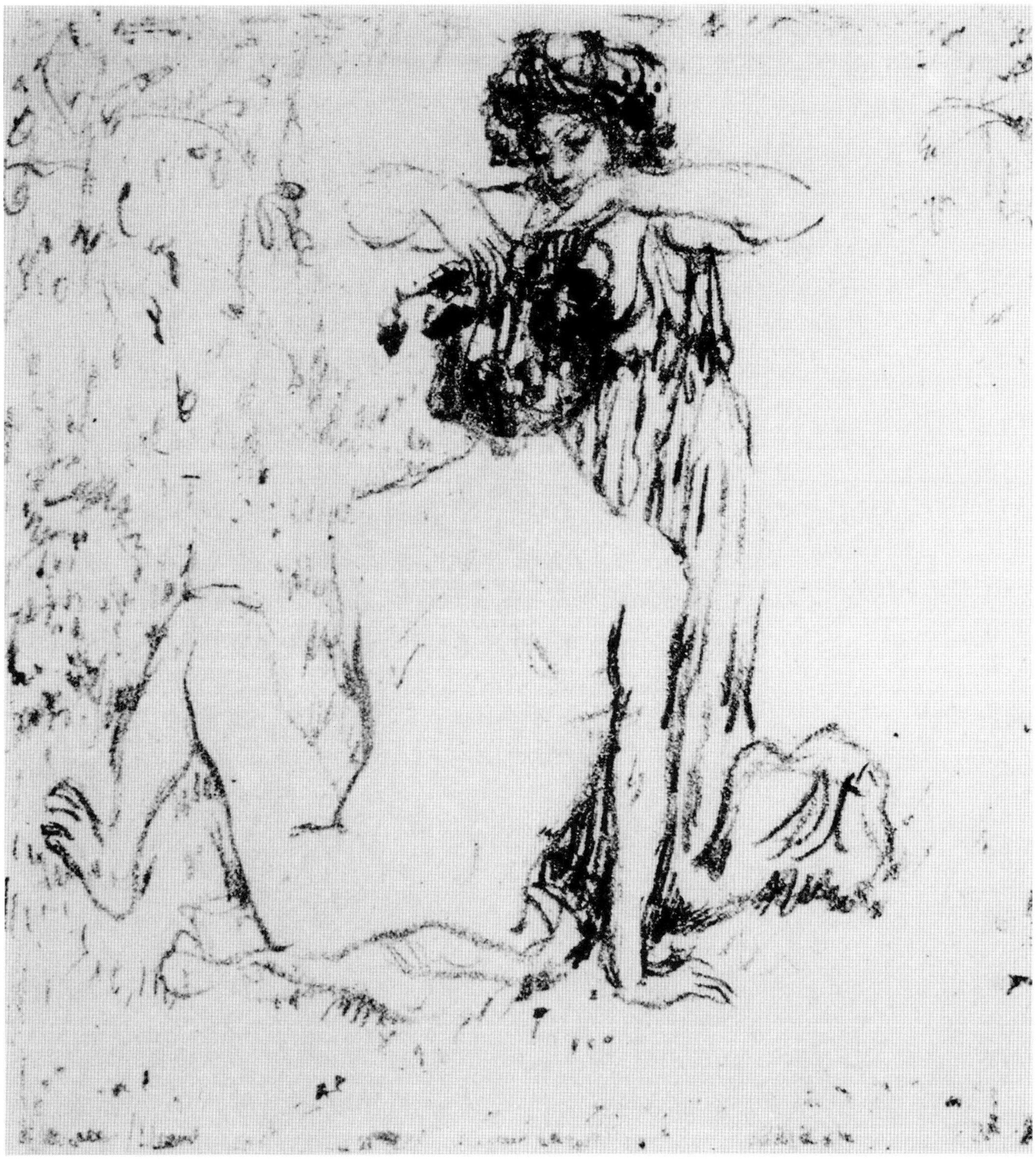

57
Chloë garlanding Daphnis.
From Longus, *Daphnis et Chloé*, 1902.
Lithograph in black, 15.3×14cm

under a straw hat, sits out of harm's way on the extreme right with his pipe, and the rest of the children are arranged between them. Bonnard's mother is retreating back into the house, from which his niece Renée is looking out of an upstairs window.[17] Bonnard himself saw the painting as something of a satire on the formal, self-satisfied atmosphere of bourgeois family life.[18] The subject and the realistic style may well have been suggested by Vuillard's two decorative panels for Jean Schopfer of 1898, featuring Marthe and Bonnard in the left panel (Plate 58), which avoids any densely packed formal grouping and lightens the atmosphere by angling the house towards the landscape behind. Bonnard went on to do a second version of *L'Après-midi bourgeoise* in 1902, which is less congested and freer in technique, and consequently less intense and interesting.

He was never to repeat such a formal, large-scale family grouping with satirical overtones. It was almost as though the achievement of his monumental decorations demanded temporal and psychological distance, the subservience of individual personality and relationships to an overall idea or mood. His solution in *La Famille au jardin*, *c.*1901 (Plate 60) was to adopt a high viewpoint and suspend the actions of the figures in a dream-like atmosphere of somnolent green foliage filling the pictorial field. The drama is impersonal. A niece with a vacant expression throws up her hands to catch a ball that will never land. The last rays of light flicker through the trees, dappling the path and illuminating the figures and foliage in the foreground. It has the quality of a stage set, perhaps recalling a Nabis production now lost. In *Paravent aux*

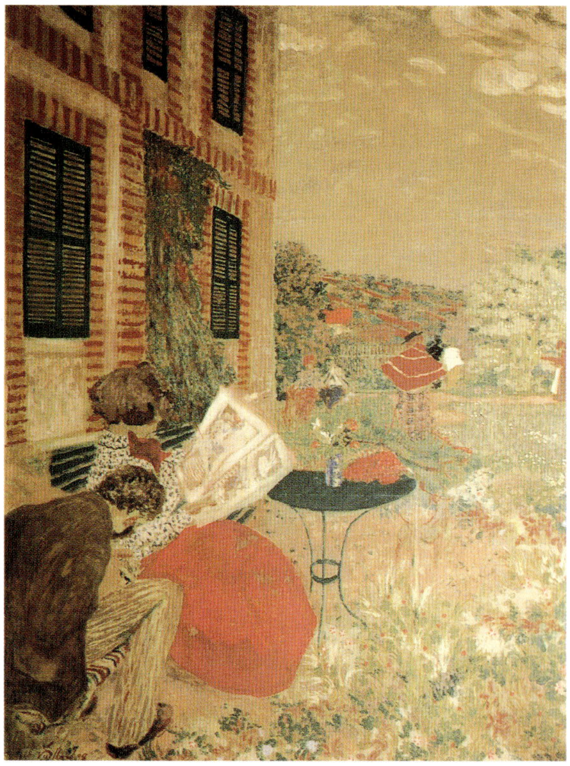

58
Édouard Vuillard
Devant la maison or *Femme lisant sur un banc*. 1898.
Distemper on canvas, 213.7×160.9cm.
Private collection

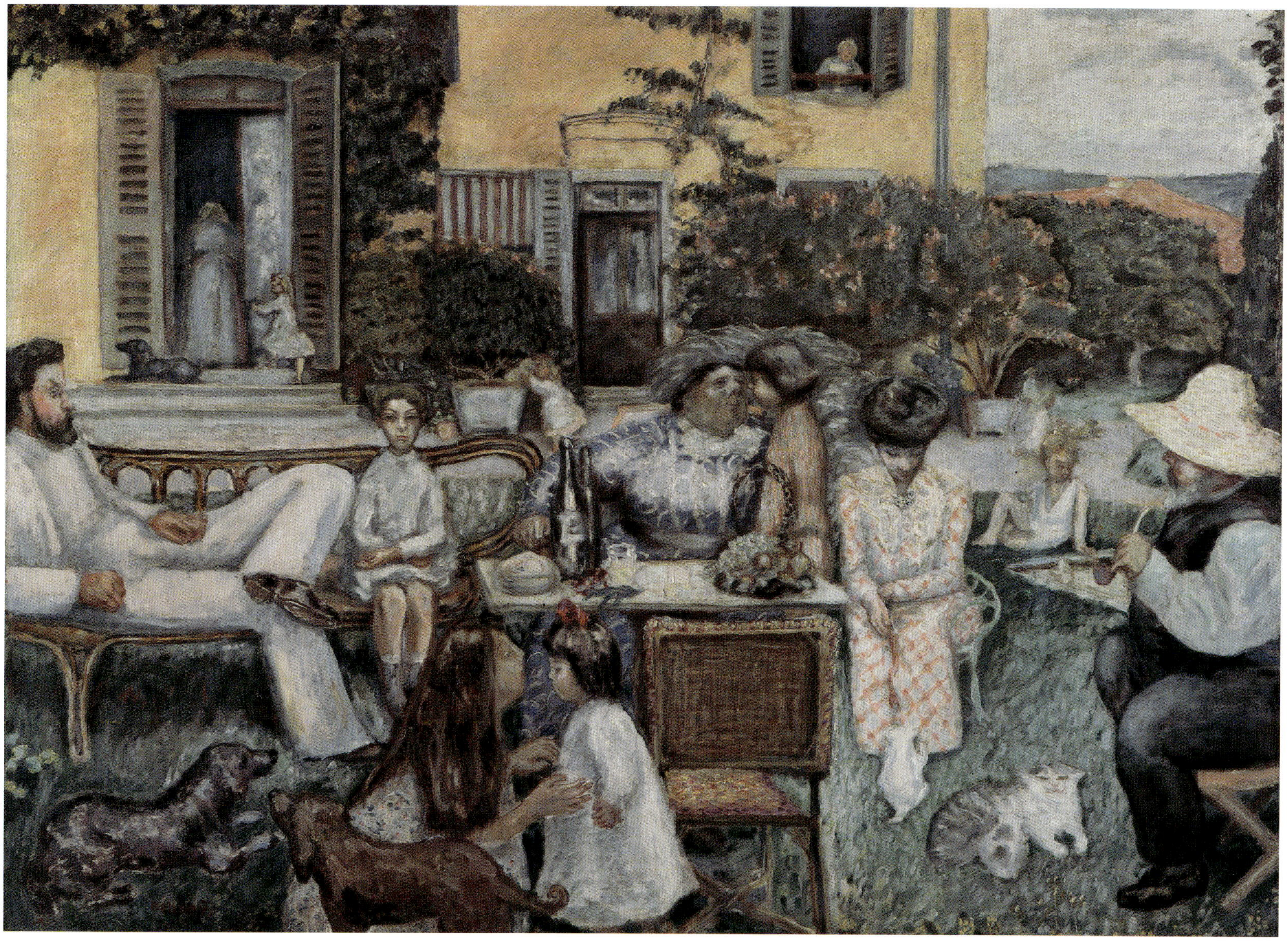

59
L'Après-midi bourgeoise. 1900.
Oil on canvas, 139×212cm.
Musée d'Orsay, Paris

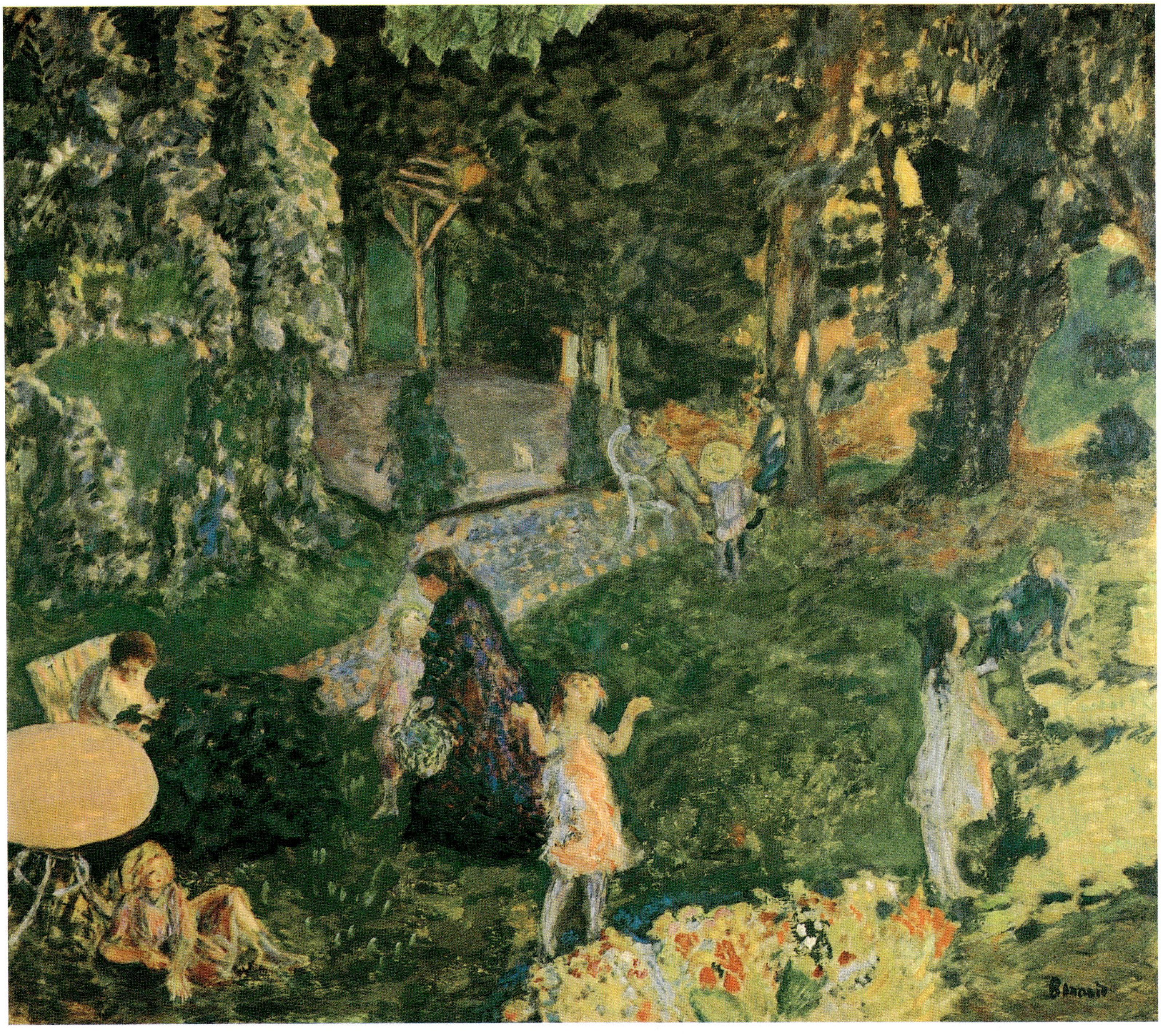

60
*La Famille au jardin. c.*1901.
Oil on canvas, 109×208cm.
Private collection

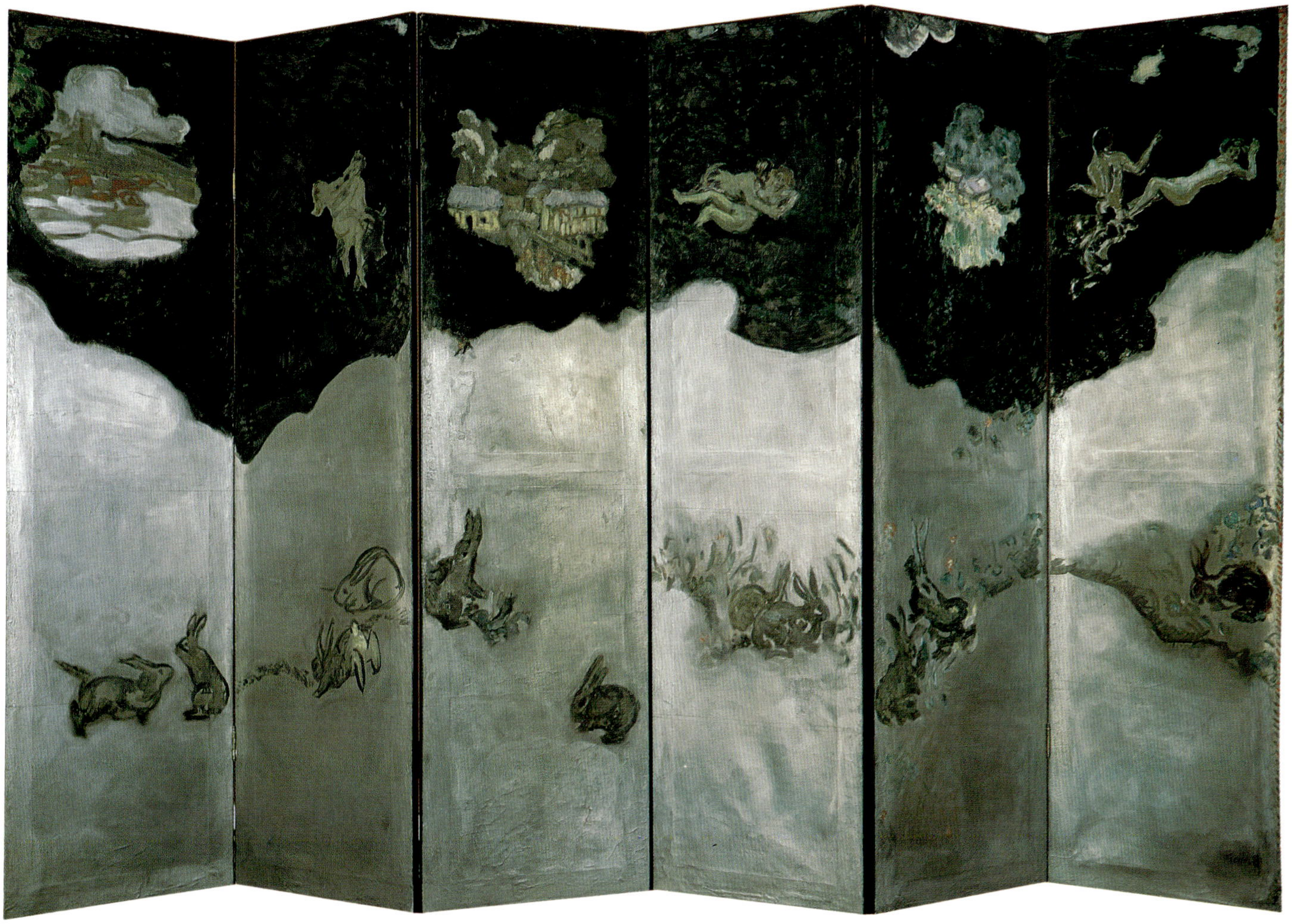

61
Paravent aux lapins. *c*.1902–6.
Folding screen.
Oil on paper mounted on canvas, 6 panels, 161×45cm each.
Musée départemental du Prieuré, Saint-Germain-en-Laye

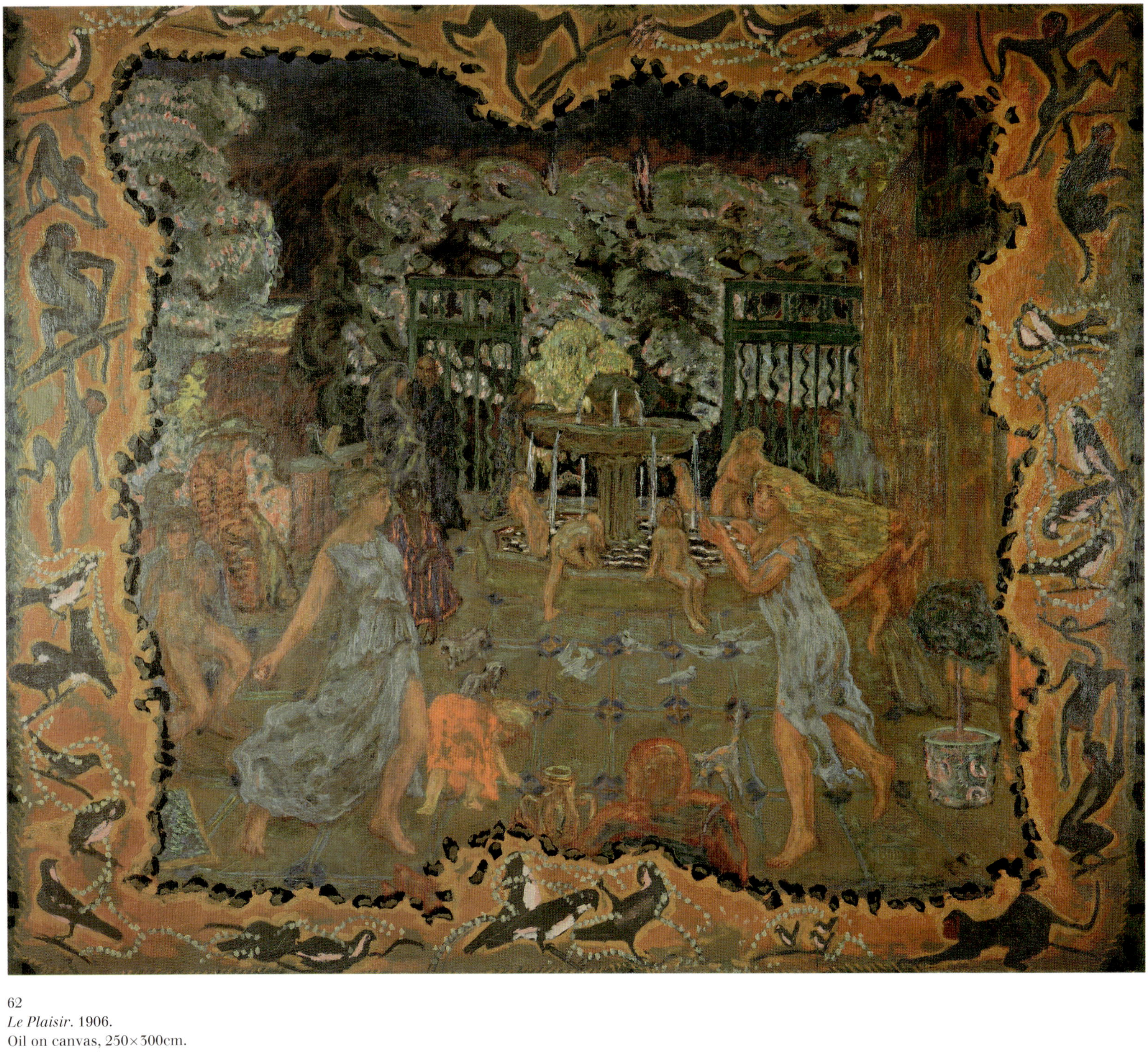

62
Le Plaisir. 1906.
Oil on canvas, 250×300cm.
Galerie Maeght, Paris

lapins, variously dated between 1902 and 1906 (Plate 61), which deals with the general theme of fecundity, he reverted to the overtly decorative format of his Japanese-inspired Nabis projects and alternated scenes of a faun enjoying a nymph with glimpses of a city and a landscape seen through a dark vegetal cloud floating over a silver field populated with amorous rabbits.

This fusion of the oriental and classical with contemporary reality was continued in Bonnard's four decorative panels for Misia, begun in 1906, in which the undulating cloud at the top of the screen was developed into a dynamic pictorial border of exotic birds and playful monkeys surrounding each of the compositions. In *Le Plaisir* (Plate 62) the pond at Le Clos becomes a classical fountain with the Terrasse children as putti playing in it. Maenads in diaphanous blue shifts run in from the wings. A group of robed figures, including what looks like a Chinese sage, attended by a little black boy, and a lady in a large garden hat sitting on a bench, observe the proceedings from the left. The pastoral tranquillity of this happy scene conflicts oddly with the barbaric energy of the border. Bonnard may have been responding to Misia's flamboyant personality, but more importantly the border reflects the decorative dynamism of Matisse, who had transformed the essentially nostalgic subject of an earthly paradise into something primitive and shocking.

Nothing in contemporary French painting to date would have prepared the viewer for Matisse's seminal masterpiece, *Le Bonheur de vivre*, 1905–6 (Plate 63), which caused a sensation when exhibited at the Salon des Indépendants in March 1906. The Neo-Impressionist dots and dashes of his first great imaginary composition *Luxe, calme et volupté*, 1904–5, are expanded into broad areas of pure, flat colour, articulated by sinuous arabesques, to provide the setting for a harem of oriental women in the West. The solitary piping shepherdess looks back over her shoulder as she leaves them suspended in an ideal state of being.[19] A ring of dancers tread out a rhythm by the sea to accompany as it were the yearning ambition set out in Mallarmé's 'L'Après-midi d'un faune':

I desire to perpetuate these nymphs.
So luminous,
Their light rosy flesh, that it hovers in the air
Drowsy with tufted slumbers.

What must have made *Le Bonheur* especially unsettling for Bonnard was that there is nothing in the painting that had not been anticipated in his own work. After all he himself, inspired by Gauguin and Japanese art, had pioneered the combination of flat colour and line in his decorative style of the early 1890s, and Mallarmé's convulsively erotic fantasy of nudes languishing in a landscape was a subject that continued to obsess him. But there is no doubt that the initiative had passed from Bonnard to Matisse. It is not a question of Matisse copying Bonnard, rather of one artist doggedly pursuing the same sources and coming to different conclusions. Gauguin is the prime case in

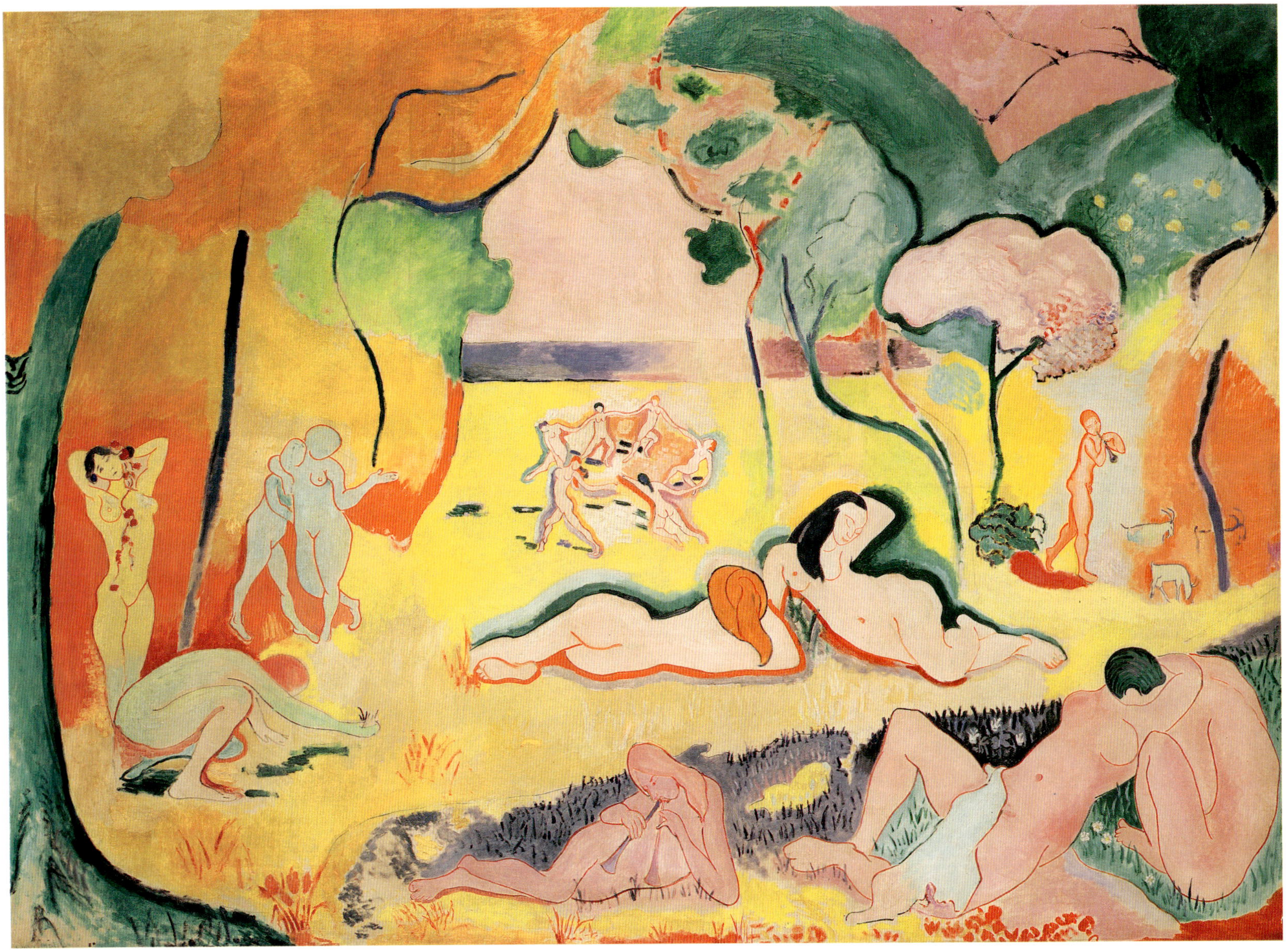

63
Henri Matisse
Le Bonheur de vivre. 1905–6.
Oil on canvas, 174×238.1cm.
Barnes Foundation, Merion, Pa.

point. Bonnard had earlier domesticated Gauguin, whom he came to regard as a classical artist; now Matisse – having seen in the summer of 1905, through the auspices of Maillol, the greater part of Gauguin's last Tahitian canvases which were being stored near Collioure – was struck by the raw impact of Gauguin's intensely coloured surfaces, which transformed both figures and setting in accordance with the expressive content or mood of the subject. Bonnard followed Matisse's example and went down to the south of France in February 1906, staying several days with Maillol, but there is no evidence that he even saw the Gauguins, and he remained seemingly untouched by the need to find an equivalent for the heady sensations of the south in exuberant brushstrokes and explosive combinations of colour.

We can recognize this as a watershed in Bonnard's art. Faced with the overtly decorative style of Matisse, who had assumed the leadership of the avant-garde, he went in the opposite direction, his art becoming more atmospheric and naturalistic, his settings resolutely French. Not for him the disquieting power of Gauguin's later works or of the tribal sculpture that fascinated modern artists bent on reinvesting the human figure with its primordial significance. It was almost as though he made a conscious decision to remain loyal to his sources in the nineteenth century, and consequently his name drops out of modernist discourse. Matisse's competition was to come from the young Spaniard Pablo Picasso, who on seeing *Le Bonheur de vivre* abandoned his own classical multi-figure composition *The Watering Place* as anaemic, too much like a Puvis de Chavannes.[20] Nobody from now on was going to make Picasso look tame. Conservative patrons not bold enough to buy a Matisse or a Picasso could settle for a Bonnard. Picasso always claimed to loathe Bonnard. When Matisse himself reverted to a more naturalistic style towards the end of the First World War, Jean Cocteau wrote dismissively in *Le Rappel à l'ordre*: 'The sun-soaked fauve has become a Bonnard kitten.'[21]

Contrary to what one might expect, Bonnard and Matisse each valued in the other something he himself had left undeveloped, or even abandoned. Bonnard continued to admire Matisse's large decorations, their astonishing energy and audacious combinations of flat colour with line. He visited Matisse in 1909 when he was working on La Danse for Shchukin, and proudly felt that he had been present at the birth of the enormous Barnes murals,1931–3. Bonnard in turn set the agenda for Matisse's intimist interiors of the early Nice period, from 1918 to 1930, and it was in these years that their correspondence began. This pattern was repeated in the 1940s when light permeating a domestic interior again became the subject of Matisse's easel paintings. Their mutual admiration continued to the end. Faced with Zervos's hostile article 'Pierre Bonnard est-il un grand peintre?', published in *Cahiers d'art*, shortly after Bonnard's death in 1947, Matisse scrawled over it, 'Yes! I assure you that Pierre Bonnard is a great painter for today and surely for the future.'[22]

Until recently Bonnard's decorative panels have not received the critical attention they merit, as though they remain something of an embarrassment in his *œuvre*. The mixing of the real and ideal has caused confusion. Their style is neither resolutely lin-

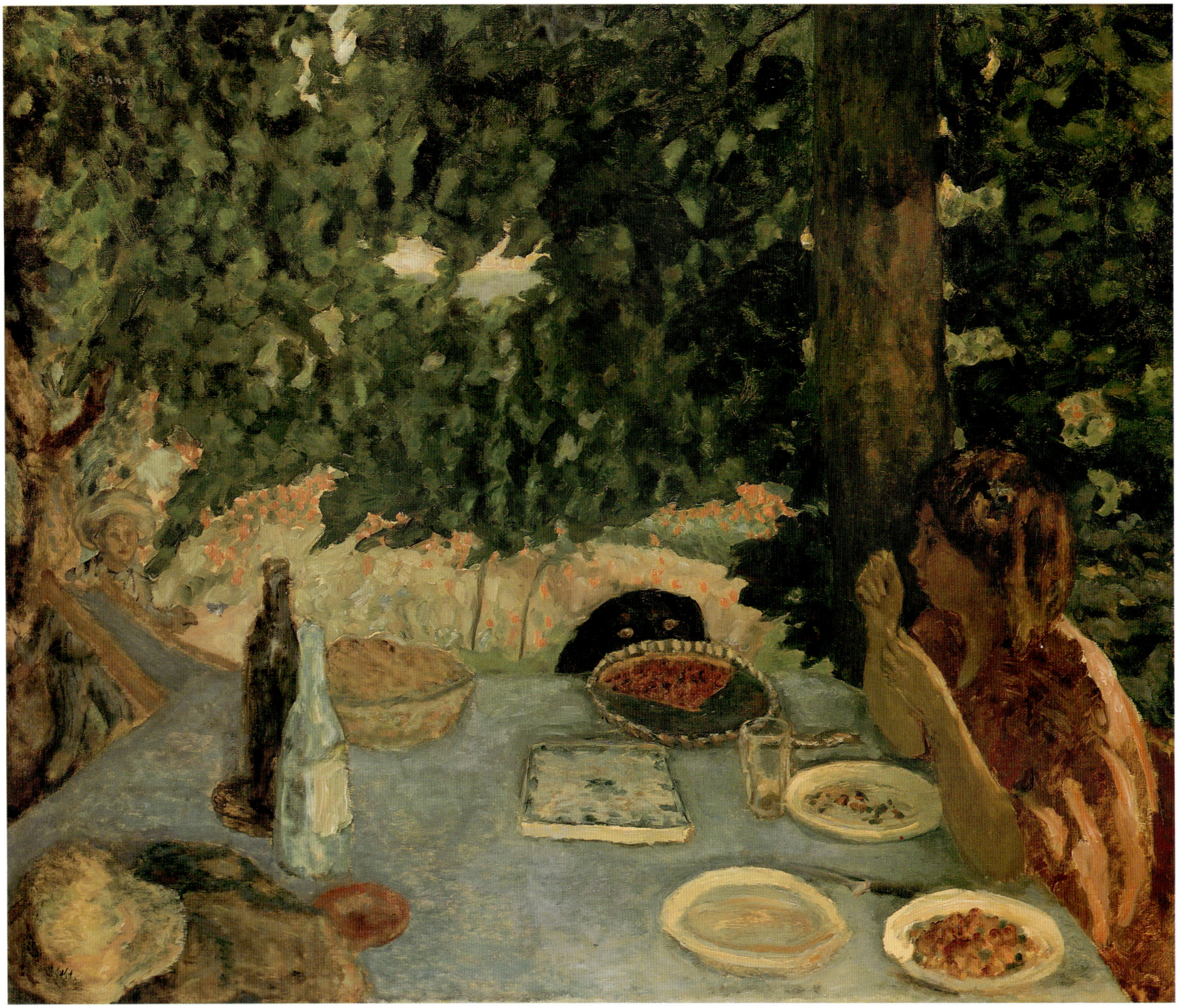

64
La Tarte aux cerises. 1908.
Oil on canvas, 115×123cm.
Private collection, Zürich

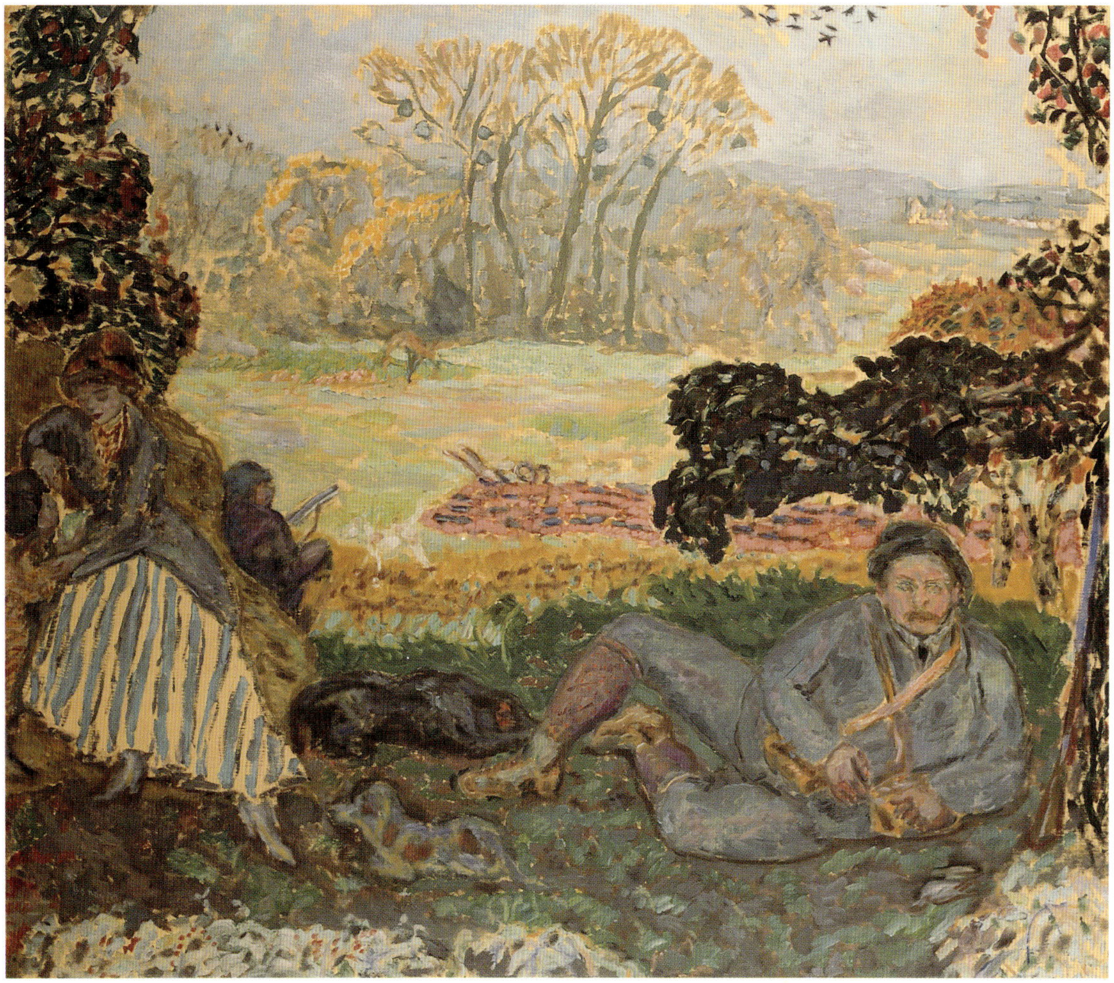

65
La Chasse. 1908.
Oil on canvas, 109×126cm.
Konstmuseum, Göteborg

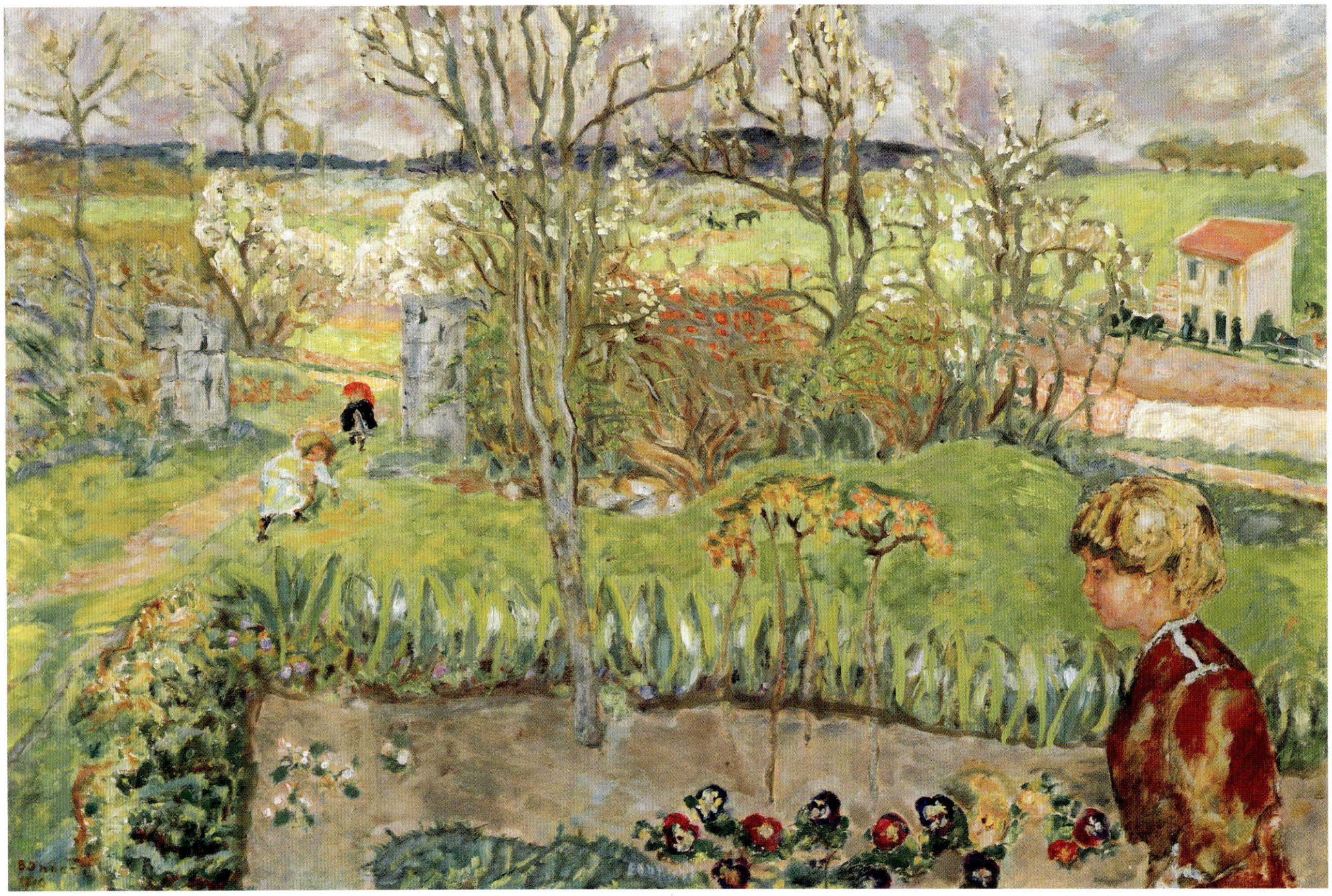

66
Premier printemps. 1908.
Oil on canvas, 87.6×132.1cm.
The Phillips Collection, Washington, DC

ear, nor dogmatically naturalistic. They do not seem to engage directly with any of the issues facing either art or society. Although *Bonheur de vivre* originated in an actual landscape, Matisse shifted the balance towards the imaginative re-creation of an ideal where the figures interact with the setting to evoke an overall mood which is the painting's subject. Bonnard, on the other hand, cut back and forth between different realities, genres, and conventions of representation. The disjunctions of style and subject-matter result in a fragmentation of consciousness that could be described in the 1990s as post-modern. It was not that he was either ignorant of or hostile to contemporary developments such as Fauvism and later Cubism; it was just that, coming from a background in the 1890s, he responded to developments in the evolving culture of painting in terms that are not ostensibly modern. This may well be taken as a sign that he lacked the imaginative capacity to forge an identifiably novel and modern style, but in saying this we are defining a crucial feature of his work. His complex notions of the pastoral lie at the root of his picturing of landscape, and the atmosphere of *Daphnis et Chloé* was to haunt his art.

Bonnard's landscapes slip similarly between genres and periods. Freed from the family atmosphere at Le Clos, a dining-room table in *La Tarte aux cerises*, 1908 (Plate 64), is removed from the darkened interior and placed as a stage overlooking the Normandy countryside. Following *Le Bonheur de vivre*, foreground figures are often employed to establish the mood of the landscapes, in which the tense atmosphere of *L'Après-midi bourgeoise* gives way to the reverie of 'L'Après-midi d'un faune'. Marthe sits at table contemplating the food. A red-faced hunter in the realist tradition of Courbet reclines in the foreground of *La Chasse*, 1908 (Plate 65), with his dozy dogs.[23] In *Les Petits Faunes*, 1909 (Plate 67), a little faun, watched by his companion, pipes in the spring. Nature as the only true source of art is dreamed into existence by art.

Bonnard always drew but seldom – if ever – painted before the motif. On one level his landscapes are to be interpreted as naturalistic representations, and on another as allegories. The idea for *Premier printemps*, 1908 (Plate 66), probably came with the memory of a particular moment when a gap appeared in the rain clouds on the horizon, catching the blossom and two children in the gateway in a burst of light. The girl, lost in thought, entering the foreground on the right with a posy of pansies, was probably added at a later stage. She could well be a Flora in modern dress. Bonnard would have been thoroughly familiar with the story of Flora, the goddess of flowers, who followed Zephyr the west wind in springtime strewing the ground with blossoms. The painting then becomes a meditation on the nature of spring, the freshness and innocence of childhood, and the transience and regeneration of life.[24] The same landscape with the children in the gateway appears again later that year in *L'Orage à Vernouillet*, transformed almost out of recognition by the advent of summer and by the driving rain. The change in the season and weather brought a change in palette, and the viewpoint is shifted to give a completely different spatial reading. With the harvest in, ploughing started and the leaves turning gold, *La Chasse* could represent autumn in an allegory of

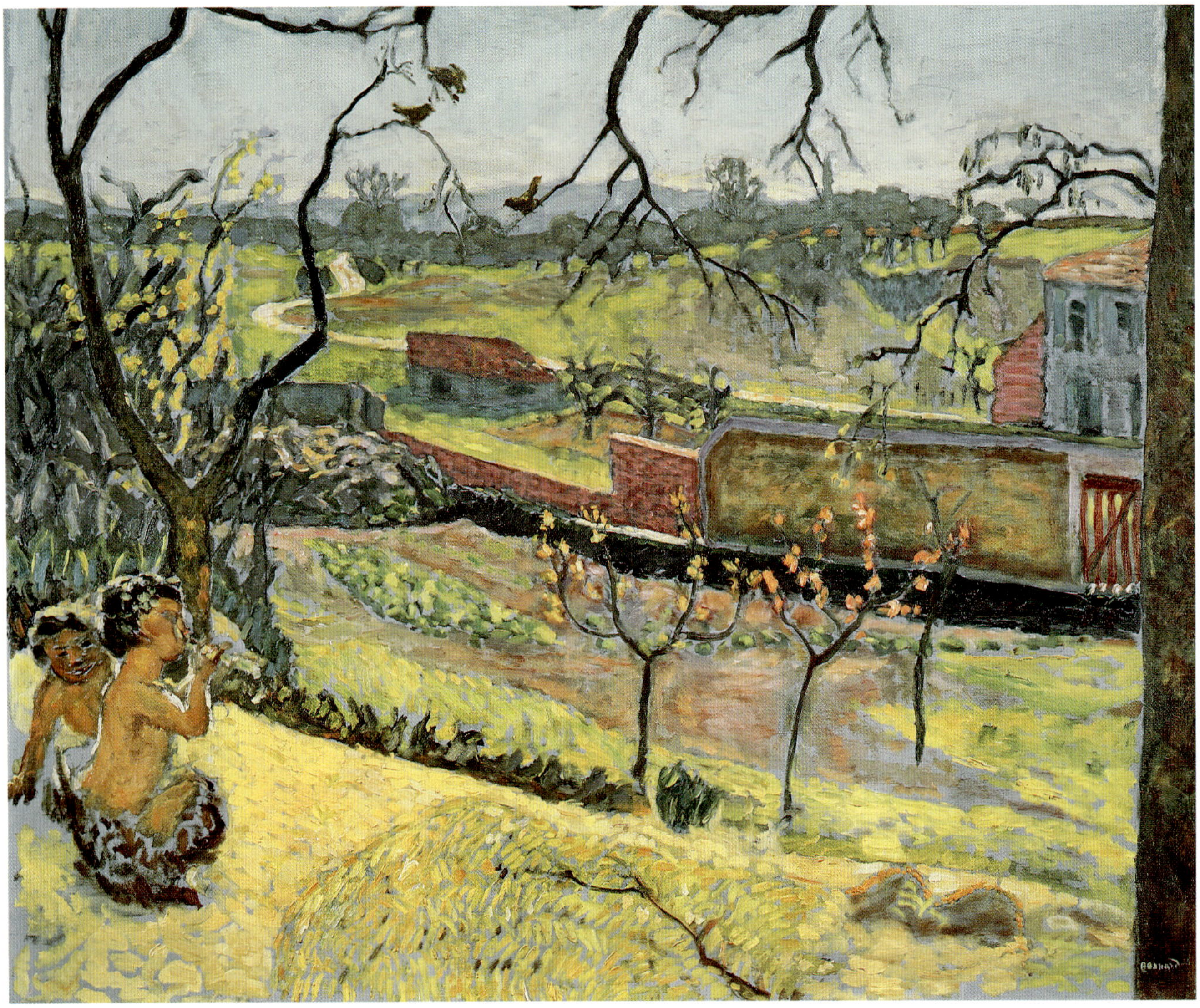

67
Les Petits faunes. 1909.
Oil on canvas, 103×126cm.
Hermitage, St Petersburg

the seasons. The four seasons had been the subject of Bonnard's first major decorative project, *Femmes au jardin* (Plate 21), exhibited at the Salon des Indépendants of 1891, and he was to repeat the subject in his series for the Russian collector Morosov in 1912.

The landscapes reveal a new interest in colour and atmospheric light, but here again Bonnard draws on a variety of conventions to different ends. *La Tarte aux cerises* (Plate 64) takes up Matisse's subject of the dinner table set out as a feast for the eye, rather than for the stomach. Objects act as vehicles for colour, and the white cloth is laid out like a screen to reflect the play of light. The dark green leaves of the tree are drawn across the background to concentrate attention on the drama of the table, where the intense black of the dog sets off the deep red of the cherry tart. Monet had employed a white cloth on a table set outdoors for similar ends in *Le Déjeuner*, *c.*1873–4, which was part of the Caillebotte bequest, but by comparison *La Tarte aux cerises* is much less naturalistic in colour and construction. Bonnard would wilfully distort for pictorial ends. The dark grey flowerbed in the foreground of *Premier printemps* is tipped towards the surface to lead the eye to the children in the gateway. Like the Fauves, Bonnard employed a mixture of techniques on the same canvas. In *La Chasse*, for instance, the cream ground of the canvas comes through to describe the stripes of the woman's dress, while the strip of plough behind is painted in a deep crimson red with Neo-Impressionist blue dashes to represent the turned sods. In *Les Petits Faunes* Bonnard adapts the technique advocated in contemporary manuals on decoration to give unity to a room and employs a predominant yellow base colour to create an overall mood suggestive of spring and burgeoning growth.[25] This conscious manipulation of the pictorial elements to generate mood distinguishes his approach from that of the Impressionists, even though Monet himself was moving in this direction.

Despite the fact that he spent less and less time in Paris after 1900, Bonnard at first maintained his parallel interest in city subjects, which he exhibited regularly at both the Salon des Indépendants and Salon d'Automne. The recurrence of the subject at the end of this period came with the commissions for decorations from Morozov and the critic Georges Besson (see Plates 72 and 73).

Monet had taken the city into the country in his paintings of urban leisure in the Seine valley, and Bonnard in turn brought the hazy atmosphere of the countryside into the city. In *Le Pont* (Plate 68), from the suite of lithographs *Quelques aspects de la vie de Paris*, published in 1899, Bonnard's new-found interest in Impressionism is reflected in the way the busy traffic is dissolved in a dream-like mist,[26] whereas in his later cityscapes it is only the background that is blurred into an overall atmosphere and the figures in the foreground remain in sharp focus. A dichotomy is thus established between the human beings and their environment which can be read as a sign of their fundamental alienation in the city, a rift that could only be healed by a return to the pastoral. Whether of high or low life, the figures remain detached and isolated in their social groupings, and the mood as in Verlaine's poetry is one of wistful melancholy.

Bonnard's preoccupation with the pastoral mode did not so much alter the formula

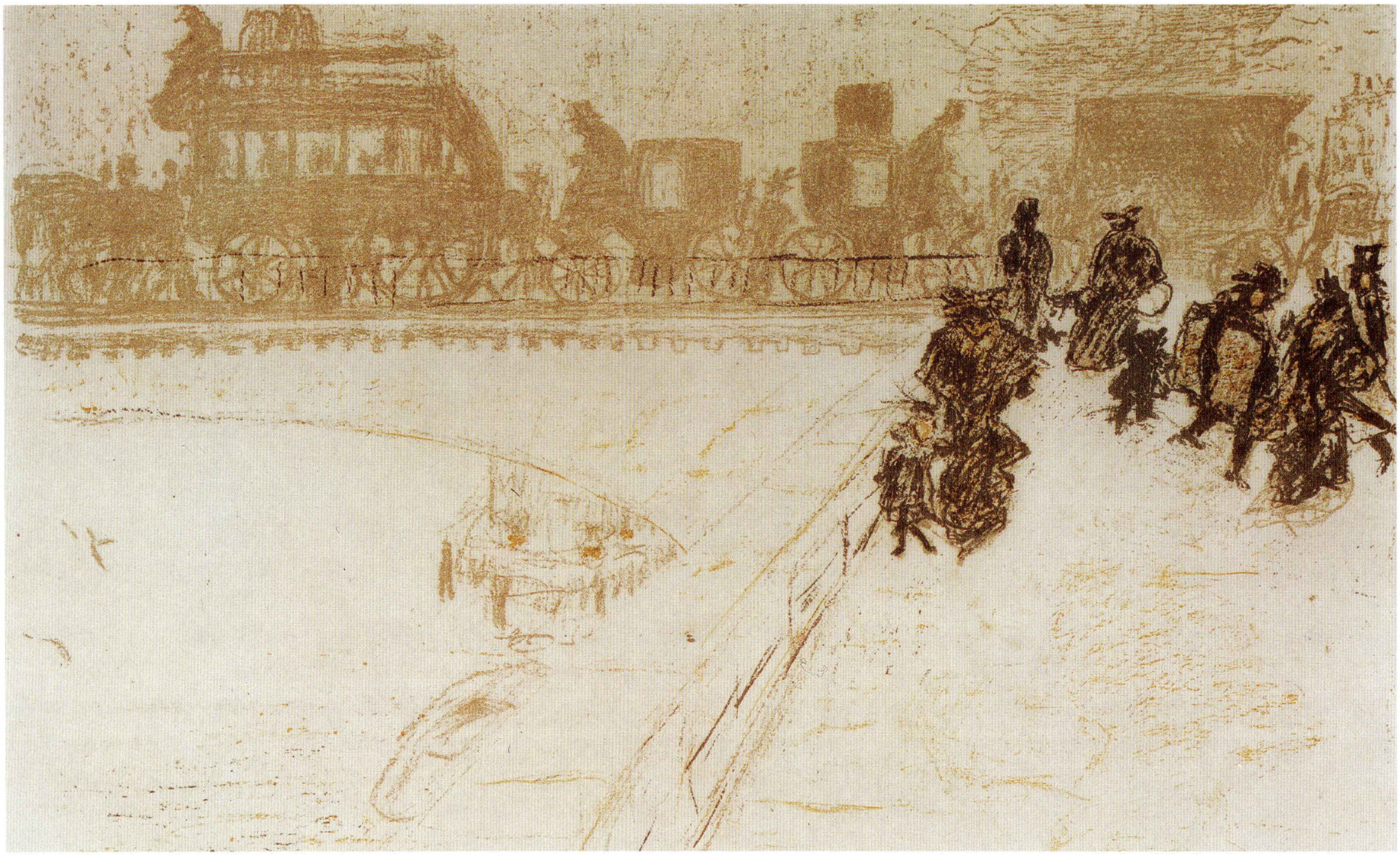

68
Le Pont. 1899.
Lithograph in 4 colours, 27×41cm

of his commercially successful city subjects as change their mood. It was the human dimension that brought him back to the city, even though he found it difficult to work there.[27] He placed the emphasis on people, not architecture. In his view of the city's inhabitants he adopted the Olympian detachment of a benign *flâneur* leisurely enjoying the spectacle of their comings and goings. Crowds drift by as in a dream or in a sequence from an early silent film. The idea for the decoration *La Place Clichy*, 1912 (Plate 73) was probably suggested by an actual mirror in the Café Wepler, which provided the setting for the composition.[28] Dramatic close-ups are employed to feature the people passing in the foreground, but there is no drama. Two ladies of the night, one dark, the other red-headed, are caught crossing the Place Clichy (Plate 70); a majestic young woman floats across the foreground of *Le Pont des Arts*, *c.*1905 (Plate 69), like a figurehead on a galleon. Their expressions are dead-pan. The pudding-faced child in *Le Pont du Carrousel*, *c.*1903 (Plate 71), is the only one to give anything away, even though his look is one of profound boredom.

The drama lies in a generalized perception of the heroism of modern life, with people passing through the city like myriads of ants, compulsively acting out their parts in a pattern which alters according to area and class. The formal grouping of the high-life scenes in the fashionable area around the Seine, emphasized by the rigid rhythm of the piers and arches of the bridges, contrasts with the chaos and vital energy of the low-life scenes in the neighbourhood of the Place Clichy. In the former a woman's function is to look beautiful, perhaps to look after children, and in the latter to earn a living. Bonnard was interested in the changing patterns of work from early morning to late at night. The central focus in *Matin à Paris*, 1911 (Plate 72), is on an overladen donkey cart returning from market to revictual the shops. In its companion piece, *Soir à Paris*, a flower seller tries to attract the custom of people returning from work. The year before he died Bonnard once again took a room in a cheap hotel overlooking the square in front of the Gare San Lazare and explained what he saw in the scene below: 'What a charming spectacle it is to see this world of workers escaping from the station like bees from a hive. They run to make their living, they are going to search for their fodder. For an elderly man like myself these goings and comings become touching, they assume a certain grandeur. From the height of my balcony they are no bigger than insects, they are depersonalized, yet represent a symbol of the workforce. I see them in the morning, they flow like a swarm of ants, to return in the evening in long processions. I can imagine that they are carrying home to the cells of their honeycombs the spoils of their day. Brave little people, I love them with all my heart.'[29]

It was said to have been a casual remark by Félix Fénéon that his Paris street scenes were very popular that led to Bonnard abandoning the subject.[30] His final variation on the theme was *Le Café du Petit Poucet*, 1928, painted as a pendant to *La Place Clichy* of 1912. However, the idea of Bonnard as the isolated loner pursuing a career outside the dictates of fashion and the commercial constraints of the market is not entirely supported by the evidence of his art. In 1905 he produced a whole series of attractive young

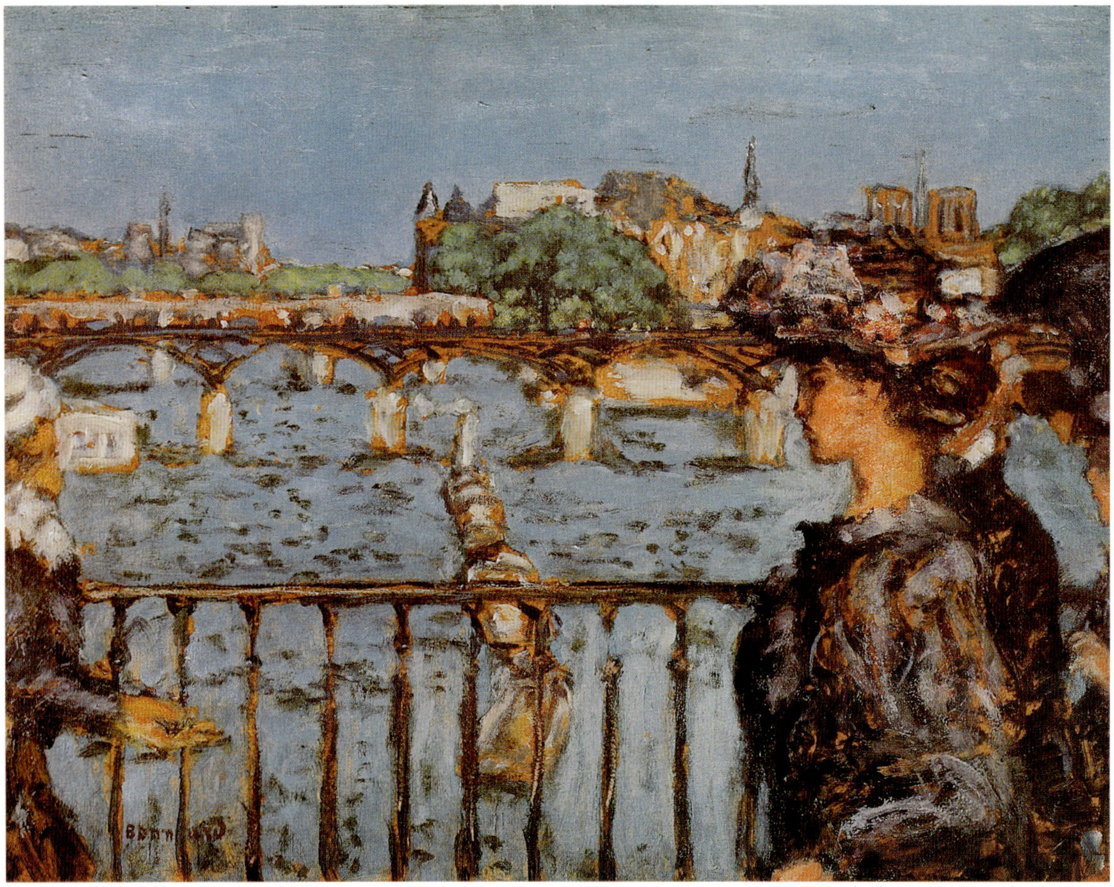

69
Le Pont des arts. *c*.1905.
Oil on cardboard mounted on panel, 55×70cm.
Private collection

70
Deux élégantes, Place Clichy. *c*.1905.
Oil on panel, 73×62cm.
Private collection

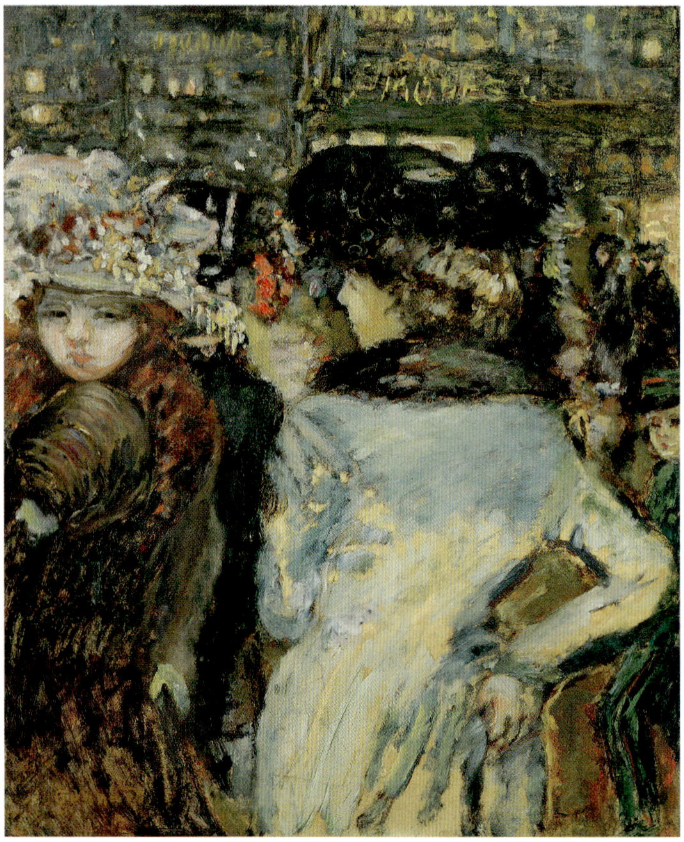

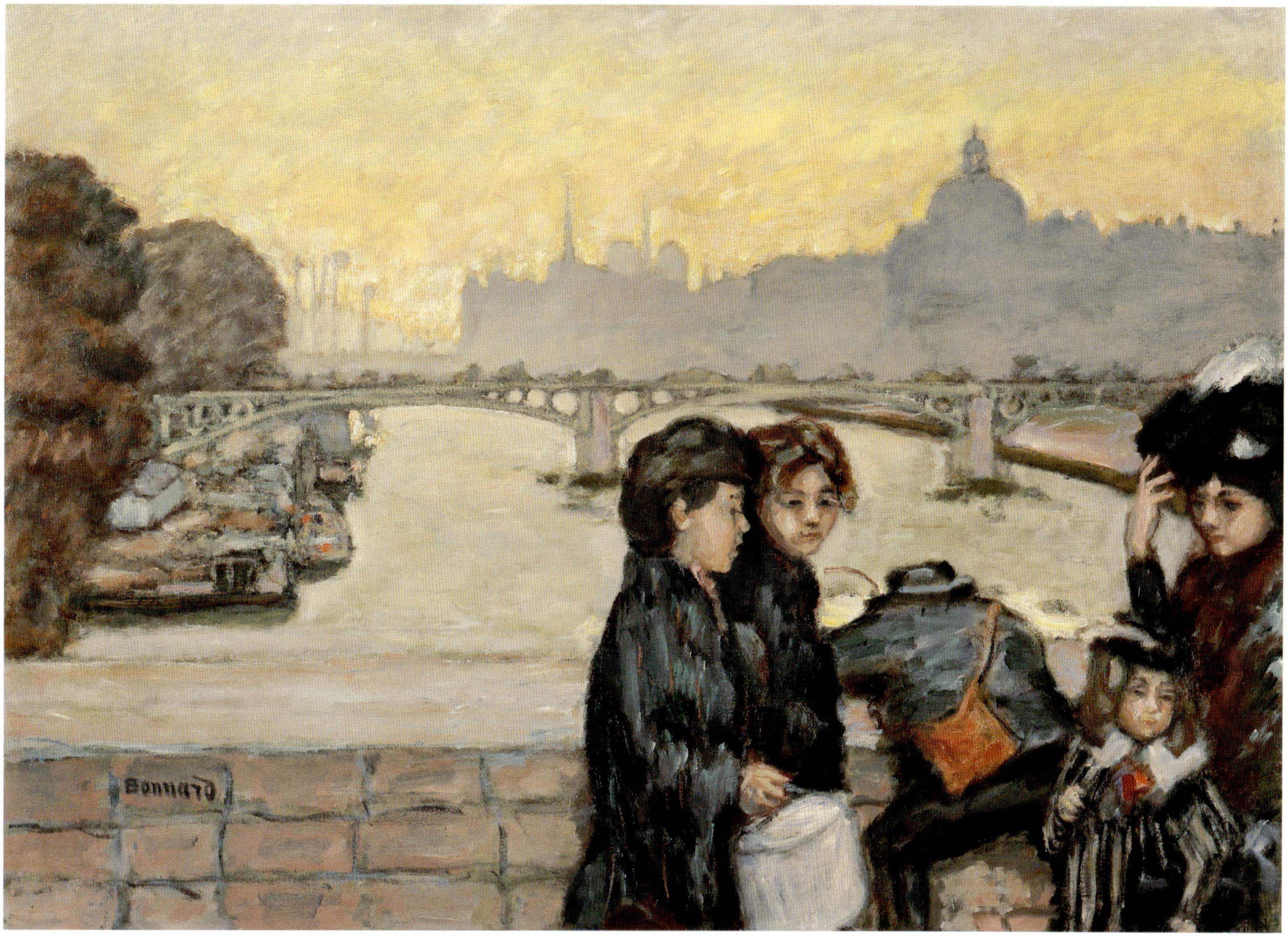

71
*Le Pont du Carrousel. c.*1903.
Oil on canvas, 71.4×100cm.
Los Angeles County Museum, gift of Mr and Mrs
Sidney F. Brody

72
Matin à Paris. 1911.
Oil on canvas, 77×123cm.
Hermitage, St Petersburg

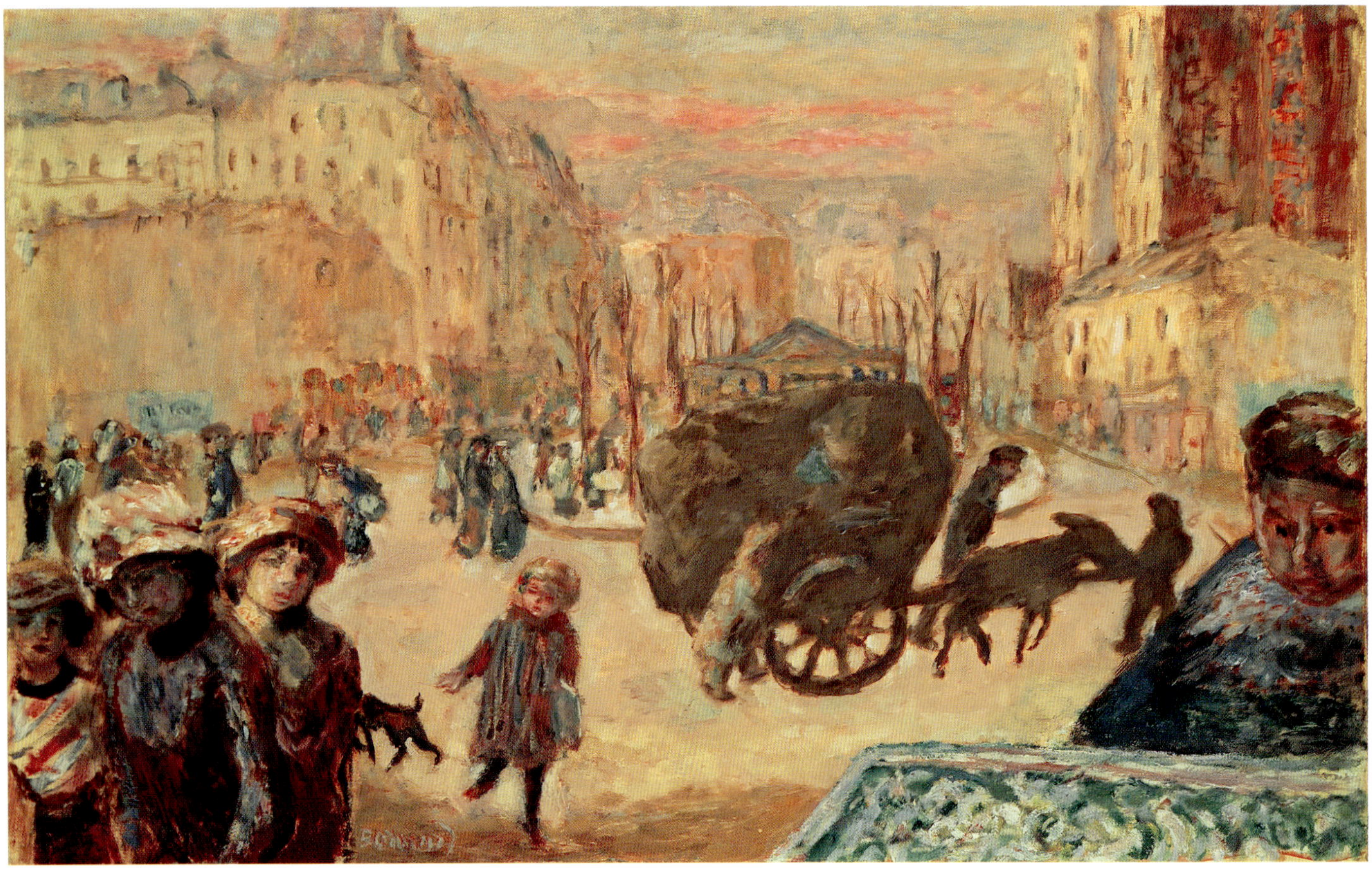

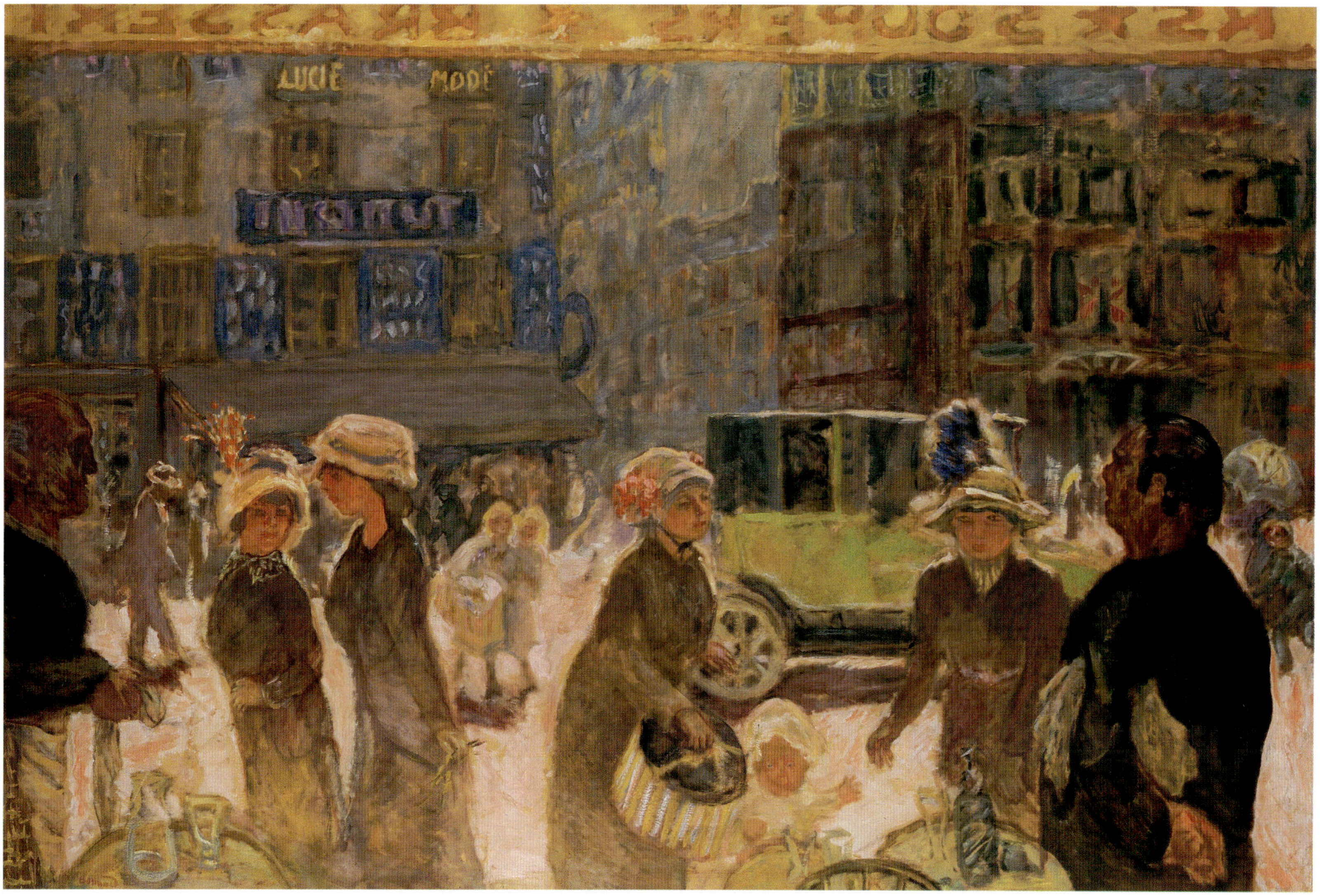

73
La Place Clichy. 1912.
Oil on canvas, 139×205cm.
Musée des Beaux-Arts et d'Archéologie, Besançon,
gift of Georges and Adèle Besson

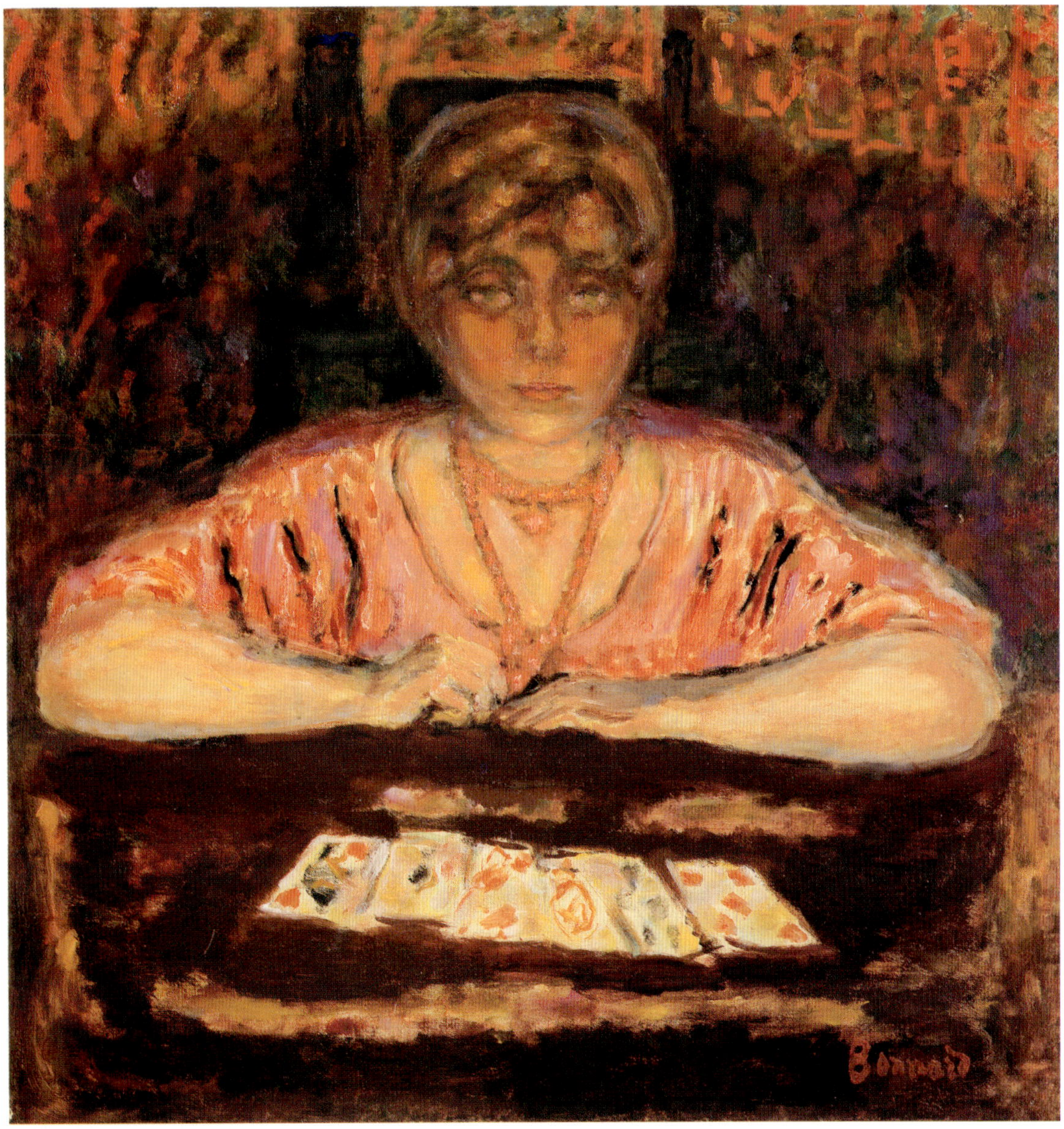

74
La Réussite. 1911.
Oil on canvas, 53.5×52.5cm.
Private collection

women, both dressed and undressed, seen either in close-up as portrait heads or modestly occupied in some gentle task, such as sewing, reading or looking into a full-length mirror. To be shown naked usually meant that they had to be caught in the act of undressing or going about their toilet. They hover salaciously between the naked and the nude. Bonnard drew close to Renoir in his wholehearted commitment to charm. The models are pictured without personality, as Bonnards, in the same way that Bonnard regarded Renoir as 'above all a painter of Renoirs'.[31]

In April 1906 Bonnard had a one-man exhibition at Vollard's, and in November that year the first of his one-man exhibitions at the Bernheim-Jeune gallery, which was to represent him for the rest of his career. The continued support of the Bernheim-Jeune gallery, where Fénéon worked, was to prove absolutely crucial for Bonnard's career. Félix Vallotton, a member of the Nabis, introduced Bonnard to his brothers-in-law Josse and Gaston Bernheim shortly before 1900, and their friendship developed into one those rare instances in the history of art of complete mutual trust between artist and dealer. Without a formal contract, the Bernheims acted as his bankers and financial advisers, paid his bills and maintained his prices in the sale room, even during the financial crash of the 1930s, when his reputation was far from secure.[32] The next generation of the family, Jean and Henry Dauberville, have continued to support Bonnard's reputation, publishing in 1965 the four volumes of the *catalogue raisonné*, which lists some 2,173 paintings.[33]

Bonnard in turn was canny enough to cultivate the friendship of key dealers, critics and patrons, on occasion painting them and members of their families. Portraiture posed considerable problems for Bonnard. His decorative style, as we have seen, involved the subjugation of individual character in the interests of an overall mood. This did not matter with Marthe, who created the domestic atmosphere out of which his art grew. Not that she was necessarily a benign presence. In *La Réussite*, 1911 (Plate 74), she stares fixedly ahead, like a demented clairvoyant, with the cards laid out in front of her on the table.

Another sitter who played roles that Bonnard was happy to record was Misia, whom he painted in various guises, from a coldly fashionable lady in flowing long white dress, with Thadée out of the limelight happily playing with his dog (Plate 75, 1902) to the impressive rococo portrait of her plumped up in the role of a somewhat blousy eighteenth-century hostess in her plush apartment (Plate 76, 1908).

Growing tired of poor Thadée, who was in any case running out of money, Misia had an affair with the thoroughly unpleasant newspaper tycoon Alfred Edwards, whom she married on 24 February 1905 after getting divorced the previous year, callously explaining in her autobiography: 'Thadée was a child and Alfred a man.'[34] Power and conquest were at the root of their relationship, which petered out in their separate affairs and divorce precisely four years later. Misia then took up with the glamorous Spanish society artist José-Maria Sert, an inveterate womanizer who came complete with sombrero, and entered the circle of Diaghilev and the Ballets Russes. She married

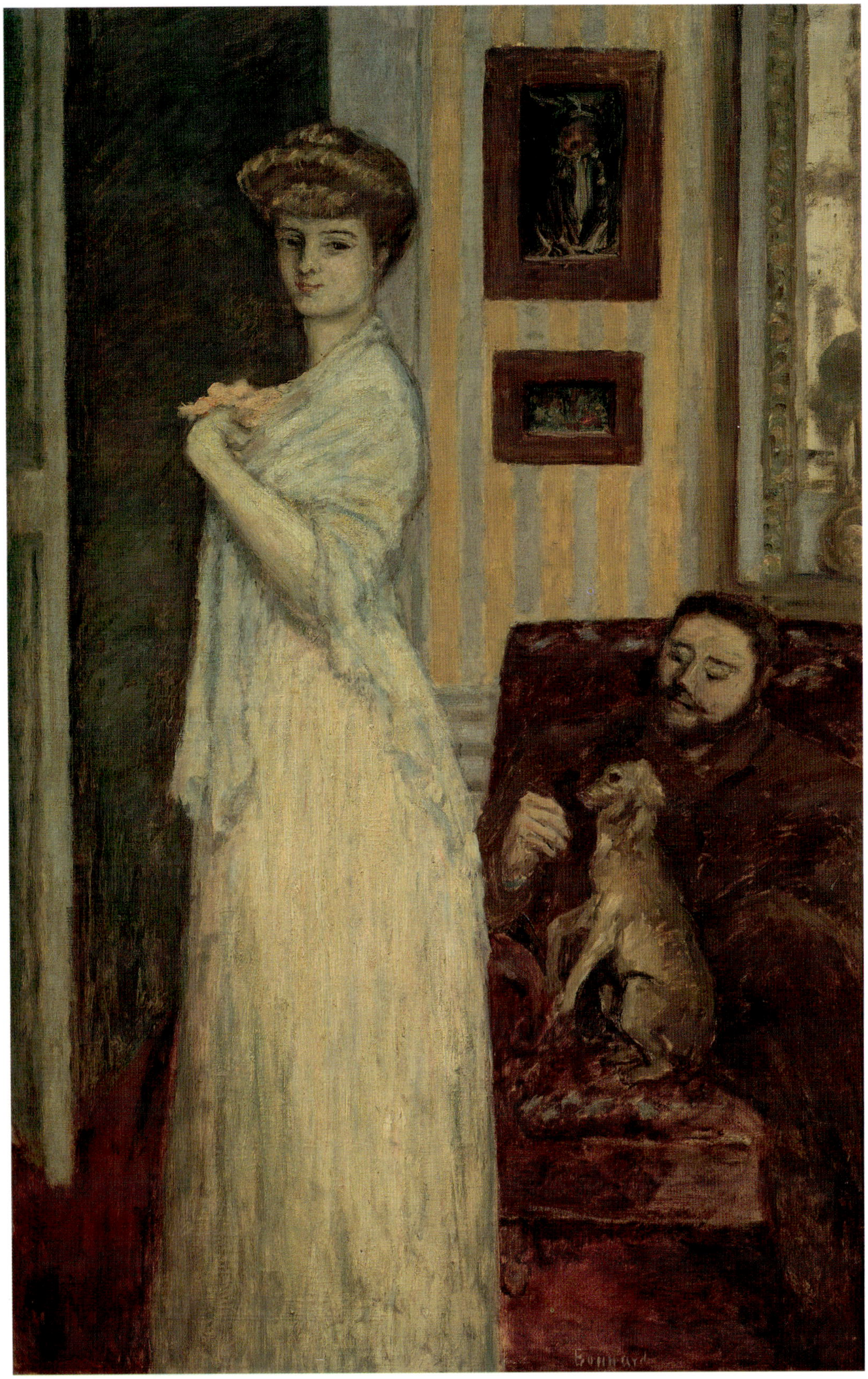

75
Misia et Thadée Natanson. 1902
Oil on canvas, 130×86cm.
Musée Royal d'Art Moderne, Brussels

76
Misia. 1908.
Oil on canvas, 145×114cm.
Fondaçion Colección Thyssen-Bornemisza,
Madrid

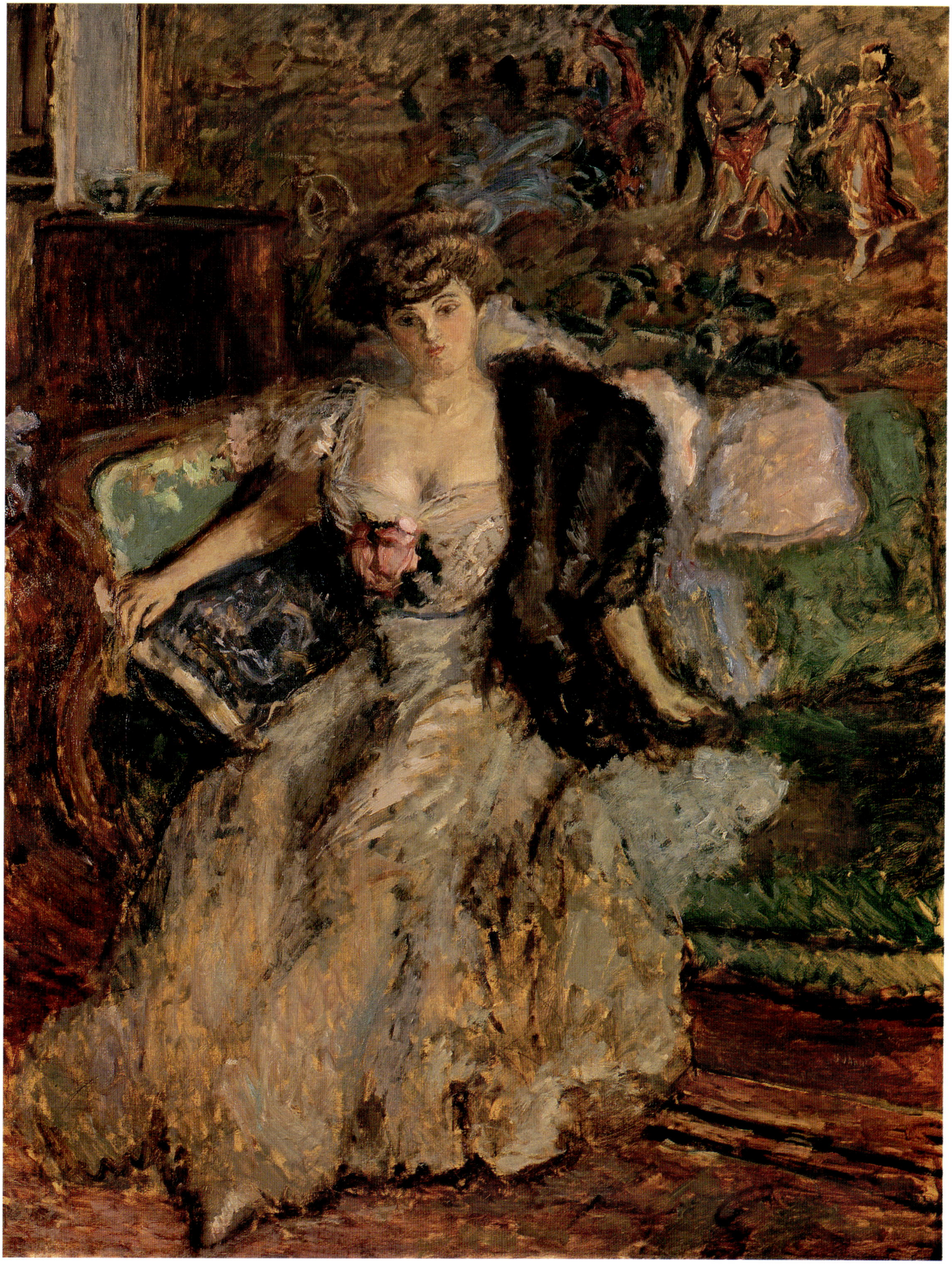

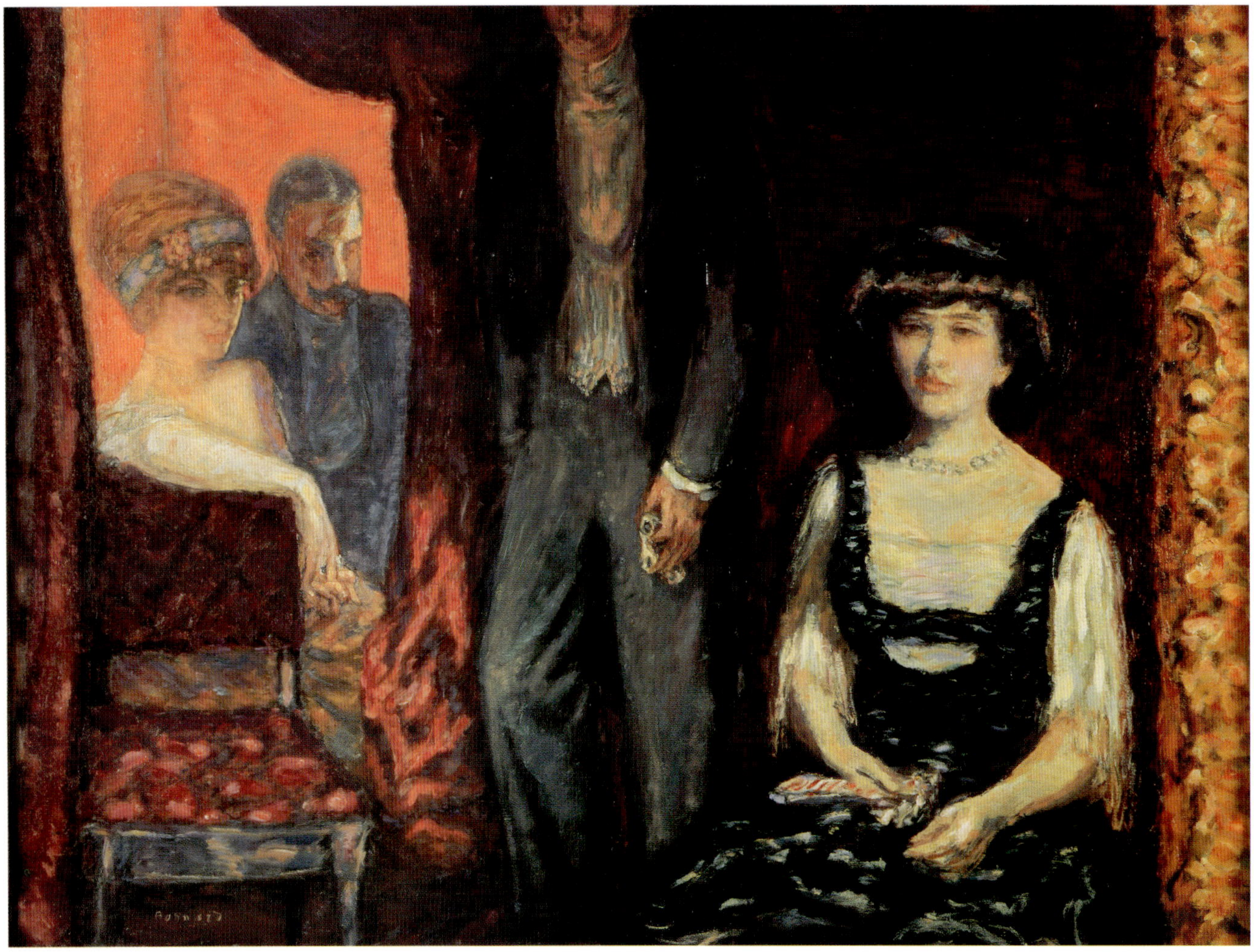

77
La Loge. 1908.
Oil on canvas, 91×120cm.
Musée d'Orsay, Paris

Sert on 2 August 1920 and with Coco Chanel set up a salon that established the mood of the 1920s, just as she had done with Thadée in the 1890s. Sert eventually left Misia for a younger woman, and their divorce on 28 September 1927 marked the beginning of her decline. Through all her vicissitudes, Bonnard never abandoned Misia, although, as Vuillard observed, he managed discreetly to keep his distance.

With less familiar sitters there was often a conflict between the twin demands of achieving a likeness and making a painting. Bonnard's solution was to let the setting help define the personality and social status of the sitter. When asked by the German painter Curt Herrmann to paint his wife Sophie, Bonnard wrote back in January 1905 saying that he should travel to Berlin because he prefered to paint people in the milieu in which they lived. His asking price was 2,000 francs.[35] In the *Portrait d'Ambroise Vollard*, *c.*1904–5 (Plate 78), he placed a cat on the sitter's lap for him to stroke and thereby keep awake.[36] In *La Loge*, 1908 (Plate 77), which depicts the Bernheim brothers and their wives (who were sisters) in their box at the opera, the painting took over from portraiture and Gaston lost the top of his head. The brothers' wealth and social status are shown in their beautifully dressed wives. Mathilde on the right wears the same dress from the Callot-Soeurs in which Renoir painted her, and the plush velvet curtain is pulled back dramatically to reveal Suzanne on the left.[37] She objected to the way Bonnard had distorted her arm; his answer was that 'faults sometimes give life to a picture.'[38] Bonnard later painted Josse and Gaston in the sumptuous setting of their office as successful businessmen (Plate 79): they could be international bankers, even the colour scheme glows gold.

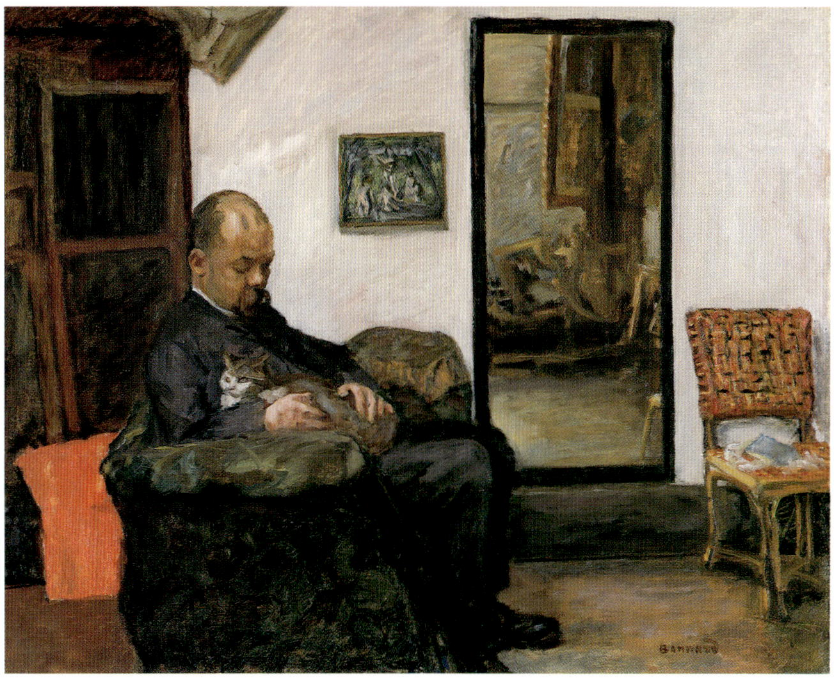

78
Portrait d'Ambroise Vollard. *c.*1904–5.
Oil on canvas, 74×92.5cm.
Kunsthaus, Zürich

Bonnard's habitual practice was to do numerous sketches and drawings of the sitter which would then serve as the basis for further painted studies. The final portrait was executed back in the studio, sometimes over a period of six months or more. His routine was not one designed to put sitters at their ease. The critic Georges Besson remembers him rubbing his hands energetically before beginning, smoking a pipe while working and crunching sweets from a small paper packet.[39] Bonnard was reluctant to do portraits, however much he liked the people and wanted to please them, and often it required a small incident for him to see a way of dealing with a commission, as Mme Heddy Hahnloser recalled in the case of *Promenade en mer*, 1924 (Plate 80), the celebrated group portrait of the Hahnloser family: 'Arthur several times asked his friend Bonnard to paint a picture including one or more of us ... One afternoon when we were going back to the islands with a good wind blowing, I appeared wearing an old pale blue jersey. "That's it," cried Bonnard, "the enchantment that makes a painting." The purity of "Bonnard blue" had so caught his imagination that he settled down at the other end of the boat, drew out his sketchbook and started to draw.'[40]

While it is surely right to stress that the idea for *Promenade en mer* originated in a spontaneous incident, it is equally true to point out that Bonnard's compositional solutions often had a lengthy gestation. In this instance Manet had similarly 'chopped' a boat in half with the frame to provide a setting for his outdoor 'portrait' *En bateau*, 1874 (The Metropolitan Museum of Art, New York), and Bonnard himself had rehearsed the composition in at least three previous paintings, *En barque*, *c.*1907 (Musée d'Orsay, Paris), *Promenade sur l'eau*, 1912 (private collection, New York), and *Signac et ses amis en barque*, 1914–24 (Kunsthaus, Zurich), before executing a preliminary version of the portrait in 1924.[41]

Bonnard felt that his increased concern for composition distinguished his art from that of the Impressionists, and this concern was inseparably linked with his treatment of the female nude. Renoir, his mentor in the treatment of the portrait and the monumental nude, had turned to Cézanne in the 1880s for ways of structuring natural subjects,[42] and Bonnard included a painting of bathers by Cézanne on the wall in his portrait of Vollard, *c.*1904–5 (Plate 78). Vollard reported Cézanne on leafing through Bonnard's *Parallèlement* as saying 'That's good ... c'est dessiné dans la forme.'[43] *Les Jarretières rouges*, *c.*1905 (Plate 81), with the model posed like Vollard to the left of the mirror in Bonnard's studio in the rue de Douai, follows on from *Nu aux bas noirs*, *c.*1900 (Plate 52), in its concern for the solidity of the female form.

Although Bonnard's focus was increasingly on the nude as a subject in its own right, he still retained a naturalistic pretext for nakedness. His nudes are presented either at their toilet, undressing and washing, or carrying with them the history and meanings of their origins in his illustrations for *Parallèlement* and *Daphnis et Chloé*. A pose such as that in *Nu en hauteur*, 1906 (Plate 82), goes back to the photograph of Marthe standing naked in the garden at Montval (Plate 83), which formed part of Bonnard's preparatory work for *Daphnis et Chloé* and for a sculpture (Plate 84) he subsequently undertook

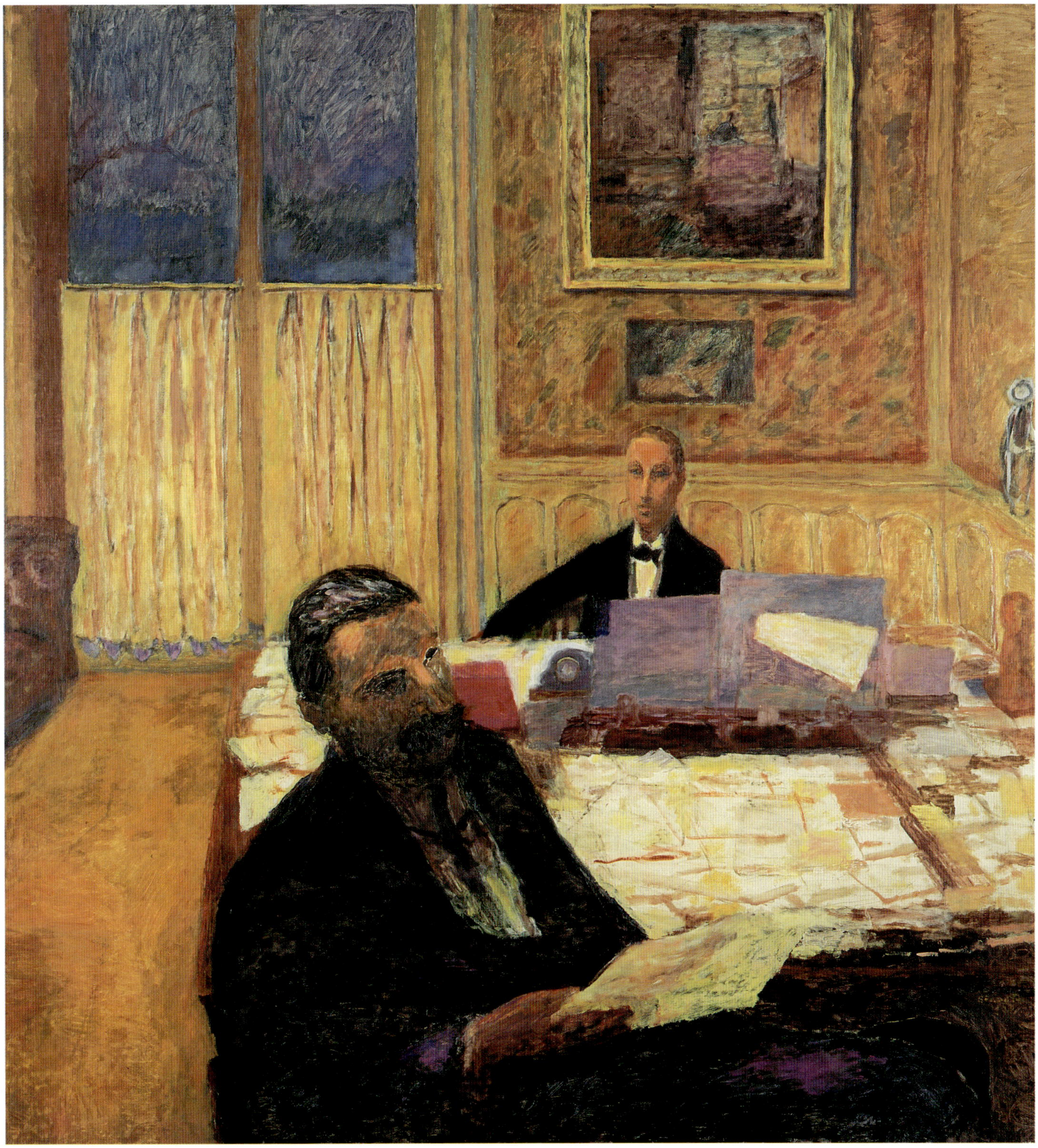

79
Josse Bernheim-Jeune et Gaston Bernheim de Villiers. 1920.
Oil on canvas, 165.5×155.5cm.
Musée d'Orsay, Paris

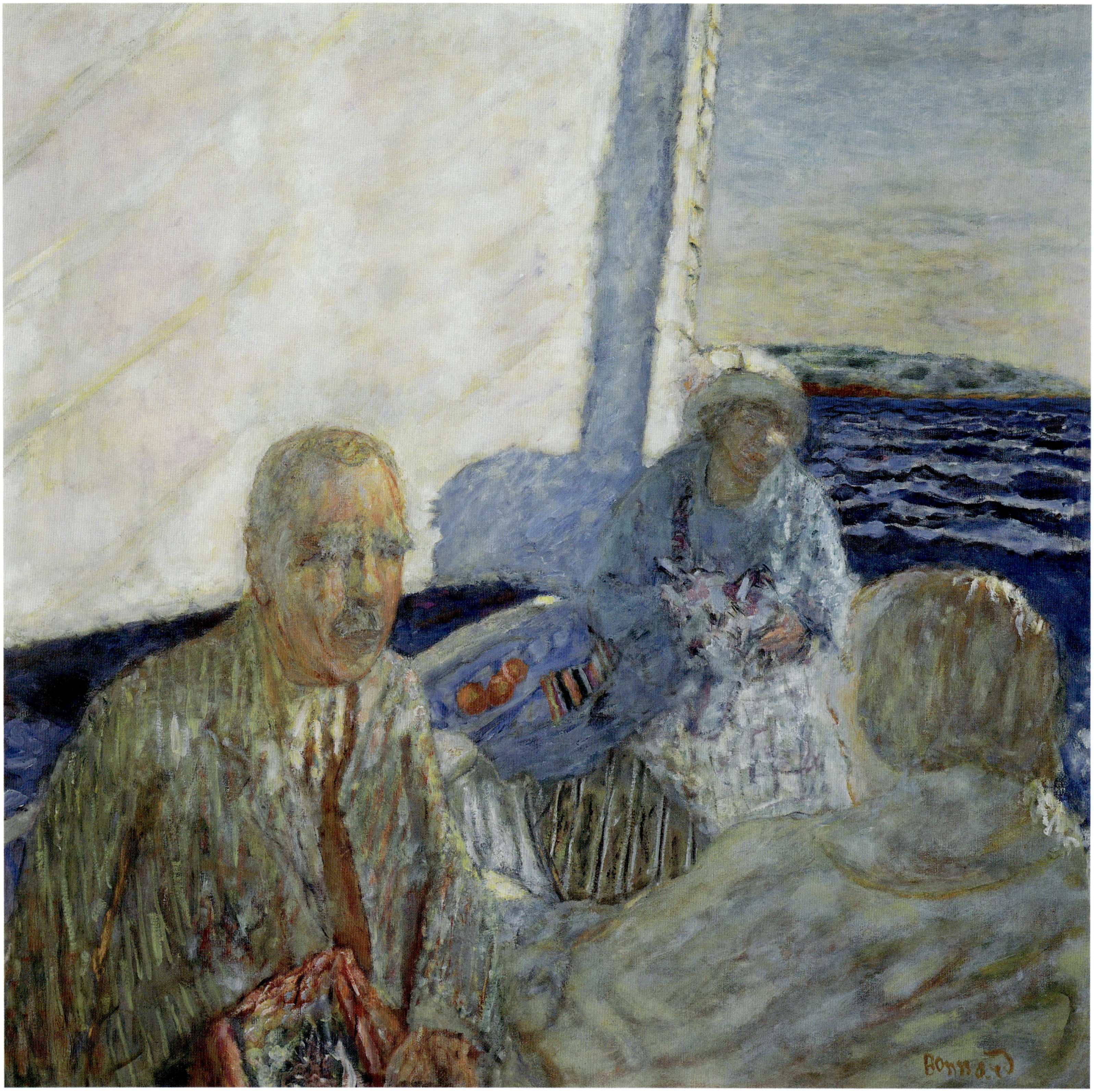

80
Promenade en mer (la famille Hahnloser). 1924.
Oil on canvas, 98×103cm.
Private collection, Switzerland

81
Les Jarretières rouges. *c*.1905.
Oil on canvas, 61×50cm.
Private collection

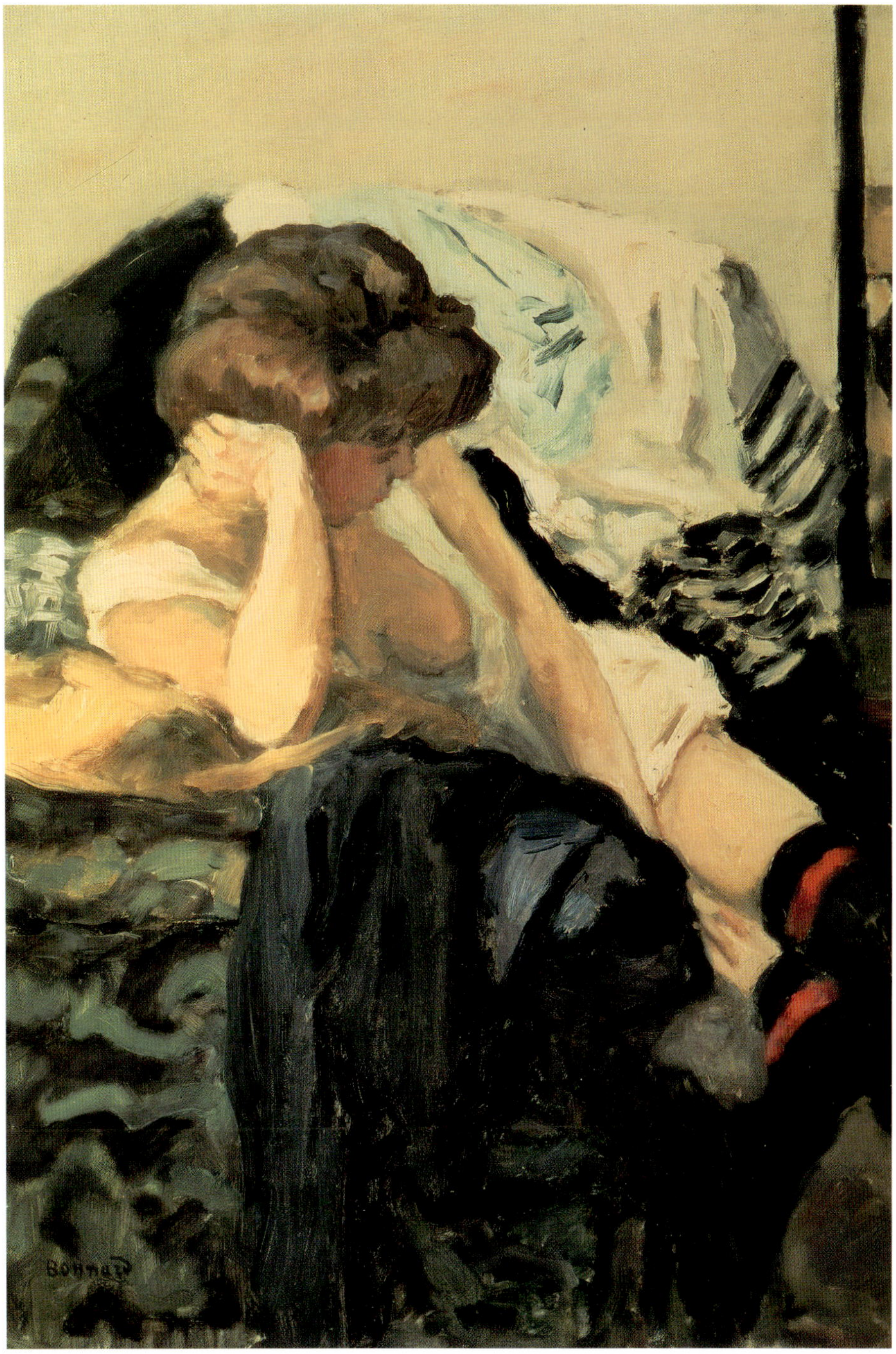

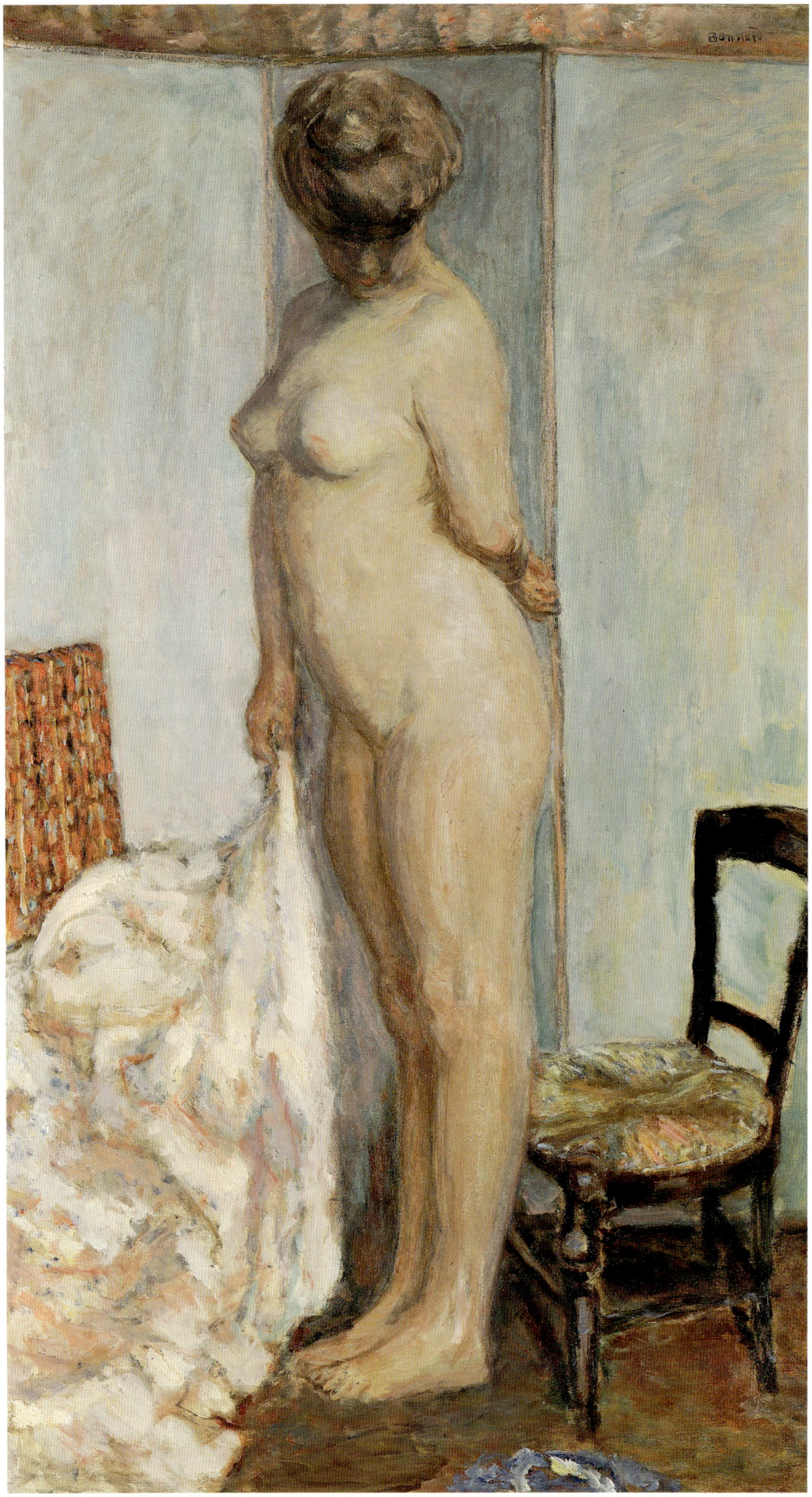

82
Nu en hauteur. 1906.
Oil on canvas, 140×80cm.
Private collection, Geneva

for Vollard at Maillol's instigation.[44] But whereas the photograph and the sculpture deal with the nude as an image of innocence, the heavier, more classical volumes of *Nu en hauteur* convey the concept of the nude as the monumental embodiment of nature. However, *Nu en hauteur* still hovers uneasily between the pin-up and the nude. It was a combination of the influences of Degas and Marthe – art and life – that enabled him to transform the nude into one of the most exciting subjects in his *œuvre*.

Bonnard first explored the subject of a woman at her toilet in prints before turning to painting it. The origin of the pose in *Femme penchée*, 1907 (Plate 85), lies in his earlier lithograph, *Le Tub*, 1894 (Plate 25), showing Marthe – like one of Degas's bathers – crouched in a tub washing herself. The cut-off, unusual viewpoint of *Femme penchée* also demonstrates Bonnard's continuing debt to Japanese prints and Degas, whose poses could come as much from art as from life. A drawing by Michelangelo of a nude male climbing up a bank out of water provided the pose for the woman in Degas's pastel *Le Bain matinal*, *c.*1890–5 (Plate 86).[45] By contrast, Bonnard's interest in the subject was sustained as much by life as by art. Marthe's obsessional need to bathe provided him with a ready-made subject.[46] He would sketch her in the bathroom, often working a few feet from her, which accounts for the extraordinarily close viewpoint of *Femme penchée*. The actual painting was carefully composed and carried out in the studio. Marthe's legs were set open like the struts of a bridge, with the lines of the floor-tiles rushing away in perspective between them. The background was darkened to concentrate attention on the figure and the warm flesh tones and cool shadows were transposed into the higher key of blue and red, with accents of yellow, to establish the dominant colour scheme of the composition.

In 1907–8 Bonnard entered his maturity as a painter, largely through Degas, who provided him with the means to escape the naturalistic straightjacket imposed by the model and to engage with the subject of the nude as art, drawing the spectator into the unfolding logic of a painting in such a way that the figure is read as part of the setting. Art for Degas was artifice, the manipulation of the pictorial elements to create the illusion of life. Light for the first time became a key element in Bonnard's construction of a work. The nude in *Dans le cabinet de toilette*, 1907 (Plate 87), throws back her towel (more a flimsy drape) and exposes her body to the light; in *Nu à contre-jour*, 1908 (Plate 88), she tilts back on her high heels to welcome the light, like a lover in a pose reminiscent of Degas's sculpture *Étude de nu pour 'La Danseuse habillée'*, 1879–80 (Plate 89). The light from the window continues down through the reflection in the tub to provide part of the geometric structure of the composition. This development of light into a constructional element further distanced Bonnard from Impressionism and paved the way for the revelation of colour in light which came with his second trip to the south of France in 1909.

Like Degas, Bonnard began to employ mirrors to add further dimensions to a painting, expanding the space, breaking down the barrier between art and life, both absorbing and rejecting the spectator, suggesting different viewpoints and readings of the

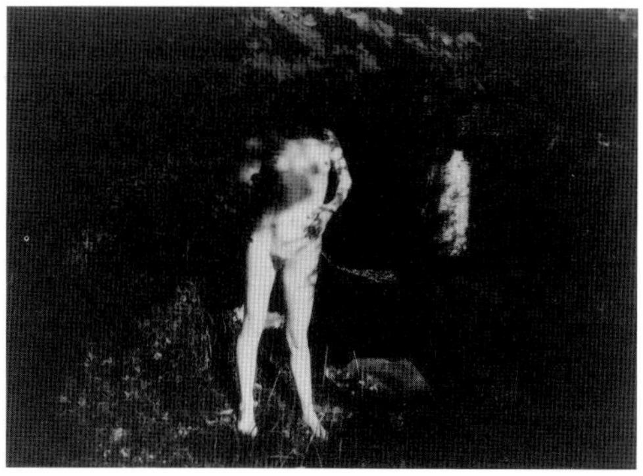

83
Marthe standing in the sun. 1900–1.
Photograph.
Musée d'Orsay, Paris

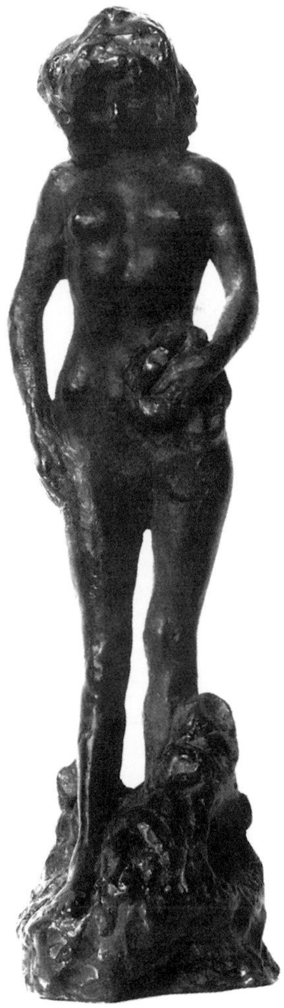

84
Nu debout. *c.*1906.
Bronze, 27.9cm high.
Private collection

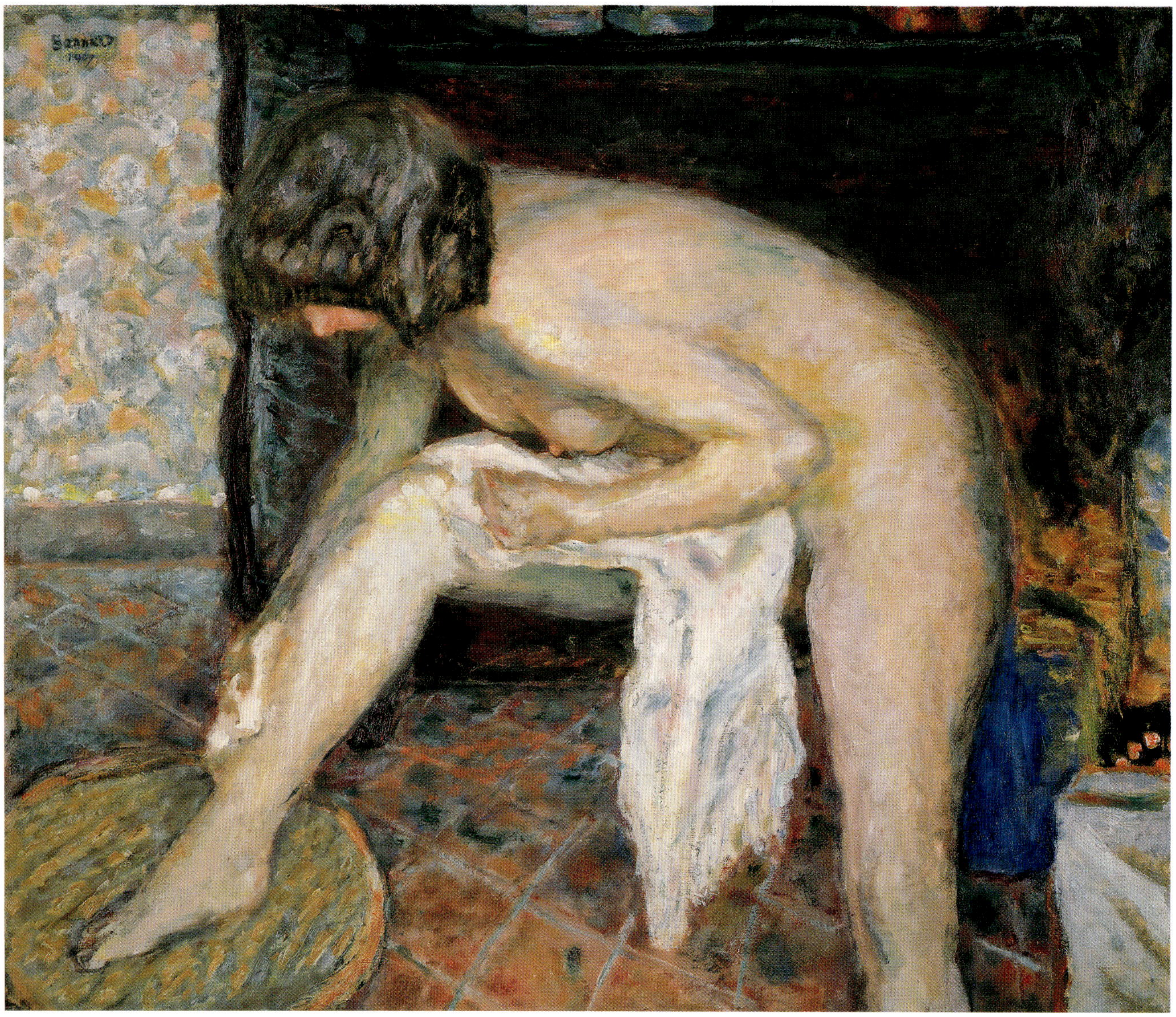

85
Femme penchée. 1907.
Oil on canvas, 72×85cm.
Niigatashi City Art Museum

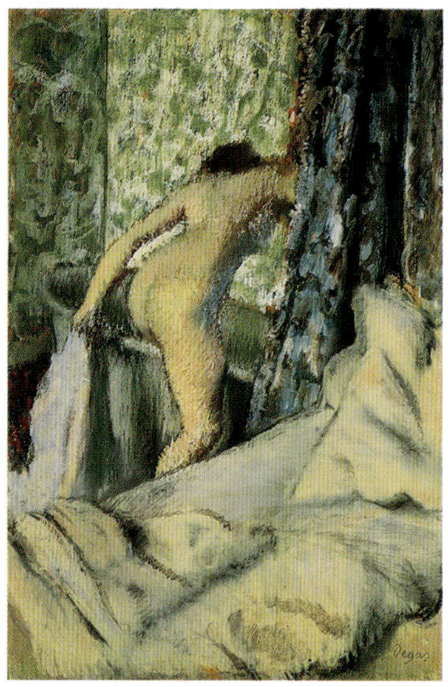

86
Edgar Degas
Le Bain matinal. *c*.1890–5.
Pastel on paper, 70×43cm.
The Art Institute of Chicago
Potter Palmer Collection

87
Dans le cabinet de toilette.
1907.
Oil on board, 107×72cm.
Private collection, Lausanne

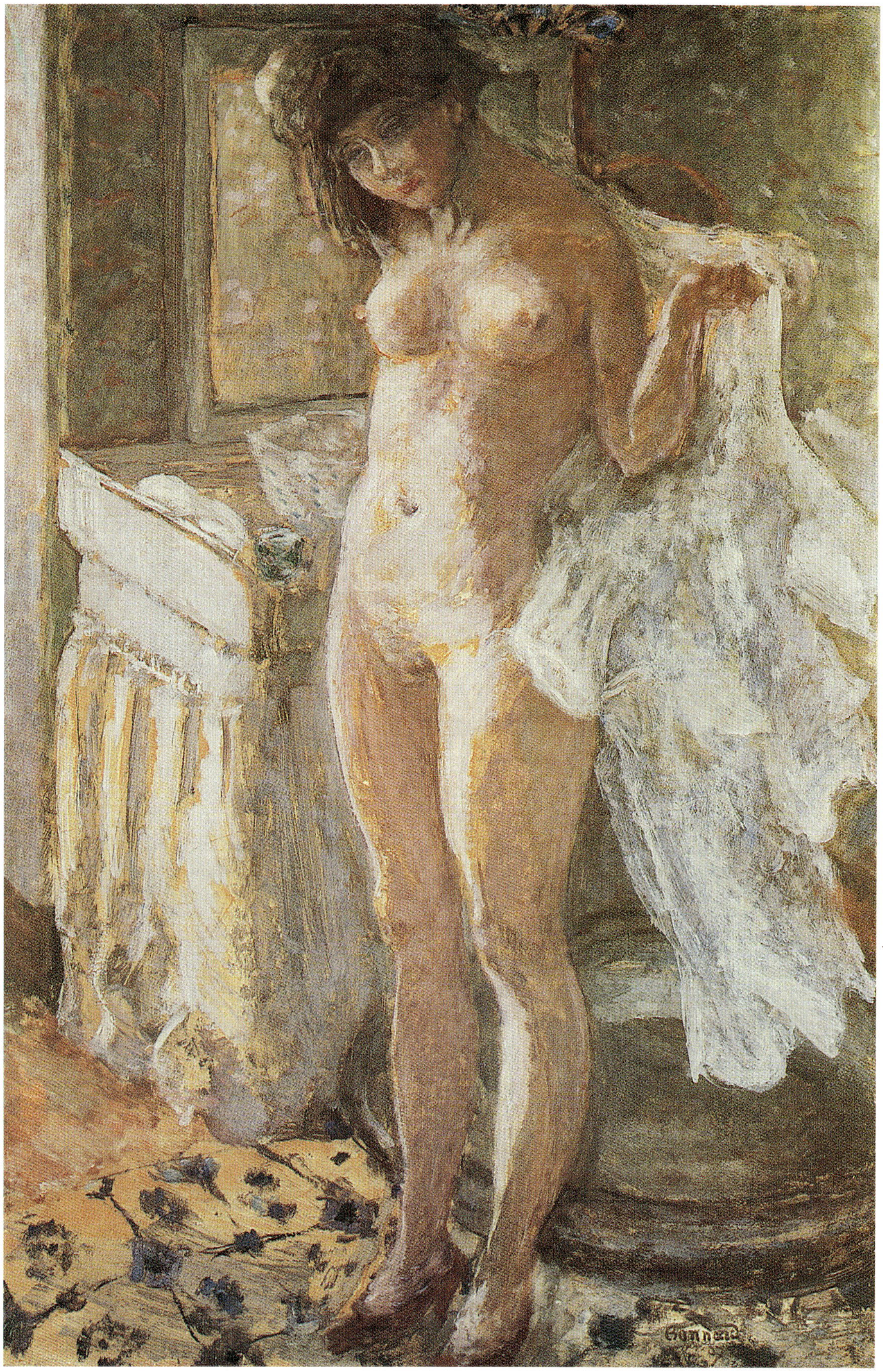

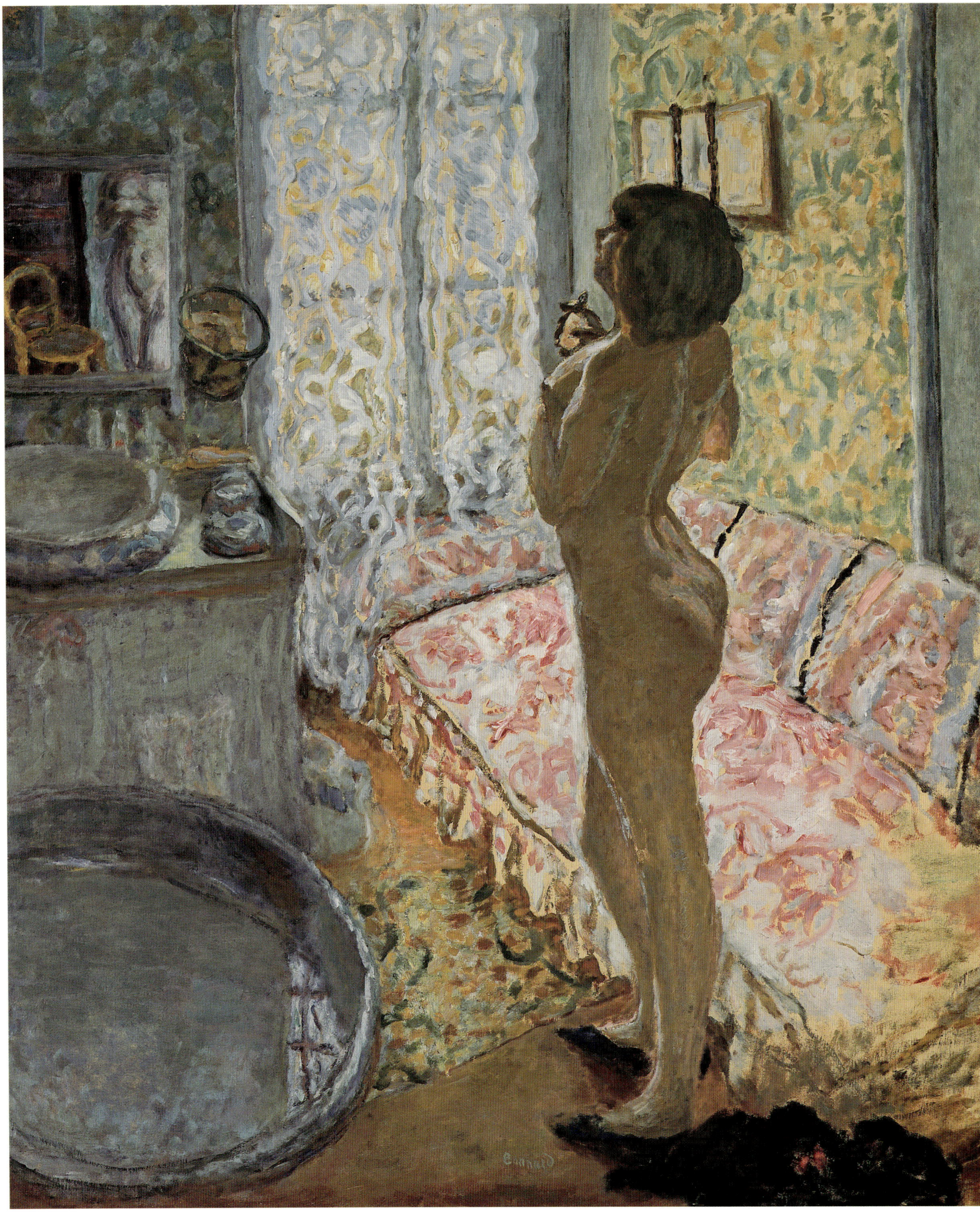

88
Nu à contre-jour. 1908.
Oil on canvas, 124.5×108cm.
Musées Royaux des Beaux-Arts de Belgique, Brussels

nude, referring to classical statuary, confronting living flesh with a deathly white reflection and creating a complex allegory on the nature and transforming power of art. In *Effet de glace*, 1909 (Plate 90), the action takes place in the mirror, where a psychological balance is achieved between the nude compressed into the frame on the left and the spatially ambiguous play of the dish on the shelf and the tub on the floor on the right. The device of the mirror opened up a sequence of permutations which Bonnard was to explore. For instance, in *Table de toilette et miroir*, *c.*1913 (Plate 91), a so-called normal reading is reversed and the reflected scene in the mirror appears more real than the rest of the objects in the room; only the flowers are left to mediate between the two domains. As in the poetry of Mallarmé, the mirror became a metaphor for levels of reality, a theme which the Belgian Surrealist René Magritte was to turn into a programme in the 1930s.

89
Degas
Étude de nu pour 'La Danseuse habillée'. 1879–80.
Bronze, 72cm high.
Private collection

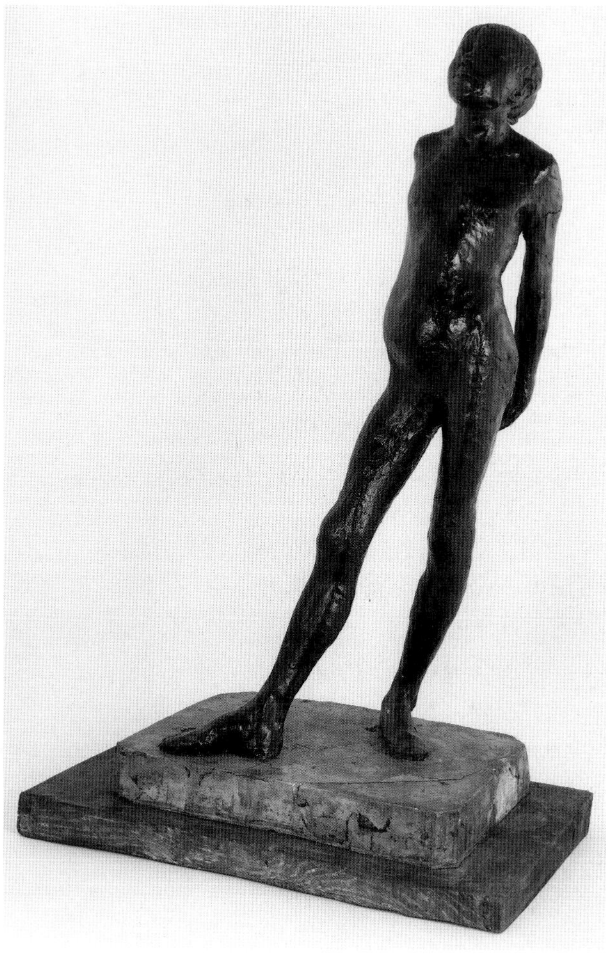

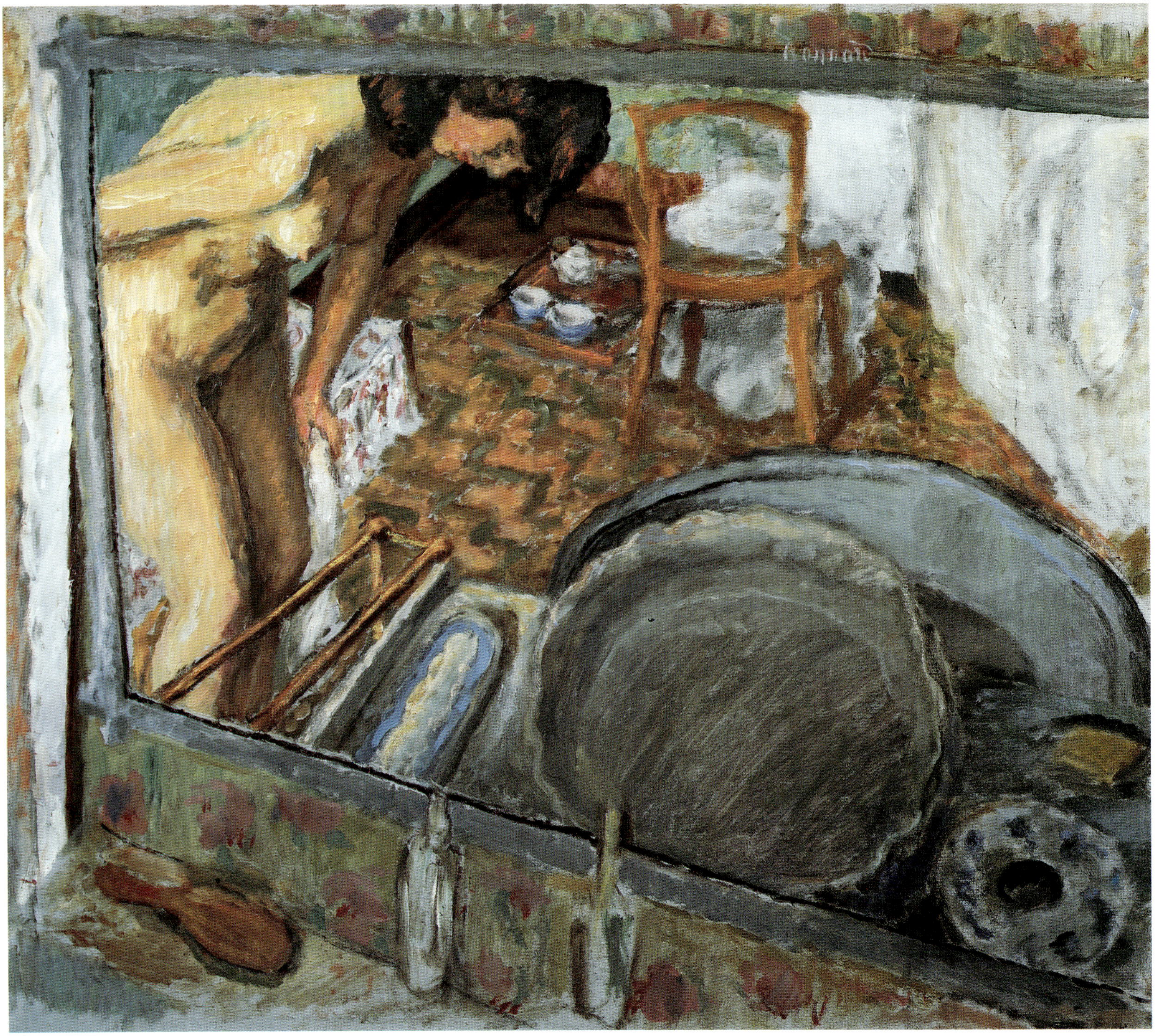

90
Effet de glace. 1909.
Oil on canvas, 73×84.5cm.
Private collection, Switzerland

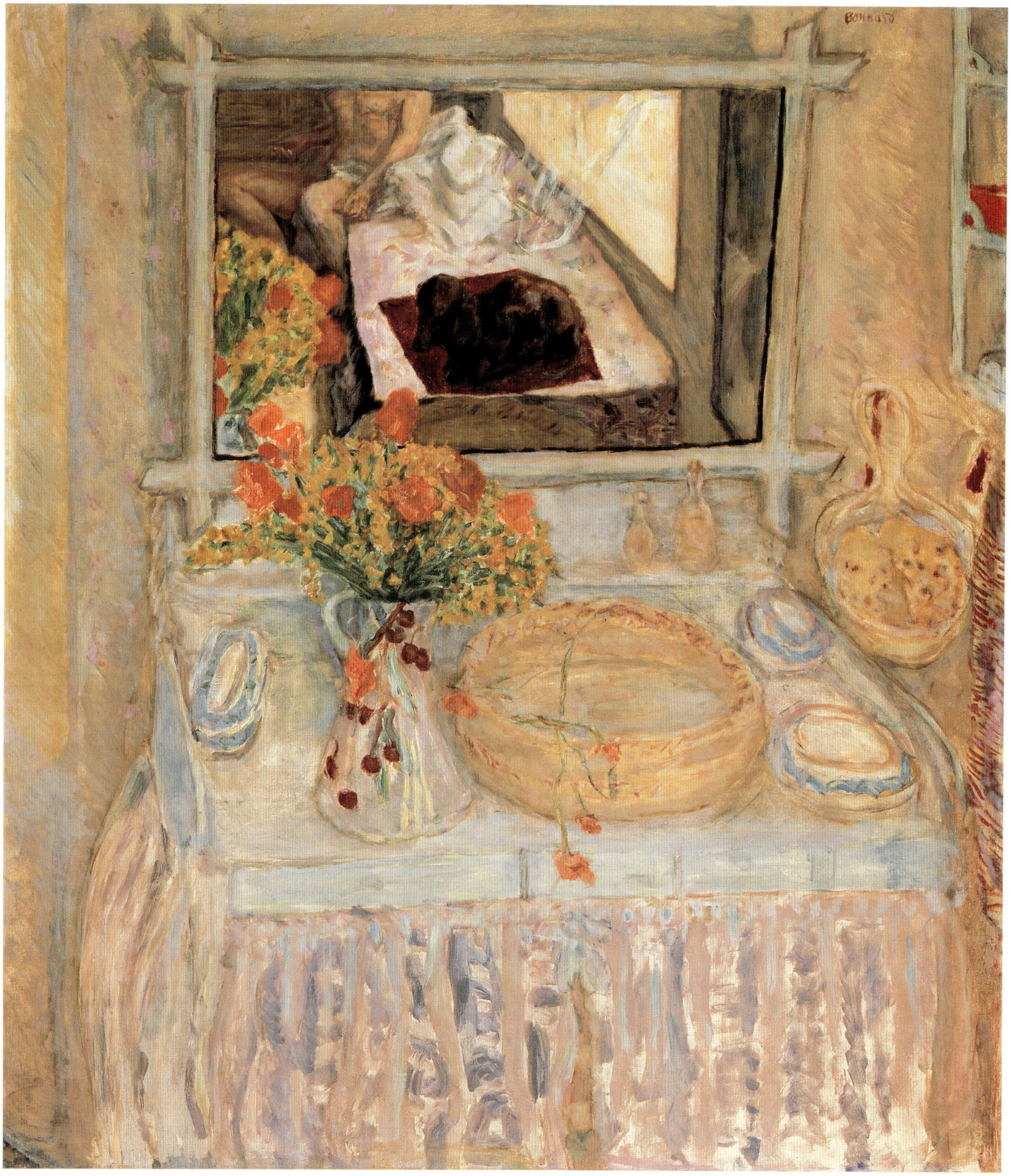

91
*Table de toilette et miroir. c.*1913.
Oil on canvas, 124.5×109.3cm.
The Museum of Fine Arts, Houston, John A. and
Audrey Jones Beck collection

Chapter 3

Realism and idealism: north versus south

As foreign commentators attempted to come to grips with the rapid advances of modernism in three enormous international exhibitions – the Sonderbund exhibition organized by Karl-Ernst Osthaus at Cologne in March 1912, Roger Fry's Second Post-Impressionist exhibition at the Grafton Galleries, London, in October 1912, and the Armory Show in New York in February 1913 – Bonnard, often coupled with Vuillard, became identified as a respected transitional figure meriting attention. Roger Fry, writing in April 1912, described him as 'the most distinguished of those artists whose work lies just on the Impressionist side of Post-Impressionism', and he selected a little street scene, 'with its delicate and witty observation', to illustrate his gifts.[1] Ironically, Bonnard's critical reputation closed him down in terms of an earlier style, just when his art was opening up.

This situation changed with the advent of the First World War. By the winter of 1914 Braque, Derain, Léger, Vlaminck and many other artists associated with the evolution of modernism were at the front. Bonnard was too old for active service; Matisse, who was two years younger, tried to enlist but was turned down because of his age. To alleviate his guilt Bonnard joined Denis and Vuillard (also too old to fight) at the front and produced a sketchy painting of a rain-soaked devastated village with an old man squatting forlornly by a ruined cottage (*Dans la Somme, village en ruines*, *c.*1916). The war took a terrible toll. Out of a total of some 8,570,000 men aged between 18 and 46 available for compulsory military service, 7,935,000 were finally mobilized; 1,322,000 were killed in battle, 3,000,000 were wounded (388,8000 permanently), and 513,000 were captured.[2] Picasso, a non-combatant as a foreigner, was not alone in feeling that a complete way of life had come to an end.

The assumption that economic and cultural activity came to a halt, especially with the occupation of the industrial regions in the north and east, has recently been challenged by historians, who have shown that pre-War trends and divisions in French society often continued in ways that had unforeseen long-term consequences.[3] Modernism itself came under attack by conservative critics as an enemy product foisted on French culture by Jewish dealers with German names, such as Bernheim (who represented Bonnard), Wildenstein, Weill, Basler and Kahnweiler.[4] The pendulum swung back to two styles associated with tradition: classicism and realism. Jean Cocteau, the young French poet, was a key figure in the promotion of an eclectic classical style in Paris during the war. Already in 1914 he had assisted on *Le Mot*, a new magazine founded ostensibly to defend modernism against accusations of being pro-German, but which

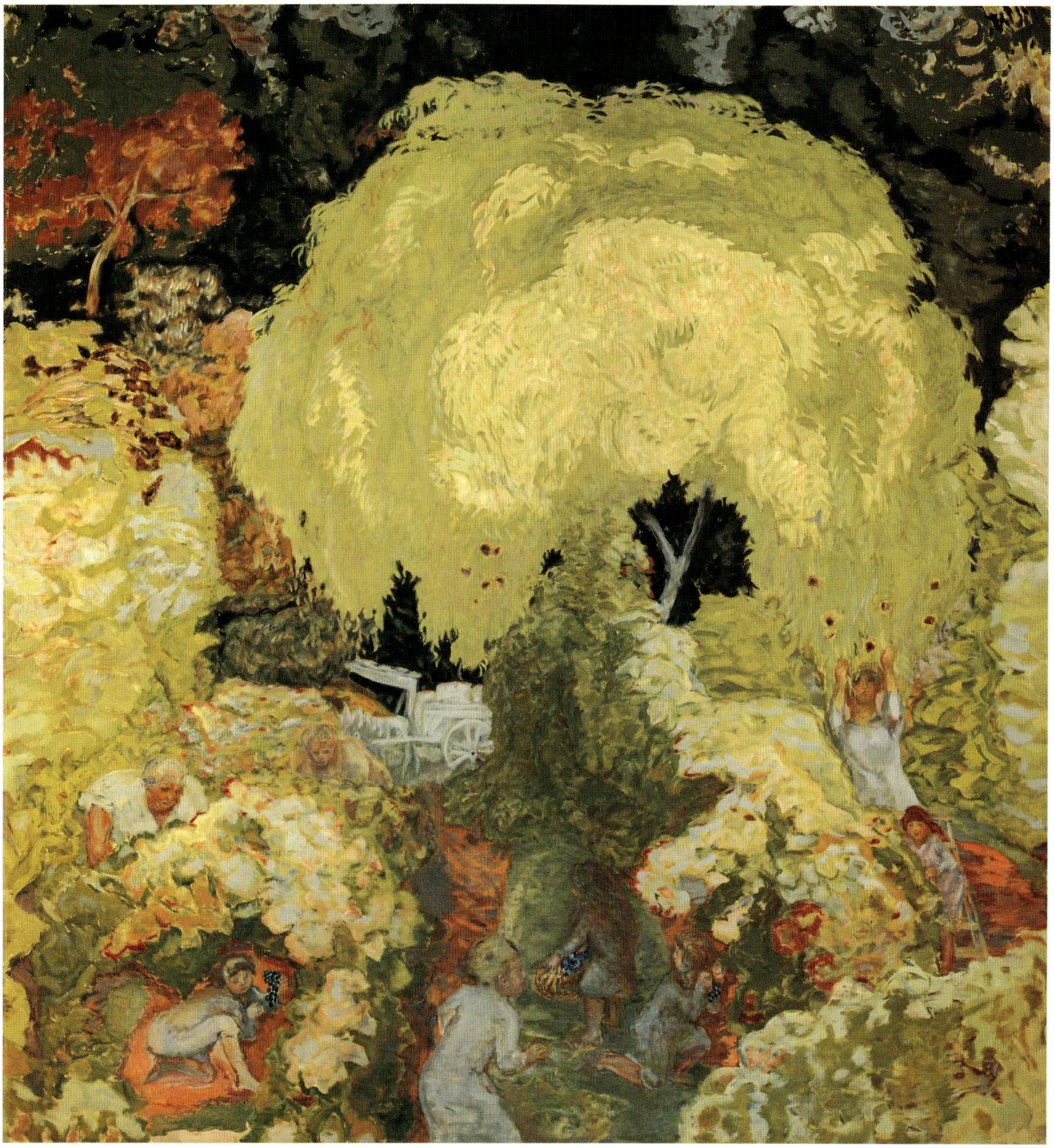

92
L'Automne. Les Vendanges. 1912.
Oil on canvas, 365×347cm.
Pushkin Museum, Moscow

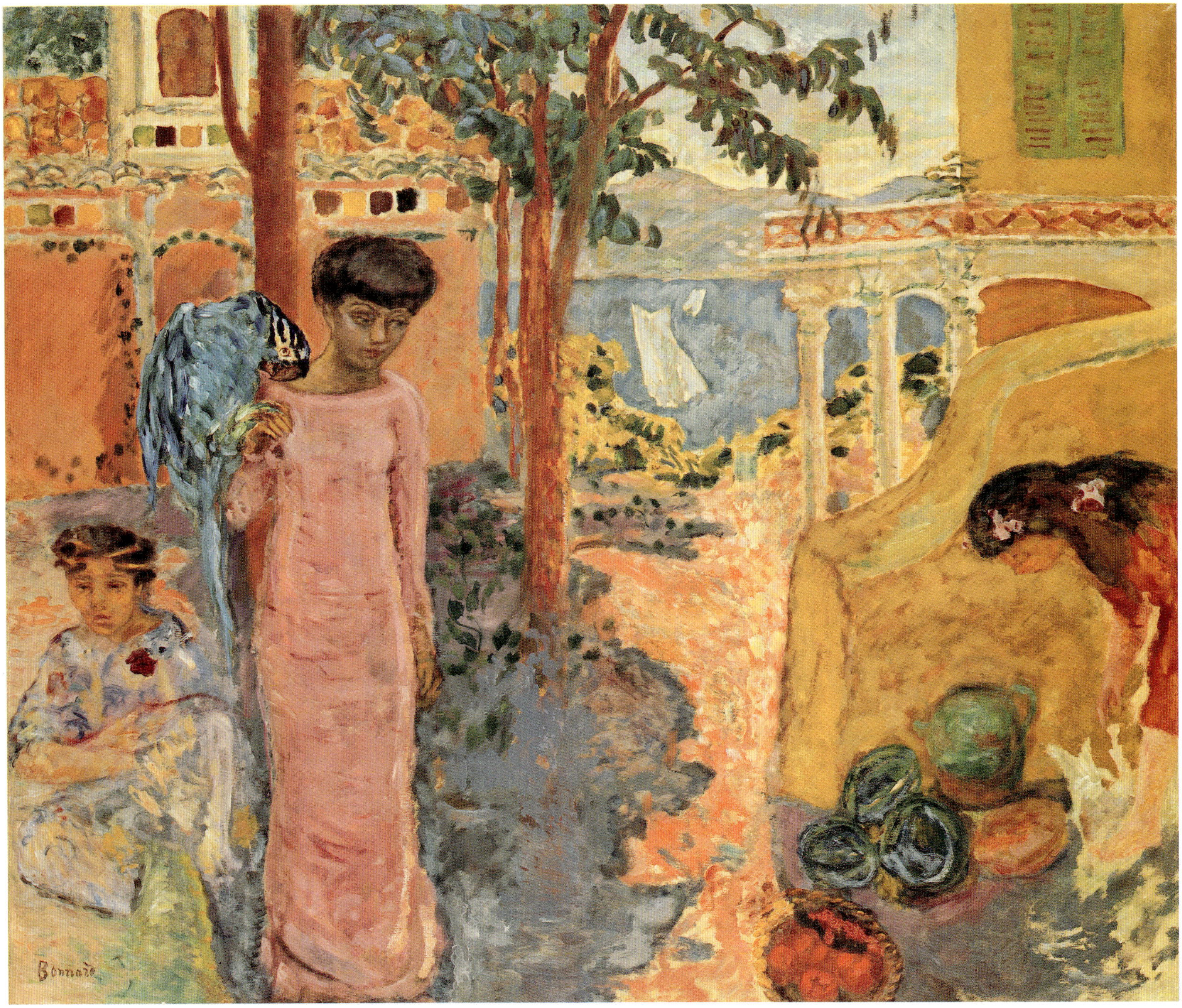

93
Femme au perroquet. 1910.
Oil on canvas, 104×122cm.
Private collection

ended up by condemning all 'isms', especially Germanism, as being antithetical to individual expression.[5] His hero Picasso, at the same time as evolving a rigorously simplified form of Synthetic Cubism, capitulated – according to modernist contemporaries such as Delaunay – to conservative critics and produced works in a neo-classical style, derived principally from Ingres. For Matisse the forceful structure and sombre palette of Cubist realism was the appropriate style for the times, and it triumphed in his paintings from late 1914 to the winter of 1916. Soon after 1916 he abandoned what he called these 'modern methods of construction' for a more relaxed combination of traditional realism and classical line drawing. The revival of realism and classicism led to a re-evaluation of Courbet and the late work of Renoir.

The classical utopia once again became both a place of retreat and a repository of civilized values under attack from Germany. However, France was not alone in laying claim to the classical tradition. The classical revival, or 'Return to Order', was a European cultural phenomenon. It was eventually embraced by the fascists, and the taint of fascism in turn has led to its neglect by historians.[6]

Given Bonnard's indifference to 'isms', coupled with his continuing interest since *Parallèlement* and *Daphnis et Chloé* in the integration of the classical into everyday life, there is every reason to expect that he would have been received back into the mainstream of contemporary art. But this does not seem to have happened. Bonnard's classicism, like Bonnard's realism, appeared too soft-focused and ambivalent for the times. His art employed the vocabulary of classicism outside the readily identifiable characteristics of a classical style. Instead of masculine strength, intellectual clarity, disciplined linear contours and tightly structured compositions, Bonnard's art was informal and unassertive. From the evidence of his contacts and paintings Bonnard's politics can loosely be described as a form of anarchic conservatism. Responding to criticism he was to make a concerted effort to emphasize form and structure, but there was nothing doctrinaire about the way he went about it.

The programme established in *Daphnis et Chloé*, dealing with the complexities of contemporary reality in a classical style, was given renewed momentum by Bonnard's belated response to two thoroughly familiar places in the annals of modern art, Saint-Tropez in the south, the home of Signac and Neo-Impressionism, and Vernon in the north, near Monet at Giverny. It was part of Bonnard's unstated objective to come to terms with these northern and southern settings, with their respective cultural associations, in a series of monumental decorations which established an artistic agenda for his landscape paintings through to the end of the 1930s.

Bonnard had become increasingly drawn to the south since his first first stay there in 1906. A visit to Algeria and Tunisia in 1908 provoked no immediate response in his art, but on going down to Saint-Tropez in the summer of 1909 he had what he called 'the revelation of a *Thousand and one nights*', and went on to describe 'the sea, the yellow walls, the reflections as full of colour as the light. After a fragrant mid-day meal we went to call on some neighbours and I had the vision of a very dark girl in a pink dress down to her feet with an enormous parakeet, uncaged, against the yellow, red and green background ... I think I shall soon be longing for the green grass and the clouds.'[7] His delayed reaction to one of the crucial experiences in the culture of painting, the discovery in the nineteenth century of colour in shadow, is on the face of it astonishing. It was as though he could shut his mind to formative issues in the history of contemporary art until he was ready to experience them on his own terms with all the freshness of a revelation.

Saint-Tropez had become a Mecca for aspiring young colourists since Signac settled in this small Mediterranean port in 1892. The Neo-Impressionist painter Henri-Edmond Cross and Félix Fénéon had houses nearby at Cabasson. Matisse had made his breakthrough to an art of colour at Saint-Tropez in 1904. In his review of the famous Salon d'Automne of 1905, the critic Louis Vauxcelles, who inadvertently gave the Fauves their name, described the painters flocking down to this enchanted land as 'migratory birds'.[8] Among them was Henri Manguin (1874–1949), whom Bonnard met at Saint-Tropez in 1909. Manguin's conservative form of Fauvism served as a bridge for Bonnard between classicism and heightened colour. Manguin had painted his wife posed dreamily before Mediterranean views, and a classical nude reclining in the landscape, both subjects which Bonnard was to take up.

Femme au perroquet, 1910 (Plate 93), one of Bonnard's first major decorative

94
Les Cascades. 1912.
Oil on canvas, 76×100cm.
Private collection

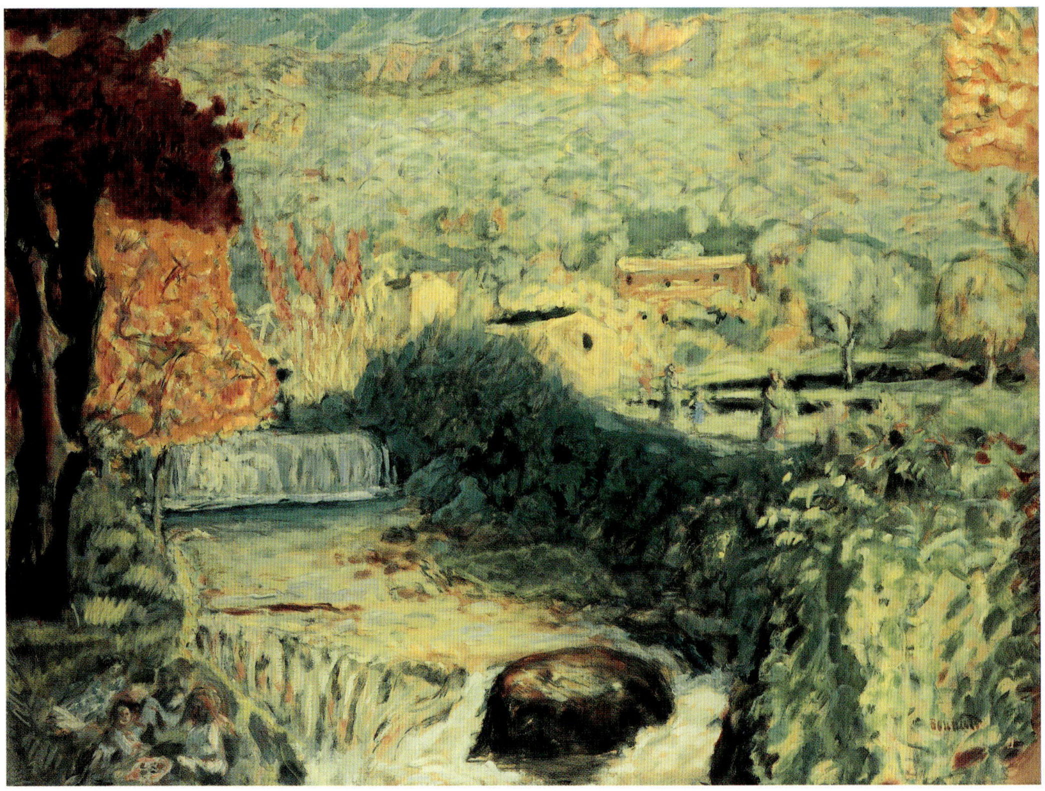

panels on a southern subject, contains all the ingredients of a composition from the Signac circle: the mixing of the real and ideal in a group of female figures absorbed in the enveloping warmth of a Mediterranean setting. Signac's house La Hune (The Crow's Nest), designed by the Neo-Impressionist painter and architect Henri van de Velde in 1898, stands just outside Saint-Tropez on a hill overlooking the sea. For both Signac and Bonnard an earthly paradise was a place remembered. *Femme au perroquet* exactly fits Bonnard's description. The wall of the house on the right is yellow, as he recalled, and the deep blue shadow is as colourful as the light areas. But whereas the precedents for Signac's vision of timeless beauty and harmony lay in Japanese prints and classical landscapes from Poussin to Puvis de Chavannes, Bonnard – as in the decorations for Misia – was still dreaming of Gauguin's vision of the South Seas. Tourists were still something of a novelty in Saint-Tropez, let alone an exotic woman carrying a blue parrot to complement her dress.

To compete successfully for the patronage of the two major collectors of contemporary art, the Russians Sergei Shchukin (1854–1936) and Ivan Morozov (1871–1921) an artist like Bonnard had to be able to produce mural-size canvases. The two Russians collected French modernist art on such a scale that they could influence the market. Morozov spent between 200,000 and 300,000 francs on pictures in Paris each year.[9] They amassed virtual museums charting the evolution of modern art from Impressionism onwards. Although their tastes overlapped, the younger Morozov, who was the more cautious and private of the two, favoured the Nabis, especially Maurice Denis, while Shchukin preferred Matisse and Picasso. In 1907 Morozov commissioned five panels illustrating the story of Psyche from Denis for the decoration of the concert hall in his mansion on Prechistenka Street, which were exhibited at the Salon d'Automne of 1908, and Shchukin replied with the commission of *La Danse* and *La Musique* from Matisse, which were exhibited at the Salon d'Automne of 1910.

To stake his place in this competitive market Bonnard exhibited his 1906 panels for Misia at the Salon d'Automne of 1910, which was dominated by decorative paintings. Whether the strategy was conscious or not it certainly proved successful. Morozov, who liked landscapes and was himself an amateur landscape painter, had commissioned in January 1910 the two city views discussed in the last chapter, *Matin à Paris*, 1911 (Plate 72), and *Soir à Paris*. He now went on to commission the immense triptych *Mediterranée* (Plate 95) for the area above the main staircase of his mansion, which was exhibited at the Salon d'Automne of 1911. Two more panels were commissioned in 1912, *Le Printemps* and *L'Automne. Les Vendanges* (Plate 92).

Mediterranée stands not so much as a critique of *La Danse* and *La Musique*, for Bonnard admired Matisse, but as an alternative, almost perverse, way of going about making a monumental mural painting. Both projects are multi-figure compositions in a Mediterranean landscape, but there the similarity ends. The essential features of a classical mural painting are compositional clarity and the distinct separation of figure and ground: the message had to be read at a distance. Bonnard opted for the other

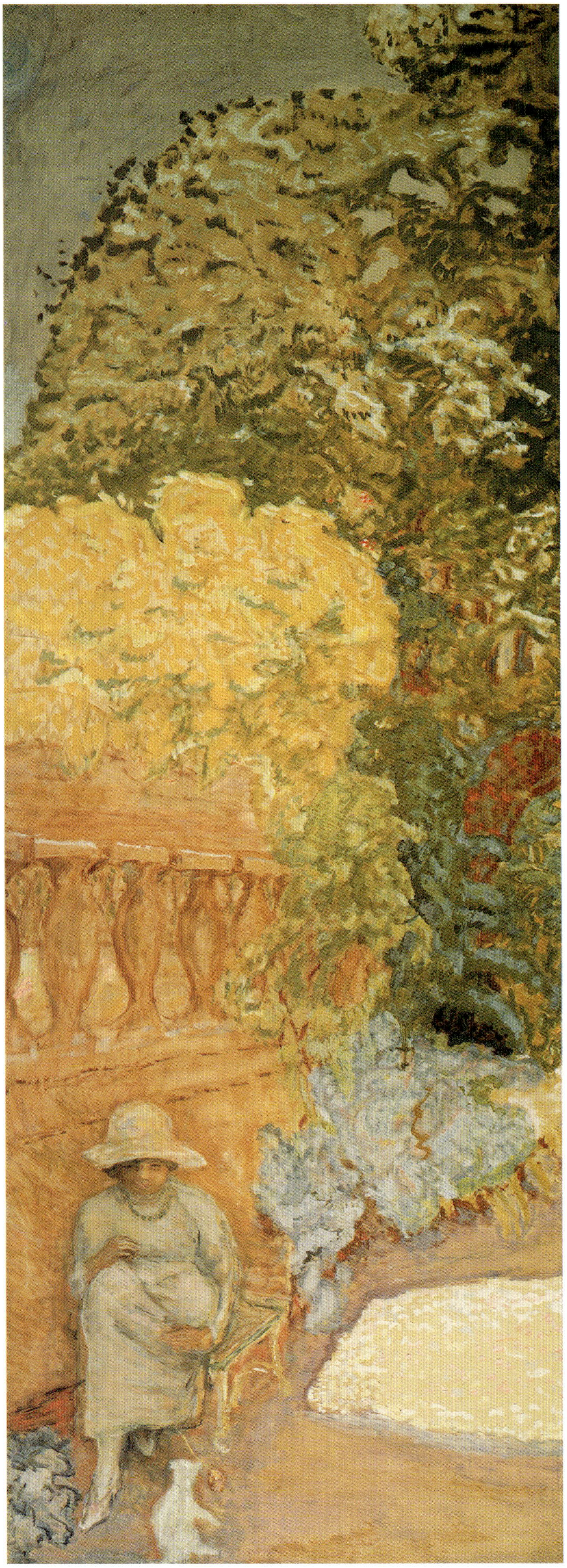

95
Mediterranée. 1911.
Oil on canvas, central panel 407×142cm,
left and right panels 407×149cm each.
Hermitage, St Petersburg

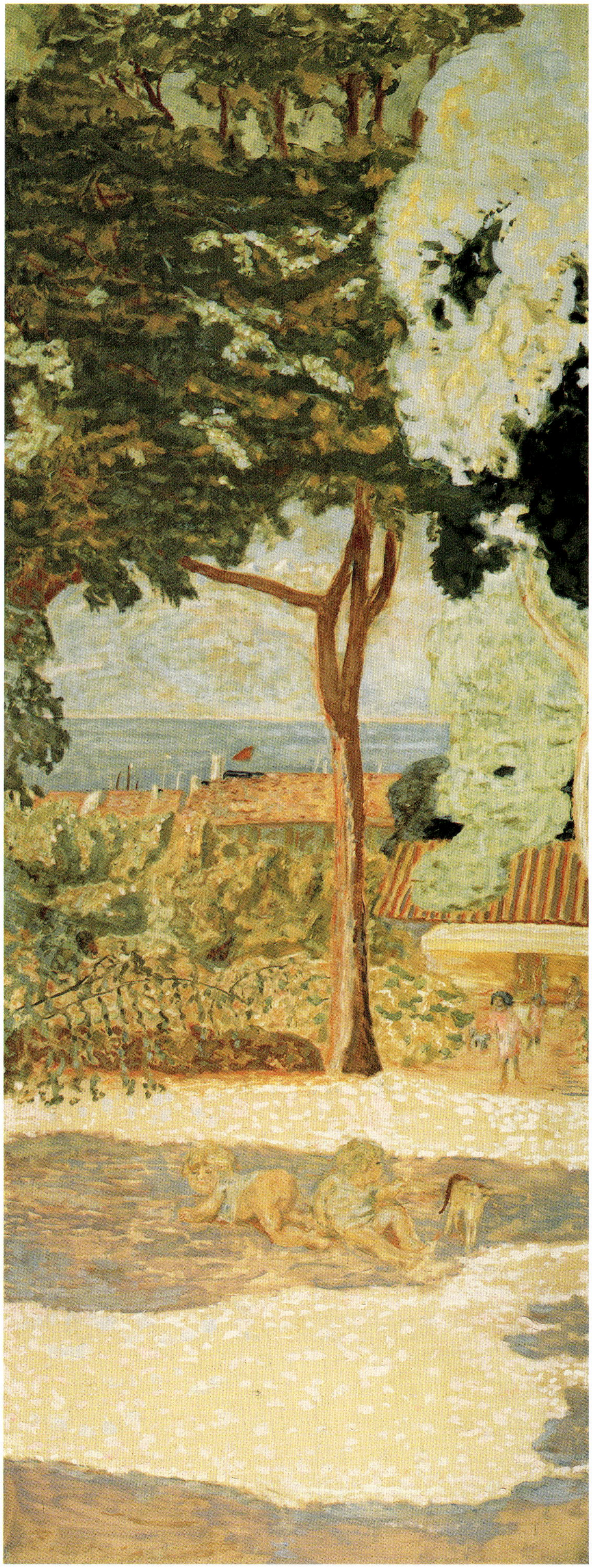

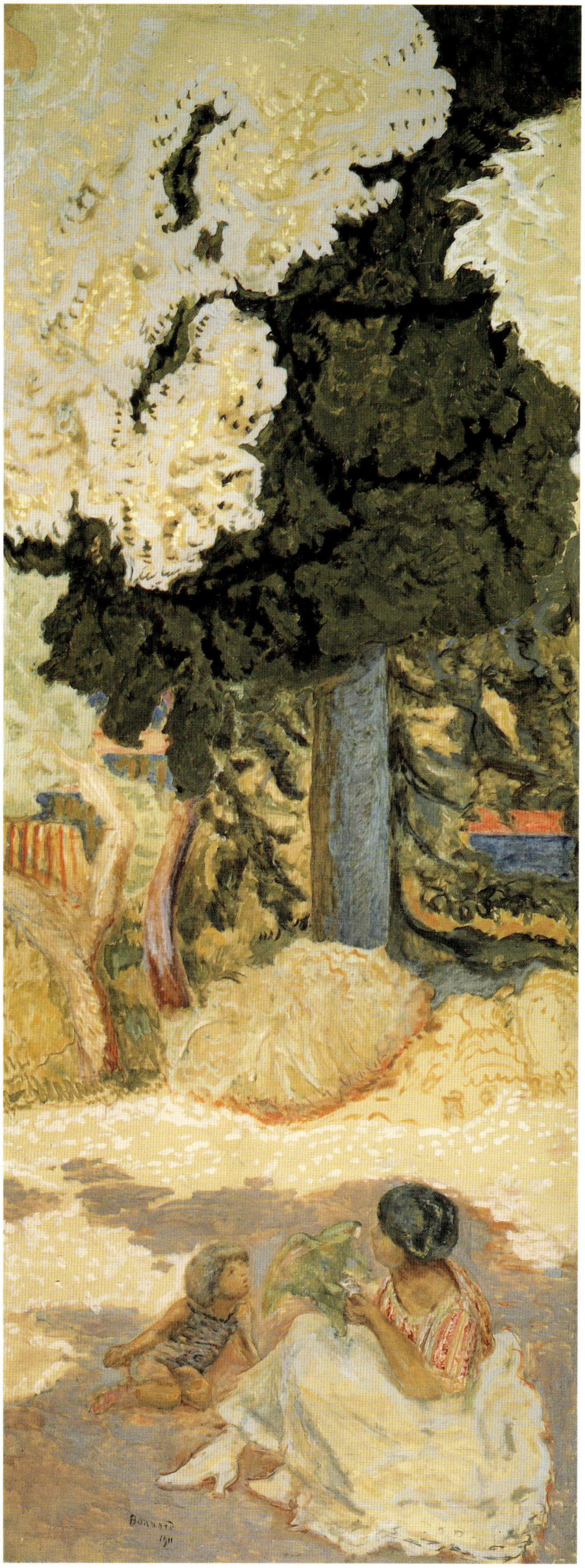

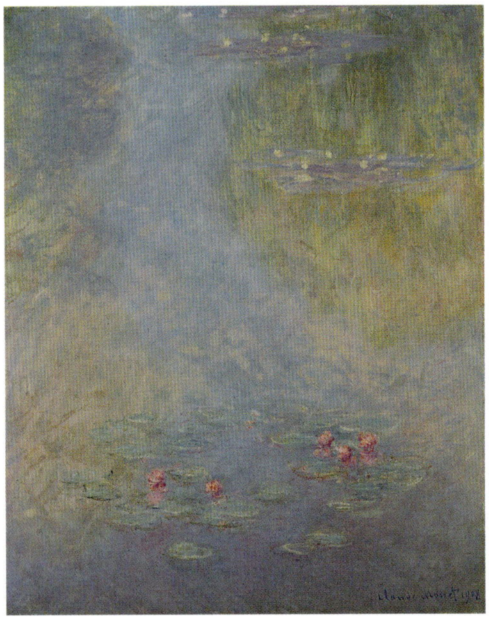

96
Claude Monet
Nymphéas. 1908.
Oil on canvas, 100×81cm.
National Museum of Wales, Cardiff

extreme. Instead of the remorseless pounding rhythm galvanizing Matisse's dancers around the surface, his figures are again the Terrasse family, taken on holiday for a change to the Mediterranean and absorbed pantheistically into the atmosphere of the garden. The foliage of the trees billows like clouds behind the two columns of the architectural setting, framing the intense light which becomes the subject of the painting.

For a realist from the north like Bonnard, southern light was a prerequisite for his emerging art of colour, and he made repeated trips there, staying at Saint-Tropez again, Grasse, Cannes and Antibes before buying the house at Le Cannet in 1926 which became his permanent base in the south. He had to feel that his art grew out of the direct perception of nature. Even a seemingly idealized landscape in the feathery pastoral tradition of the eighteenth century, such as *Les Cascades*, 1912 (Plate 94), was based on an actual view of the river and hills behind Grasse which Bonnard loved. The surviving sequence of drawings in an unpublished sketchbook shows that the waterfall in the foreground first caught his eye and that he then explored the possibility of adding Cézannesque bathers, before settling for the domesticity of the picnicking family in the foreground and the women and children walking along the far riverbank. An anonymous reviewer wrote in *The Times* of 21 October 1912: 'M. Bonnard's Cascade is wonderfully skilful and charming; but it lacks lucidity. This picture has a general air of untidiness owing to its lack of relief, and bewilders the eye instead of guiding it.'[10]

Seemingly indifferent to criticisms that his art was charming but formless, Bonnard continued his exploration of an alternative decorative tradition stemming from Claude Monet. The transient vision of Impressionism was for Bonnard a northern phenomenon associated with green fields and cloudy skies in the countryside of the Seine valley and Normandy coast. In 1910 he first rented, and then bought in 1912, Ma Roulotte, a house overlooking the Seine outside Vernonnet, across the river from Vernon and only a short distance from Monet at Giverny.

With the growth of *plein air* painting in the nineteenth century a virtual army of landscapists had descended on the area. This move was part of the development in tourism which saw a remarkable boom between 1860 and 1910, largely facilitated by the development of the railway. A poster was produced, presumably by the local *syndicat d'initiative*, proclaiming: 'Vernon à une heure de Paris', and numerous illustrated guide books were published to help the tourist discover the countryside.[11]

Monet came to Giverny in April 1883 and remained there until his death in 1926, drawing artists to this tiny village from all over the world. The first American painters began arriving in 1885, and during the next fifteen years Giverny became an established artists' colony,[12] firmly equated with Impressionism, in the same way that Saint-Tropez was associated with Neo-Impressionism. Bonnard's arrival in Vernonnet coincided with the decline of the colony – every motif had so thoroughly been converted into art that amateurs could take over – and there was no question of his becoming the focus of a new grouping. He was antisocial and avoided his neighbours, who were unaware that a distinguished painter was living by them; his house was difficult to find.

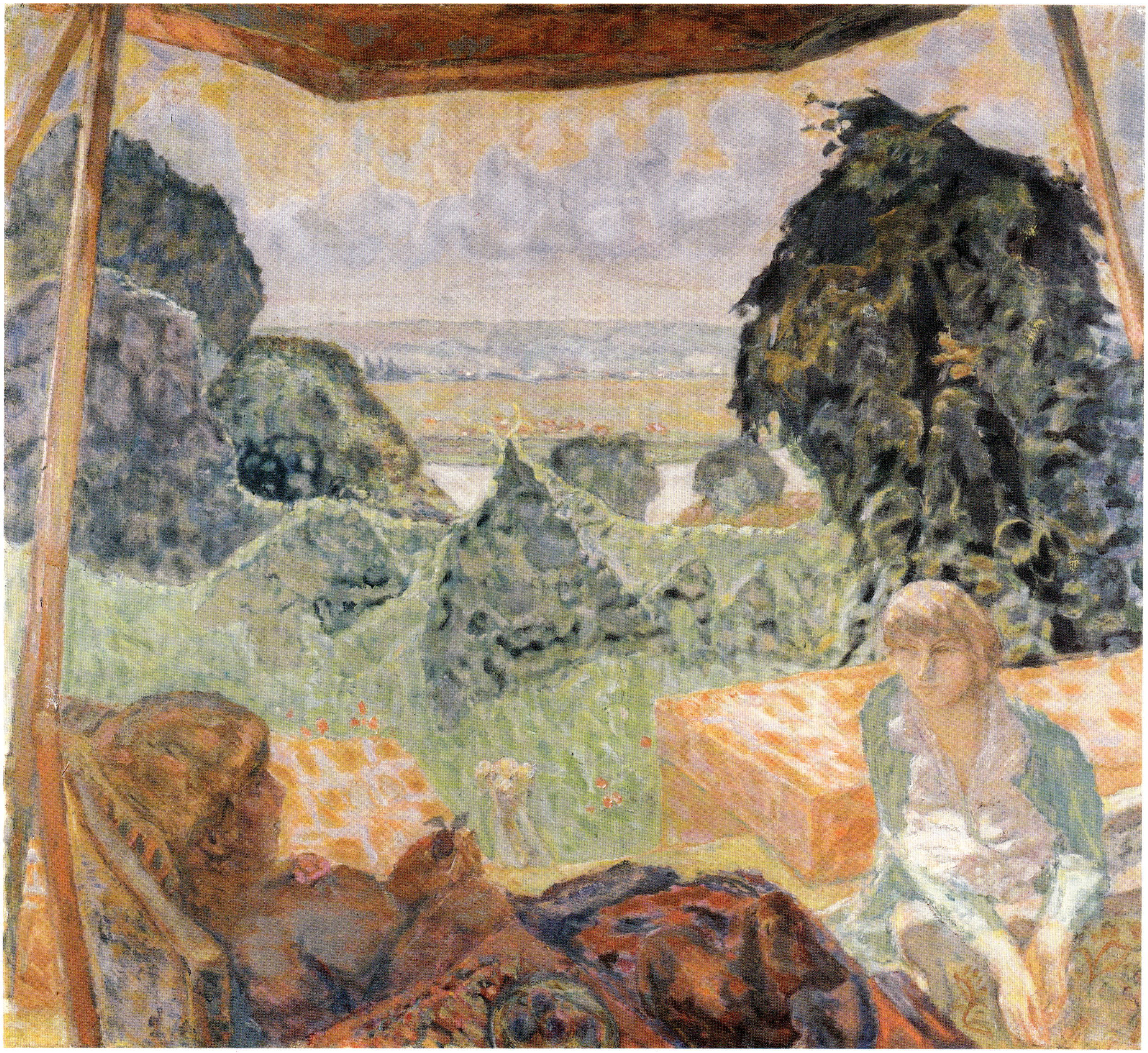

97
L'Été en Normandie. 1912.
Oil on canvas, 114×128cm.
Pushkin Museum, Moscow

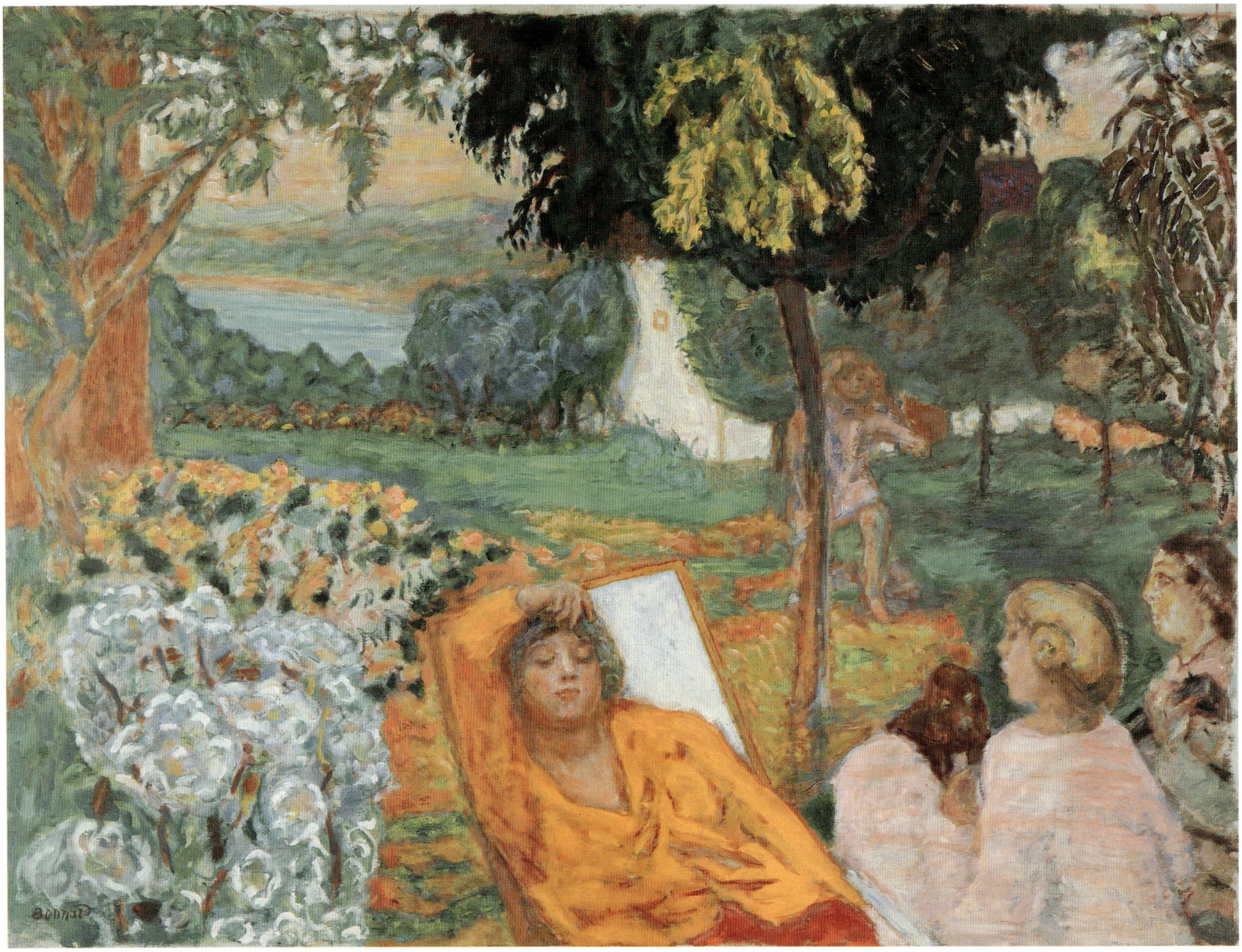

98
Soir or *La Sieste*. 1914.
Oil on canvas, 84×113cm.
Musée des Beaux-Arts, Berne

There are three compelling reasons why Bonnard should want to come to this area and pick up the tail end of a fading vision. Firstly, he found the motifs around his house Ma Roulotte endlessly stimulating, and he tackled them with all the enthusiasm and freshness of an artist oblivious to what others had done before him. He needed, as he said, the lush pastures and passing clouds of the north as a fitting complement to the heat and timelessness of the south, in the same way that an intense red engenders a green after-image. Secondly, an important strand in his art was concerned with the perpetuation of a particular vision of landscape, an earthly paradise deeply rooted in cultural memory, which is by definition immune to progress, and he followed the Impressionists in locating it in the Seine valley. Since *Parallèlement* and *Daphnis et Chloé* he had attempted to heal the cultural divisions between city and country and between the rival attractions of a southern and northern paradise. And thirdly, Monet was in the process of redefining Impressionism in terms not readily apparent to his immediate followers.

Irrespective of any reservations that Monet had of Bonnard's unevenness as a painter, they exchanged visits, corresponded and discovered in each other's company a certain companionship during the war. Both artists were evolving decorative art forms derived from nature, and they shared a love of Japanese art. Monet had gradually excluded the world outside his garden from his art and focused increasingly on his waterlily pond. On seeing just photographs of the garden, Proust felt that nature had been transformed into one of the 'six gardens of paradise'.[13] By 1908 Monet's waterlily series (Plate 96) had led to the dissolution of the boundaries between the elements in an overall atmosphere of light, and the subject was not just flowers floating on water but the play between surface and depth.[14] The sheer size of these decorative canvases precluded outdoor working, so like Bonnard he came to rely on memory to preserve the initial naturalistic effect. In 1912 Monet exhibited his latest new series, and he was to

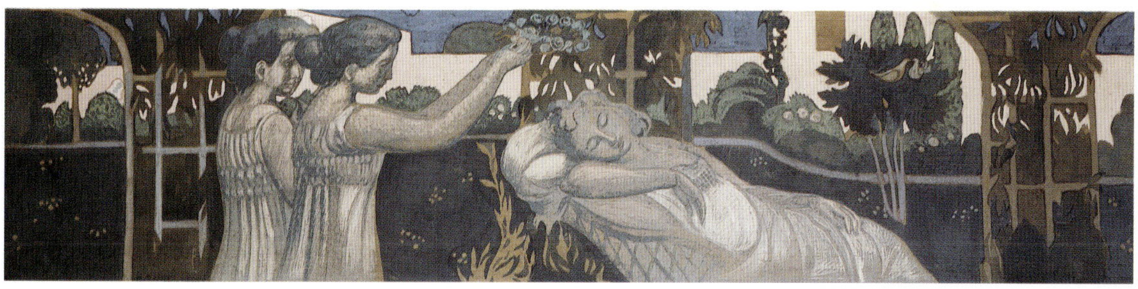

99
Maurice Denis
The Crown of the Betrothal. 1895.
Tempera on canvas, 53×219cm.
Musée départemental du Prieuré, Saint-Germain-en-Laye

concentrate for the remaining years of his life on the nineteen immense panels of the two *Nymphéas* cycles. Georges Bernheim failed to buy the panels, which were finally installed in the Orangerie in 1927, the year after Monet's death. These waterlily decorations, housed in a prestigious site in the centre of Paris, posed a radical alternative to both modernism and the classical tradition, the originality of which was not fully appreciated at the time, because the advent of Fauvism in 1905 and Cubism in 1908–9 had caused Monet to be stereotyped in terms of the instantaneity of an earlier form of Impressionism. But some commentators recognized that Monet had gone beyond naturalism to achieve a near-oriental identification with the rhythms and laws of nature.[15]

There is nothing quite like Monet's Orangerie cycles in Western art. It is possible that Bonnard's Japanese-inspired screens may have played a part in their genesis, but Monet took formlessness to a point where Bonnard did not care to follow. By contrast, Bonnard's landscapes with figures continue in the tradition of the Nabis and his own *Daphnis et Chloé*. They are not so much moments of nature as states of the human soul. Marthe is posed as a *repoussoir* form in the foregound of *L'Été en Normandie*, 1912 (Plate 97), to establish in her reverie the mood of the composition; in *Soir* or *La Sieste*, 1914 (Plate 98), she reclines in a deck-chair. In the former a silent female watches attentively, and in the latter children are posed beside her like attendant angels in a quattrocento altarpiece. Both compositions have close affinities with such Symbolist decorations as Maurice Denis's panels for his own bedroom, *The Crown of the Betrothal* and *Birth*, 1895 (Plate 99), on the theme of 'Frauenliebe und Leben' from the Schumann Lieder cycle, in which a profound feeling of peace is attained through love of a particular woman;[16] but whereas the grey-blue and mauve colour scheme of the Denis is carefully contrived to communicate the content, Bonnard chose those moments of the day that matched the required poetic mood – early morning and evening. Thus in his continuing adherence to nature as the source of art, Bonnard came close to Monet's rejection of the Symbolists' departure from the visual truths of the external world.[17]

Bonnard's opportunity to bring together his obsessive themes in a decorative cycle came with the commission from his dealers, the Bernheim family, for four panels: *Symphonie pastorale* or *Campagne* (Plate 100), *Méditerranée* or *Monuments, Le Paradis terrestre* (Plate 101), and *Les Travailleurs à la Grande Jatte* or *Citée moderne*, which were executed between 1916 and 1920. Southern landscapes are either combined or juxtaposed with northern landsapes, the temporal with the timeless, city with country, work with leisure, the classical Golden Age with the Garden of Eden, and art with nature. Figures are strung across the foregrounds of the four panels to enact their parts in the narrative. *Symphonie pastorale* and *Le Paradis terrestre* deal with idealized landscapes. *Symphonie pastorale* is a southern landscape in the pastoral tradition of *Daphnis et Chloé*, and several levels of reality are fused in the same composition. The human race is in harmony with nature and the gods: a woman milks a cow, a man leads his horse down into the fields, while a classical goddess, perhaps Diana, detains a little stag from leaving the scene. Children play naked in the warmth of the red earth; a

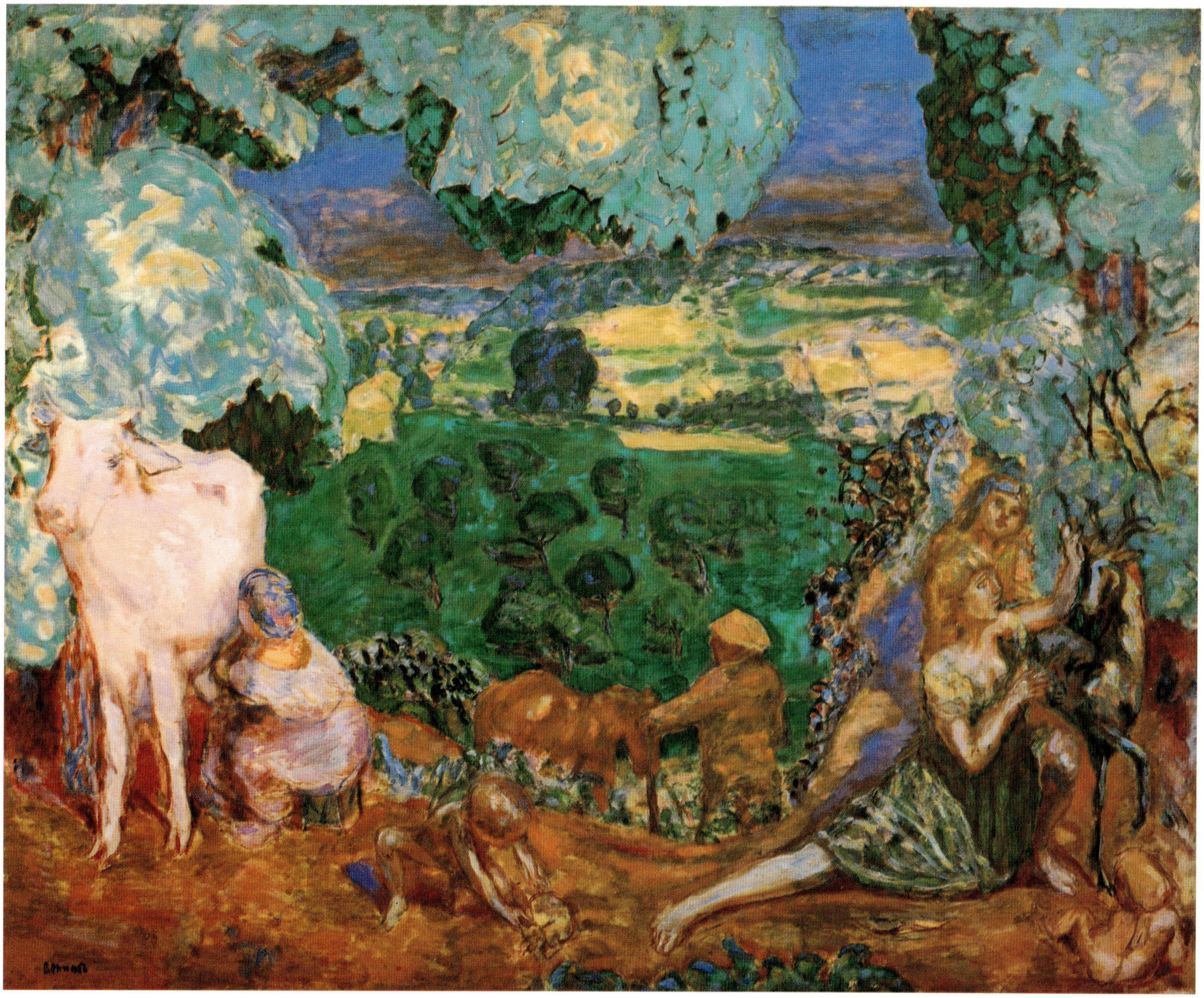

100
La Symphonie pastorale. 1916–20.
Oil on canvas, 130×160cm.
Private collection

general state of innocence prevails in this landscape of the Golden Age. *Le Paradis terrestre* is more northern, restless and melancholy. A consciousness of sin, guilt and mortality has entered the Garden of Eden. The woman lies back in a state of post-coital abandon, while the man stands awkwardly aware of his nakedness by a tree, now separated from his monkey companion by consciousness. The sun is setting on this earthly paradise. The vegetation of high summer is heavy to the point of being overblown. There is something autobiographical about this composition, as though it laments the passing of youthful passion.

In *Les Travailleurs à la Grande Jatte* and *Méditerranée* the intense activity of workers in the city is contrasted with the timeless leisure of the Mediterranean inhabitants.[18] The former is a subtle inversion of Seurat's *Un Dimanche à la Grande Jatte*, 1885–6, which invested the subject of urban leisure with the grandeur and permanence of a classical composition. Bonnard's working population is not composed of muscle-bound heroes; their heroism is that they carry on the daily struggle for survival. They meet on the bridge over the Seine, the compressed group of commuters on the left facing the manual labourers on the right. *Méditerranée* tackles head-on the legacy of the classical tradition as a memory preserved in statuary. It is a strictly French preserve. Through the proscenium-like arch of the foreground stage the Vatican *Ariadne* and other classical sculptures overlook a small Mediterranean port reminiscent of Saint-Tropez. The women filling their pitchers at the fountain on the left are the inheritors of a classical figure style and they are treated with greater solidity than the sculpture. A feeling of fragility, even of impending doom, runs through the cycle, as though under threat from Germany French civilization was once again proving as vulnerable as stage sets. The cycle in turn anticipated Picasso's neoclassicism in his sets for the ballets *Pulcinella* and *Le Tricorne* of 1920.[19]

Bonnard's final major decorative project of the war years, *L'Été* (Plate 102), is something in the nature of a space-filler rephrasing several familiar themes. It was commissioned by the Hahnlosers for an office in their house in Winterthur. In a letter to Mme Hedy Hahnloser-Buhler of 26, July 1917, Bonnard commented on the large surface to be covered' ... more than double the size I had in mind at the outset – and therefore I have had to look for subjects that are more decorative than expressive,' and he went on to describe what he had sketched out in a very matter-of-fact tone: 'Two naked figures are placed in a small valley surrounded by trees, and in the foreground there are modern characters – sleeping figures and young girls.'[20] Unfortunately, he had misunderstood the final dimensions of the space and the canvas had to be sent back to him.

The sheer size of *L'Été* gives it the appearance of a theatre back-drop organized in three distinct horizontal bands or time zones. It combines children lazing in the garden at Le Clos, from his decoration *La Famille au jardin*, *c.*1901 (Plate 60), with the incongruous subject of two female nudes reclining in a middle ground curtained by trees from Matisse's *Le Bonheur de vivre*, 1905–6 (Plate 63). The high viewpoint ensures that we become aware of the entry from the wings back-stage of a mysterious woman

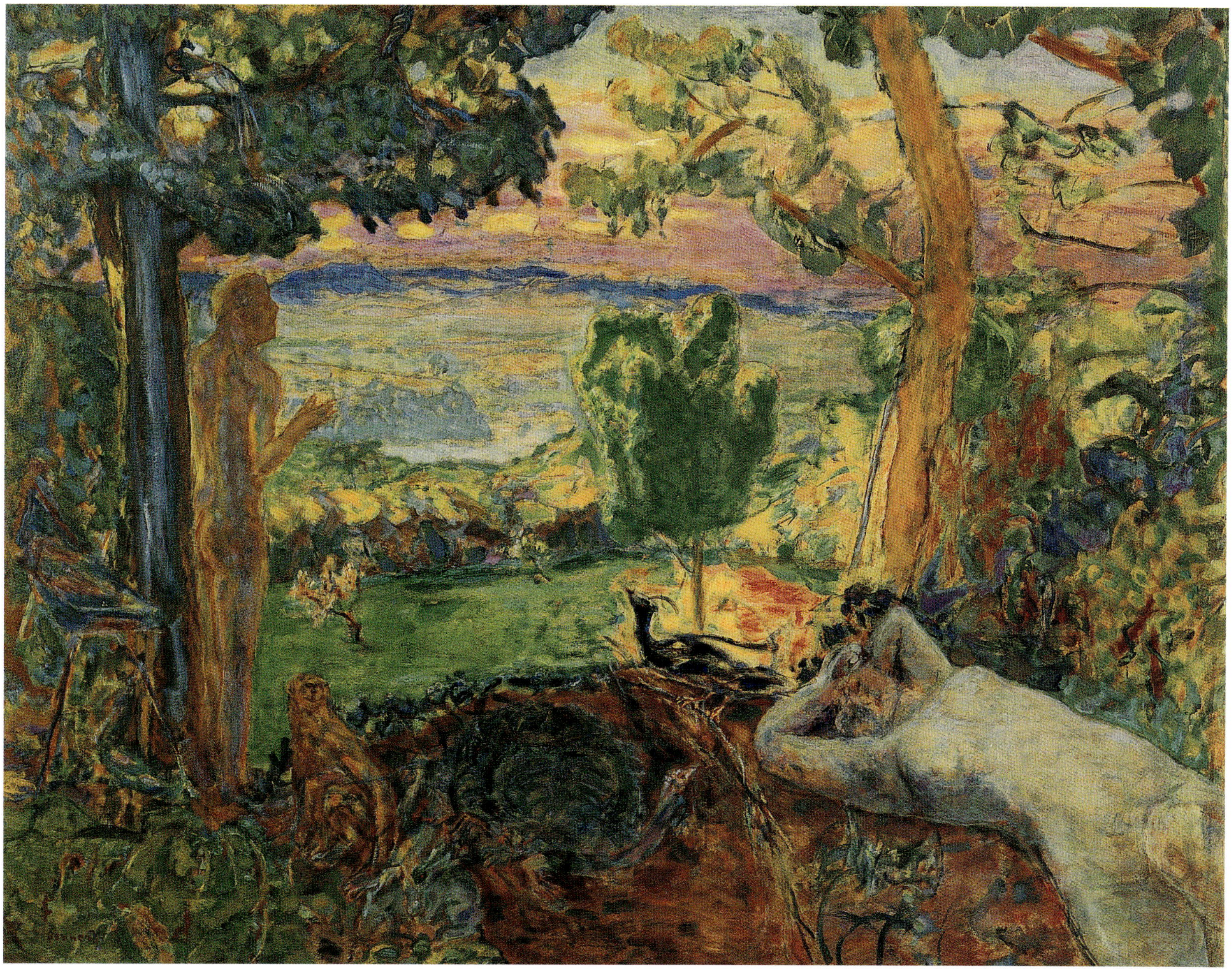

101
Le Paradis terrestre. 1916–20.
Oil on canvas, 130×160cm.
Private collection

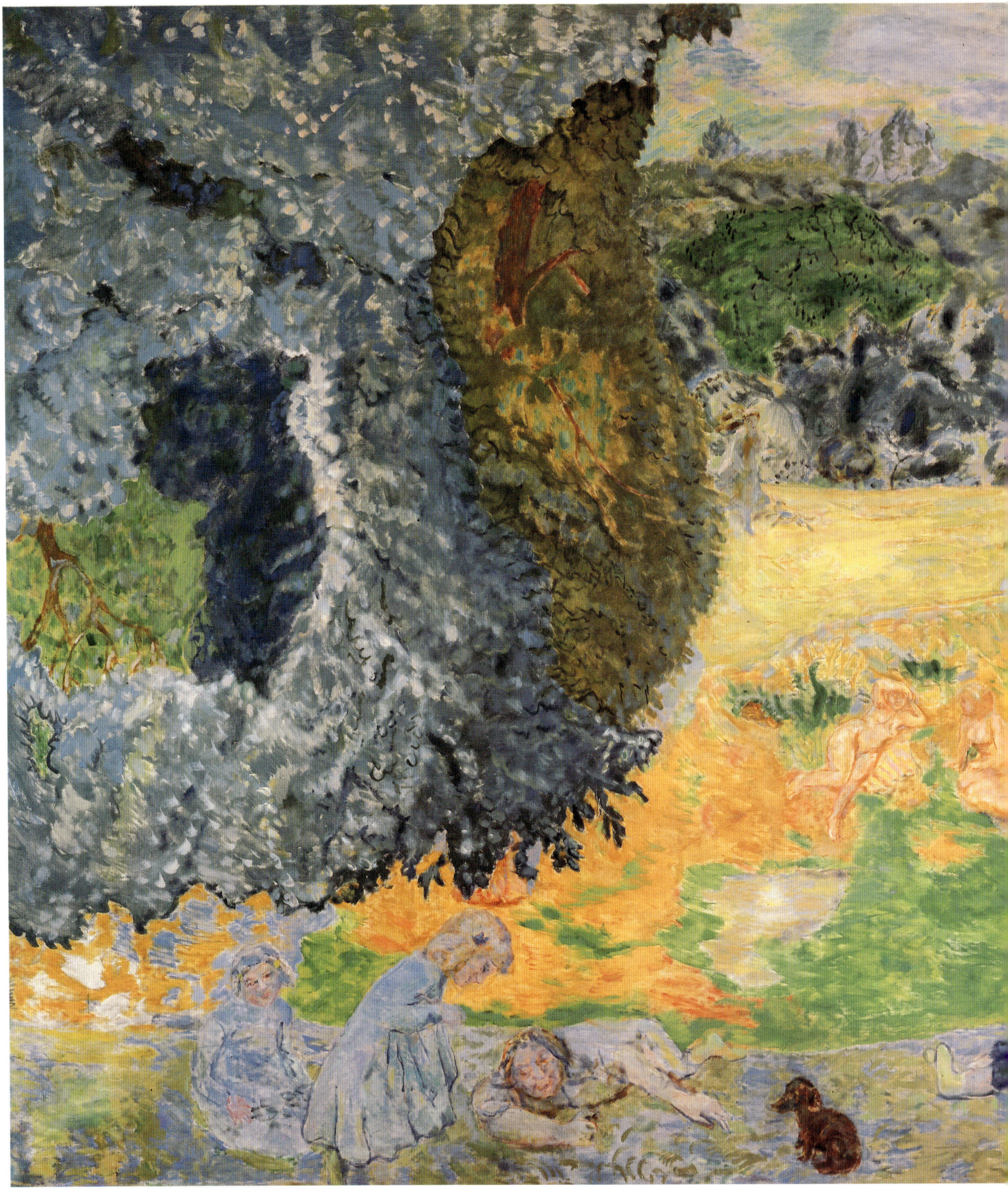

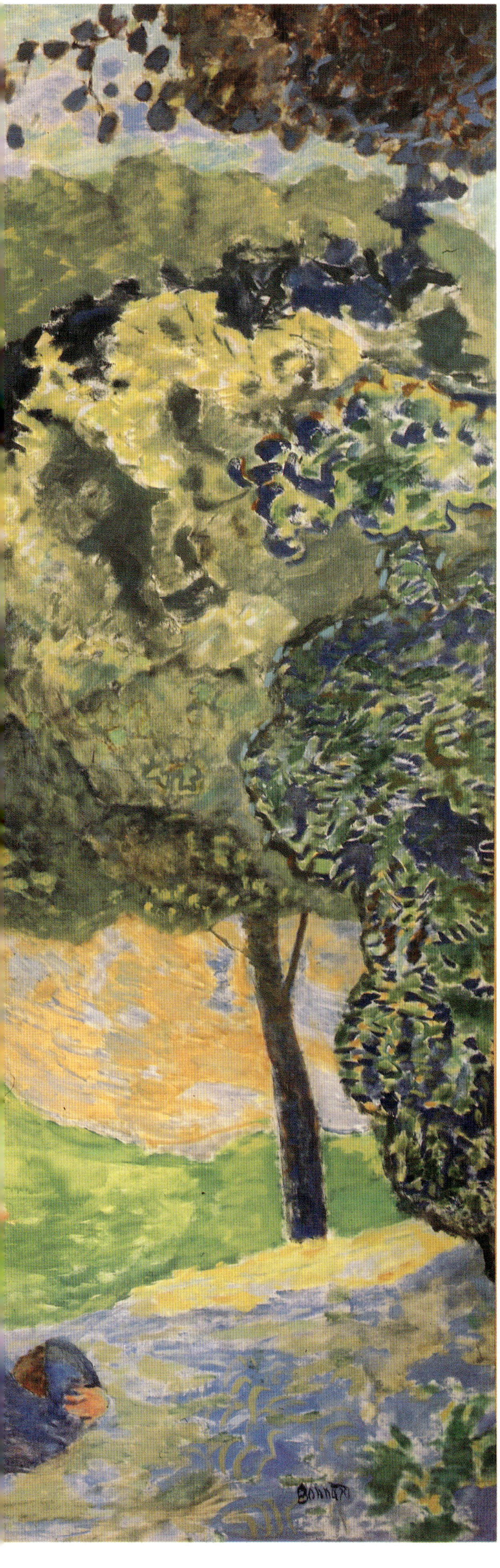

102
L'Été. 1917.
Oil on canvas, 260×340cm.
Fondation Maeght, Saint-Paul-de-Vence

and her dog, like Diana the huntress, with long hair and flowing dress. The figures blend in with their respective bands within an overall soft, dappled atmosphere of grey-blues drifting into mauves and greens. The only dramatic notes come with the unexpected inclusion of startling patches of colour in the main masses of foliage. He was not given another commission to execute a large decoration in the pastoral tradition until *La Pastorale*, 1937 (Plate 125), for the Palais de Chaillot.

Bonnard's ambivalent attitude to Monet's Impressionism, reinforced by the contemporary reassertion of traditional values, brought on what amounted to a mid-life crisis around 1913. His crisis was not so much one of what to paint as how to paint it. Feeling that he had been sacrificing form and composition to colour, he took himself, he said, back to school. He told his nephew, Charles Terrasse: 'I drew ceaselessly. And after drawing comes the composition, which must be balanced. A well-composed painting is half done.'[21] Bonnard's crisis brought to a head a conflict which could not be resolved simplistically because it went beyond questions of style to his very vision as a painter. For the emphasis on form in its turn carried with it connotations of materialism, of a world tied down in time and dominated by objects and human beings, whereas Bonnard was essentially a painter of mood and atmosphere.

His solution as it emerged was novel and totally idiosyncratic. Instead of equating colour in traditional academic terms with emotion and drawing with the mind, he reversed the process, maintaining: 'Drawing is sensation. Colour is reasoning.'[22] He was too shy to be readily identified as the artist at work, and too aware of the controlling power of both the subject and high-keyed colour to be able to paint before the motif. Thus his little drawings, quickly sketched in a pad secreted in his hand, assumed an extremely important function in his art; they represented his codified sensations of specific experiences and served as the starting point for paintings executed in the studio. These drawings are at first sight slightly disappointing, because they appear to have the status of *croquis*, thumb-nail jottings from life, rather than of more substantial-looking statements that could hold their own with paintings in an exhibition. But it is only after examining them closely that their obvious charm gives gives way to an appreciation of the sensibility at work, searching for and fixing a graphic notation of his sensations before the motif. Nobody before Bonnard had so developed the *croquis* that it could capture fleeting changes of atmosphere and mood. In this way he was able to take on and make his own subjects which the Impressionists sought to realize in paint.

Bonnard did not want to reject Monet so much as to integrate form and structure within an overall atmosphere of light, without departing from the premise of realism. He often came close to his subjects, adopting extremely wide angles, so that the constituent parts of a painting are spread across the surface.[23] He decribed a painting as 'a sequence of marks which join together and end up forming the object, the fragment over which the eye wanders without a hitch'.[24] His overwhelming debt to Monet was in the recognition of the transforming power of light, and he coupled this with the Nabis conception of a painting as a decorative object in its own right.

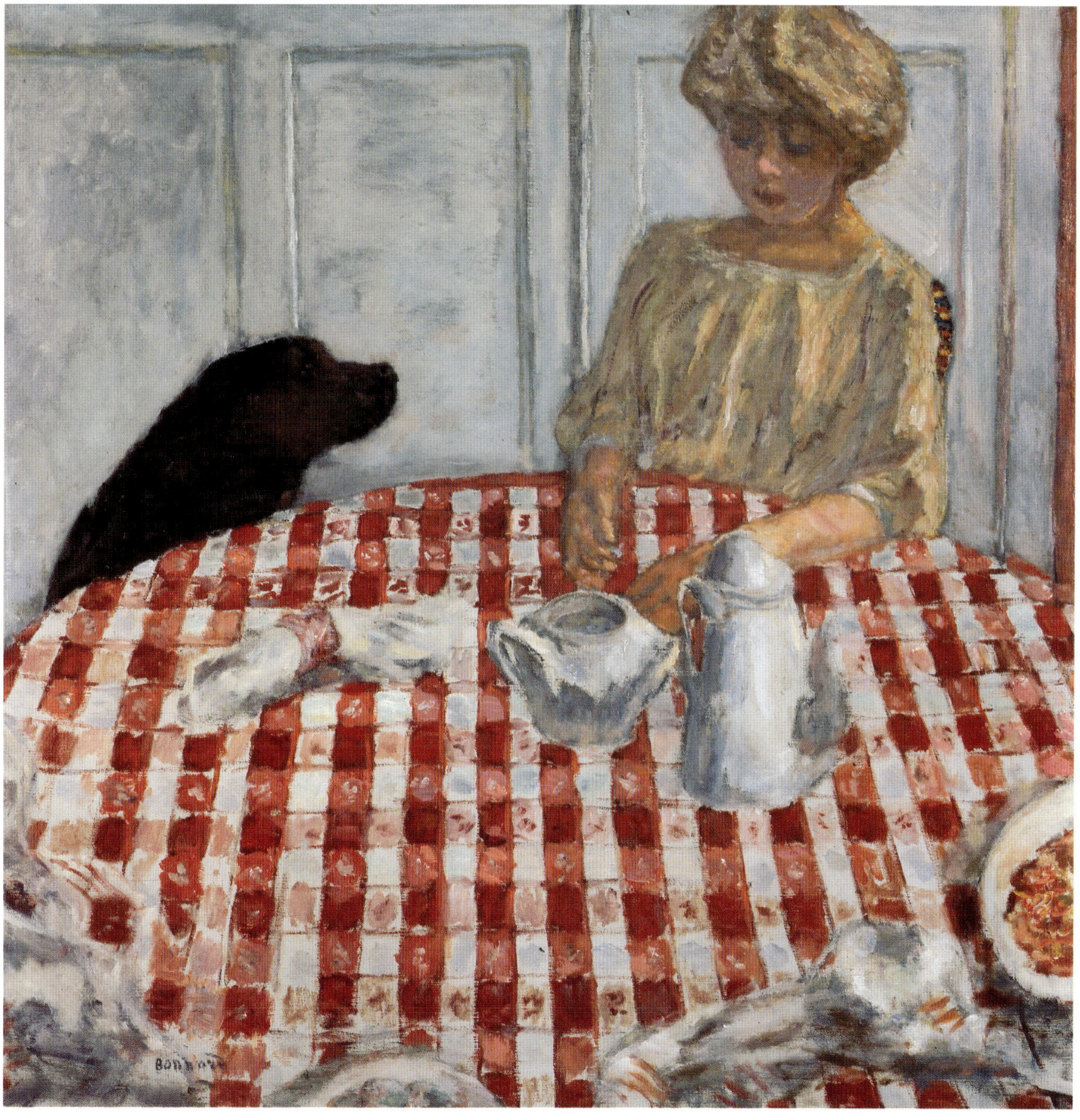

103
La Nappe à carreaux rouges. 1910.
Oil on canvas, 83×85cm.
Private collection, Switzerland

Bonnard was fully aware of what Matisse was doing with colour and the Cubists with space, but he absorbed their discoveries on his own terms, finding subjects where abstract concepts could be treated in a seemingly naturalistic way. This is nowhere better seen than in his development of the subject of the interior opening onto the exterior in his masterpiece, the glorious *Salle à manger à la campagne*, 1913 (Plate 105), which is a complex compendium of sources and themes. The subject was deeply rooted in Bonnard's art. In *La Porte ouverte*, 1909, he had placed a table immediately in front of a door to act as a springboard from interior to exterior. In *La Nappe à carreaux rouges*, 1910 (Plate 103), he took up again the idea of *La Collation*, 1899 (Plate 41), and *Le Déjeuner*, 1899 (Plate 42), of the table tilted up as a stage with the spectator joining Marthe and the dog Dingo as the audience. *Salle à manger à la campagne* combines both these ideas, using the table as the fulcrum around which the composition turns from interior to exterior across the surface of the canvas.

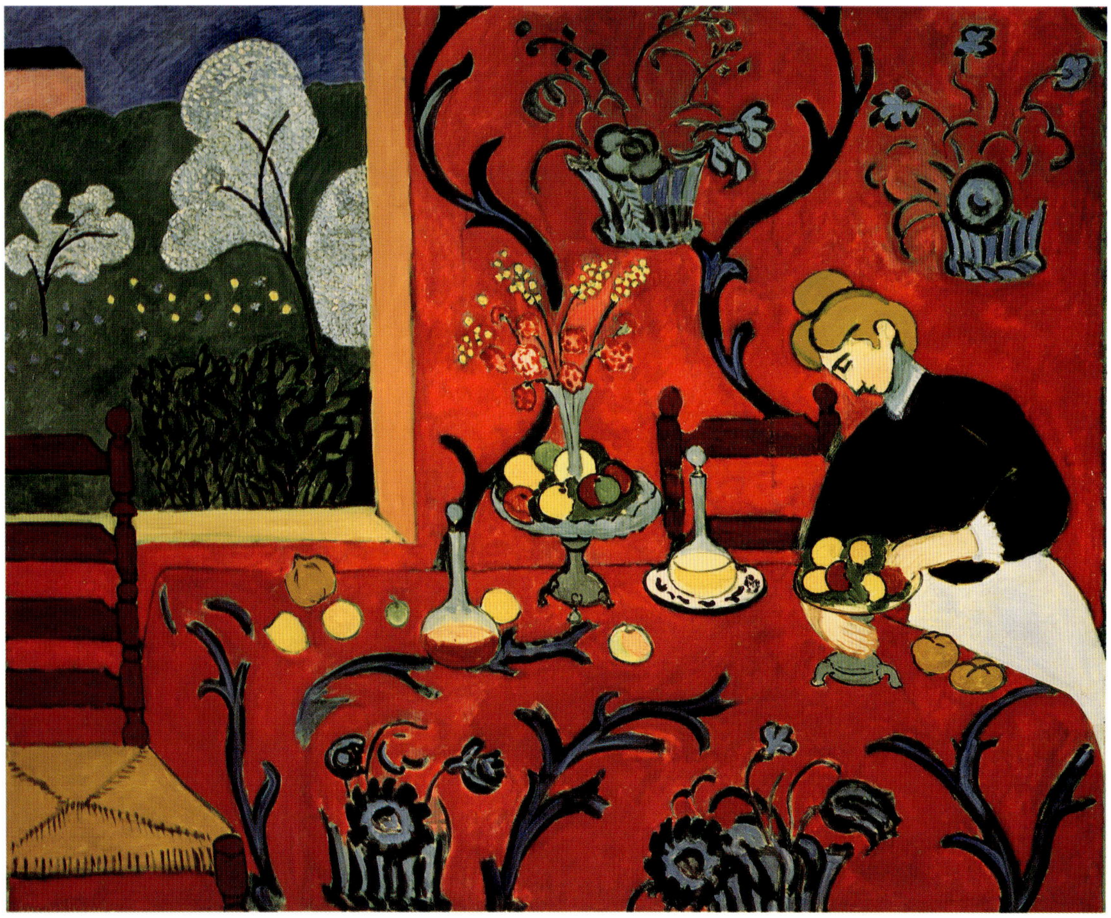

104
Henri Matisse
La Desserte (harmonie rouge). 1908.
Oil on canvas, 180×220cm.
Hermitage, St Petersburg

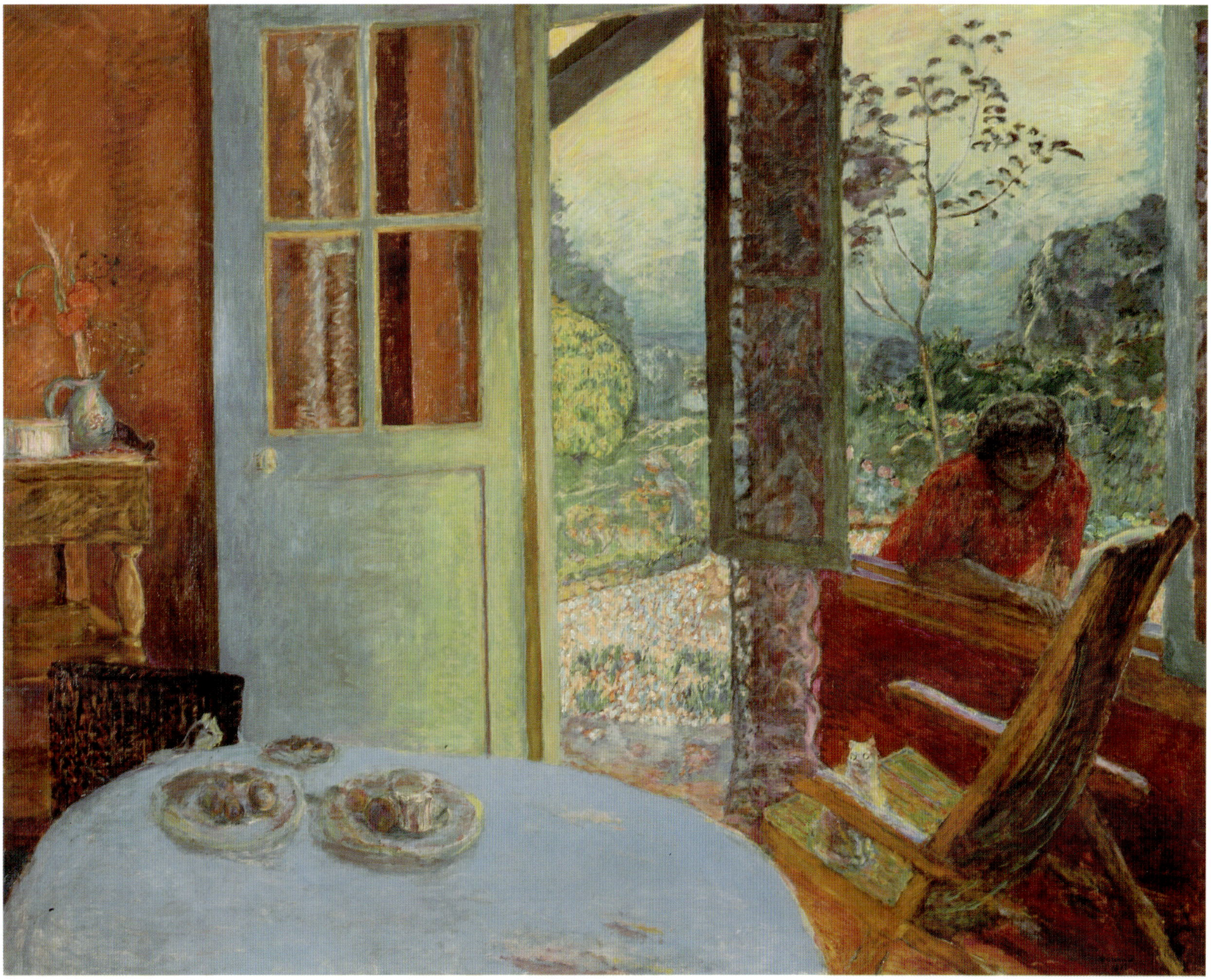

105
La Salle à manger à la campagne. 1913.
Oil on canvas, 168×204cm.
Minneapolis Institute of Arts

On one level the painting can be seen as Bonnard's response to Matisse's transformation of the domestic interior into a monumental decoration in *La Desserte (harmonie rouge)*, 1908 (Plate 104), which at one stage was *harmonie bleue*. Quite typically, though, Bonnard's composition grew out of his prolonged experience of a particular place, the little dining room overlooking the garden at Ma Roulotte, in front of which he photographed Marthe (Plate 107). He recorded the view from the room in a pencil drawing (Plate 106) which probably acted as the starting point for the painting.[25] By contrast with Matisse who changed his colour scheme from blue to red for pictorial reasons, Bonnard selected the deep red for the interior because it *was* – and still is – painted in red. There the immediate similarities between the painting and drawing end. Sitting in the room one is aware of the cosy confines of a cottage dining room, whereas in the painting Bonnard opened up and flattened the space across the corner of the room. The glass-panelled door and windows are peeled back to provide a complex geometric framework of interlocking rectangles, as rigorous in their spatial organization as any Cubist composition, and the view of the garden dropping down to the river becomes a type of eighteenth-century idealized landscape pictured in Watteau's *Embarkation for the Island of Cythera*, 1717 (Plate 108), with a woman, perhaps Marthe, picking flowers.

Among other things, the painting is about processes of looking and awareness within silence, about the changes occurring in the transformation of a small room into a glorious vision of an earthly paradise. Marthe looks in at the window, two cats size each other up from the security of their respective chairs, and the spectator is drawn into the unfolding logic of the painting through the door and windows, which open as much

106
La Porte ouverte. *c*.1910.
Pencil on paper, 10.8×17.5cm.
Private collection

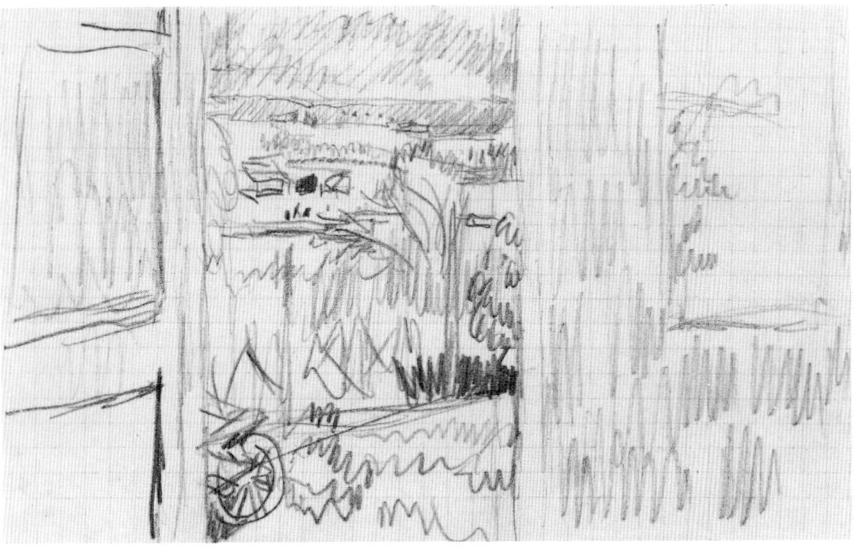

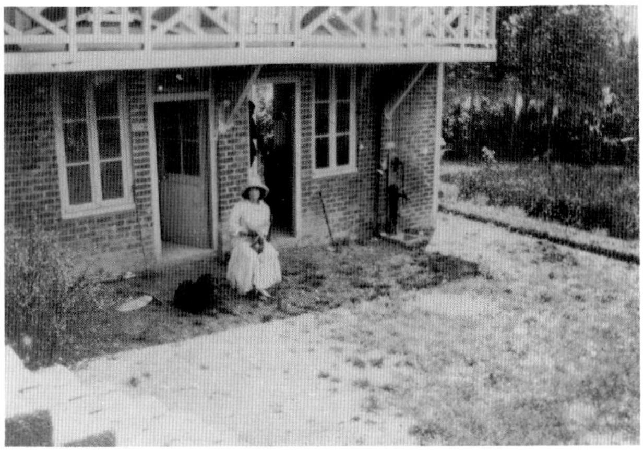

107
Marthe with Black at Ma Roulotte. *c*.1910–15.
Photograph.
Musée d'Orsay, Paris

on to colour as the view. Colour in Bonnard's terms is the rational, organizing principle uniting the composition, which is delicately suspended between interior and exterior, between the opposing forces of red and green. The warm red of the interior on the left is reinforced on the right by the appearance of Marthe wearing red. Above all, the painting demonstrates his new-found interest in reflected light competing with colour in a subtle series of transitions from the cool blue and violet tints of the table-cloth to the green of the garden outside. To counteract any suggestion of a too programmed colour scheme, Bonnard introduced a powerful note of black in the back of the chair behind the table. The pervasive atmosphere is one of gentle nostalgia, of existence fleetingly registered on the boundaries between reality and the dream.

In making out a case for Bonnard's divergence from Impressionism, it is easy to overlook, or at least pay insufficient attention to, the landscapes which form a substantial part of his *œuvre*. His house, Ma Roulotte, with its veranda and small terrace, provided a platform overlooking a subject that he found endlessly fascinating: the Seine and the immense, usually cloud-filled sky. His numerous paintings of the river were not planned as a series systematically recording the changing effects of light, for his interest in what was happening in this great theatre of nature varied according to what caught his eye. The wonderfully atmospheric drawing, *La Seine, près de Vernon*, c.1920 (Plate 111), is a good example of the sort of incident which he habitually recorded in small sketches. A dark curtain of rain has come down and a small sapling is caught in a burst of light illuminating the water. It is achieved in an extraordinary variety of marks, from agitated loops which evoke the sensation of wind tossing the foliage, to heavy scouring describing the rain driving through the cloud. He got to know the river

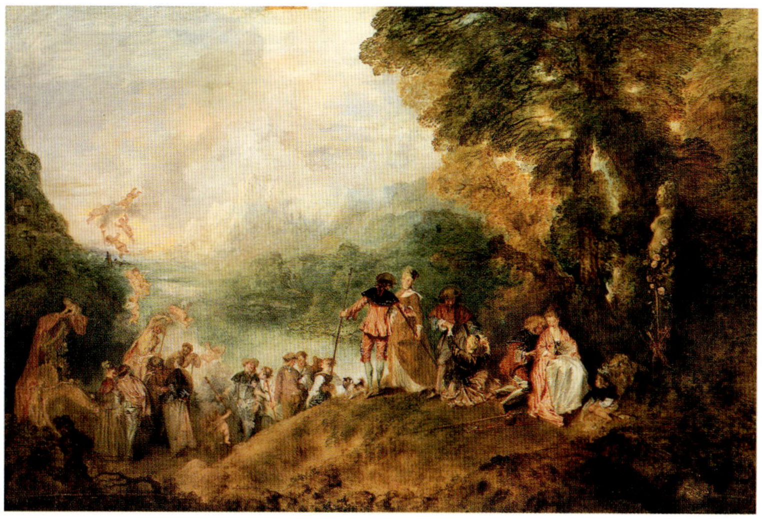

108
Jean-Antoine Watteau
Embarkation for the Island of Cythera. 1717.
Oil on canvas, 129×194cm.
Musée du Louvre, Paris

extremely well on his daily walks and often explored it in his boat, kept on the little tributary, the Bras de ma Campagne, running between the Île Saint-Pierre and the bottom of his garden.[26] Apart from the erosion of the island and the expansion of the industrial zone of Vernon on the far bank, the view from Ma Roulotte is much the same today.

While wanting, like an Impressionist, to preserve in the painting executed in the studio the freshness and immediacy of its starting-point in nature, Bonnard sought to go beyond the Impressionist position and to achieve through a greater emphasis on composition and colour an equivalent of the experience in paint. *Le Pont de Vernon*, 1915–20 (Plate 109), for instance, is carefully composed to concentrate attention on the river. The rhythmic repetition of the arches of the bridge, which was blown up in 1940 to impede the German advance, leads the eye to the far bank at Vernonnet, where the low golden light of late evening glows through the silhouetted trees, casting deep blue shadows on the mauve-tinged water. Bonnard particularly liked the effects of late evening, what he called *'l'heure bleue'*. This beautiful, moody painting was given to Mlle Renée Monchaty, Bonnard's lover for a time, who sadly committed suicide in 1923.[27] The slightest change in weather or focus could present the river in an entirely new light and provide the subject for another painting.

Bonnard's commitment to landscape painting continued in the 1920s. In 1922 alone

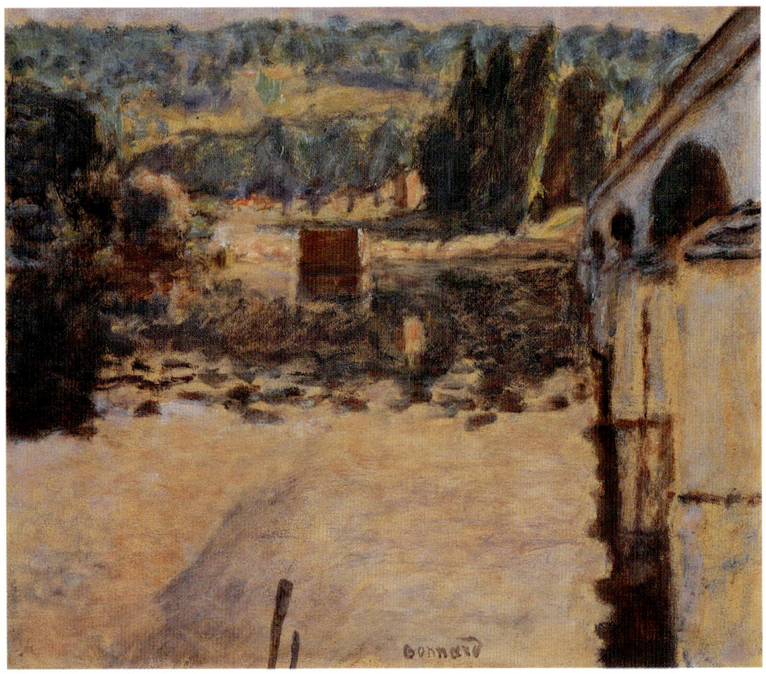

109
Le Pont de Vernon. 1915-20.
Oil on board, 31.5×38.5cm.
Private collection

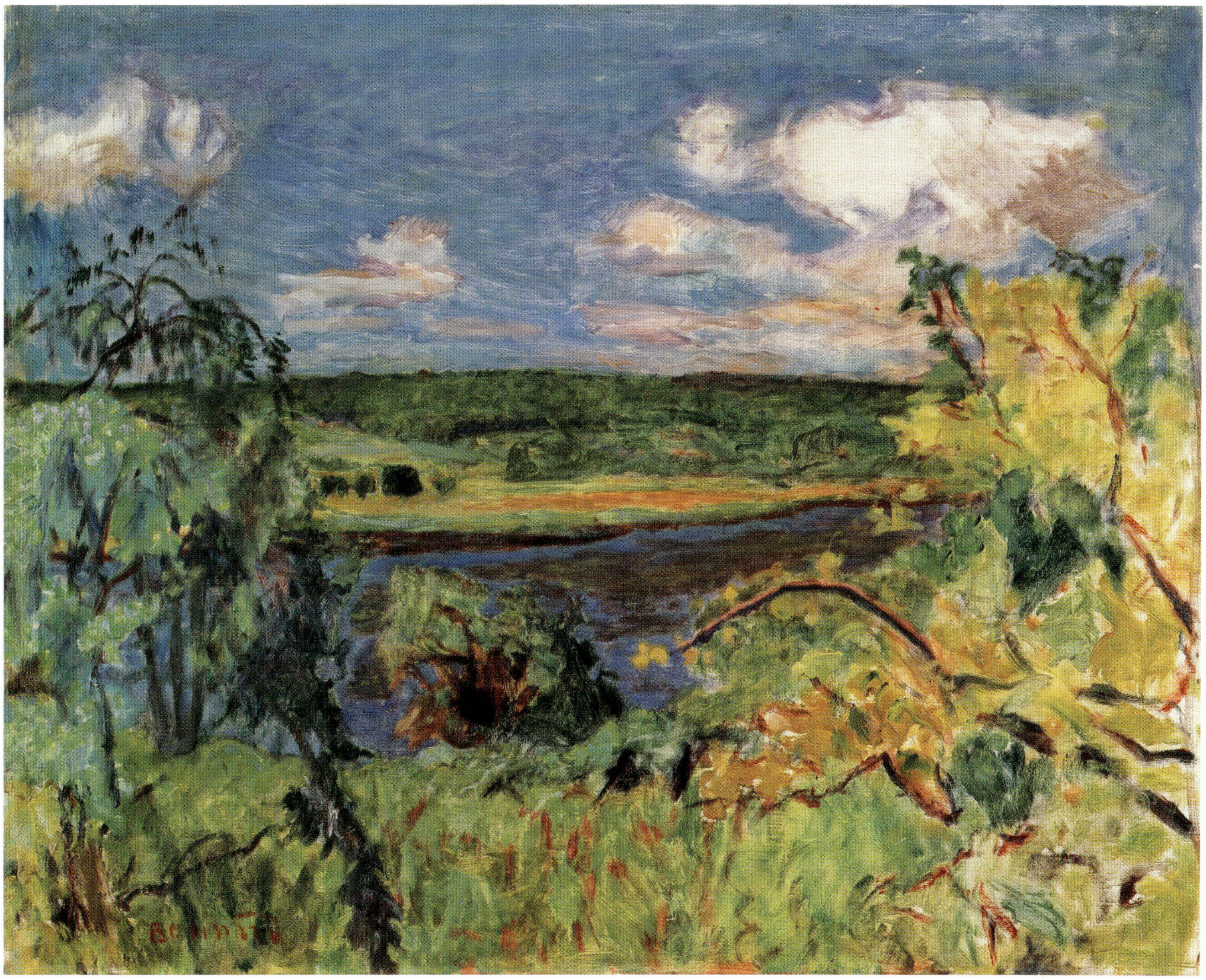

110
Lumière de soir, près de Vernon. 1922.
Oil on canvas, 50.3×63.1cm.
Aberdeen Art Gallery

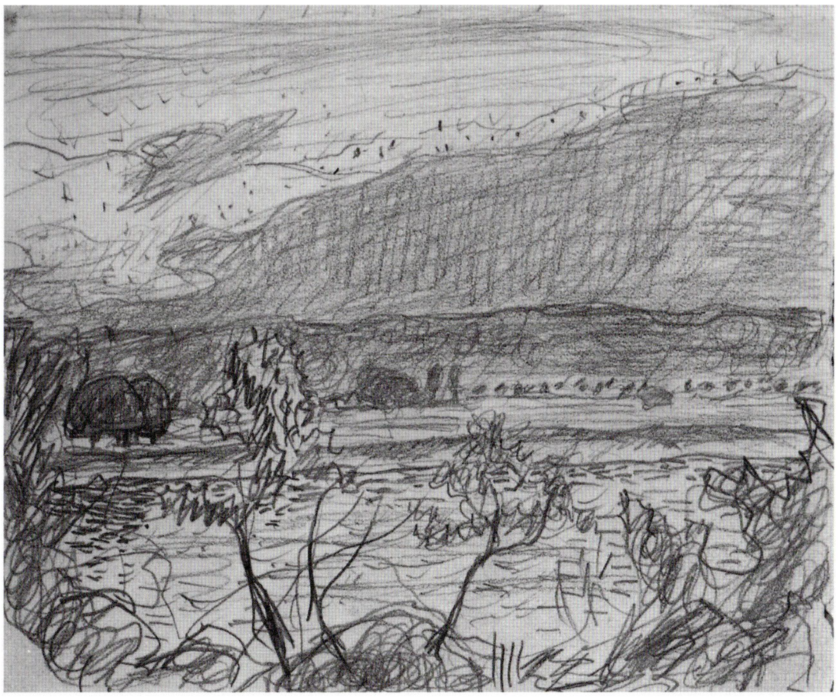

111
La Seine, près de Vernon. *c*.1920.
Pencil on paper, 11.4×14.9cm.
Mr and Mrs C. Fisher

he painted some twenty-two landscapes, splitting his motifs between Normandy and the south of France. Even when he settled in Le Cannet above Cannes, he always visited Normandy each year. Bonnard's nephew, Charles Terrasse, told the photographer Brassaï, 'Like Boudin, one of his favourite painters, he considered the light of the north more interesting than that of the south ... Indeed, my uncle believes that nowhere is the sky so beautiful, so varied, as in Deauville, Trouville, Honfleur. And he also likes the types of trees found in the north – elm, lime, chestnut, apple.'[28] The contrasting experience of southern light and vegetation made Bonnard bring out more intensely those qualities he felt distinguished the northern landscape, lush greens, cloud-filled skies and constant changes in the weather. He concentrated increasingly on capturing the mood of the most transient effects. Consequently, his landscapes often became technically more varied and interesting. In *Lumière de soir, près de Vernon*, 1922 (Plate 110), the movement of the vegetation in the light-filled foreground contrasts with the deep blue of the river and ushers in the billowing clouds from the distant horizon. An examination of the paint surface shows that such spontaneous effects were skilfully contrived within the context of the picture. The dark blue-green tree on the left was raised – like adding another story to a building – to balance the light ochre tree on the right and to disrupt the over-obvious division into four horizontal bands, alternating tonally between light and dark in the transition from foreground to sky.

Contemporary observers were struck by the mobility of Bonnard's environment, vision and lifestyle. The river, the sky and even – according to his nephew Charles Terrasse – his house, aptly named Ma Roulotte, the caravan, seemed mobile.[29] Unlike Monet, Bonnard was no gardener; art was the process by which he ordered nature and the garden was allowed to run wild. His obsessional morning walks were extended into frequent car trips. The building of the garage at Ma Roulotte symbolized his need for mobility. But the dichotomy inherent in his art between the transient and the permanent, between realism and idealism, persisted as a constant source of inspiration. His restlessness found an outlet in mobility, but the achievement of movement in decorative painting required sustained concentration in time and place.

In three large-scale paintings, *La Terrasse*, 1918 (Plate 113), *La Terrasse à Vernon*, 1928 (Plate 115) and *Décor à Vernon*, 1920–39 (Plate 116), Bonnard took up Monet's challenge to make out of the Normandy landscape a monumental decorative art form. By changing the composition and colour scheme, the same view from the little terrace at Ma Roulotte is given in each case a completely different reading. The setting in *La Terrasse* is opened up in an angle of over 180 degrees, and the scale of the two figures down in the garden diminished to give the impression of a vast panorama opening up before the spectator. But instead of distancing the spectator from the view by linear perspective, Bonnard treats the horizontal canvas format as the equivalent of the field of vision and allows the eye to wander in the painting as in a landscape.[30] This was a major formal innovation in his work, which is all to easy to describe but extremely difficult to achieve. Art is not nature. To offset the natural pull of the horizon on the right,

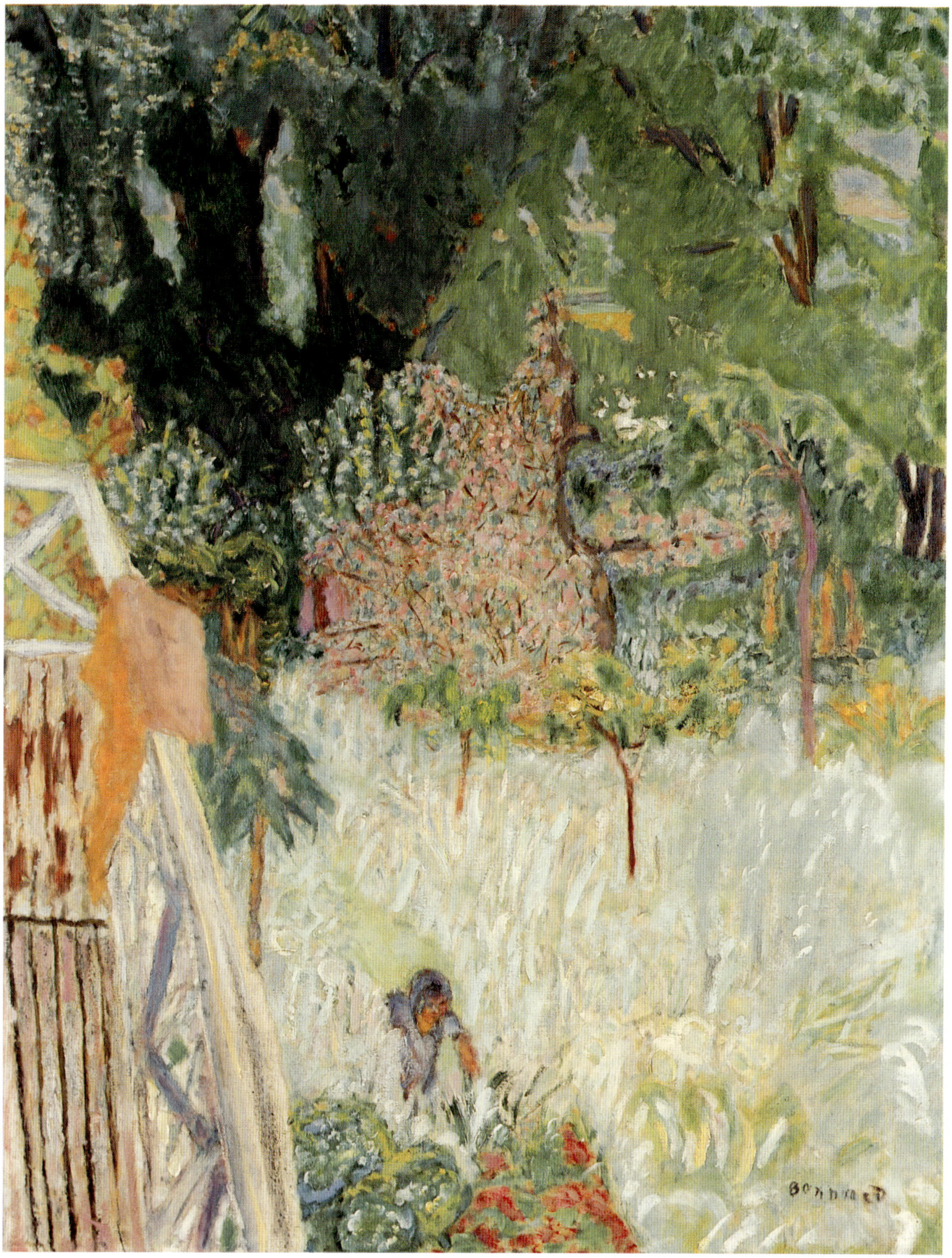

112
Balcon à Vernonnet. 1920.
Oil on canvas, 100×78cm.
Musée des Beaux-Arts, Brest

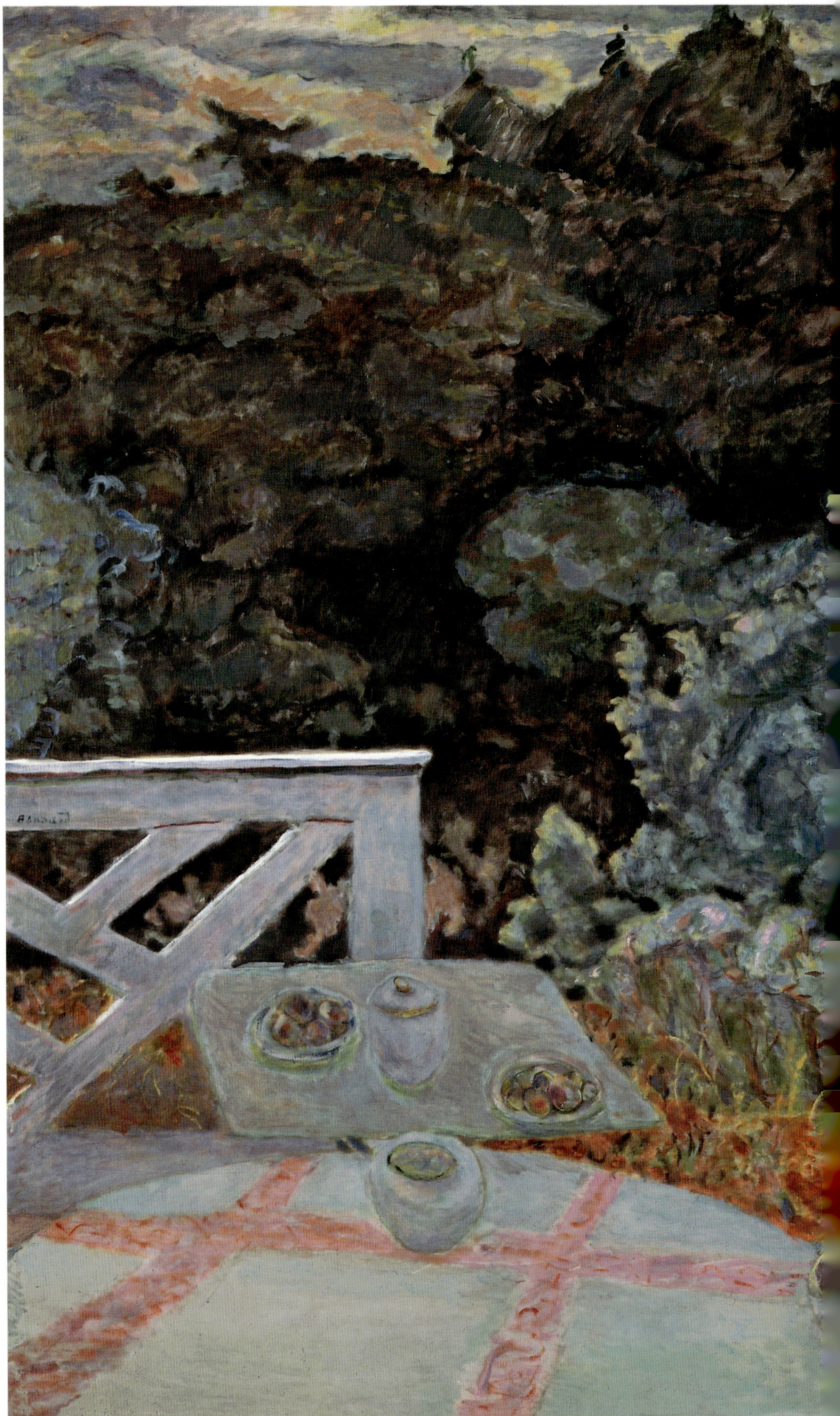

113
La Terrasse. 1918.
Oil on canvas, 159.5×249.5cm.
The Phillips Collection, Washington DC

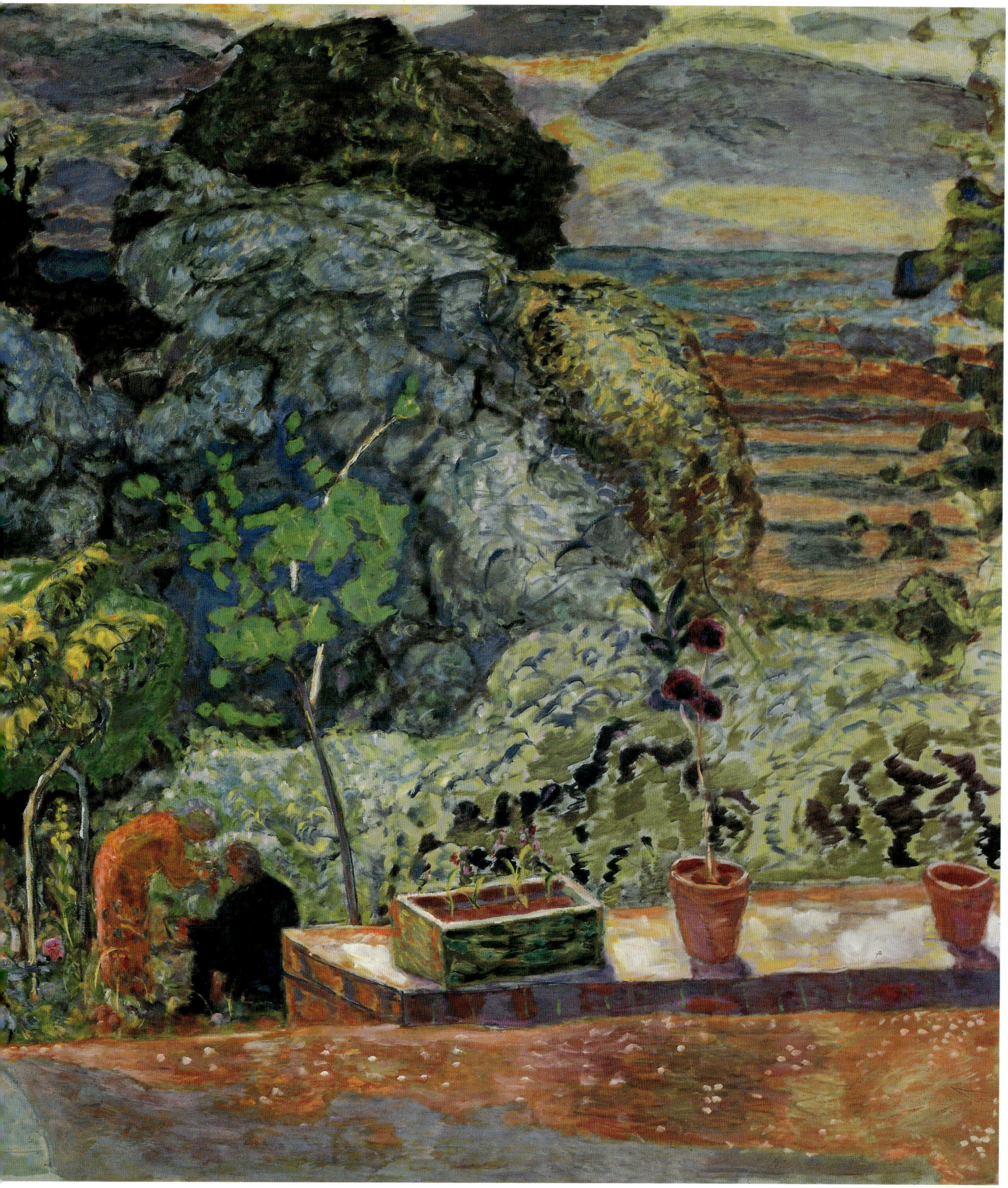

115
La Terrasse à Vernon. 1928.
Oil on canvas, 242.5×309cm.
Kunstsammlung Nordrhein-Westfalen, Düsseldorf

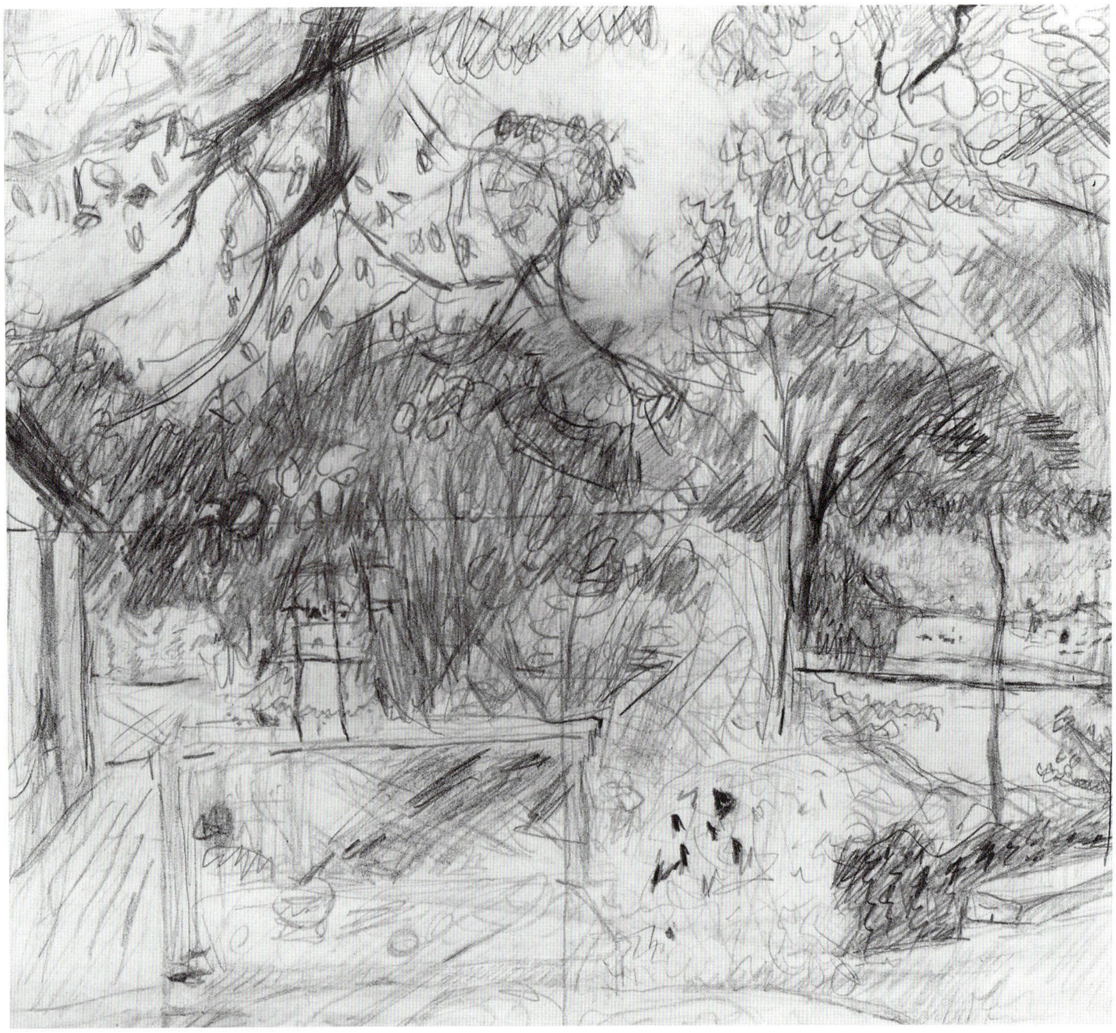

114
La Terrasse à Ma Roulotte. *c*.1928.
Pencil on paper, 27.5×30.5cm.
Private collection

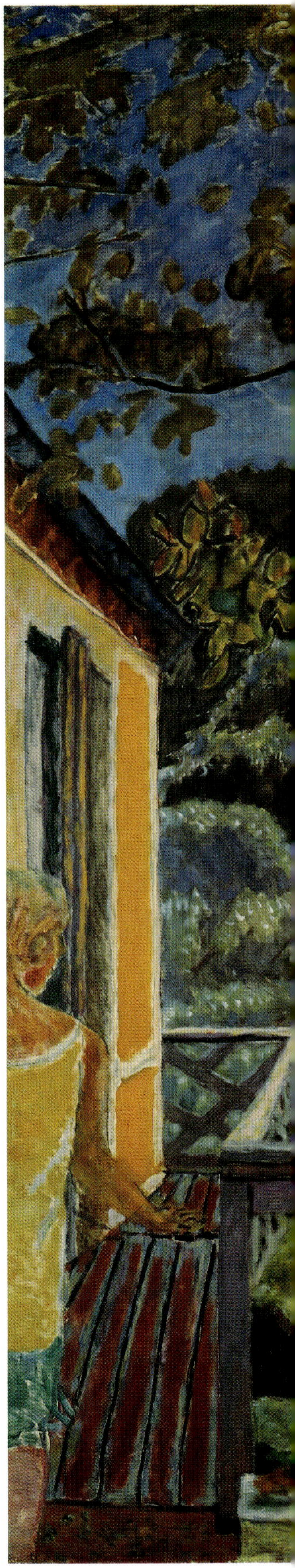

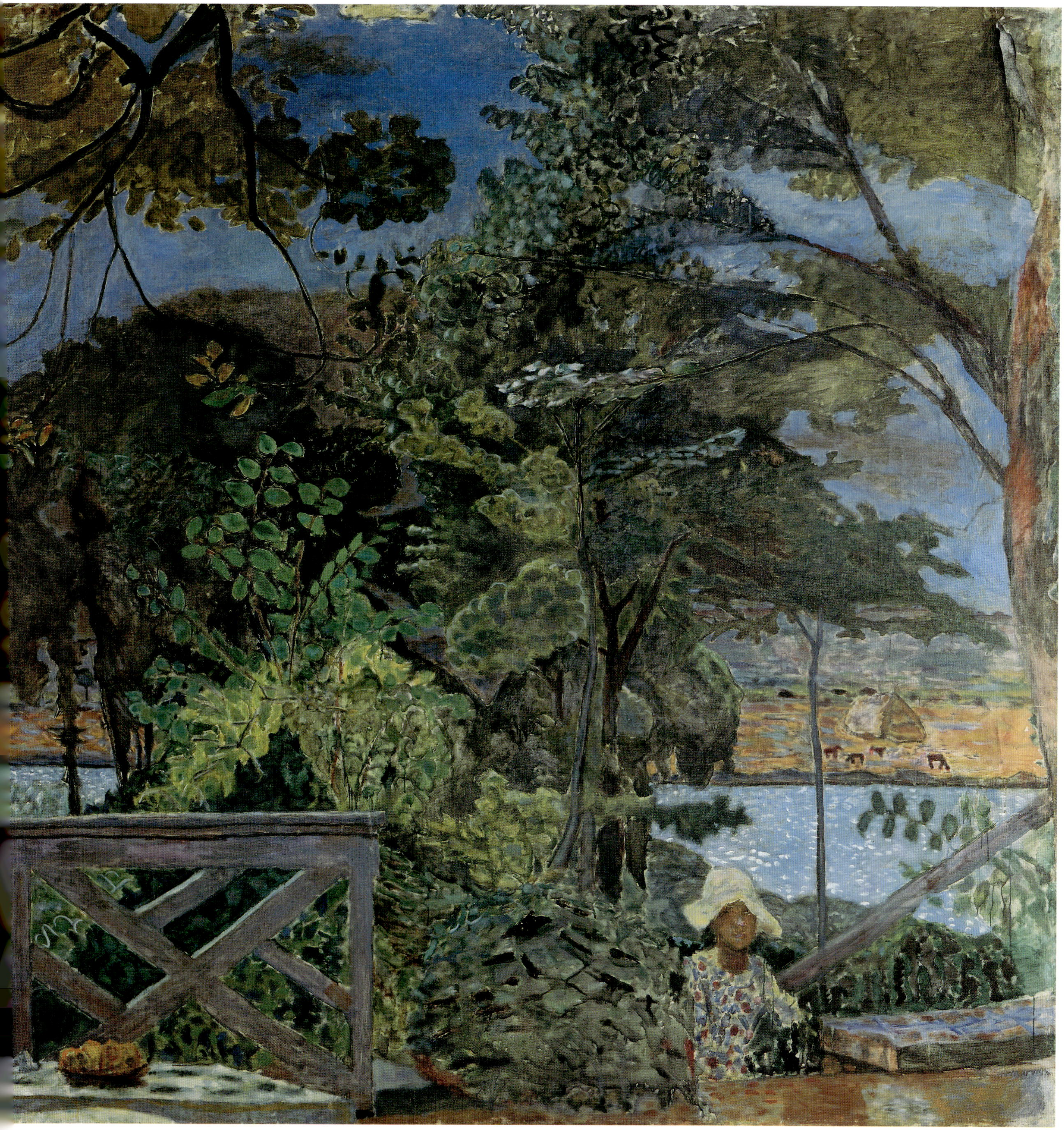

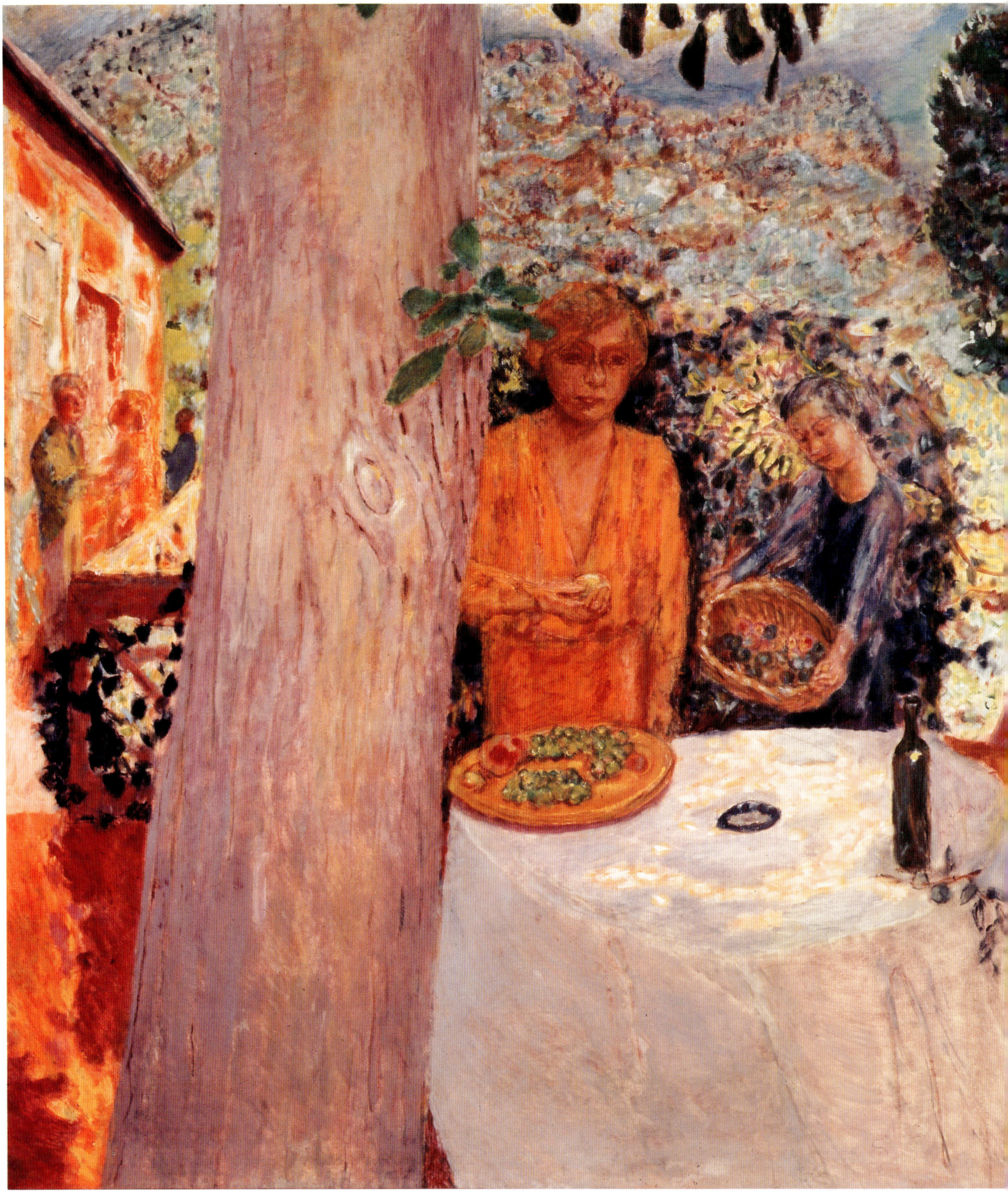

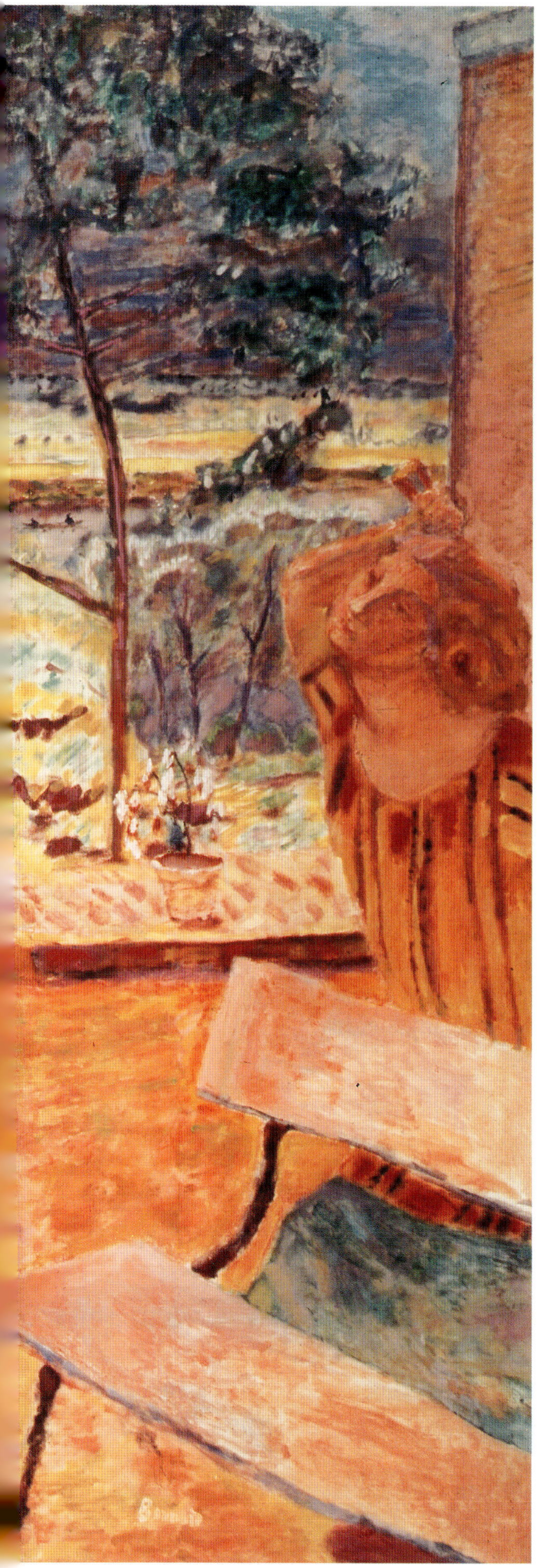

116
Décor à Vernon. 1920–39.
Oil on canvas, 147×192cm.
Metropolitan Museum of Art, New York

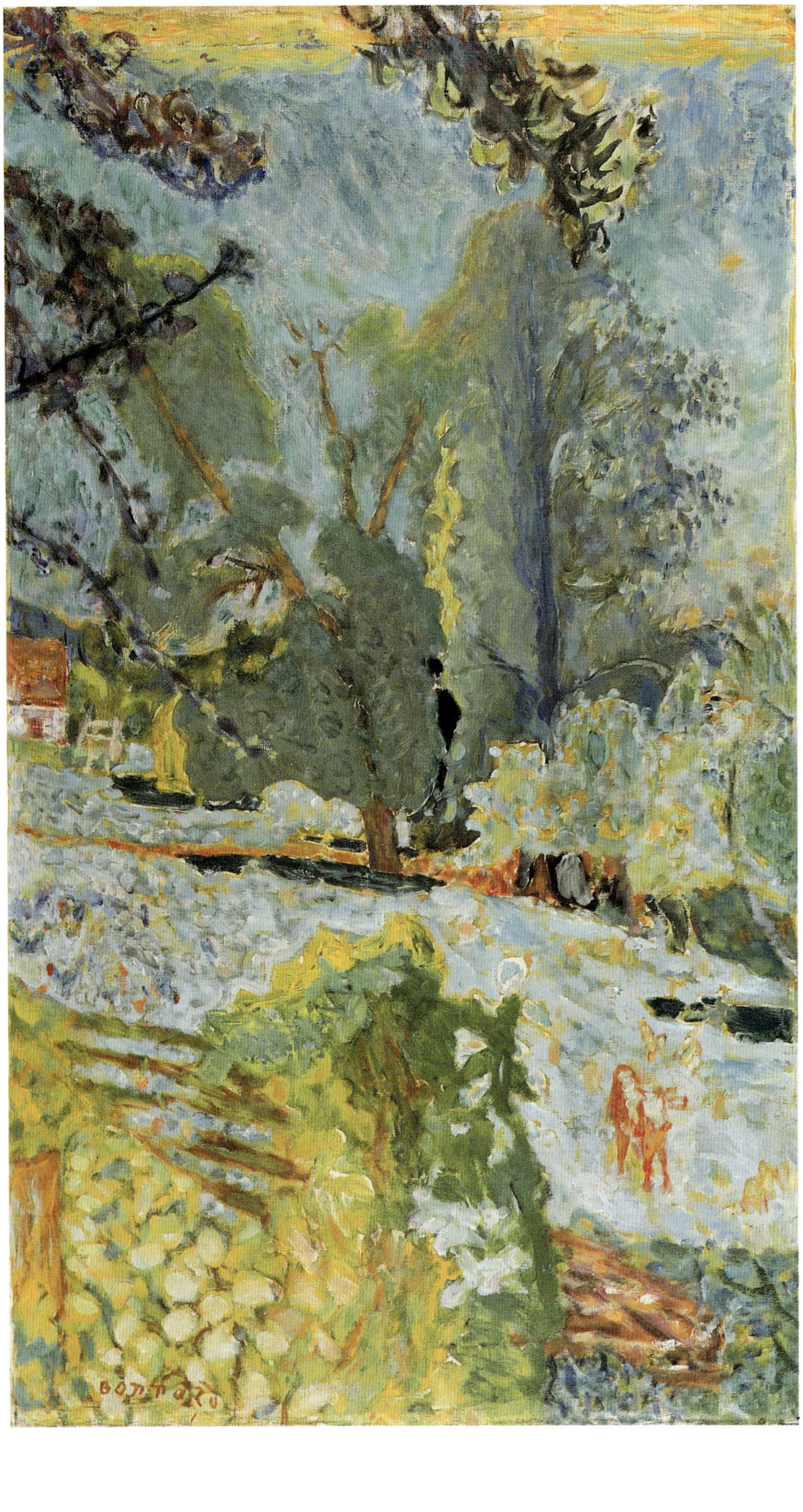

117
Paysage normand. 1920.
Oil on canvas, 105×57.9cm.
Musée d'Unterlinden, Colmar

the spectator is guided along the lines of the tablecloth on the extreme left into the dense foliage of the trees on the island. The river which dominates the view from the terrace is ruthlessly excluded. The stillness of evening was selected to communicate the quiet pastoral feeling of being at one with nature. The light is fading fast, and the warm colours are caught in a residual glow uniting foreground and background in receding bands of warm and cool tones.

La Terrasse à Vernon, painted some ten years later, is sharper and more dramatic. The clarity and colour of the south had further changed Bonnard's vision. The spectator is brought right up against the landscape, pressed against the picture plane. Bonnard could now handle the drama of the great river at dusk, which becomes the new subject of the painting. As in reality, it appears close to the terrace, filling the middle ground (on occasion the bottom of the garden would be flooded by the tributary in front of the island). A comparison with the sketch (Plate 114) shows how faithful Bonnard remained to his original conception in the disposition of the principal forms and tonal masses.[31] The main changes were done, firstly, to assert the foreground and two-dimensionality of the surface as a decorative entity in its own right, by bringing in the tree trunk on the right and by further emphasizing the framing branches, in the manner of Cézanne. Secondly, Bonnard focused on the inclusion of the two women, one enticing the parrot back into captivity on the left and the other climbing up to the terrace on the right, by blocking the view though the trees on the island in the middle of the composition, thus forcing attention to the sides. The warm colours are introduced in association with form to glow like lamps against the darkening trees in the middle ground and to create the sensation of depth in the transition from the foreground to the band of light catching the far bank in the background. Drips of green run down the surface in the bottom right-hand corner to further assert the foreground.

The atmosphere of the third great Normandy decoration, *Décor à Vernon*, is very different. Painted over a period of some twenty years, it looks more like a view from Le Cannet, bathed in southern light, than the terrace of Ma Roulotte. The oranges and reds of a hot summer's day are giving way to the deliciously cool violet and blue shadows of evening, in a dialogue which is extended symbolically to take in the transition from the real to the ideal, the contemporary back to the classical. The viewpoint on the terrace is withdrawn behind the chestnut tree, which acts like a divide between two panels of a screen: the one on the left contains informally grouped contemporary figures chatting on the balcony and that on the right a formal group of classically inspired figures on the terrace. Marthe, attended by a handmaiden offering a basket of fruit, poses as Pomona, the Roman goddess of fruit, solemnly holding an apple, while a woman enters on the right clutching a tennis racket in the lethal pose of a Roman legionary dispatching a Gaul from a relief in the Louvre.[32] In other words, the painting recapitulates southern themes from the four Bernheim panels (Plates 100, 101) in the landscape of the north. It is one of those strange paintings that remained in the artist's studio and evolved with his changing concerns.

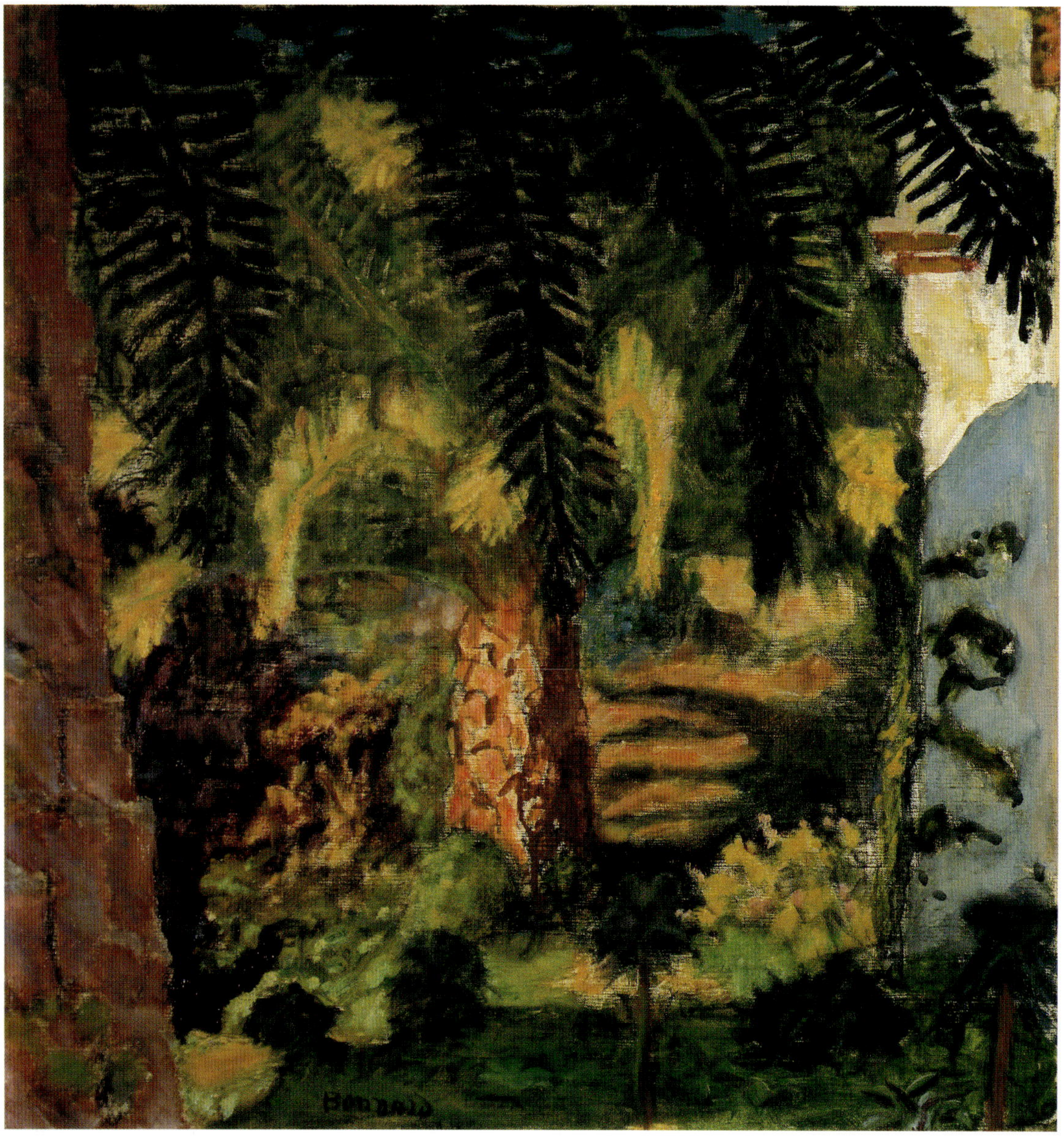

118
Le Palmier au Cannet. 1924.
Oil on canvas, 50×48cm.
Manchester City Art Galleries

The notion that Bonnard was a challenging formal artist, extending the language of painting, may seem difficult to accept, because his innovations look so unforced and natural, and at the same time so outside the concerns of the contemporary avant-garde, that they pass unnoticed. Part of his success depended on his ability to disrupt habitual ways of looking at things. If the conventional way of representing landscape was to emphasize the sky, then he would if necessary avoid it. His quest to re-create the expansive sensation of pictorial space of the Vernonnet decorations on a smaller scale resulted in one of his most important formal solutions. By excluding the sky and focusing on the vegetation, the whole surface became an organic tapestry, continuing as it were beyond the framing edges of the canvas, leaving depth to be established through relationships of form and colour. In *Balcon à Vernonnet*, 1920 (Plate 112), the balcony is dramatically pressed up against the surface, and a cloth, split between orange and pink, is tossed over the rail to introduce the colours which are played out in the foliage to create depth. In the 1920s he began to employ the heightened colours associated with southern landscapes to create mood, feeling and pictorial drama, as well as space. In *Paysage normand*, 1920 (Plate 117), a red seam opens out across the middle of the painting like a molten fissure in a volcano. Whereas in *Balcon à Vernonnet* pink, white and pale yellow-green convey an atmosphere of spring, the heavy middle-greens and blues of *Paysage normand* suggest late summer.

Bonnard increasingly rephrased ideas between northern and southern landsapes, to the point where it is sometimes difficult to distinguish between them. He worked from memory, aided by drawings, and thought nothing of rolling up an unfinished canvas, sticking it on top of his car, and continuing it when he moved between Normandy, Paris and the south. On one occasion he arrived at his destination to find that the roll had blown off en route. Just as he had transposed the heightened palette of the south into the north, so too did he pursue his northern exploration of the garden motif in the south. *Le Palmier au Cannet* (Plate 118) was the second of two paintings of this garden executed in 1924 featuring the magnificent palm tree. Bonnard was fascinated by the way palm branches filtered the light and formed arches, drawing the eye down through the vegetation. The main chromatic accents come in the reddened glow of the palm trunk and path behind, and the formal leitmotiv of the arch is repeated in the shape of the blue shadow on the wall framing the composition on the right. He employed the same device in *La Palme*, 1926 (Plate 121), to frame a view of Le Cannet.

It is easy to appreciate why Bonnard was attracted to the village of Le Cannet. The air was said to be good for Marthe's fragile health, and, more importantly, the houses on the hill command a stupendous view over Cannes, the bay, the Golfe de la Napoule and the mountains of the Esterel. The path of the Canal de la Siagne, which Bonnard often followed on his morning walks, curves round the side of the hill like the back tier of a natural amphitheatre, providing at each turn an ever-changing spectacle, breathtaking in its scope. At one point the houses drop away in a patchwork of pink to be taken up in the ascending rhythm of the mountains of the Esterel; at another they overlook

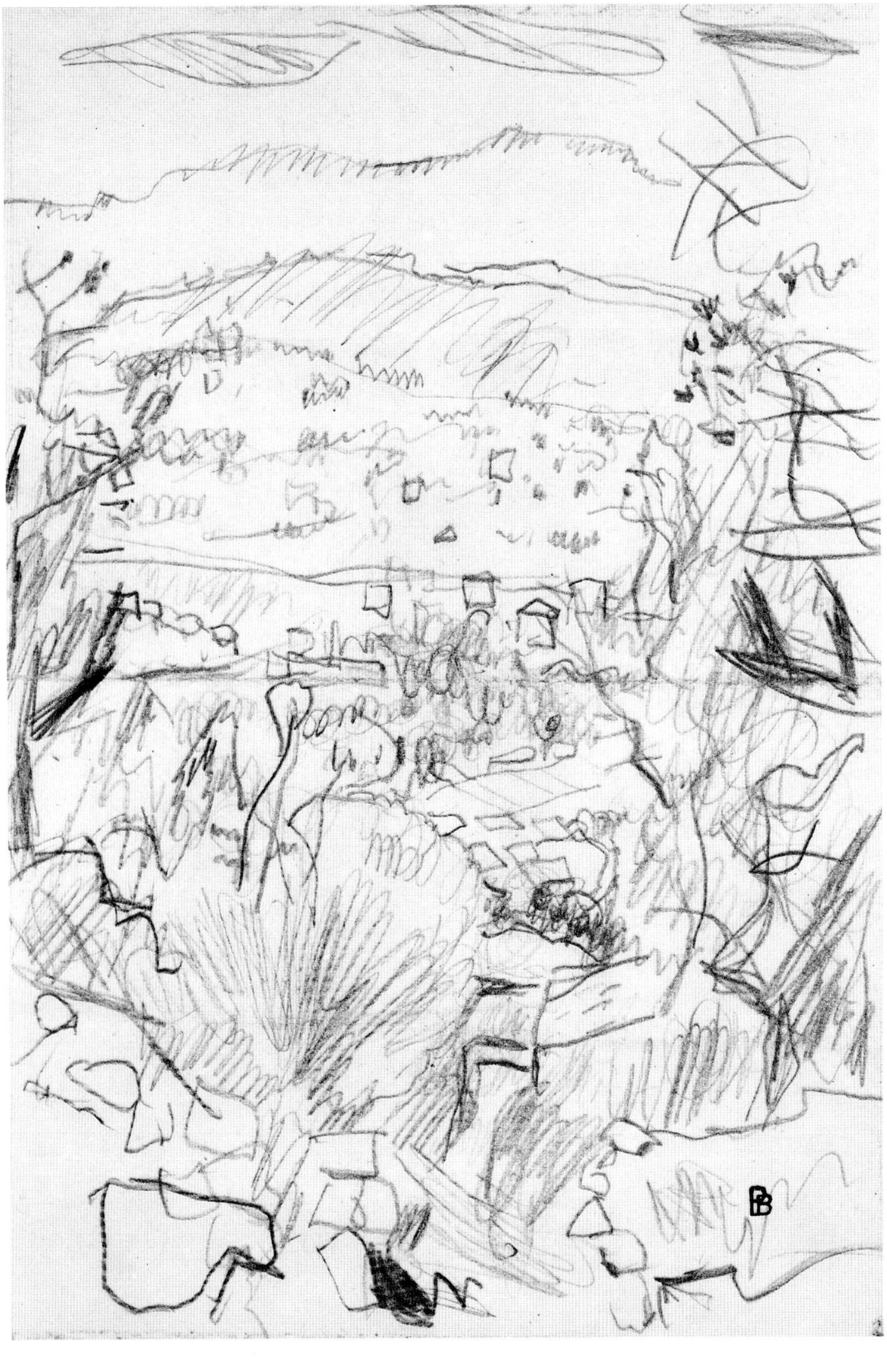

119
*Vue du Cannet. c.*1938.
Pencil on paper, 17.8×14.3cm.
Private collection

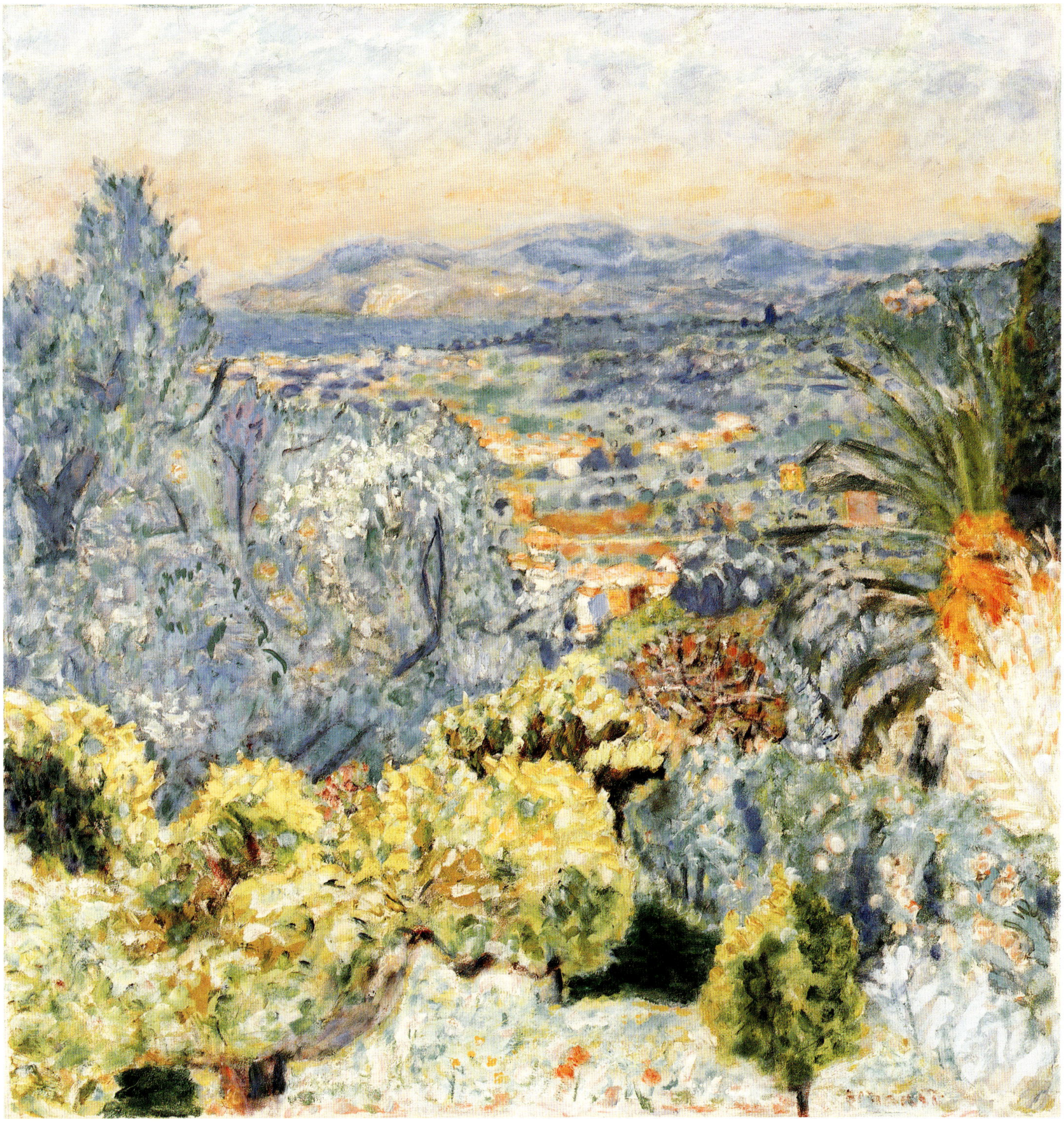

120
La Côte d'Azur. *c*.1923.
Oil on canvas, 79×76cm.
The Phillips Collection, Washington, DC

the bay of Cannes. Cypresses stick up at intervals like dark vegetal columns silhouetted against the crystalline sky. By selecting his vista Bonnard could feel either in the country, among the olives, or down in the town. The sheer variety of motifs, perceived under different conditions through the seasons, provided him with sufficient subjects for the rest of his career.

Bonnard was struck by the architectural nature of the vegetation in the south and by the way that light isolates colours and shapes, suggesting a way of dealing with the view from Le Cannet in both paintings and drawings through poetic correspondences across the landscape. The pink roofs in the painting *La Côte d'Azur*, *c.*1923 (Plate 120), act like stepping-stones through the blue haze of the middle ground in the transition from the foreground vegetation to the distant mountains of the Esterel. The challenge of representing this view continued to obsess him. The bold, rectangular shapes of the stones strewn across the foreground of the drawing *Vue du Cannet*, *c.*1938 (Plate 119), are so repeated in the background that they describe the houses on the opposite hill, creating in the process the sensation of depth. Bonnard's solution to the problem of reconciling depth with the decorative assertion of the surface in the painting was to treat the landscape as a kind of tapestry into which the view was woven.[33] Even the trees in *La Côte d'Azur* look as though they are made out of wool.

Bonnard's art was always very much based on reality, but a distinction can be made between his northern and southern landscapes: whereas in the former he was more concerned with capturing the transient effects of weather, in the latter the permanence of atmosphere drew him into an alternative Mediterranean vision of a classical Golden Age. Cézanne and Renoir, rather than Monet, became his mentors in the south. The greens of his first terrace decoration at Vernonnet (Plate 113) gave way to the pervasive golden light of his two main southern decorations of the 1920s, *La Palme*, 1926 (Plate 121), and *Paysage du Cannet*, 1928 (Plate 122). The flickering branches of *La Palme* act as conductors framing Le Cannet in light. The vines in the foreground have turned gold. The landscape is shot with golden threads, and a Pomona figure holds what looks like a golden apple.[34] In *Paysage du Cannet* the view from behind his house, Le Bosquet, is opened up in a panorama of the surrounding hills. A Virgilian shepherd, looking remarkably like Bonnard himself, reclines in the right-hand corner of the golden foreground with his sheep.[35] The message is clear: Le Cannet is classic ground and the purpose of the decorations is to continue the theme of *Symphonie pastorale* (Plate 100) and unite the past with the present in a harmonious vision of the Golden Age. Remove the mythological figures and both paintings look like decorative landscapes of Le Cannet.

In the 1930s, while remaining faithful to nature, Bonnard felt increasingly free to transpose the landscape into a higher key. His palette became brighter, his compositions bolder and more simplified. *Paysage d'automne*, *c.*1932 (Plate 123), looks like a landscape at Le Cannet, when in fact it is the view from the hill above Ma Roulotte at Vernonnet.[36] (Bonnard had painted four landscapes from different positions on the hill

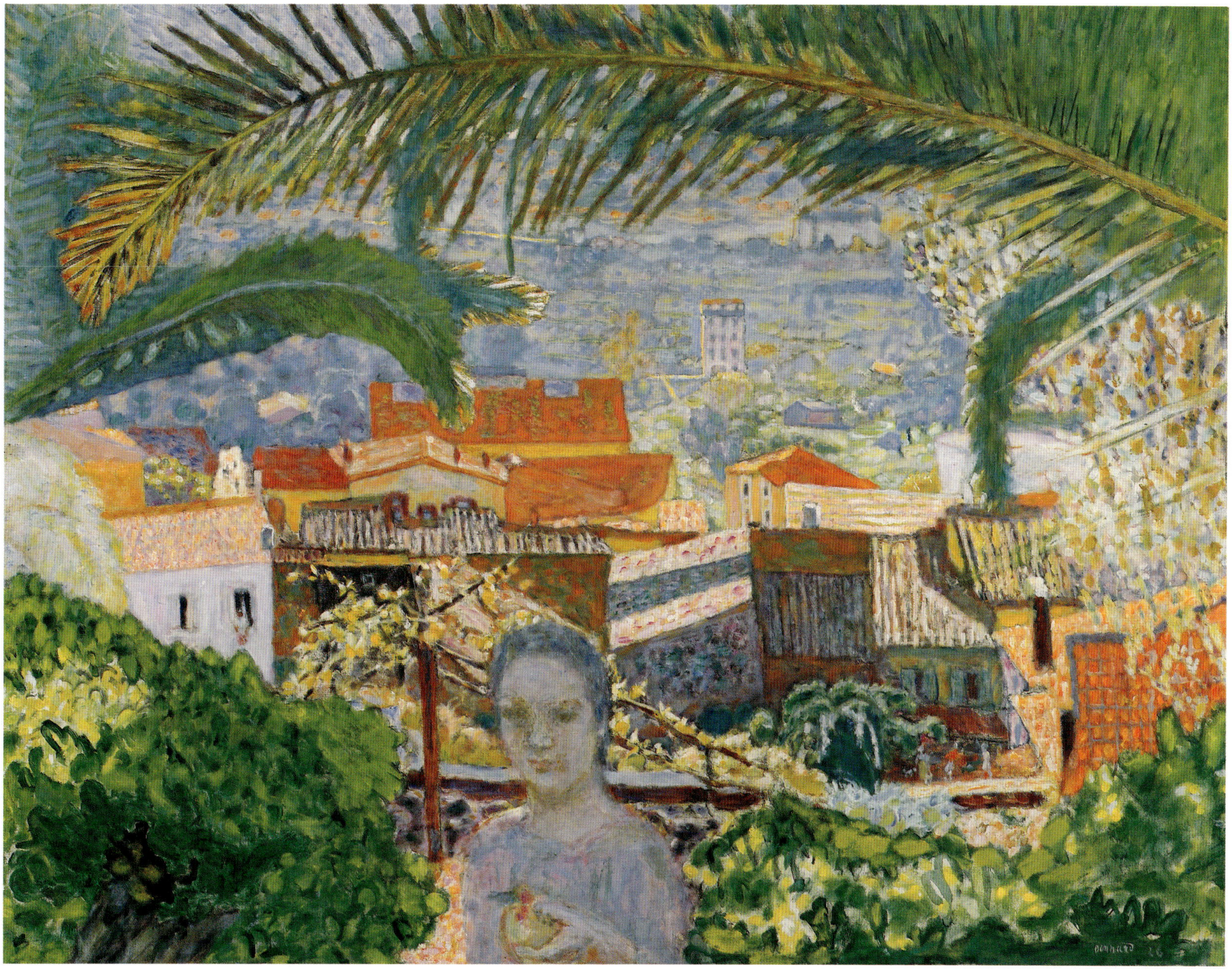

121
La Palme. 1926.
Oil on canvas, 114.3×147cm.
The Phillips Collection, Washington DC

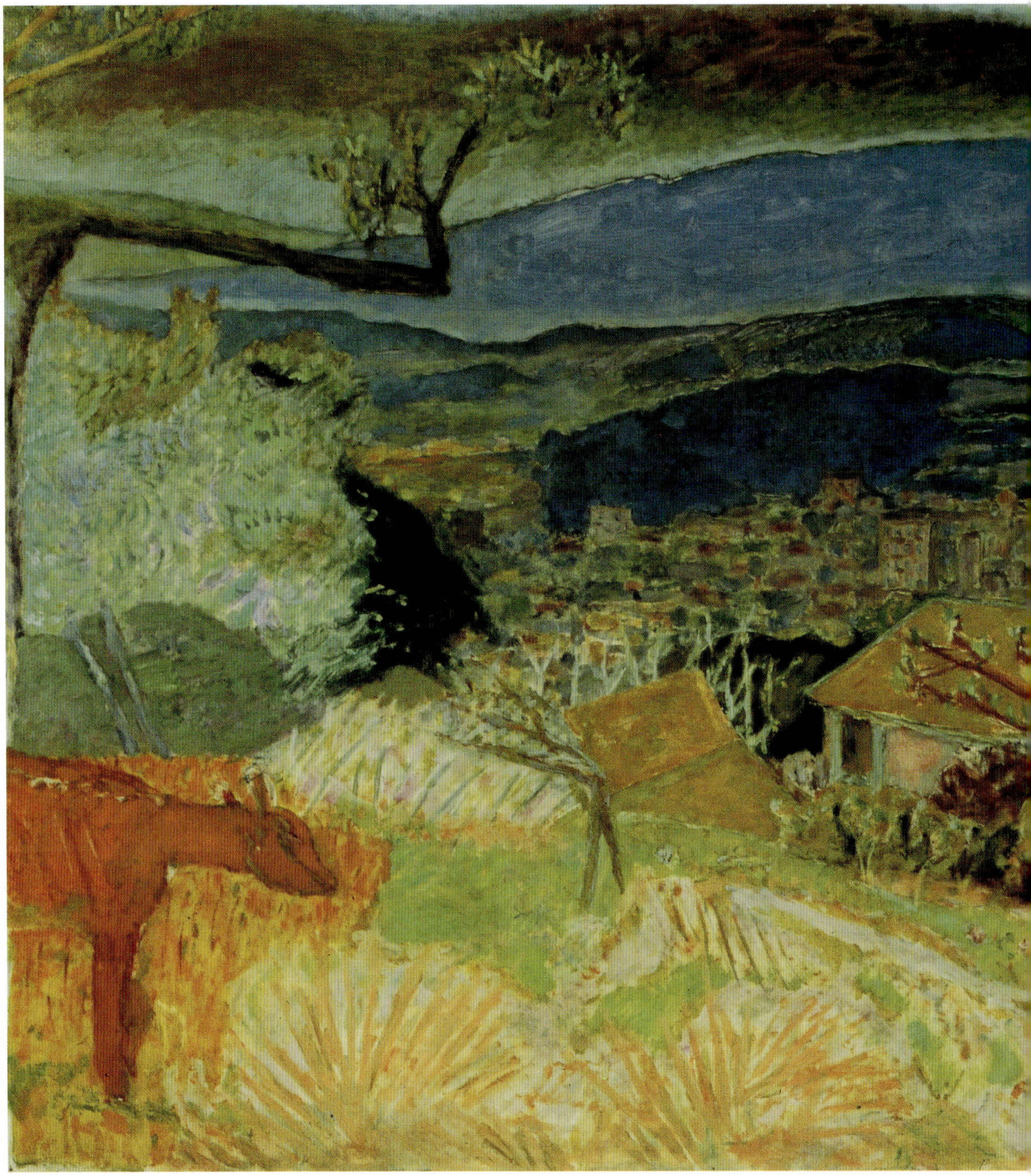

122
Paysage du Cannet. 1928.
Oil on canvas, 123×275cm.
Galerie Maeght, Paris

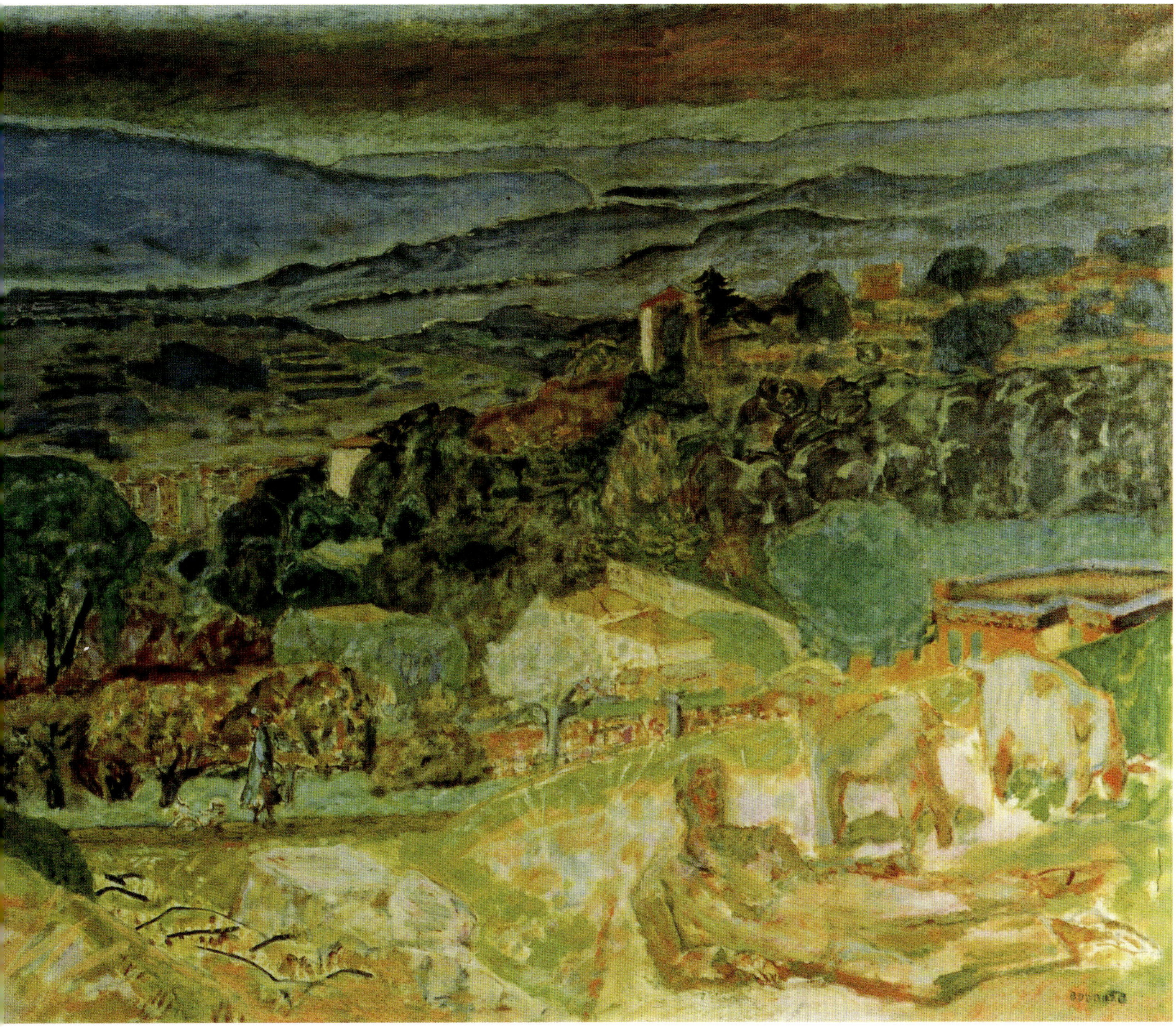

in 1922.[37]) What appears to be a river on the right, bathed in reflections, with red and yellow cabins on the far bank, is the roof of a building with two chimneypots still wet after rain. The actual river is represented by the dark blue line above the pale blue gabled end to the building in the centre of the composition. The main forms are flattened into units surrounded by continuous contours, and the colour scheme is dominated by the three pigment primaries, red, yellow and blue.

This extremely decorative painting was intended as a cartoon for a tapestry, which was never woven, commissioned by Marie Cuttoli, who was responsible for reviving interest in the medium by getting leading artists to provide cartoons for the Manufacture de Beauvais.[38] Whereas *Paysage d'automne* made a tapestry out of a landscape, *Le Jardin*, *c.*1936 (Plate 124), further developed the concept in *Balcon à Vernonnet* (Plate 112) of a paradise garden tapestry taken back into nature. The garden of Le Bosquet is sealed off in a virtual riot of colourful vegetation cascading down the surface. Pulsating areas of energy are dramatically balanced either side of a yellow path, which leads into colour rather than a view.

Bonnard's opportunity to combine the tapestry of nature with the pastoral in a large-scale project came with the commission to do a mural for the Universal Exhibition of 1937 in Paris. The commission brought full circle the Nabis ambition to integrate art

123
Paysage d'automne. *c.*1932.
Oil on canvas mounted on board, 43×66cm.
Reuters Ltd

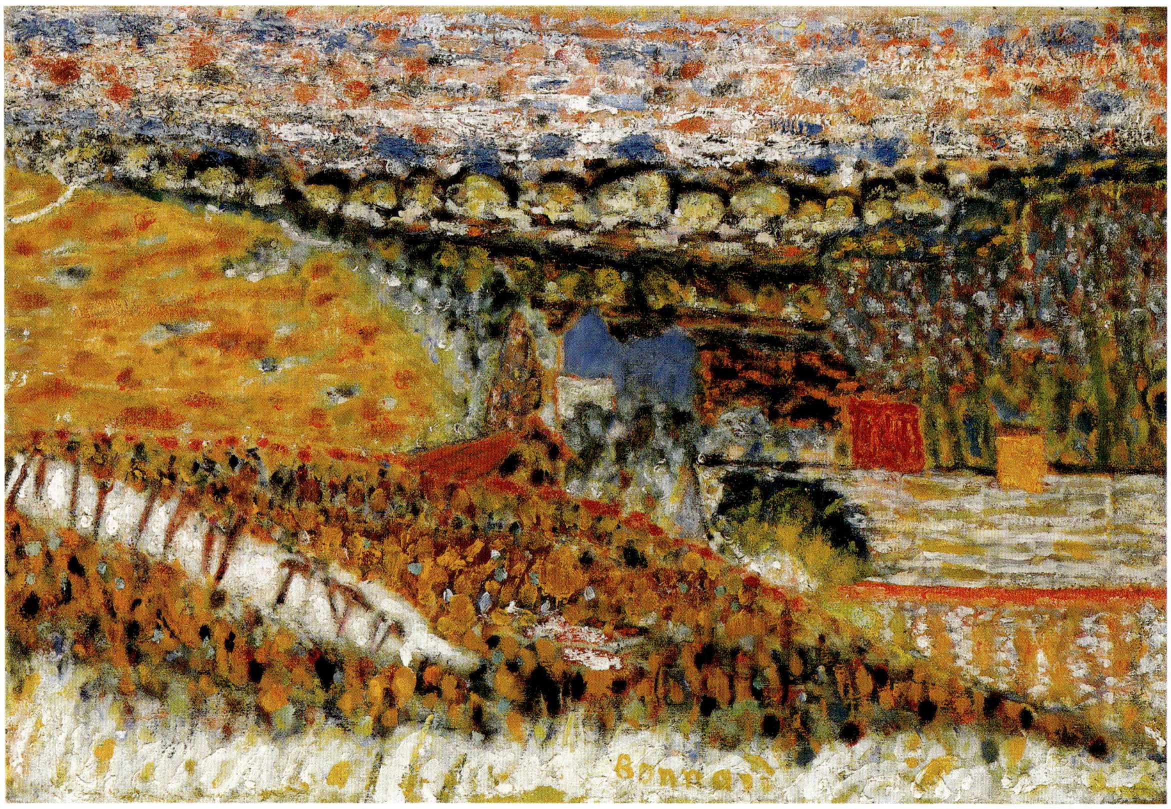

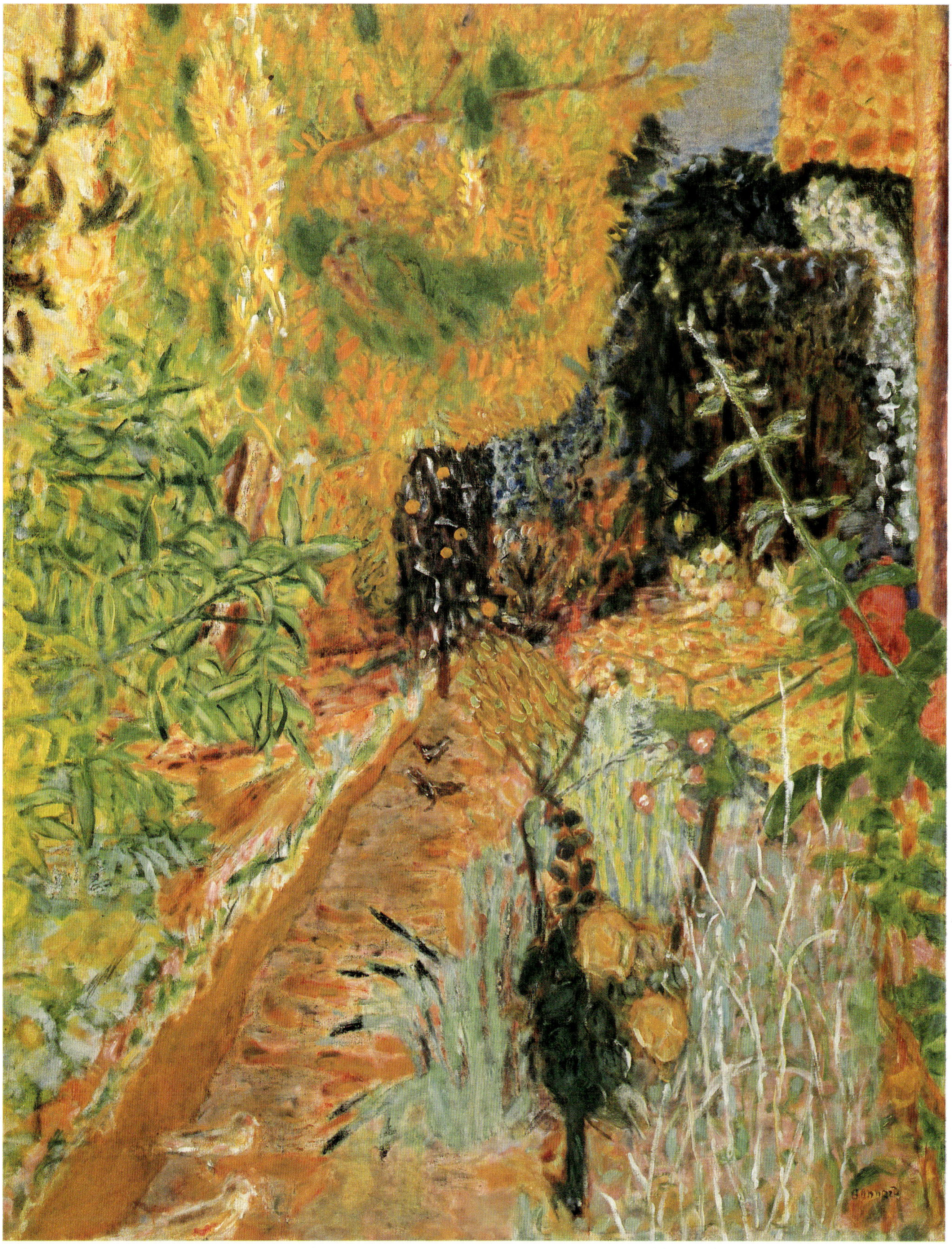

124
*Le Jardin. c.*1936.
Oil on canvas, 127×100cm.
Musée du Petit Palais, Paris

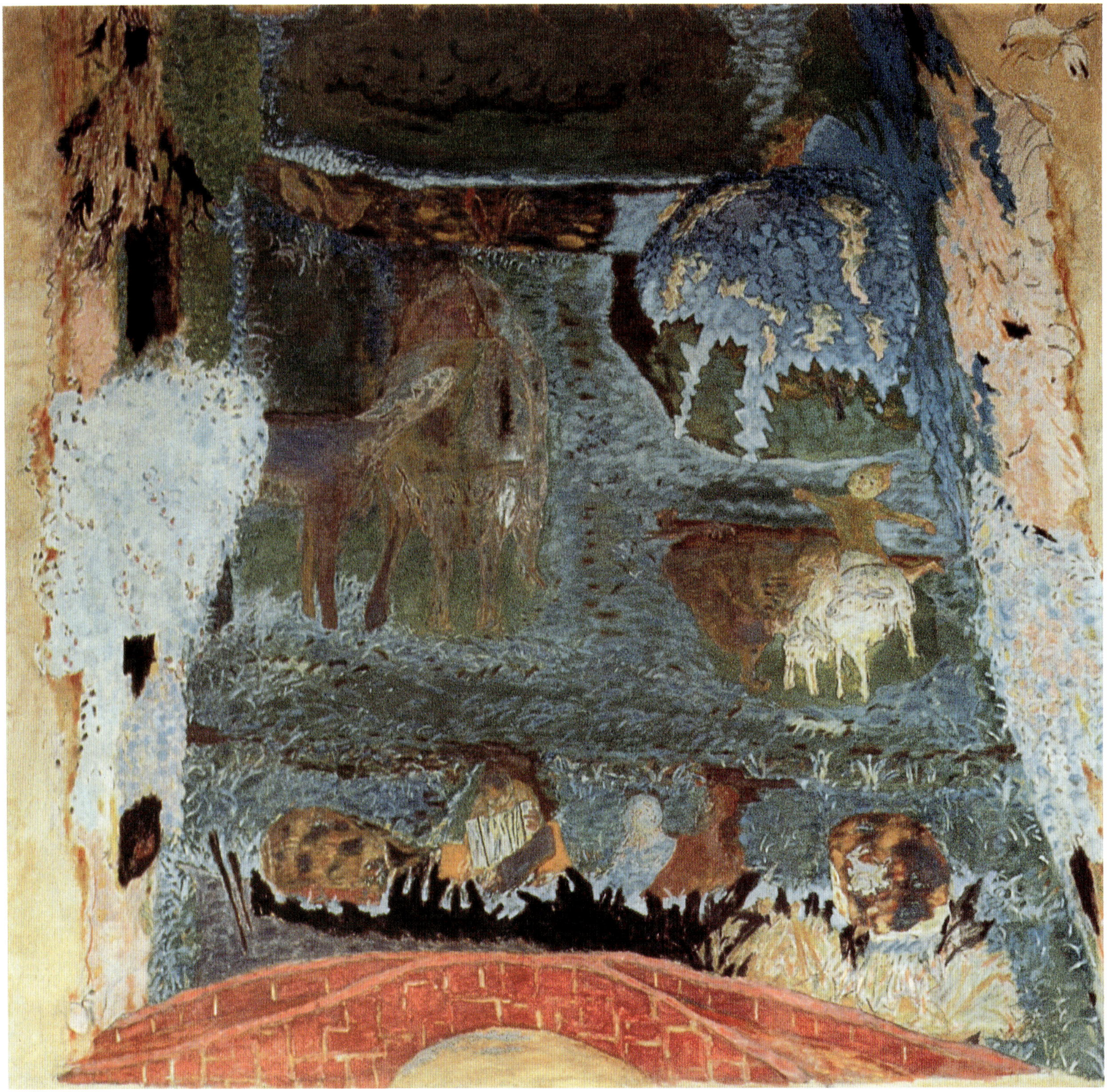

with life in a decorative art form drawing on the past. His old companions from his Nabis days, Vuillard and Roussel, were also invited to contribute panels to the programme of three allegories for the theatre in the new Palais de Chaillot. Vuillard did *La Comédie*, Roussel *La Danse* and Bonnard *La Pastorale* (Plate 125).[39] *La Pastorale* is the largest painting Bonnard ever attempted. Far from dominating the proceedings, humans are absorbed on an equal footing with animals into a vast landscape 'tapestry' governed by the forces of nature. Lightning crackles through an umbrella of blue. Water runs down the surface. A donkey looks up nervously. A little shepherd throws open his arms in a Marini-like gesture of despair.[40] Bonnard adopted a *faux-naïf* figure style to communicate a world of childhood innocence under threat. The hot colour scheme of the landscape of the Golden Age has been abandoned in favour of the greens and blues of his first pastoral decorations, based on the garden of his childhood home, Le Clos. A classical subject, the pastoral, has been inverted to give an unclassical reading. Bonnard was becoming old and pessimistic. For the third time since 1870, France was facing a resurgent Germany. *La Pastorale* commemorates the world taken at the Flood rather than an earthly paradise.

125
La Pastorale. 1937.
Oil on canvas, 335×350cm.
Palais de Chaillot, Paris

Chapter 4

The internal paradise

In the aftermath of the Great War and the devastating epidemic of Spanish flu that killed almost as many people as the war itself, relief that it was all over found expression in a decade of celebration – the 'gay twenties'. The defeat of Germany was hailed as a vindication of traditional French values. Those like Bonnard who had held out against modernism came in for renewed attention. In one of the first monographs on the artist, published in 1919, the author, François Fosca, lauded him as a delightful artist who had resisted doctrinaire systems, formulas and abstractions.[1] Claude Roger-Marx, writing in 1924, claimed that the time of injustice was over, Cubism had collapsed like a pack of cards and Bonnard was rediscovered: 'His charms had recovered their power.'[2]

Criticisms of Bonnard's formlessness persisted; words like 'fluidity' were employed to describe his style. François Fosca, while acknowledging Bonnard's debt to Impressionism in the impregnation of the decorative with light and atmosphere, also saw him as the 'victim of this impressionism which was both his strength and weakness. Slave to his sensibility, incapable of selection, of order, he is saved by his innate taste which verges on the prodigious.'[3] There was little in contemporary criticism to indicate that in his nudes and in his transformation of the interior into an earthly paradise Bonnard in the 1920s was on the threshold of a great imaginative leap.

Bonnard enjoyed a run of successful exhibitons in the inter-war years. The four Bernheim decorations, 1916–20 (Plates 100, 101), were included among some 24 paintings exhibited at their family gallery in May and June 1921. *La Terrasse*, 1918 (Plate 113), his first Vernon decoration, was well received at the Salon d'Automne in November 1923. Dealers began to compete for his work. He was given a retrospective exhibition at the Galerie Druet in April 1924. His reputation spread abroad. Duncan Phillips started that year to amass his outstanding collection of Bonnard's work. The two met in 1926, when Bonnard went to the United States as a member of the Carnegie International jury. Bonnard's first major one-man show outside France was held at the de Hauke gallery, New York, in 1928. Seven of his paintings were included in the exhibition, *Paintings in Paris*, held at the Museum of Modern Art, New York, in 1933. In 1934 he exhibited 44 paintings at the Wildenstein gallery in New York, and the following year went to London for the opening of his exhibition at the Reid and Lefevre gallery.[4] The sales drive abroad was partly a search for new markets, as the prices of Bonnard's paintings collapsed in France during the depression from 1932 to 1936.[5]

Any increase in prosperity was not, however, reflected in a change in Bonnard's life-

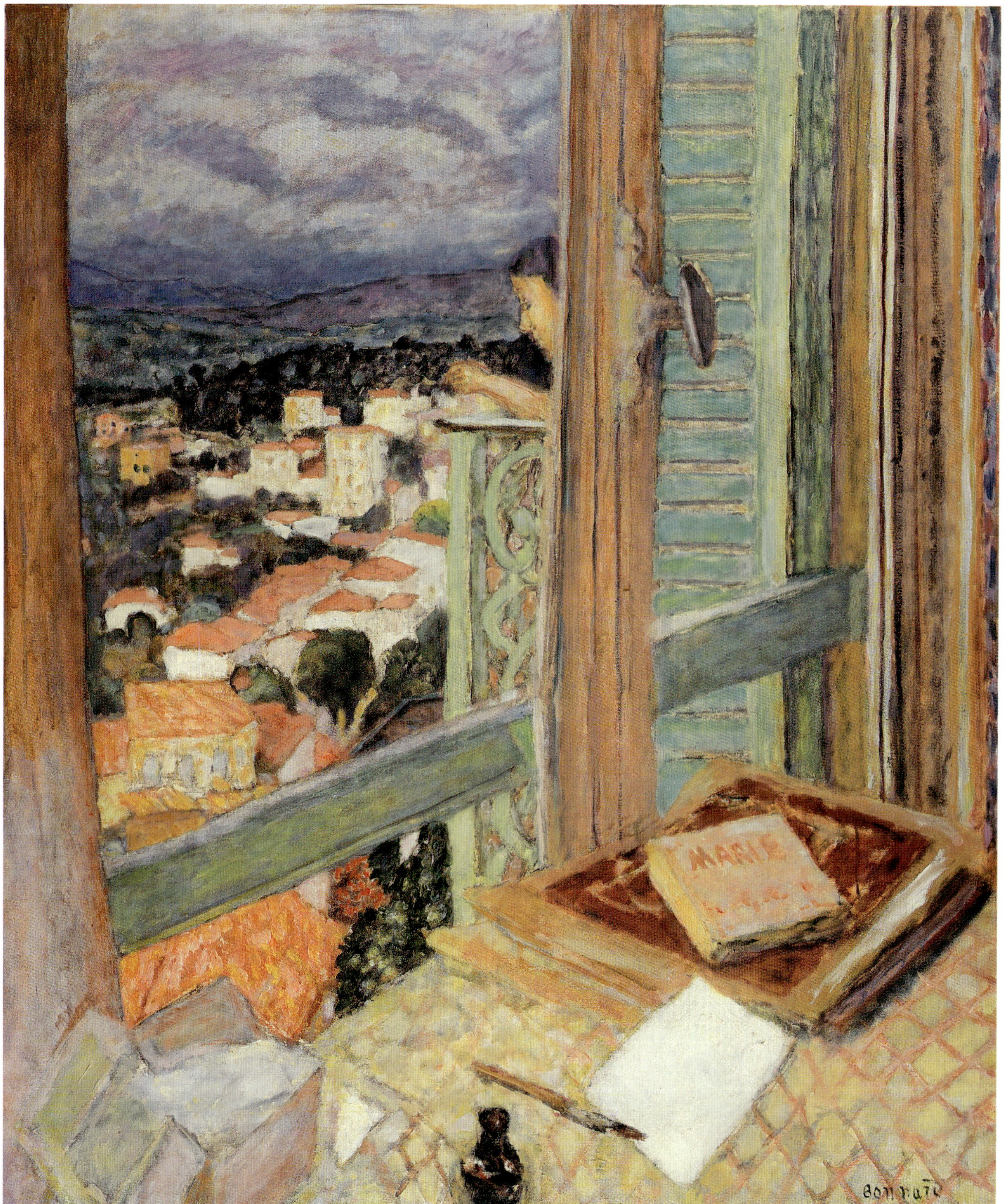

126
La Fenêtre. 1925.
Oil on canvas, 108.5×89cm.
Tate Gallery, London

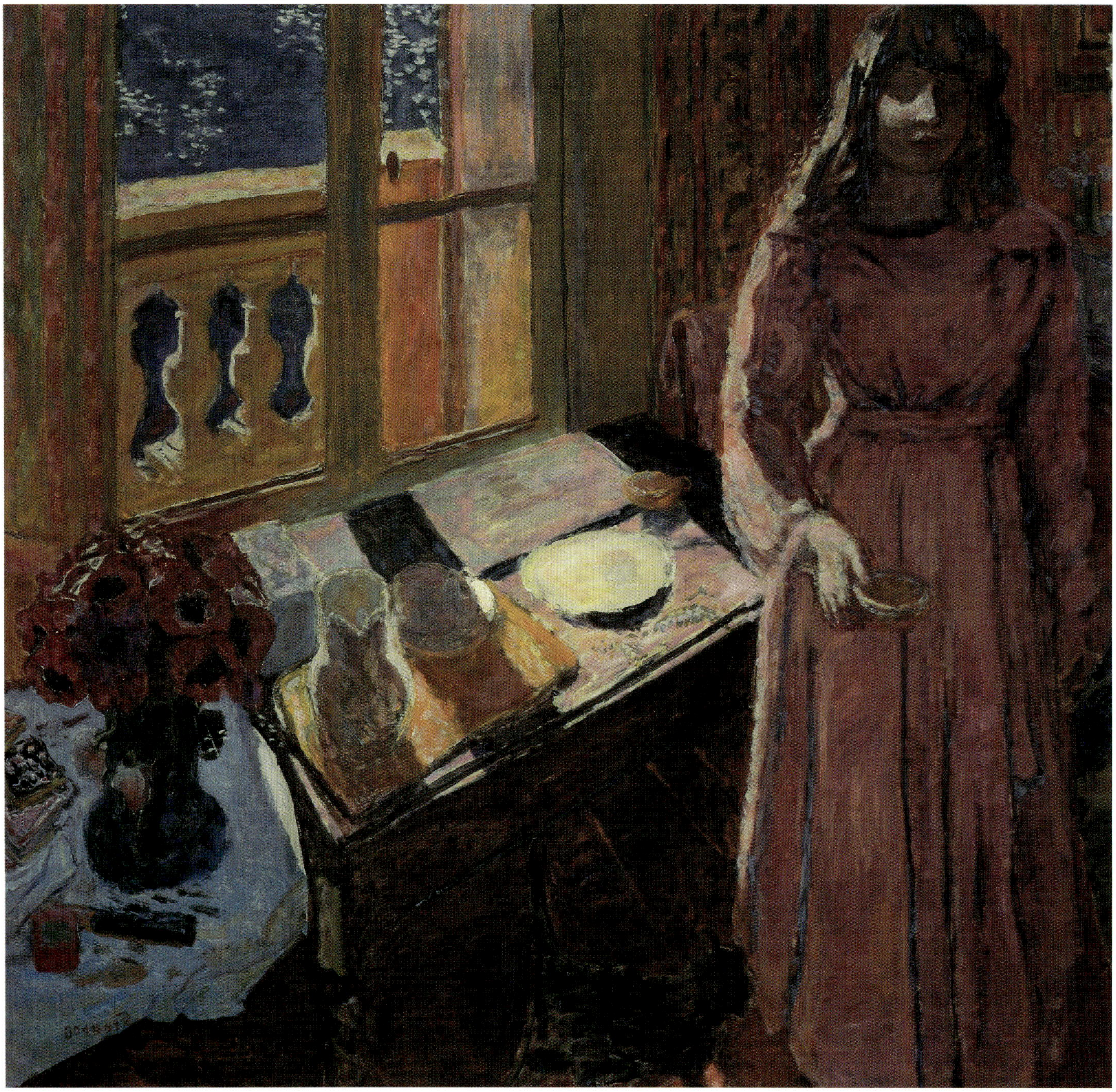

127
Le Bol de lait. *c*.1919.
Oil on canvas, 116.2×121.6cm.
Tate Gallery, London

style. There was a marked disparity between the luxury of his work and the simplicity of his homes. If anything, his horizons contracted as his career developed. Marthe became increasingly difficult. Her health declined. In 1923 he was obliged to take her to three different spas. Boredom and long solitary walks with the dog became a feature of his life with her. A comparison between his two self-portraits, *Autoportrait à la barbe*, *c.*1920 (Plate 4), and *Le Boxeur*, 1931 (Plate 5), reveals a marked decline in self-esteem. Loneliness had taken its toll. Occasionally Bonnard broke out and had affairs, only to return like an old lifer to the enclosed atmosphere to which he had grown accustomed. Far from abandoning Marthe, he in fact married her in 1925. Bonnard's life took on the outward appearance of a modest member of one of the professions in premature retirement, pottering about between house and garden. A world without work, without men, the province of women and cats. Childhood memories merged with age in an existence trapped within the atmosphere of a largely female domain. It was a place both of refuge and confinement.

In gradually withdrawing from life Bonnard developed a strand in his art which had run parallel with the landscapes and decorations in the pastoral tradition. He abandoned any claim to the high status of history painting. Instead of dealing with the public world, he looked inwards. The rooms within which he lived contained his subject-matter, and an infinitely complex dialogue ensued between art and life. His art spanned the genres. A bunch of wild-flowers had already illumined and brought the aroma of the country into a darkened interior (Plate 128); in the 1920s the intimist interior was opened up to the breadth and light of landscape; meals were spread out invitingly across a table; interiors opened out onto a view; nudes were accommodated into the domestic interior on the pretext of washing; Marthe passed in and out of the rooms, leaving a pervasive perfume. Bonnard was drawn to windows, only to encounter the flattened presence of Marthe, his muse and gaoler, pulling him back into the atmosphere of the room. Art was his solace and means of escape. For Bonnard there was evidently an increasingly poignant link between *Marie* by Peter Nansen, which he illustrated in 1897 with the youthful Marthe as the model, and their life together, and he included the novel, with the title clearly visible, beside her in *La Fenêtre*, 1925 (Plate 126). Marie was a midinette whose upper-class lover finally returned to her when she became ill.

Bonnard was a painter of sentiment as well as place. Each painting begun in the memory of a specific visual experience was transmuted through nostalgia into an earthly paradise. Time lost its meaning in a myriad of marks making up the surface. Bonnard wanted somehow to capture nature, not describe it literally.[6] The instant became an eternity possessed in the warm light of remembrance. In a memorable passage Patrick Heron described Bonnard's choice of subject as integral to its meaning: 'The quiet at the end of a meal; that lapse between two kinds of activity which makes the leisured rhythm that denotes order in daily living : a moment that is almost the epitome of civilized life in the West.'[7] The quiet, almost petrified stillness of *Le Bol de lait*, *c.*1919 (Plate 127),

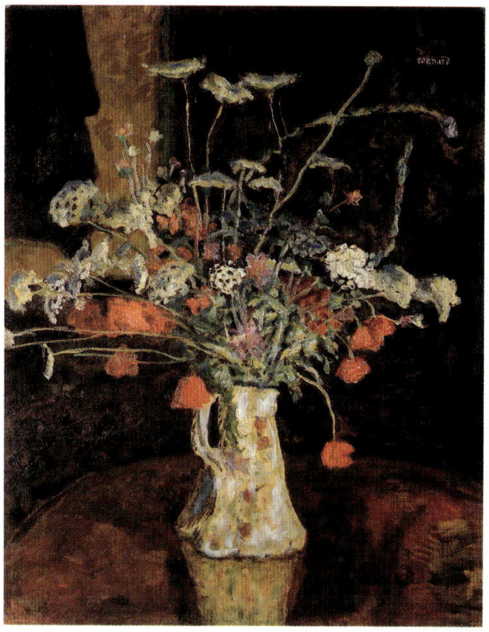

128
Fleurs de champs: ombelles et coquelicots. *c.*1912.
Oil on canvas, 77×61.5cm.
Private collection

with Marthe posed like a Greek *kore*, is brought out by the neurotic cat, tail stiff with anxiety and exasperation, waiting for its food.

Paradoxically, Bonnard was a religious painter without a religion. Christian art advocated the sanctity of the image, presented with all the symbolic clarity of sacramental furniture on an altar, whereas he wanted to dissolve it. He transferred the emotionally loaded content from the Symbolist subjects of his fellow Nabis to the interior. The lowest of the genres became the highest. There was something Zen-like about Bonnard's need to work away from the motif. Jean Clair recalled the anecdote of the Chinese artist who identified with his painting to the point where he was absorbed by it.[8] The subjugation of the human subject to the atmosphere of a room assumed the function of a meditational exercise in humility.[9] Yellow was his sign of that divine, luxurious warmth to which he aspired; the alchemy of light became his goal.

In going beyond the object Bonnard wanted to create a language which, in Symbolist terms, would 'objectify the subjective (the externalization of the Idea) instead of subjectifying the objective (nature seen through the eyes of a temperament)'.[10] He confided to Pierre Courthion in 1933: 'I believe that when you are young, it is the object, the outside world that inspires you: you are totally absorbed. Later, it is the internal, the need to express an emotion that drives the painter to choose such and such a starting point, such and such a form.'[11] His solution to the problem of matching vision with nature was to discover in nature the conditions that matched his vision. While endowing a subject with all the immediacy, warmth and sensuous richness of the thoroughly familiar, remembered in an atmosphere of affection, he disrupted conventional ways of looking at things and involved the spectator in painting as an expressive language.

Cézanne and Cubism showed Bonnard how far he could depart from a literal description without forfeiting the essential reassurance of reality. In organizing a composition Bonnard would select a limited number of objects and let them assume their own dimensions as a painting evolved. 'Distortion for visibility's sake', he noted in his diary entry for 1 January 1934.[12] Colour played a formal, constructive role, as in a still life by Cézanne. The direct influence of Cézanne is evident in the way fruit becomes colour and colour fruit in *Le Compotier*, 1924 (Plate 132).

Still-life, being the most manipulable of the genres, proved an ideal vehicle for aesthetic exploration. Without noticing we are drawn into the unfolding logic of a painting. A pool of white dissolves the black, tilted tabletop in *Intérieur avec des fleurs*, 1919 (Plate 129), appearing to flow beyond it to the right, as if reflected in a mirror, and a patch of white occupies the floor. A plane is established, splitting the foreground from the background. Bonnard's problem in this painting was to achieve a psychological balance between the two: between the spare geometric forms and predominantly black and white colour scheme of the foreground, and the exuberant organic patterns and hot colours of the background. Nature is juxtaposed with art, the flowers of the still life with the floral-patterned wallpaper.

In the south of France Bonnard heightened his colours to achieve an equivalent for

129
Intérieur avec des fleurs. 1919.
Oil on canvas, 117×90cm.
Private collection

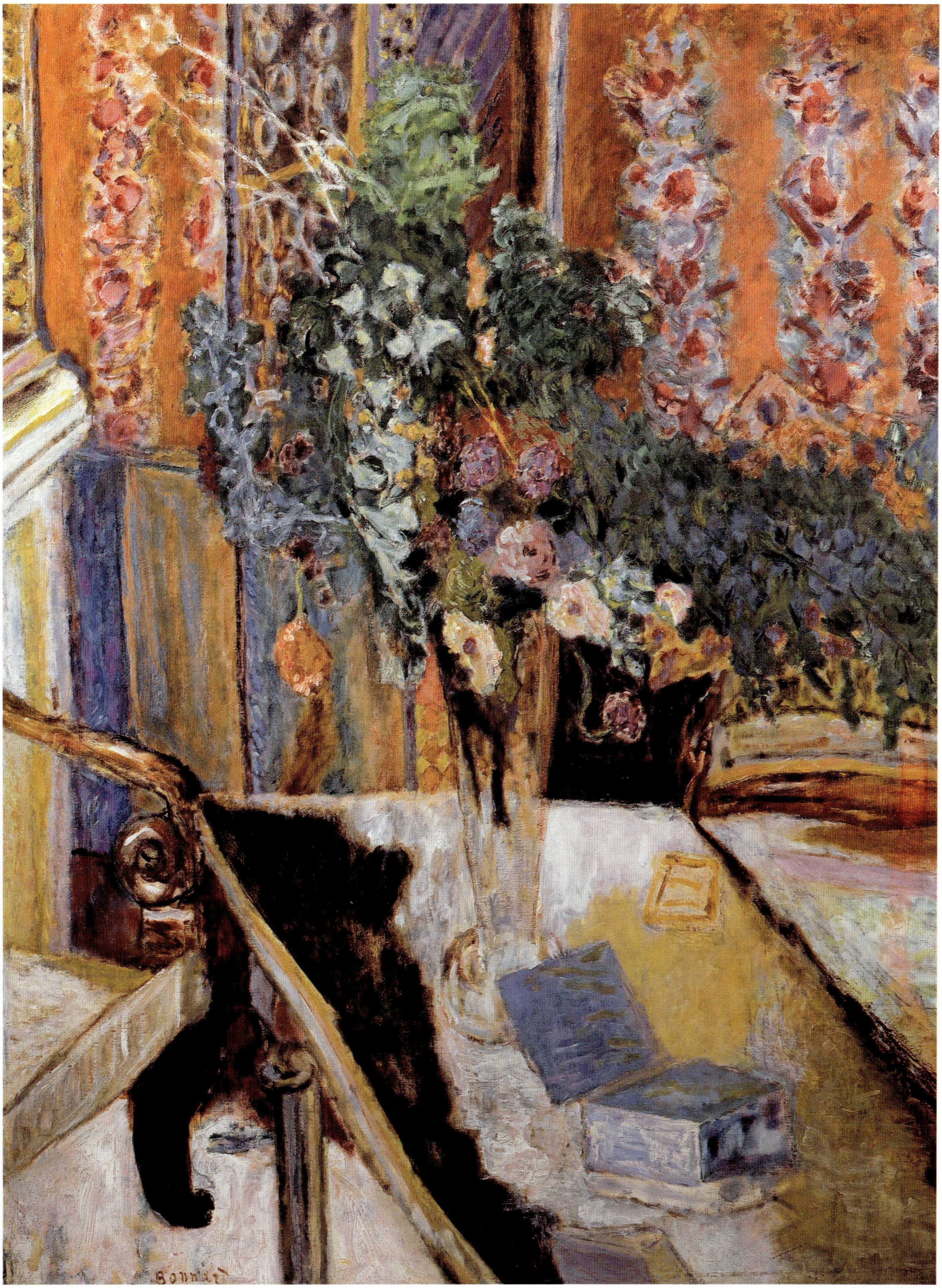
Bonnard

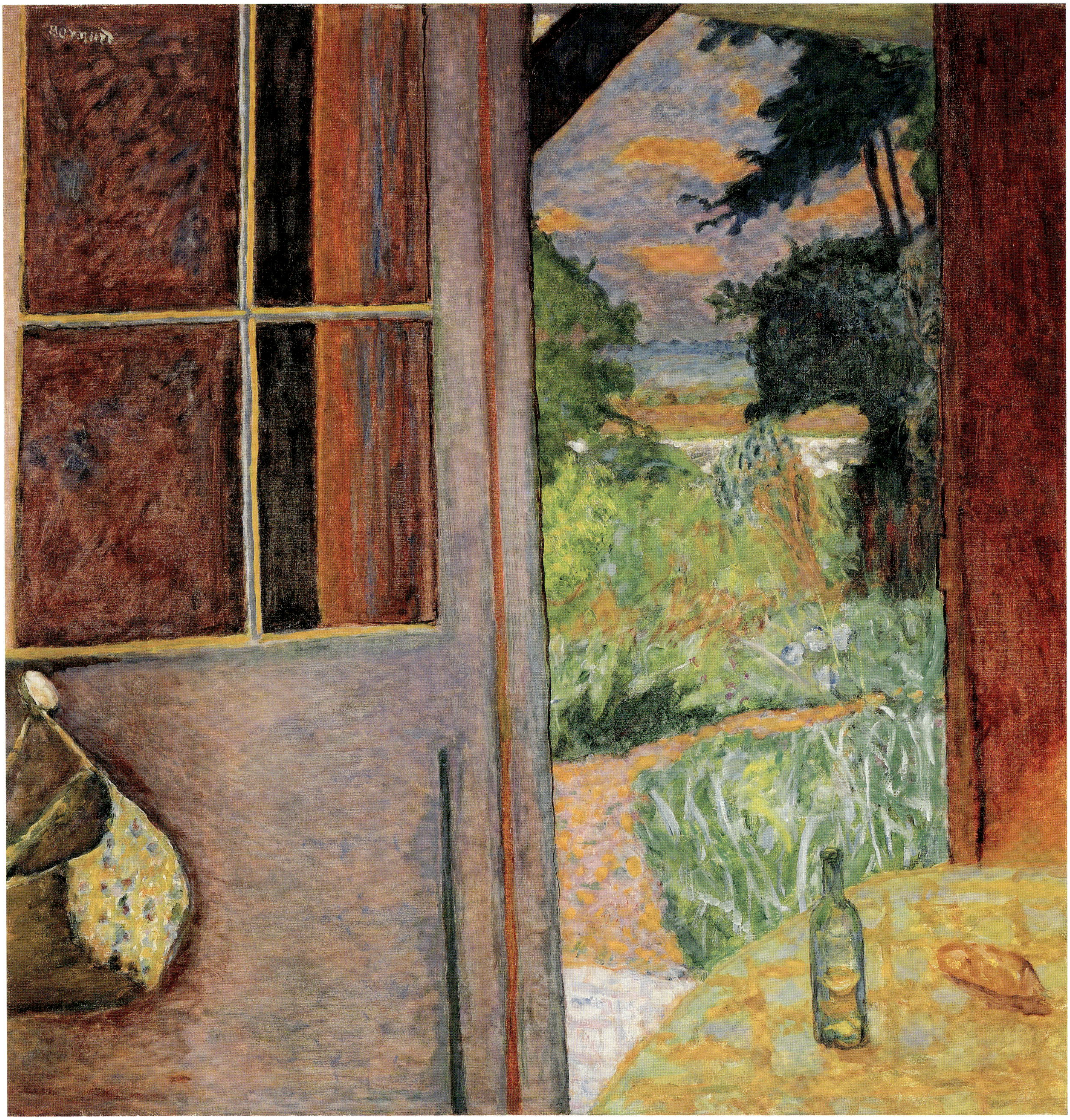

130
La Porte ouverte à Vernon. *c*.1921.
Oil on canvas, 114×112cm.
Private collection

the intensity of the light. From the evidence of his paintings he was fully aware of the complex issues involved in the representation of light. Different conventions are juxtaposed in *Intérieur avec des fleurs*: value contrast, black against white, with the contrast of complementary and adjoining hues, red against green, orange against blue, and red against orange. White and yellow are also employed as alternative signs for light. Light, in combination with colour, became a key factor in the organization of a painting. Objects are broken up by light in patterns of colour across the surface, and the dialogue between object and colour, colour and pattern, pattern and surface, surface and pictorial depth becomes part of the content of a painting. In *Le Bol de lait* the blue of the Mediterranean outside his room at Antibes is brought into the foreground of the interior in association with the ultramarine blue jug. The square shadows cast by the objects on the table join with the shapes of the table-mats to reinforce the firm geometric structure established by the window. By contrast the deep black shadows and strange, almost hypnotic concentration on form and colour in *Le Compotier* are perhaps to be accounted for by the fact that it represents a rare night scene, illuminated by electric light.[13] The band of red at the bottom balances the hot colours of the fruit and asserts the surface.

There was nothing programmatic about Bonnard's working methods and technique. Paintings begun in the memory of a visual experience encapsulated in a drawing were transformed through colour into a rich, immensely varied surface made up of a tapestry of brushstrokes, glazes, scumbles, impasto highlights and *pentimenti*. Objects were not so much painted as felt into shape within the surface over a long period. 'The principal subject', Bonnard maintained, 'is the surface, which has its colour, its laws over and above those of objects.'[14] The assertion of the surface in turn required the dispersal of attention over the whole canvas. In, for instance, *Le Bol de lait* he employed a relatively square format and balanced the striking jug of colourful peonies on the left with the presence of Marthe on the right, in order to draw attention away from the centre to what is happening on the edges. Every inch of a Bonnard became an area of discovery.[15] 'It's not a matter of painting life', Bonnard concluded, 'It's a matter of giving life to painting.'[16]

Paintings have their own momentum and developmental processes, and Bonnard was often at his strongest when the issues were most rehearsed. Without consciously setting out to work in series, he would develop themes and pictorial ideas across time. This is particularly evident in his treatment of the window motif. A window proved an infinitely flexible device. Like a painting it acts both as an opening and a barrier, a three-dimensional view and an object in its own right. It draws the spectator in, while at the same time flattening the three-dimensional within the thickness of a pane, and like a mirror it reflects what is in front of it.[17] By distancing life from function, allowing the world to be viewed aesthetically, the window in itself became a sign of the contemplative process of painting, and its ramifications went back to the very root of Bonnard's ambitions as an artist, for it enabled him to reconcile the perceptual experience of nature with the decorative surface. When taken round the Louvre by Jean Leymarie, Bonnard commented: 'In a museum, the most beautiful things are the windows.'[18]

Having established the agenda for the interior opening on to the exterior in *Salle à manger à la campagne*, 1913 (Plate 105), Bonnard developed the subject as his ideas evolved. Some eight years later, with the renewed experience of painting in the Mediterranean behind him, he returned to the same motif in *La Porte ouverte à Vernon*, *c.*1921 (Plate 130). The composition is bolder, the colours more saturated and intense. An amorphous yellow bag hangs fom the doorknob on the left to balance the bottle and yellow table-cloth on the right. A white strip outside the door is repeated in the line of the river. Strange orange clouds are suspended like barrage balloons in the sky.

Formal ideas were developed from south to north. For instance, the way the sea, seen at an angle in *Le Bol de lait* (Plate 127), fills the window, demonstrates that colour flattens form within a defined space. This enabled Bonnard to adopt a more complex view of the garden. He moved the circular table, the visual pivot, to the bottom right-hand corner and revolved the view round from the north-east towards the south to include the river, flattening the scene within the frame of the open doorway. Instead of easing the transition from the red interior to the greens of the garden through the blending of reflected lights, he enhanced and solidified the colours into a full-blooded contrast.

Colouristic ideas were similarly developed from painting to painting. An interesting innovation was the way that black became a constructional colour. The black of the chair-back in *Salle à manger à la campagne* was transformed into a solidified band of black, running parallel to the vertical glazing bar between the glass panes of the door in *La Porte ouverte à Vernon*, forming a colour composition as complete in itself as any Rothko or Barnett Newman. The potential of black as a chromatic accent, so powerful that it could compete with, and balance, a colourful motif such as a garden, was further exploited in a number of major canvases. The black of the rolled-up blind forces the eye downwards in the beautiful *La Fenêtre-ouverte*, 1921 (Plate 131), to the black cat in the right-hand corner, which is balanced by the crucial black accent on the chair on the left. Bonnard, though, always maintained a physiological rationale for his colour transformations. Seen against intense light a straw blind can look black.

In *La Table*, 1925 (Plate 133), Bonnard excluded the exterior and focused on the still-life objects and the presence of a woman eating, employing black to solve a different problem. A comparison with the preparatory drawing shows that the position of the woman was moved to the left in order to let the black door balance and enhance the white expanse of the table-cloth, creating in the process a powerful contrast which distracts attention from the colourful still-life objects. 'Make possible strong colours in the light through the proximity of black and white,' Bonnard noted in his diary entry for 4 May 1927.[19] No element was to be allowed to dominate in an expressive art of decoration. Each idea or theme, once developed, remained as a separate entity with the

131
La Fenêtre-ouverte. 1921.
Oil on canvas, 118×96cm.
The Phillips Collection, Washington DC

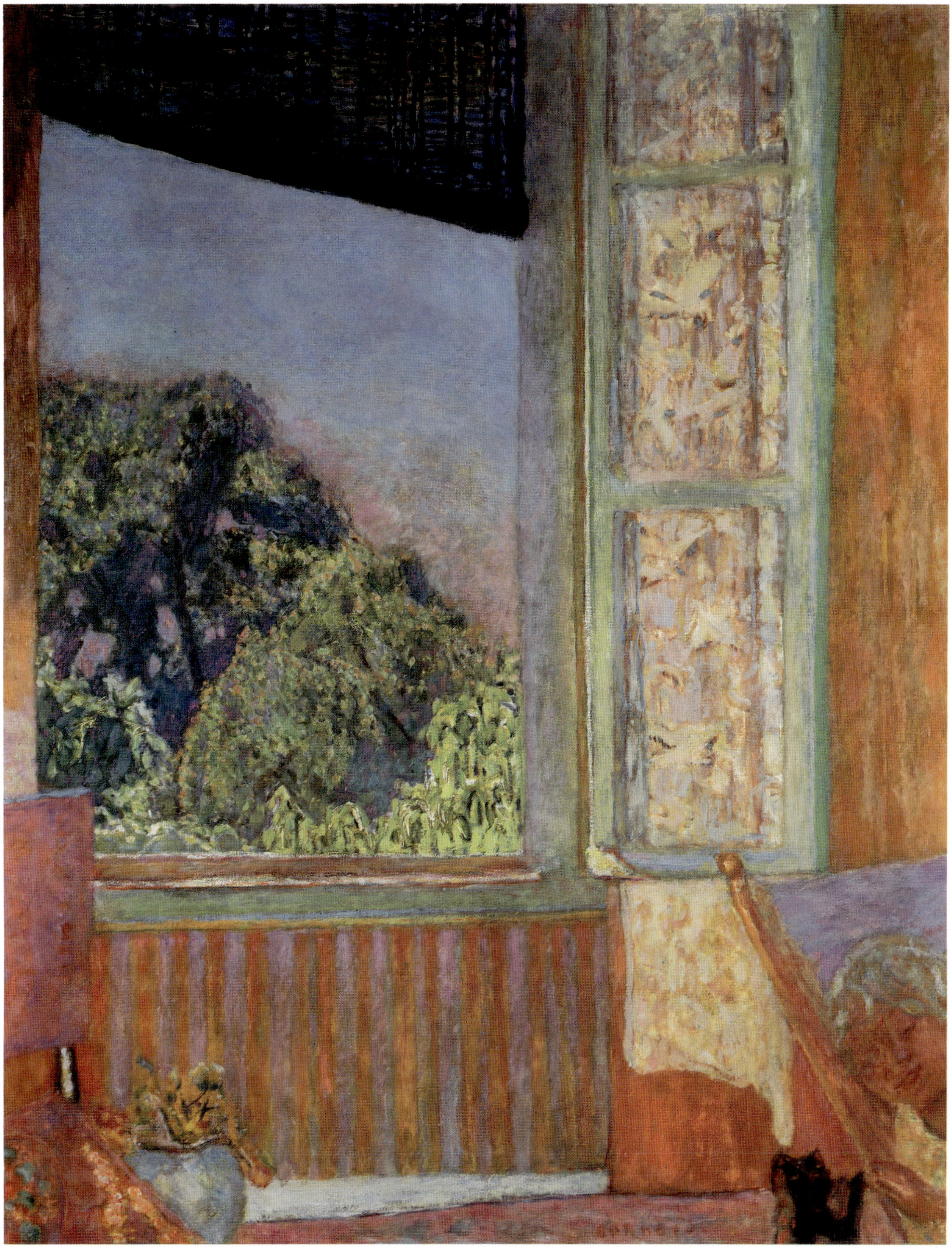

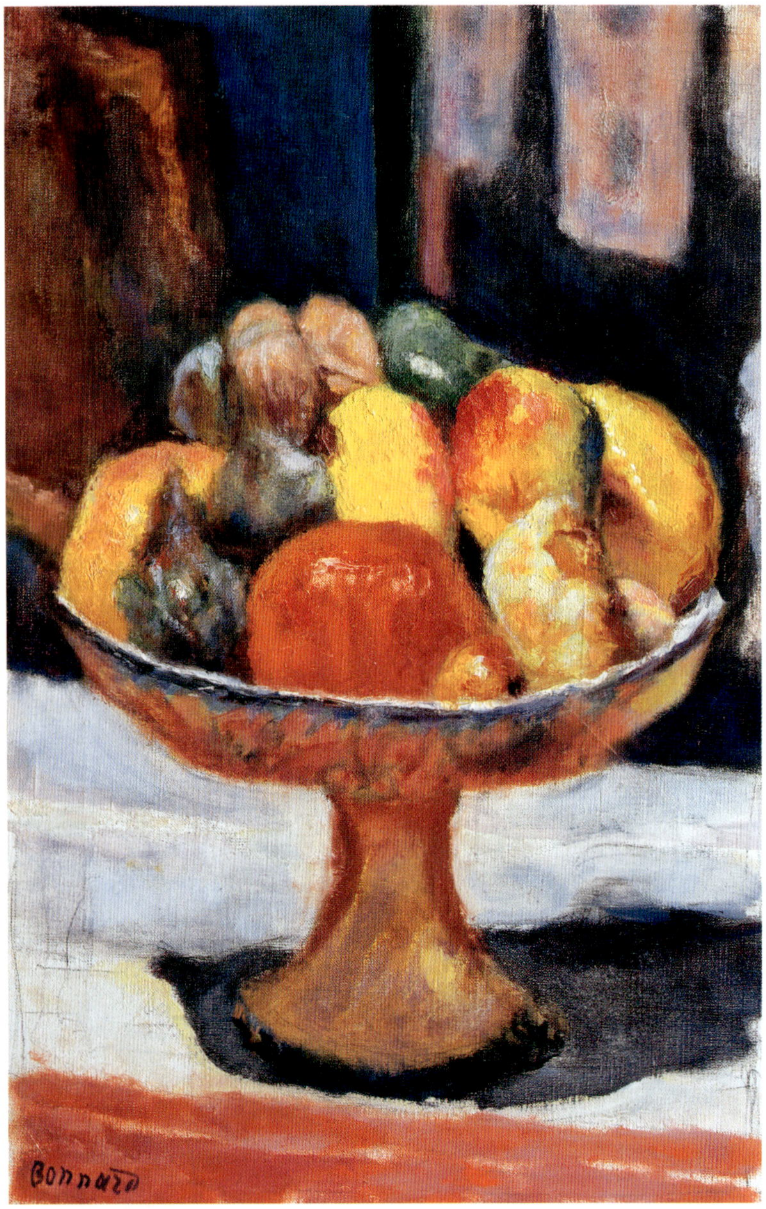

132
Le Compotier. 1924.
Oil on canvas, 74×31cm.
Private collection, Fontainebleau

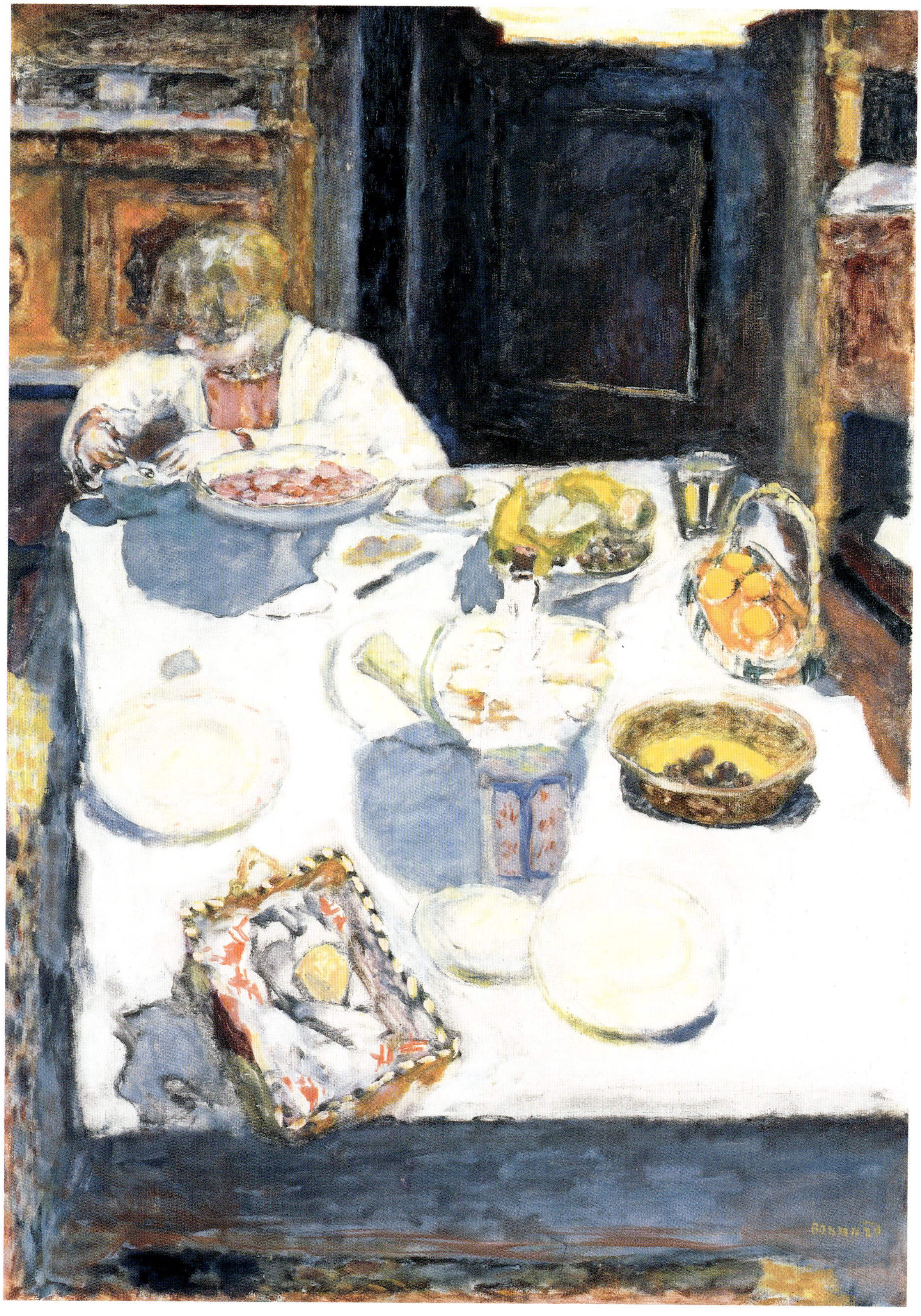

133
La Table. 1925.
Oil on canvas, 103×74.5cm.
Tate Gallery, London

potential to be rephrased in a different context. The corollary of separation was balance, a state of equilibrium or harmony which remained his ultimate goal. The extreme contrast of large planes of black and white, while undeniably dramatic, had something forced and unnatural about it, a too facile way, perhaps, of making an impressive-looking painting.

From *La Table*, Bonnard moved on to the extraordinarily ambitious problem of balancing two themes, the laden table and the window view, a combination which achieved glorious fulfilment in three major paintings, *La Salle à manger sur le jardin*, 1930–1 (Plate 134), *Salle à manger à la campagne*, 1934–5 (Plate 135), and *La Table devant la fenêtre*, 1934–5 (Plate 136). The setting for *La Salle à manger sur le jardin* was apparently a house at Arcachon where Bonnard and Marthe stayed from October 1930 to April 1931, whereas the latter two show a room in a villa at Benerville-sur-Mer which he rented from June to September 1934.[20] Although each began in the experience of a particular place, Bonnard pursued a set of pictorial issues from painting to painting: there is a definite feeling of development towards the abstract and poetic. Marthe remains in all three as a moody presence merging with the background. In *La Salle à manger sur le jardin* she stares out with unseeing eyes, cup in hand; in *Salle à manger à la campagne* she has been moved to the right of the window, leaving a phantomic form above the chair on the left; in *La Table devant la fenêtre* she exists as a partial silhouette etched into the colour of the wall.

La Salle à manger sur le jardin is the busiest and if anything the most realistic. The rigorous architectural division between the competing areas of the pale blue-and-white striped tablecloth in the interior and the view, flattened like a tapestry of yellow and green foliage in the window, is softened by the play of shadows dissolving form. A glowing orange takes over from deep red as the colour of interior warmth, establishing in the process the play between red and orange that runs as a chromatic theme through all three compositions. Orange cuts off the corner of the table in *Salle à manger à la campagne*, balancing the expansion of broad planes of colour, which find their own dimensions within the contours of form. The table is bathed in a final flush of pink before being overtaken by the blue shadows of evening, which bring the colour of the sea and sky into the interior. Finally, in *La Table devant la fenêtre* the orange glow of the setting sun has drained the interior of colour, leaving electrifying lines of red running down the surface. The central chair and window jamb form a blackened cross holding out symbolically against the departing light.

Bonnard's lifelong obsession with the subject of the female nude had been given fresh impetus by the 'return to order'. Inspired by Degas and Renoir he changed Marthe from a bird-like waif into a classical bather. The bather theme gave Bonnard the opportunity to move back from the classical sculptures in his decorative panel *Méditerranée*, 1916–20, into life. Marble was turned into flesh and a cold little bathroom into a glorious light-filled chamber. According to Charles Terrasse, whereas Bonnard had previously painted a movement, even an atmosphere, he now painted a body. [21] Marthe's

134
La Salle à manger sur le jardin. 1930–1.
Oil on canvas, 159.6×113.8cm.
Museum of Modern Art, New York

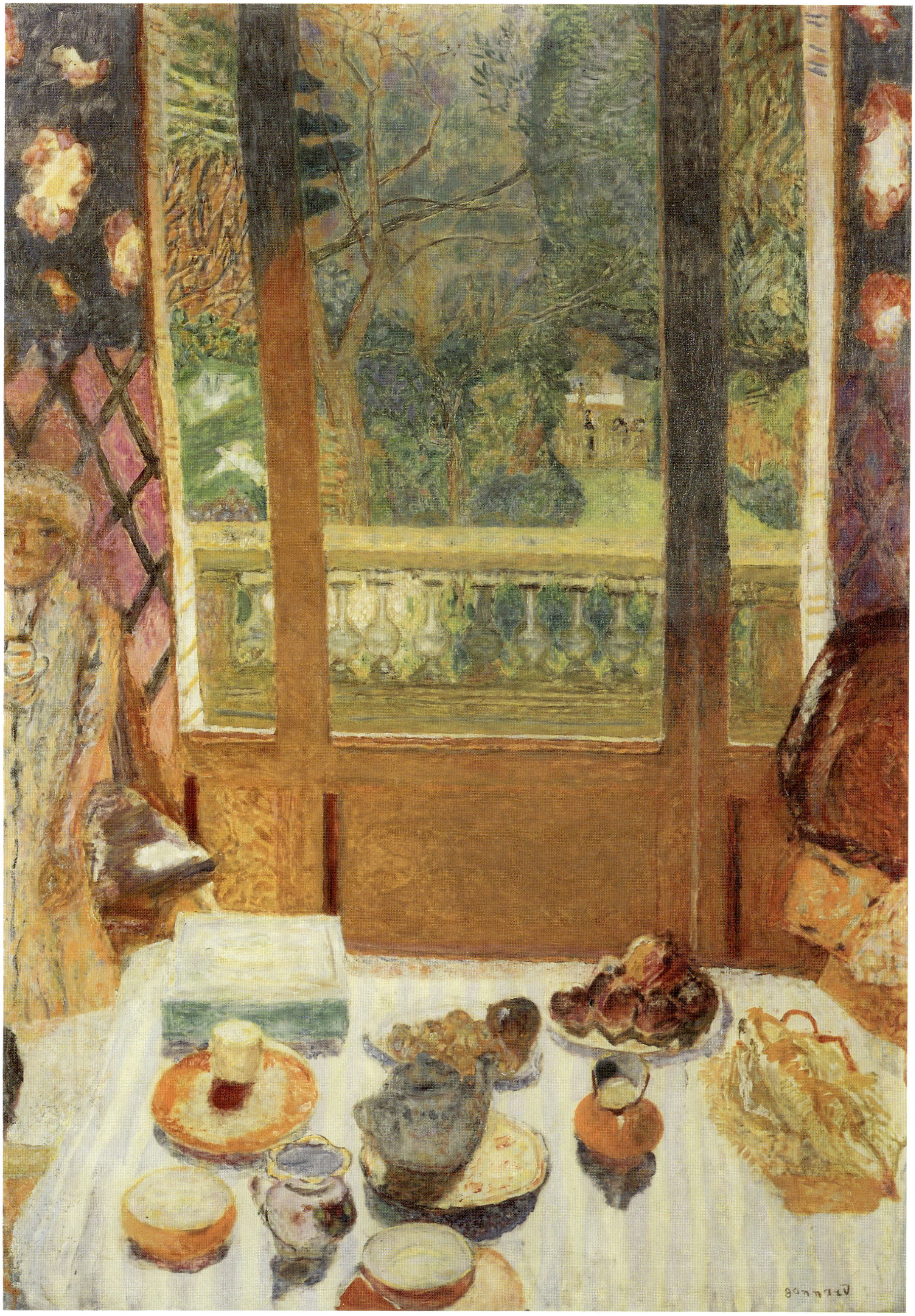

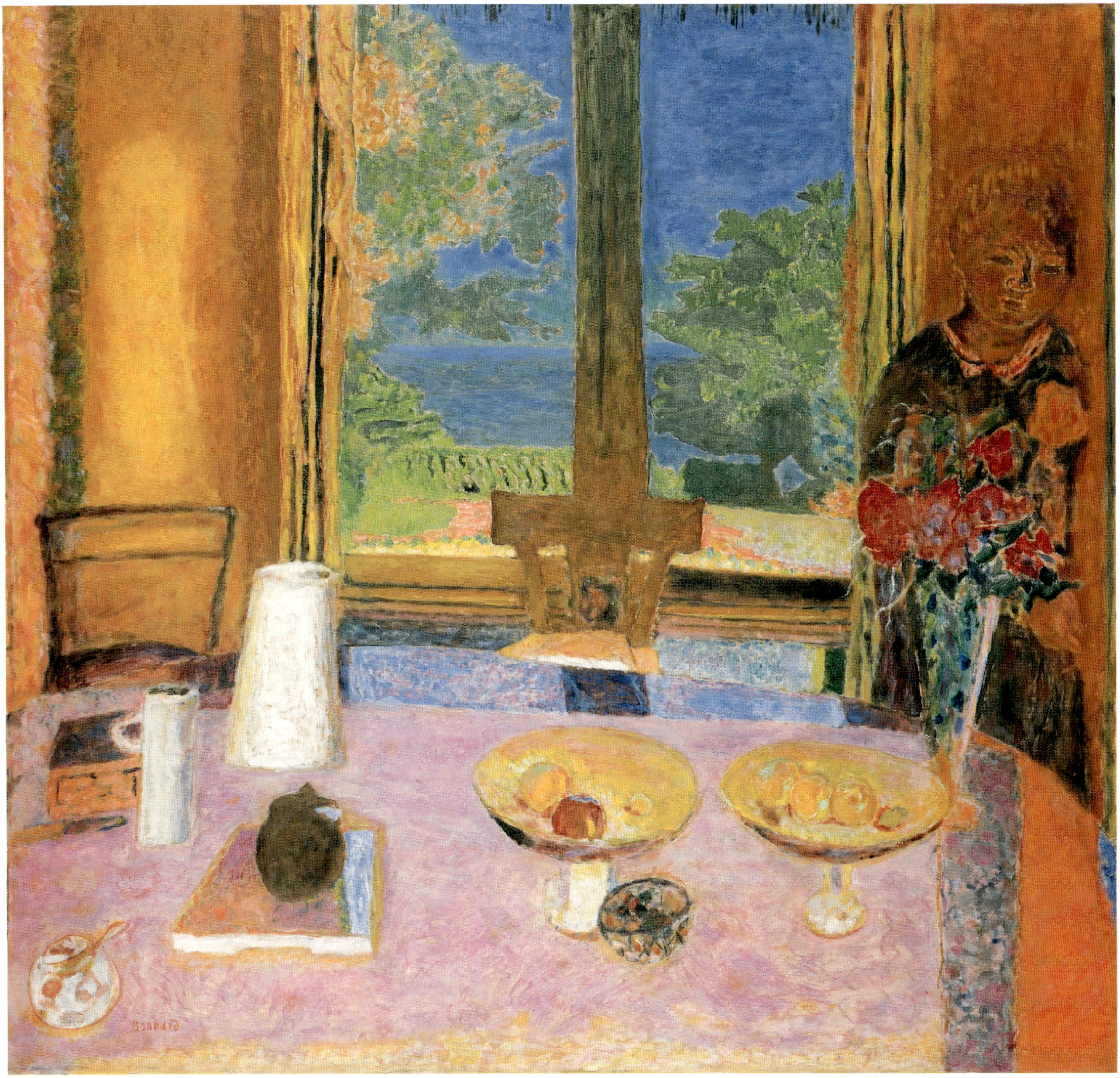

135
Salle à manger à la campagne. 1934–5.
Oil on canvas, 127×135cm.
Solomon R. Guggenheim Foundation, New York

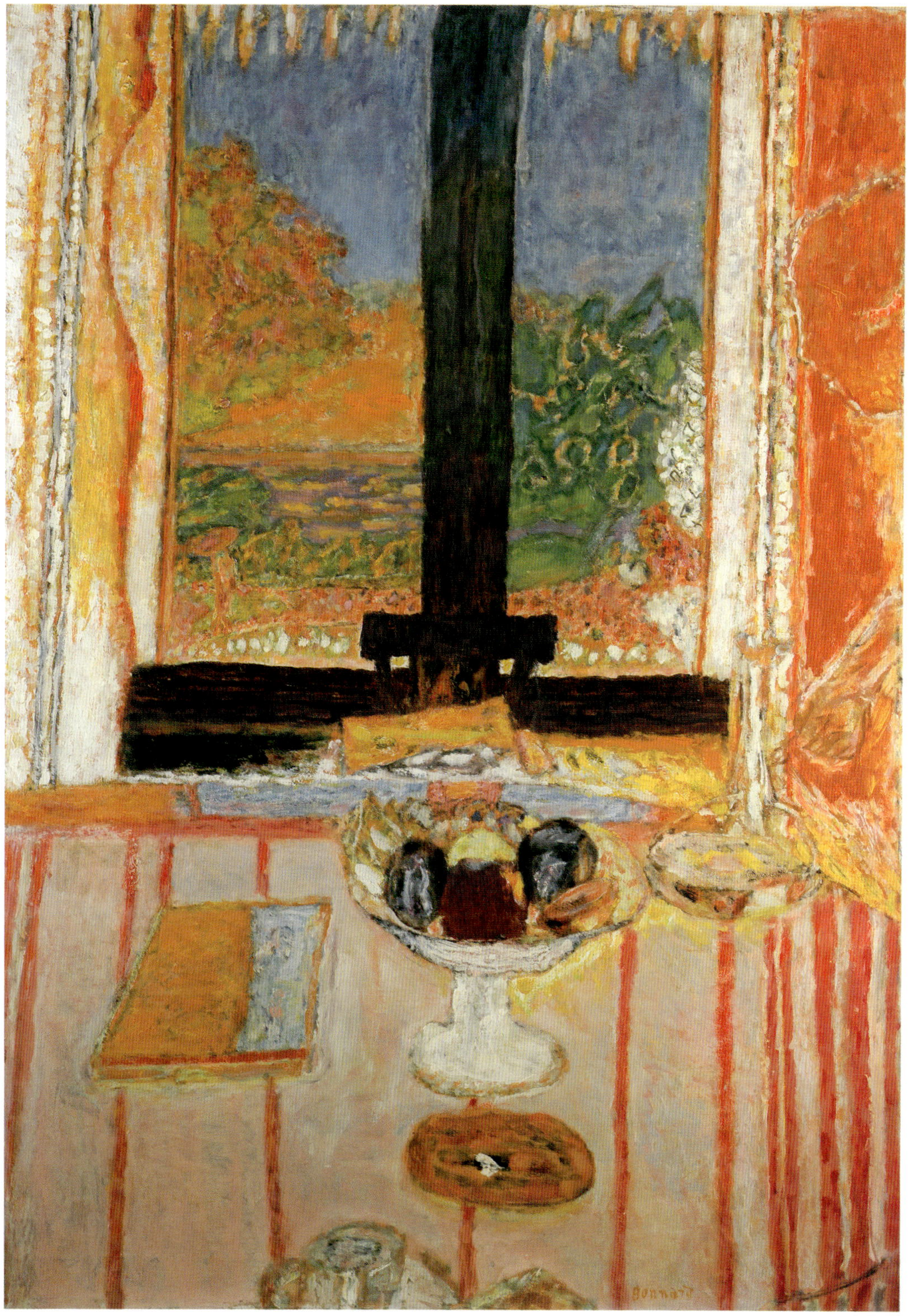

136
La Table devant la fenêtre. 1934–5.
Oil on canvas, 101.5×72.5cm.
Private collection, New York

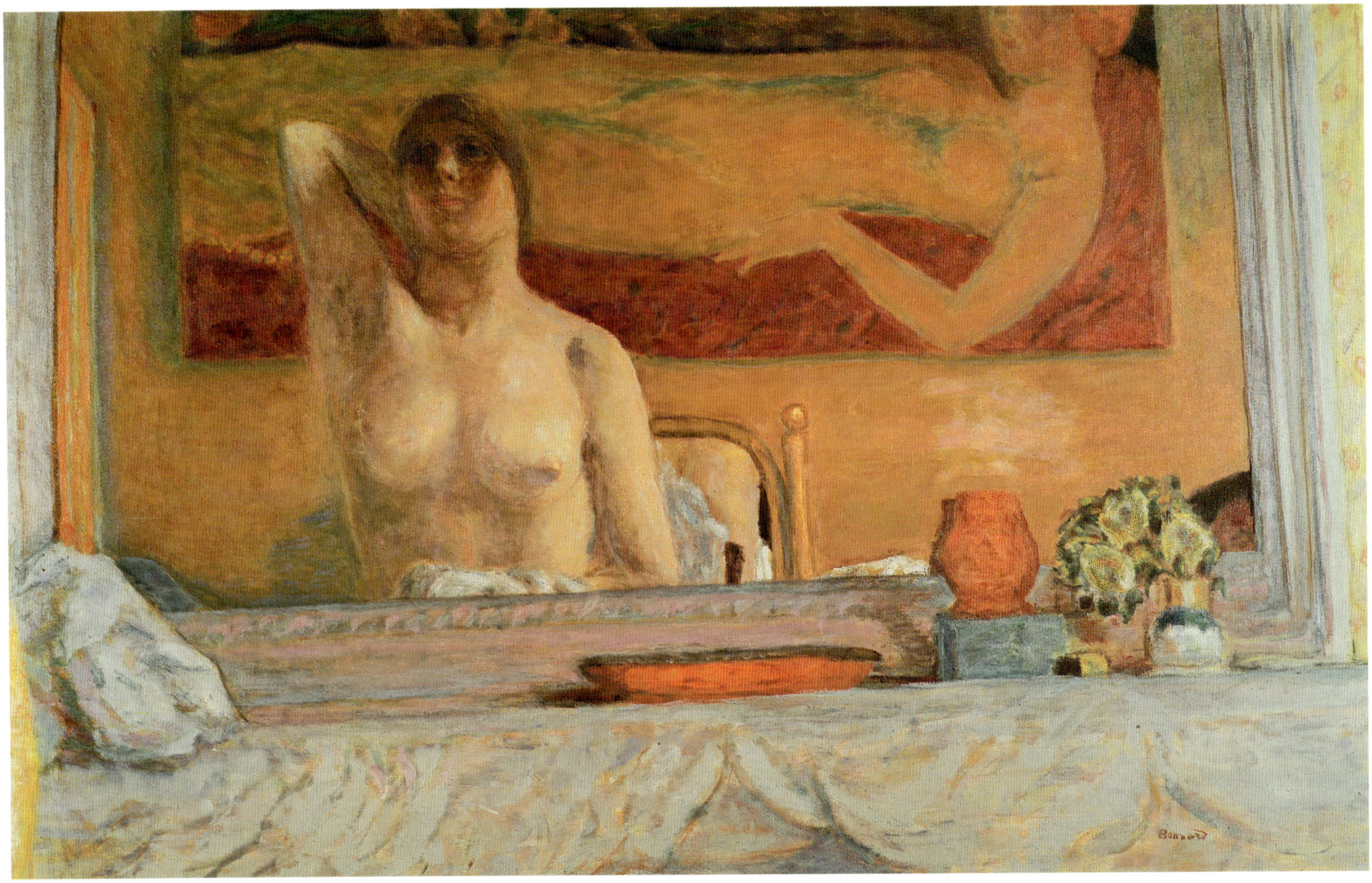

137
La Cheminée. 1916.
Oil on canvas, 81×111cm.
Private collection

body was amplified into smooth, rounded forms, her face assumed a vacant expression. A sign of sensuality, rather than sex, her body became volume material, a reflectant surface to be balanced within the confines of a picture. By contrast with his landscape practice, Bonnard idealized his nudes to the point where it is difficult to recognize the models. In the mid-1920s, to save money, he shared a model, a buxom blond called Marinette, with his friend Henri Lebasque(1865–1937) who had moved to Le Cannet, but, according to Mme Lebasque-Reymond, he found her too heavy and curvaceous to work with and preferred to paint his slim wife.[22]

Classicism in itself did not connote a distinct style. The flat colour and line, favoured by Puvis de Chavannes and Gauguin, whom Bonnard regarded as a classical artist, contrasted with the solid volumes of nudes by Cézanne, Renoir and Maillol. Bonnard had made different ways of picturing the nude the subject of his seminal painting *La Cheminée*, 1916 (Plate 137). Filtered through a system of two mirrors, a more naturalistic depiction of Marthe in the nude, seen in a preliminary version, becomes a statuesque figure based on the *Dying Niobid*, *c.*450–440 BC, juxtaposed with the painting-within-a-painting in the background, the flattened, attenuated nude by Maurice Denis which Bonnard owned.[23]

Irrespective of his artistic sources, Bonnard still needed to give his figures the semblance of life. Through Degas, who had shown him how a domestic routine such as Marthe's washing could be turned into art, he had achieved his maturity as a painter in 1908 and it was to Degas again that he turned for inspiration in his new sequence of bathers. In *Femme nue se baissant*, 1923 (Plate 138), he combined the nude bather with another of Degas's favourite subjects, the ballet dancer (Plate 89). The simple act of drying a limb is disciplined in a structural balletic pose, reminiscent of the fourth position in ballet, with the weight on one leg and the other crossed over. However, the ultimate source was life rather than art. The pose evolved from quick sketches of Marthe in the bathroom which were transformed in the studio into a monumental nude placed within a carefully constructed setting.[24] The square format compresses and concentrates attention on the figure. The emphatic vertical axis of her left leg, raised from the floor on a high-heeled shoe, is complemented by the vertical edge of the frame to the right, connected and countered by the right leg being pulled across it on the diagonal. Within the muted overall colour scheme of pale violet, with the red-brown floor glazed in purple, the chromatic accent of the yellow chair seat on the right, draped with discarded clothing, is balanced on the left by a little table with tea set out on a white cloth. The geometric divisions of the background panels suggest either doors, dado or French windows.

As he entered his fifties, like Degas before him, Bonnard became increasingly conscious of the central place of the nude within the great tradition of European art. By contrast with his Vernon landscapes in the 1920s, which became ever more concerned with capturing the most transient of effects, his nudes became more monumental. The mobility of his motifs and peripatetic life-style was mirrored by a mobility of vision within the confines of the bathroom he had built for Marthe at Ma Roulotte, along with his garage. The frozen sequences of Marthe's daily routine in the bathroom were observed with the classical detachment of Degas and structured in an outstanding series of bather compositions; the transient was made monumental and eternal, the movements of life were accommodated within the geometry of art.

Marthe can be seen crouching at the end of the bath, stretched out in the water, standing up, reaching for a towel, bending over, drying or washing in a variety of poses which might be changed between drawings, paintings and prints. The pose in *Nu rose à la baignoire*, *c.*1924 (Plate 142), evolved from a series of drawings (see Plate 141) in which Marthe gradually raised herself from the bath to form with her limbs a square, with her left foot drawn back to the right knee to introduce the diagonal. *Le Bain*, *c.*1925 (Plate 144), was commissioned by the publisher Edmond Frapier for an album of original lithographs from Manet to Matisse, published to revive interest in the medium.[25]

Bonnard was by no means isolated in his structural treatment of the nude. His use of the tiled wall in *Le Bain* as a compositional grid was adopted some four years later by Matisse in *Le Grand Nu gris*, 1929 (Plate 143), and the mutual exchanges between the two artists became a feature of their art in the 1920s. The distinction between the two paintings, though subtle, is crucial. Whereas Matisse was increasingly materializing colour to emphasize shape, Bonnard would employ colour in combination with reflected light to counteract a rigid pose and integrate the figure with the background, while at the same time, in a more complex form of realism, bringing in information from outside the immediate visual field. This is readily apparent in the way the side of the bath is so brushed in green as to suggest Marthe's body refracted in the water inside it. For Bonnard light held a transforming power, which Matisse tended to identify with the Impressionism that he had reacted against.

Bonnard habitually rephrased poses from painting to painting to give radically novel readings. The bending-over pose of for instance *Nu, jambe droite levée*, 1924 (Plate 140), cropped within the visual field, had enjoyed a long pedigree in his art, from his earliest Nabis days (see Plate 25) to the first nudes of his maturity (see Plate 85). Sargy Mann has pointed out how in the transition from the preliminary drawing (Plate 139) for *Nu, jambe droite levée* to the final painting a box was introduced into the bottom right-hand corner to flatten and extend the visual field. 'The practice of cropping the visual field almost always gives something which does not seem true', Bonnard explained. 'Composition at the second stage consists of bringing back certain elements which lie outside the rectangle.'[26] The right leg of the nude, bathed in blue shadow, merges with the background and the box, split between red and pale violet, both balances the figure and makes it read as an arch, dramatically continued on the left down the leg of the stool covered in the red towel. By contrast, in *Le Grand Nu bleu*, 1924 (Plate 147), the same pose is at first glance barely recognizable. The nude is perceived as through the haze of a steamed-up mirror, with a *repoussoir* leg left in the bottom left-hand corner. Air appears above her head and the format is enlarged and changed from the square to

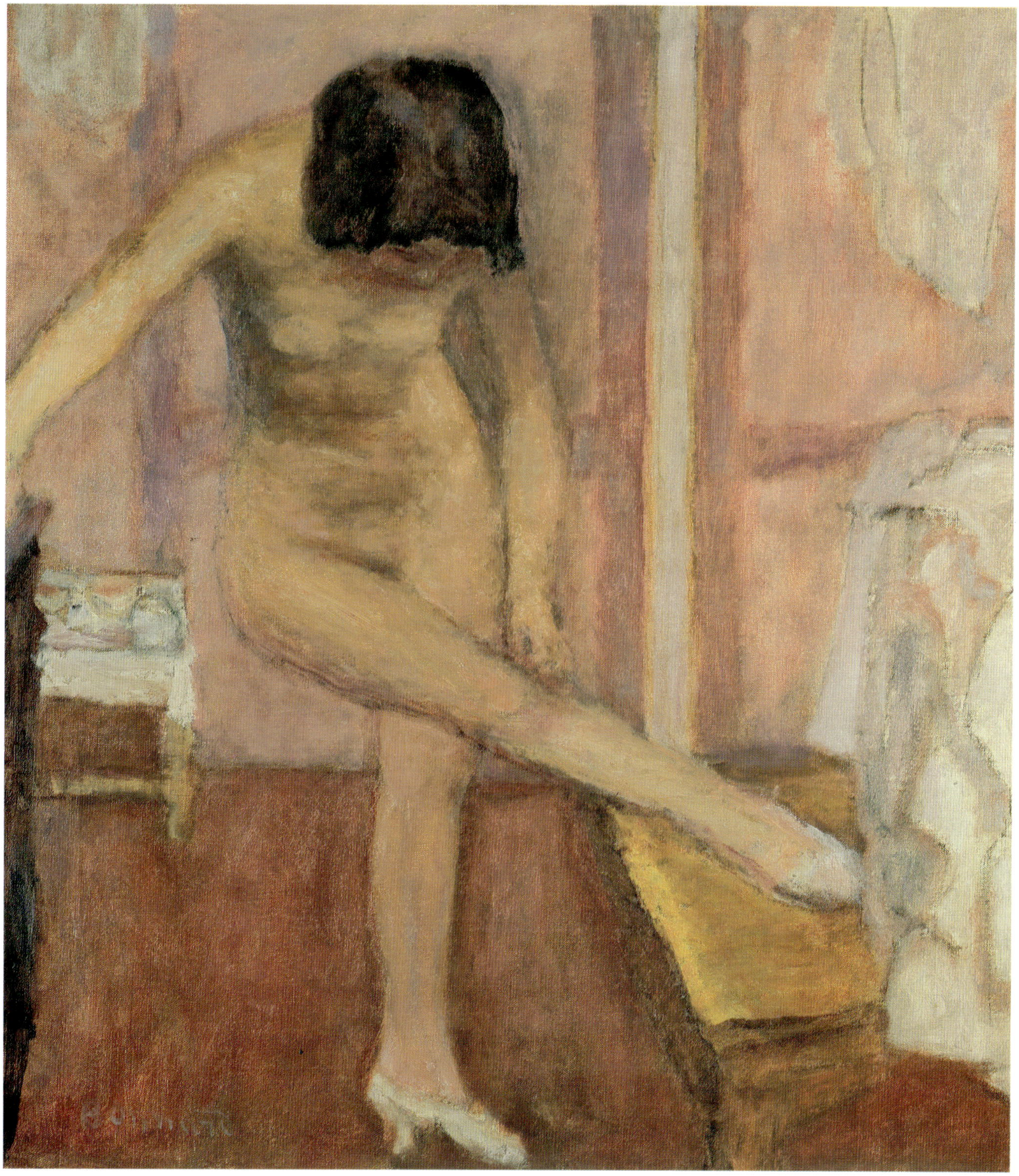

138
Femme nue se baissant. 1923.
Oil on canvas, 57.1×52.7cm.
Tate Gallery, London

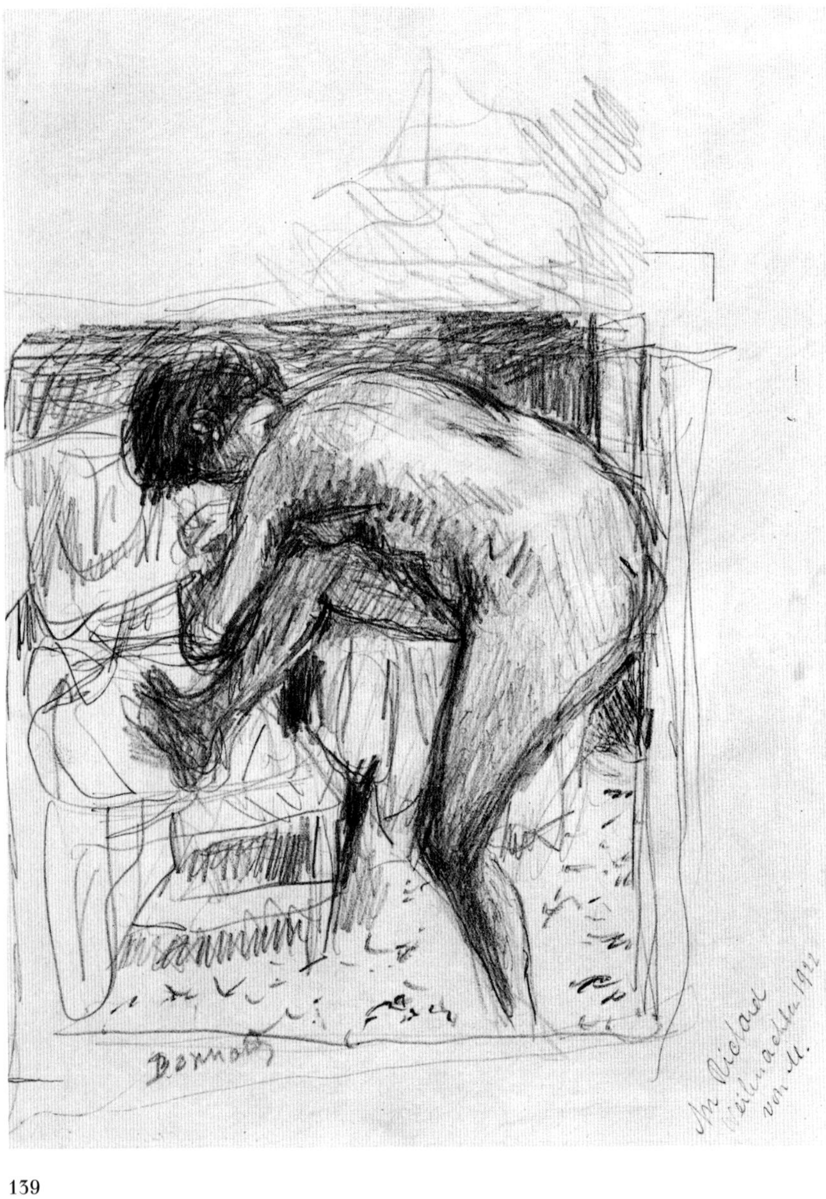

139
*Nu au bain. c.*1920.
Pencil on paper, 25×17.5cm.
Private collection

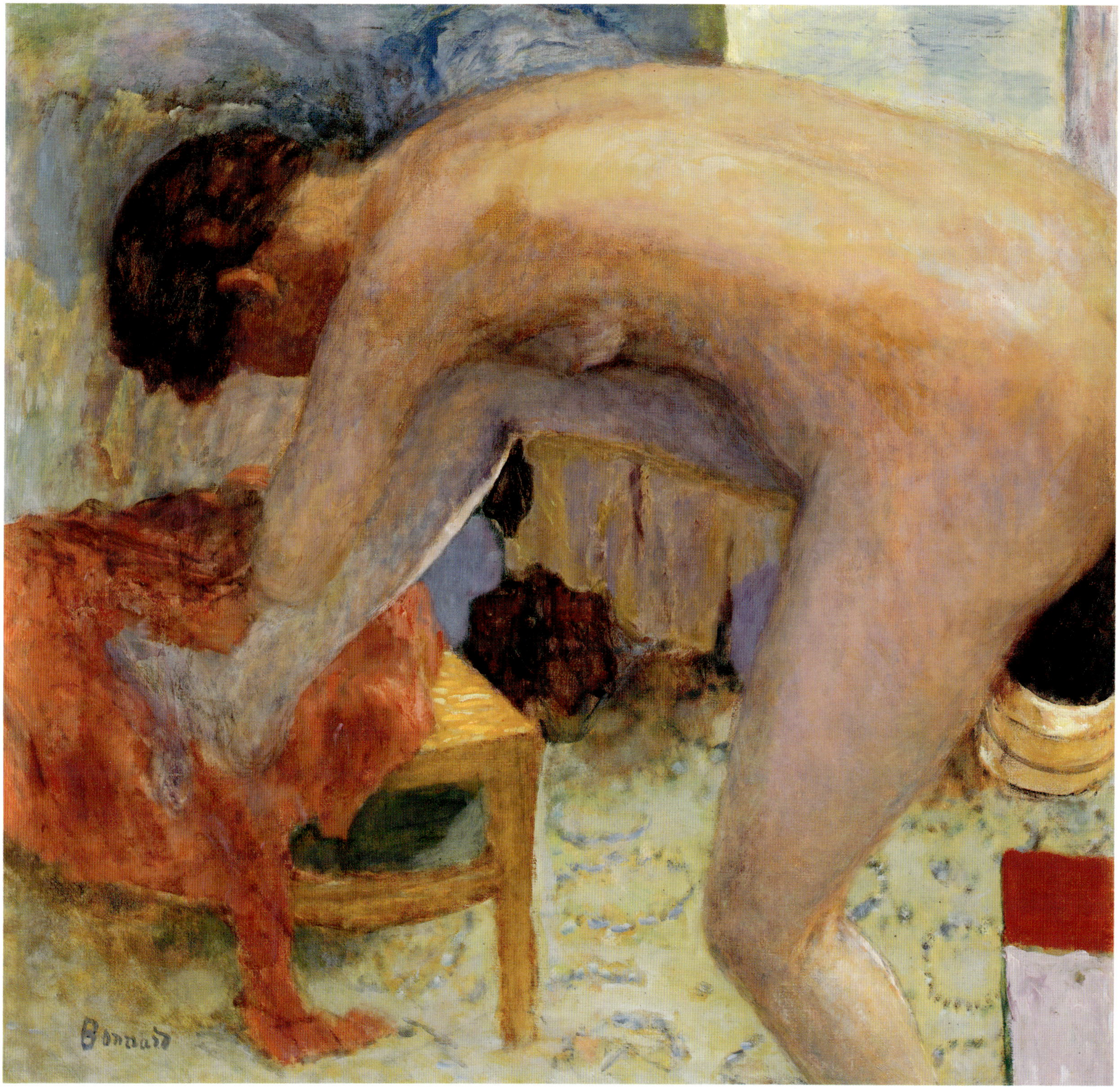

140
Nu, jambe droite levée. 1924.
Oil on canvas, 74×78cm.
Private collection

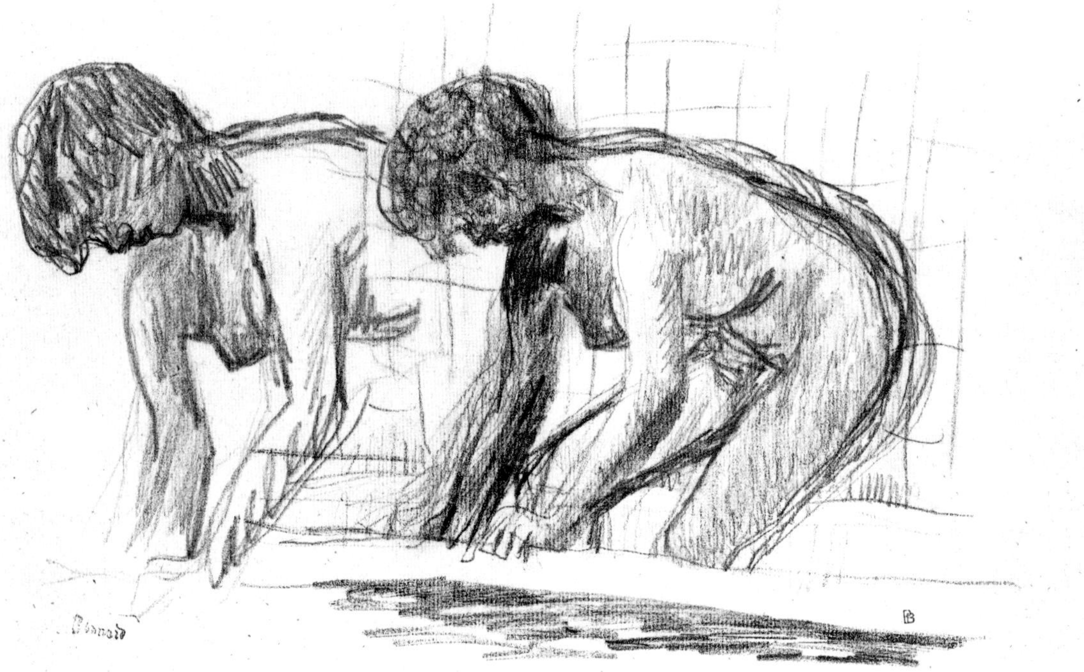

141
*Étude pour 'Nu rose à la baignoire'. c.*1924.
Pencil on paper, 24.8×32.8cm.
Private collection

the horizontal, to make the nude read as part of the overall surface pattern of the painting, as in a Japanese screen. In other words, the decorative ideal of his Nabis days was rephrased in terms of an emotive atmosphere derived from Impressionism within the loose parameters of the classical tradition.

Bonnard's concern for structure was taken to an extreme in *Le Bain*, 1925 (Plate 150). Marthe is stretched out like a corpse in the stillness of a watery grave, a modern Ophelia of the bathroom whose life-blood has drained away, leaving a crimson stain below the outside rim of the bath. Uncompromisingly rigid and anaemic in colour, it is a cold painting that speaks of uncomfortable events, troubled dreams and blighted hopes, the very tensions out of which paintings are often made, but the kind of things few artists would be foolish enough to talk about. It is difficult not to link the painting with the suicide of Bonnard's lover, Renée Monchaty, in Rome in 1923.[27] He had painted both the women in his life at the time together in *Jeunes femmes au jardin*, 1921–3 and 1945–6 (Plate 149). Marthe is the jealous presence in the bottom right-hand corner, eyeing Renée across the divide of the back of the wickerwork chair. Bonnard touchingly reworked the painting after Marthe's death in 1942, boldly surrounding Renée in a golden glow, an ultimate sign of nostalgia.[28] *Le Bain*, which began in death, ended up by giving life to a series of the most original compositions in Bonnard's career (see Plates 148, 162). Without loosing touch with either form or life, his bathers, like Renoir's late nudes, were absorbed in a tapestry of light.

Observers close to Bonnard repeatedly drew attention to his liking for the aged Renoir, whom he used to visit at his home, Les Colettes at Cagnes near Nice. Despite being crippled by arthritis and confined to a wheelchair, Renoir managed to keep working and maintain faith in art right up to his death on 17 December 1919. After the

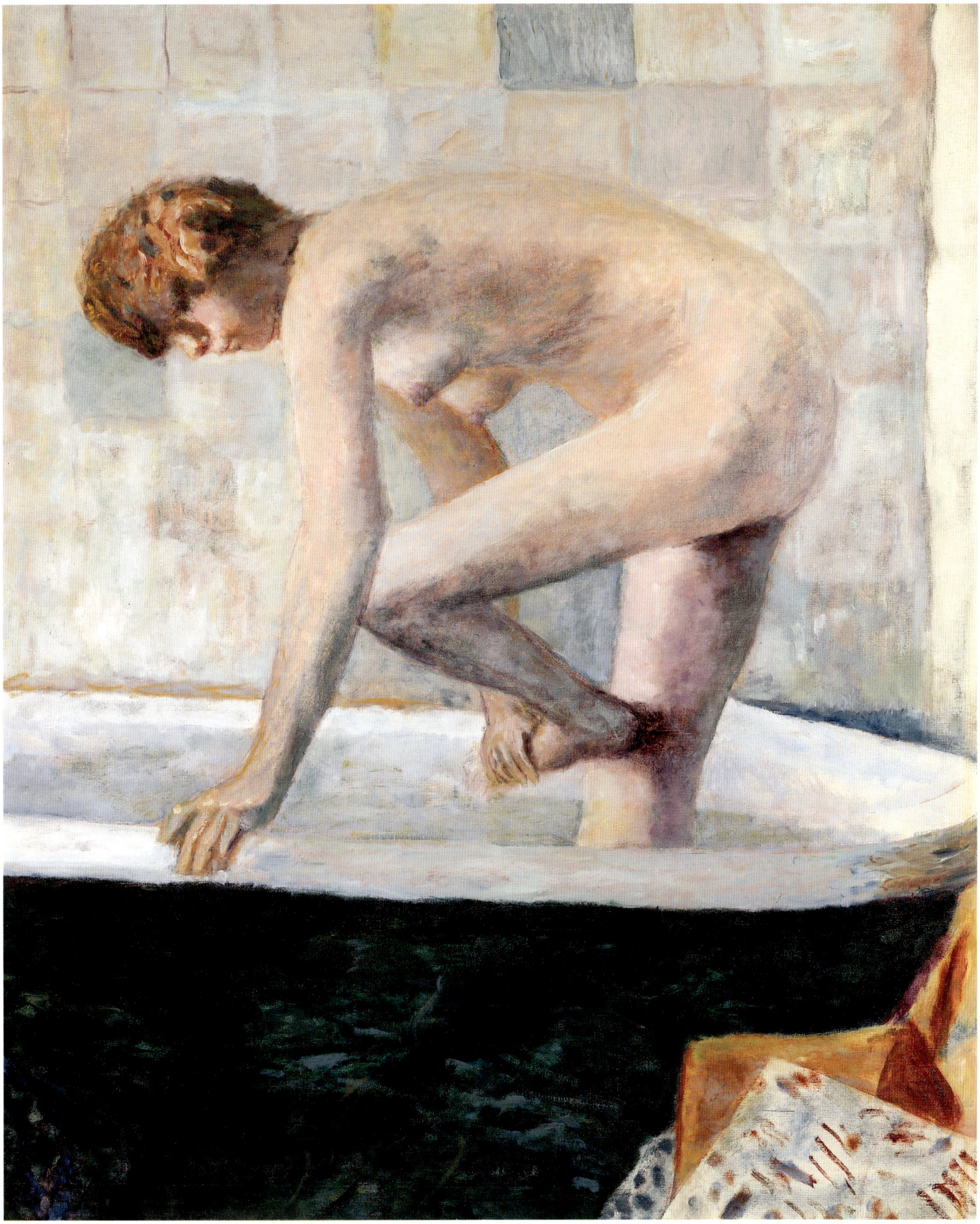

142
Nu rose à la baignoire. c.1924.
Oil on canvas, 106×96cm.
Private collection

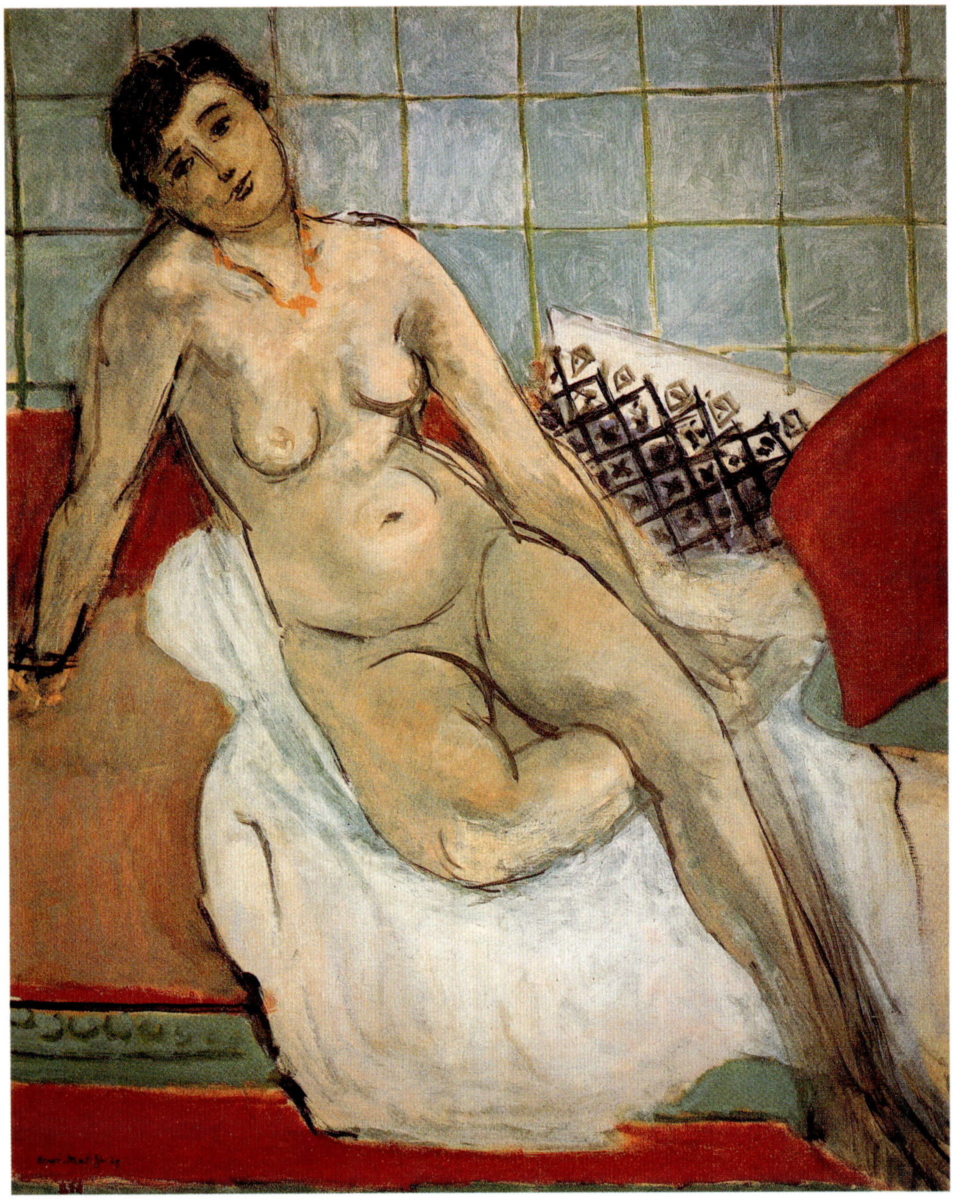

143
Henri Matisse
Le Grand Nu gris. 1929.
Oil on canvas, 102×81cm.
Private collection, New York

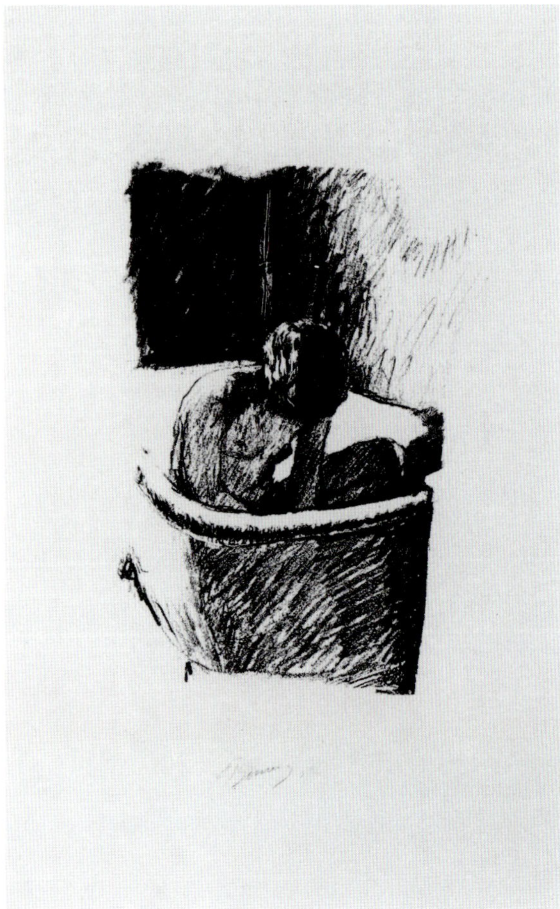

144
Le Bain (deuxième planche). *c*.1925.
Lithograph, in black, 33×22.5cm

traumas of the First World War, his last paintings, when exhibited posthumously at the Salon d'Automne of 1920, provided an antidote for the times, a lost world of remembered innocence in which nature – including human nature – was there to be loved and enjoyed. Bonnard hung colour lithographs by Renoir in Le Bosquet and, according to Thadée Natanson, the little nude that Renoir gave him was his most precious possession.[29] His influence on Bonnard went beyond questions of style, for he provided the example of a contemporary painter who had taken on the French classical tradition and made it his own. A Renoir is always a Renoir. He fused the classical with Impressionism in a glorious light-filled vision of the Mediterranean as a landscape of the Golden Age, in which nudes, his principal subject, were integrated with their settings in a painterly tradition stemming from Titian, Veronese, Rubens, Watteau and the French eighteenth century. The amplitude and ease of a Renoir, of humanity at one with itself and with nature, was something to which Bonnard aspired. In the spirit of Renoir he painted *Le Grand Nu étendu*, 1927 (Plate 146), as a classical Mediterranean goddess bathed in golden light. Preliminary drawings (Plate 145) show that it began as a nude in an interior and then was placed in a landscape setting based on Le Cannet. In an interview in *Comoedia*, published on 18 October 1942, Bonnard recalled Renoir's injunction 'one must embellish' and concluded by saying: 'I considered Renoir like a slightly severe father.'[30] His response to Renoir's advice to embellish was to exaggerate and enhance to the point where the pictorial elements became active participants in the drama of a picture. 'Represent nature when it is beautiful', Bonnard wrote in his diary entry for 16 February 1932. 'Everything has its moment of beauty. Beauty is the satisfaction of sight. Sight is satisfied by simplicity and order. Simplicity and order are produced by the legible divisions of surfaces, the groupings of sympathetic colours, etc.'[31]

Like Renoir, Bonnard ended up by creating the necessary conditions in the south out of which his art could grow. After renting villas, he finally bought on 27 February 1926 a two-storied house on the hill at Le Cannet, which he christened Le Bosquet.[32] With its pitched roof and little wooden balcony, it reminded contemporaries of a type of modest chalet built by speculators for the retired.[33] He and Marthe moved in a year later after essential alterations had been carried out. His additions were significant: a bathroom, a studio and a garage, excavated into the hill at the bottom of the garden. The two rooms on the ground floor were knocked into one and French windows were put in on both floors to open the interior on to the garden, which was enlarged by the acquisition of the adjoining land. After over twenty years of neglect, following Bonnard's death in 1947, and a protracted lawsuit, the house was finally bought back by his rightful heirs, the Terrasses, faithfully restored and eventually protected as a *Monument historique*. Bonnard's great-nephew, the painter Michel Terrasse, who has published a moving account of his great-uncle's work in the house, continues to live there with his wife.[34]

Le Bosquet provided Bonnard with subject-matter for the rest of his life. Visiting it is

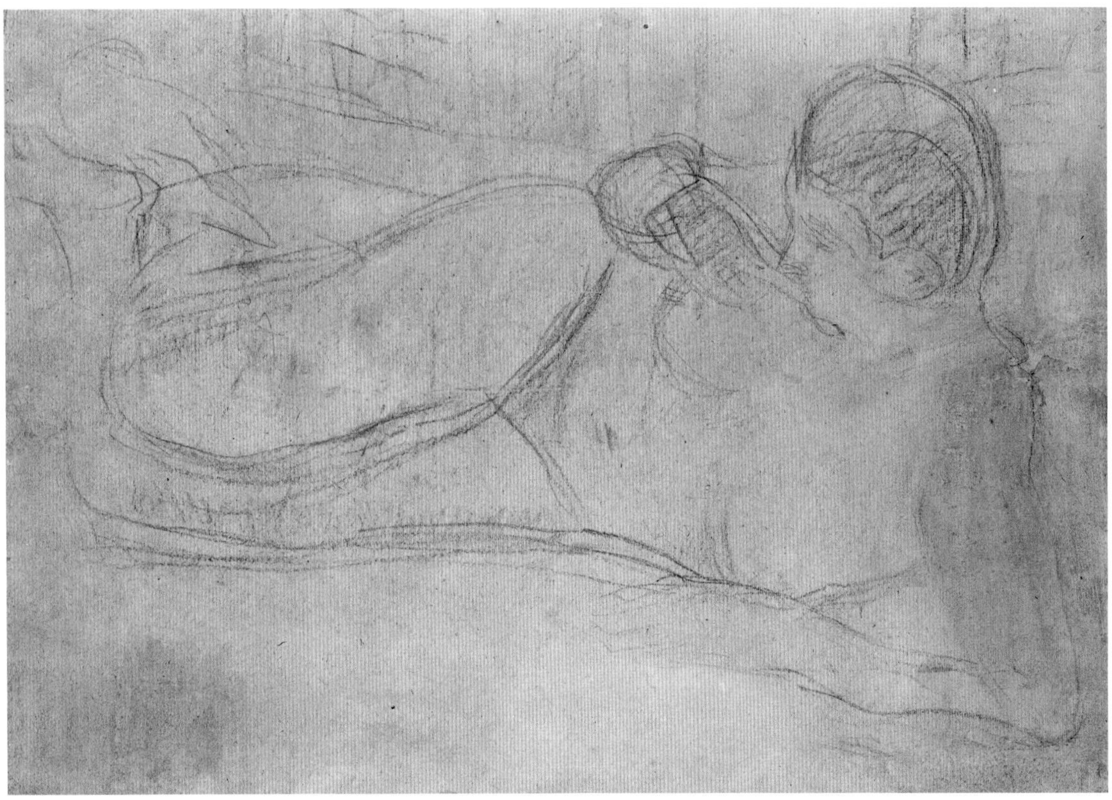

145
Étude pour 'Le Grand Nu étendu'. *c*.1927.
Charcoal on paper, 39.3×54.3cm.
Private collection

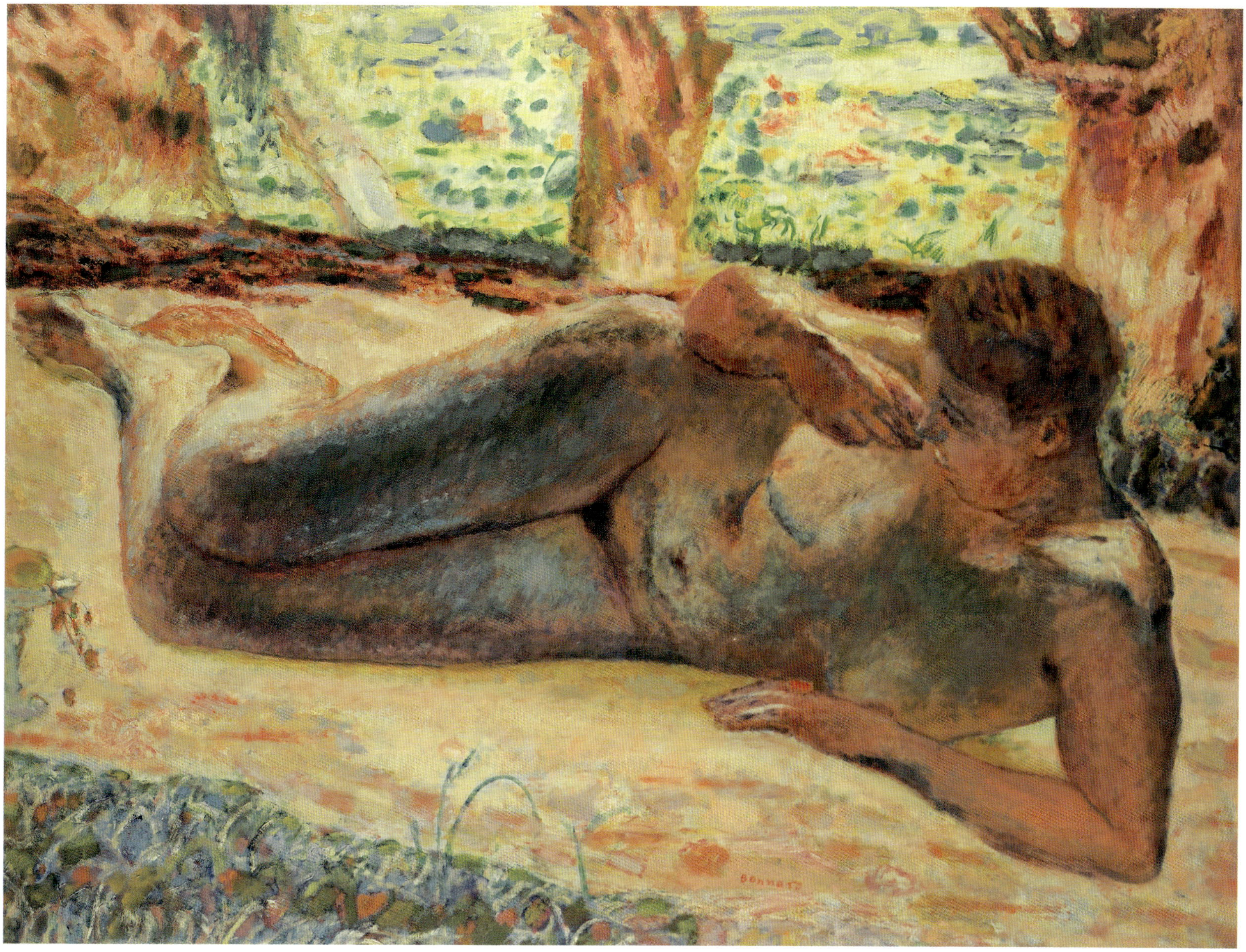

146
Le Grand Nu étendu. 1927.
Oil on canvas, 142×181cm.
Private collection

like stepping into one of his paintings. Everything is still there: the pale yellow dining room with the interior of the glass-fronted cupboard painted in red; the small sitting room on the first floor, where Bonnard and Marthe had breakfast, opening to the bathroom on the south side and the view of Le Cannet and the mountains of the Esterel framed by the French windows on the west; the bathroom itself, with the great bath wallowing like a hippopotamus with tiny patterned feet; and the studio with the raised balcony and walls, Bonnard's easel, pock-marked from tacks holding up unstretched canvases. Of some 115 paintings featuring the interior of Le Bosquet, 59 show the dining room, one the kitchen, one the staircase, 21 the small sitting room, 15 the bathroom, six his bedroom, one the spare bedroom and 11 the studio.[35] Marthe's bedroom was the only room he never painted.

Photographs do little to convey the experience of Le Bosquet as pictured in Bonnard's paintings. Wide-angled lenses, while giving the often extraordinarily wide field of vision encompassed in a single painting, tend to distance the subject, making it feel remote. While remaining faithful to the starting point of a painting in a particular experience, Bonnard would spread the confined space of a room across the surface, drawing the spectator into the painting. Rectangular units within the composition act as mirrors, doors, windows, paintings within paintings, or simply reflectant surfaces, enlarging and adding further dimensions to the space. A multiplicity of 'openings' are suggested and then closed off, returning the eye to the surface. With the lowering in price of large sheets of mirror glass in the mid-nineteenth century, the enlargement of small Parisian café premises with mirrors became a matter of everday public experience.[36] Bonnard was the first painter to extend the concept of 'mirror space' to the construction of a whole painting. The darkened intimist interior of his beginnings in the 1890s was opened up to the breadth and light of the southern landscape. Interior surfaces assumed the luminous qualities of the sea and sky united by light in a phosphorescent glow.

Familiarity became a prerequisite for aesthetic progress. Like Monet's waterlily pond at Giverny, Le Bosquet encapsulated the raw material for the experience Bonnard wanted to achieve in paint. The architecture supplied the essential disciplining structure for his compositions, and he got to know the rooms so well that he was able to rephrase them in terms of an increasingly ambitious set of plastic problems. As well as taking the memory of Le Bosquet with him when he went back to the north, he travelled with the actual canvases he was working on. In a celebrated photograph of Bonnard's room at Deauville in 1937, *Nu à la baignoire*, 1936 (Plate 148), based on the bathroom at Le Bosquet, can be seen tacked to the disconcertingly busy floral wallpaper. When asked if the wallpaper distracted him, Bonnard replied: 'Not at all. It probably would if it was one colour, but as it is the colours neutralize each other.'[37]

In his complex painterly process Bonnard placed the initial emphasis on drawing, stating: 'The whole pictorial effect ought to be conveyed by equivalents in drawing. Before adding colour, one must look at things once or a thousand times'. [38] In the course

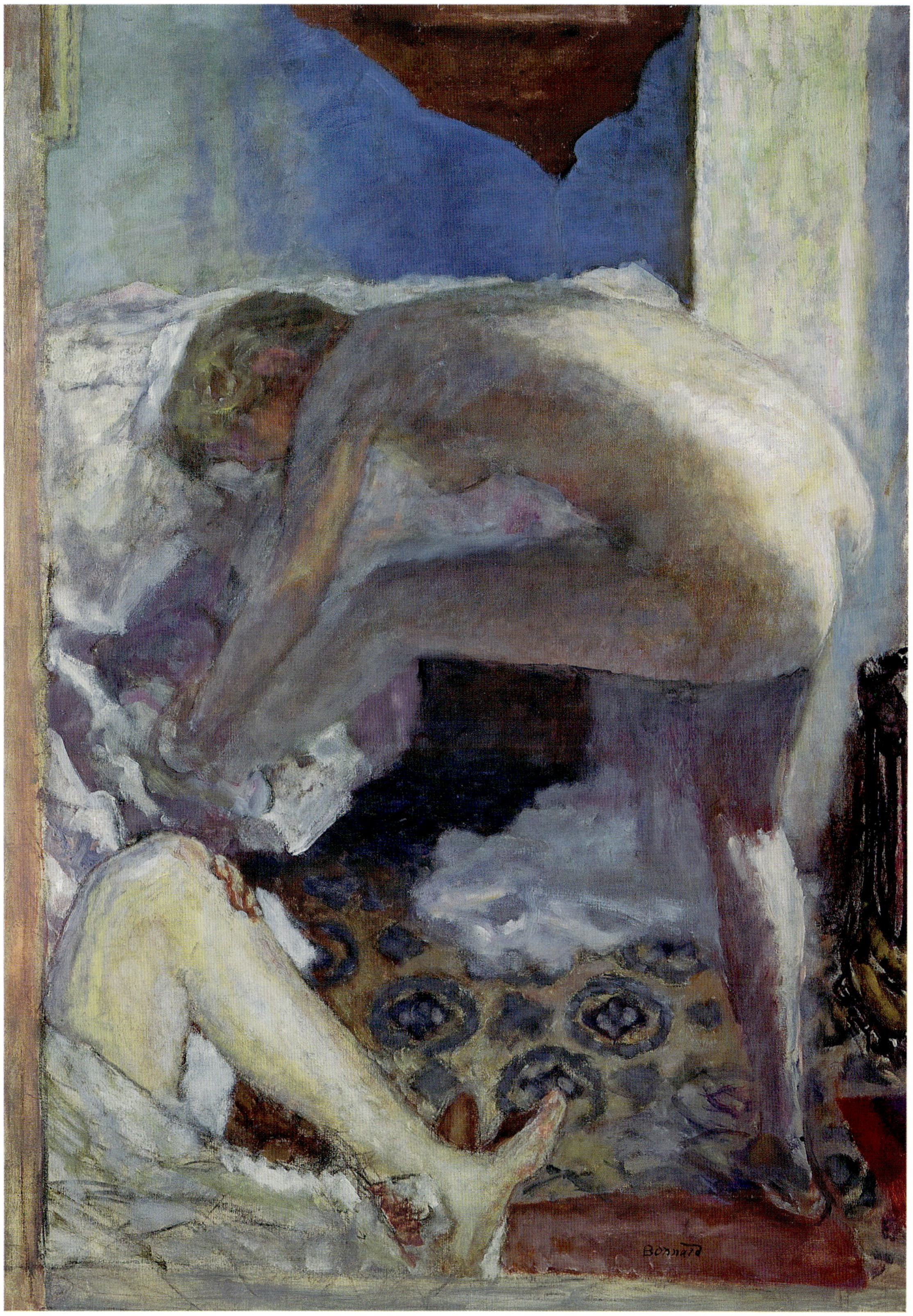

147
Le Grand Nu bleu. 1924.
Oil on canvas, 101×73cm.
Private collection

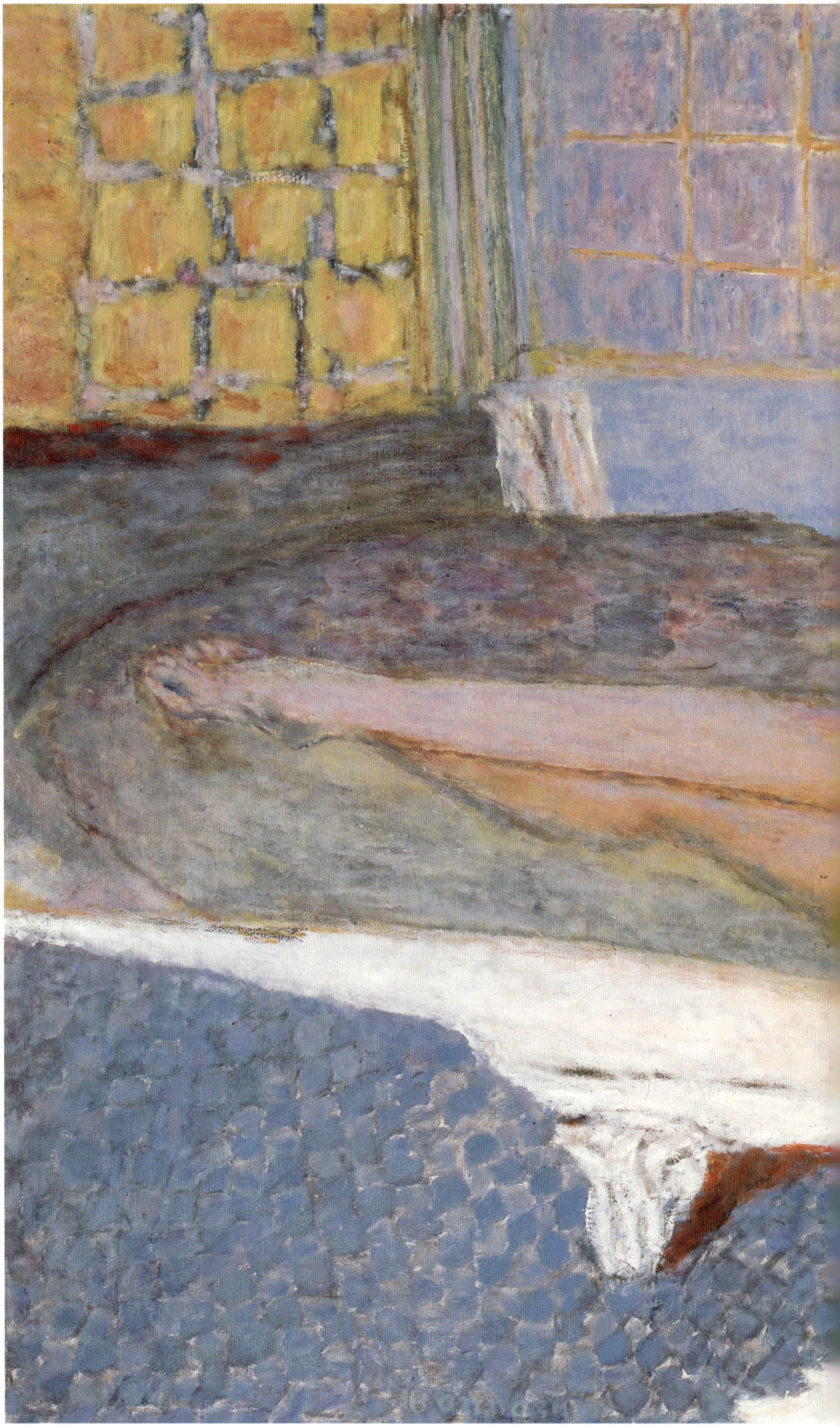

148
Nu à la baignoire. 1936.
Oil on canvas, 93×147cm.
Musée du Petit Palais, Paris

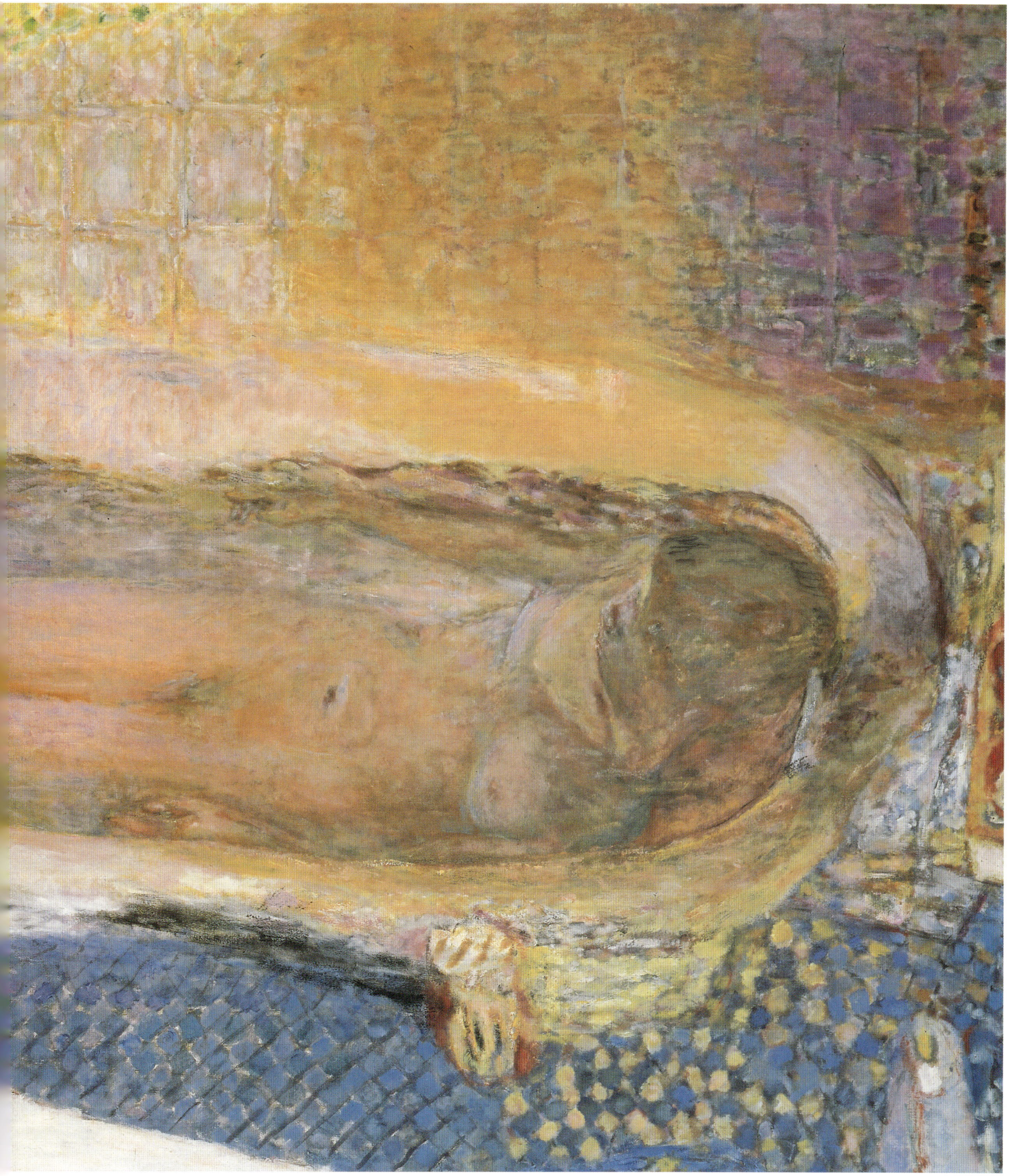

of moving from drawing to painting a theme would emerge. The simple act of clambering out of the bath in *La Sortie de la baignoire*, *c.*1926–30 (Plate 151), was enough to set in motion a sequence of ideas in which the subject became the transition from one side of the canvas to the other across the open divide of the floor. The bath mat provides a causeway of white over the sea of blue and green tiles to her clothes and towel banked up on the far side. Crouched on the bath, the nude is about to propel herself across the intervening space to collect them. The purple flush on her face is echoed in the pile of drapery on the right, setting up a secondary dialogue between the groupings of warm and cool colours.

The experimental quality of Bonnard's nudes distinguished him from Renoir and brought him into direct accord with Matisse, who was similarly engaged in the distortion of female anatomy to convey movement across space. The eight dancers of Matisse's mural for the main hall of the Barnes Foundation, finally installed in 1933, rise and fall within the rhythm of the three lunettes, both lightening the oppressive weight of the vault above and creating a dynamic surface pattern of intertwining limbs, moving in counterpoint to the flat vertical bars of the background.[39] Bonnard was deeply impressed by the Barnes mural, visited Matisse while it was in progress and wrote to him from La Baule in September 1933, 'I am delighted because I assisted at the genesis of your work.'[40] In relation to Matisse Bonnard is often perceived as a reactionary, with his feet firmly embedded in the nineteenth century, whereas both artists, perhaps responding to the freedom from convention that came with Surrealism, shared an ambition in the 1930s to break open the walls of the domestic interior, distort form and construct through colour in association with light an expanded reading of pictorial space. Space was to be materialized into colour, shaped and then dematerialized within

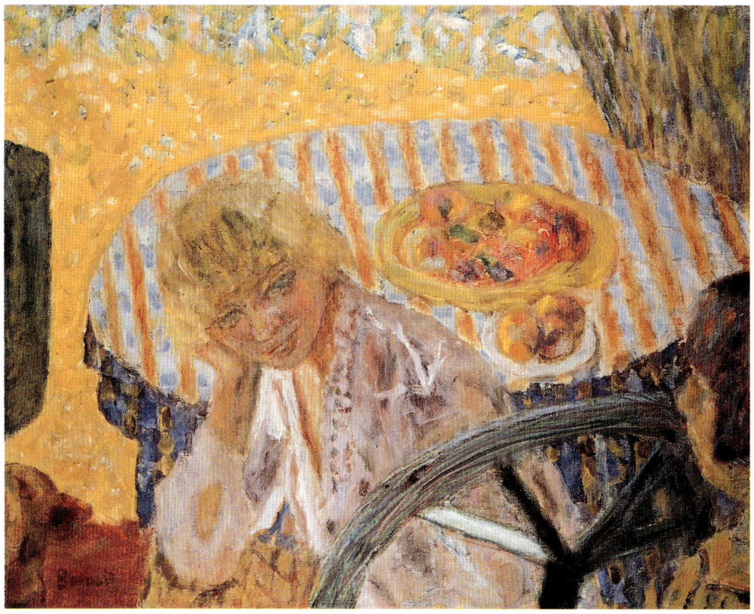

149
Jeunes femmes au jardin. 1921–3, reworked 1945–6.
Oil on canvas, 60.5×77cm.
Private collection, Paris

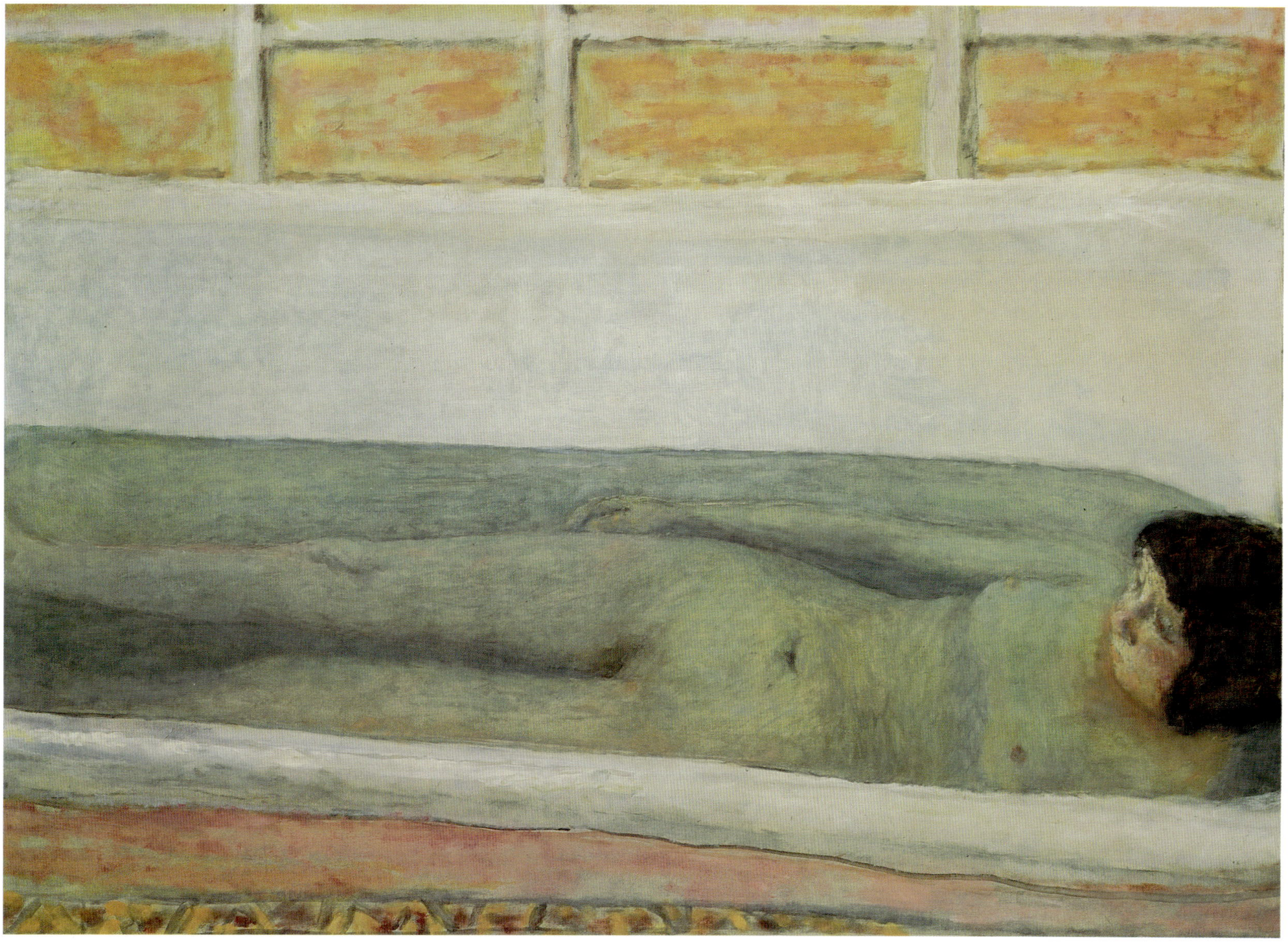

150
Le Bain. 1925.
Oil on canvas, 86×120cm.
Tate Gallery, London

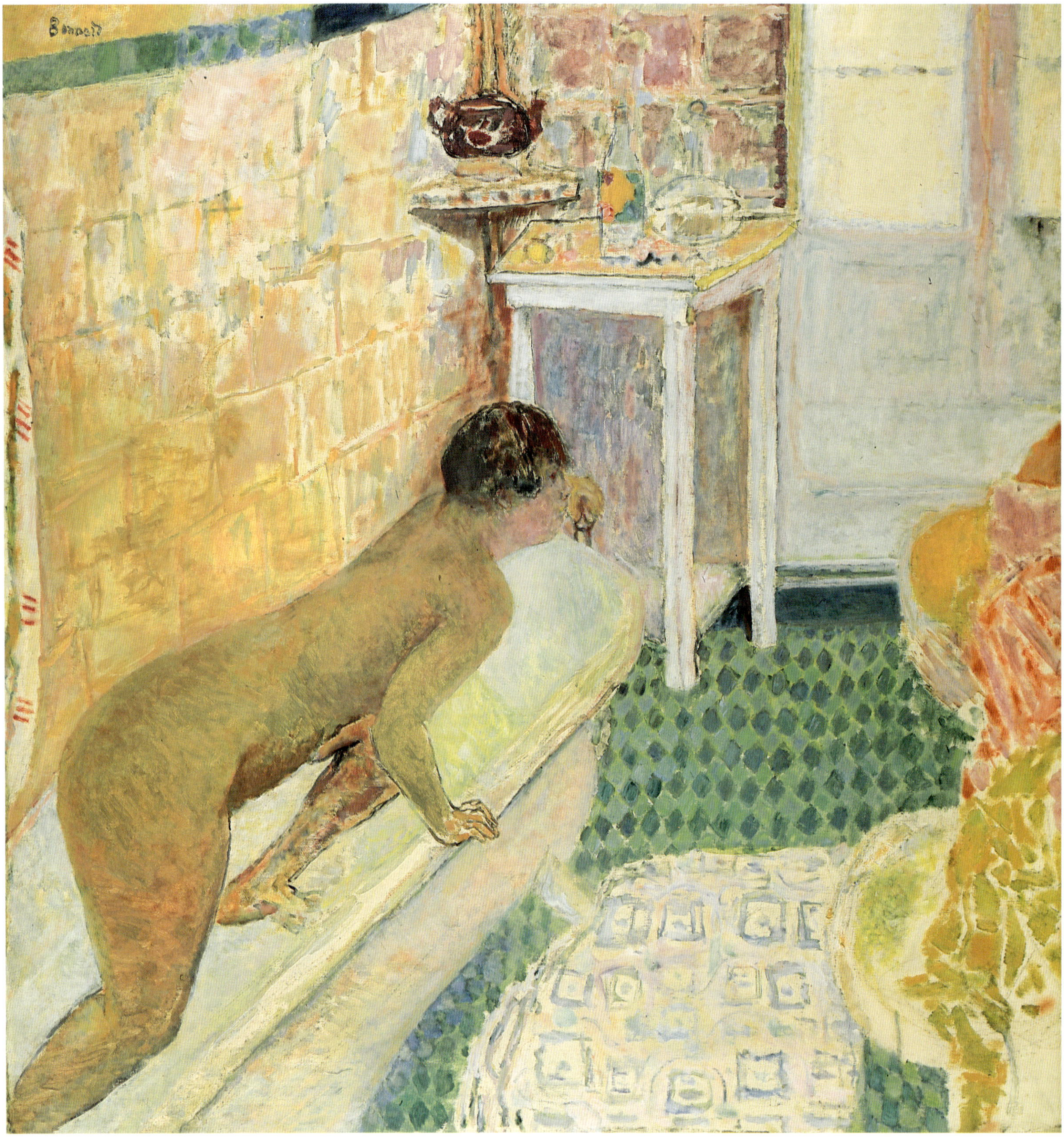

151
La Sortie de la baignoire. *c*.1926–30.
Oil on canvas, 129×123cm.
Private collection, Switzerland

a surface of light, suggesting a continuum beyond the framing edge of a canvas.

Although there is nothing overtly programmatic about Bonnard's paintings in the 1930s, each can be seen as dealing with a given set of plastic issues which are rephrased from painting to painting across the genres. White as a sign of both light and limitless space was to be balanced with colour. Colour was to assume shape within the overall pattern of light. Light was to compete with colour for the possession of form. Form was to be distorted and merged as part of the broad 'legible divisions of surfaces'. Central to the subject-matter and atmosphere of the paintings was the female presence. For instance in *Nu à la baignoire*, 1931 (Plate 152), the outline of the nude's shoulder continues the contour of the end of the bath, which then merges with the white wall behind on the left. The backgound on the right is likewise sealed off in white, and cascades of colour flow between these broad white masses like water through a gorge. 'Proximity of white making patches of colour luminous', Bonnard wrote in his diary entry for 16 April 1927.[41] The complex spatial reading given by the changes in alignment and colour of the floor tiles show that Bonnard had absorbed the discoveries of Synthetic Cubist painting on his own terms.

From an initial starting point in nature a colour scheme would assume a logic of its own. *Le Pot provençal*, 1930 (Plate 157), for instance, began with Mrs Hahnloser's gift of a bunch of garden flowers, 'fresh leaves, two dark lilac-coloured irises and a mass of orange and sulphur-yellow marigolds'. [42] The bright orange of the lower half of the jug suggests that as the flowers faded their colour was drained into the water. When asked what Marthe's arm was doing on the extreme right of the composition, Bonnard replied 'Nothing at all. I needed something in that part of the picture. I might just as well have hung a mascot on the wall, but I put in the arm, and that's all there is to it.' [43] The idea of white confronting colour was turned into a spectacle in *Nature morte au bouquet de fleurs* also known as *La Vénus de Cyrène*, 1930 (Plate 154). The white table in the foreground overlooks a colouristic performance split between burning orange on the left and deep ultramarine blue on the right, with the yellow, Bonnard's alternative sign of light, linking the two.

As in the three window paintings, *La Salle à manger sur le jardin* (Plate 134), *Salle à manger à la campagne* (Plate 135), and *La Table devant la fenêtre* (Plate 136), the move towards greater spatial complexity led Bonnard to take on increasingly ambitious subjects in Le Bosquet. The small sitting room on the first floor, containing three doors, a fireplace and a French window, posed a particularly difficult challenge, which Bonnard took on in *Le Petit Déjeuner au radiateur*, *c.*1930 (Plate 155), and the larger *Intérieur blanc*, 1932 (Plate 156). He registered his first interest in the subject in two sketches in his diary on 29 April 1929. *Le Petit Déjeuner au radiateur* combines several familiar themes: a woman absorbed in the atmosphere of a room, the dialogue between artist (reflected in the mirror) and model, and between the window view and the interior. The composition is divided into a sequence of rectangles structuring the light-filled surface. Nothing is quite what it seems. The central landscape of Le Cannet

152
Nu à la baignoire. 1931.
Oil on canvas, 120×110cm.
Musée National d'Art Moderne, Centre Georges Pompidou, Paris

153
Nu de dos à la toilette. 1934.
Oil on canvas, 105×73cm.
Musée National d'Art Moderne, Centre Georges Pompidou, Paris

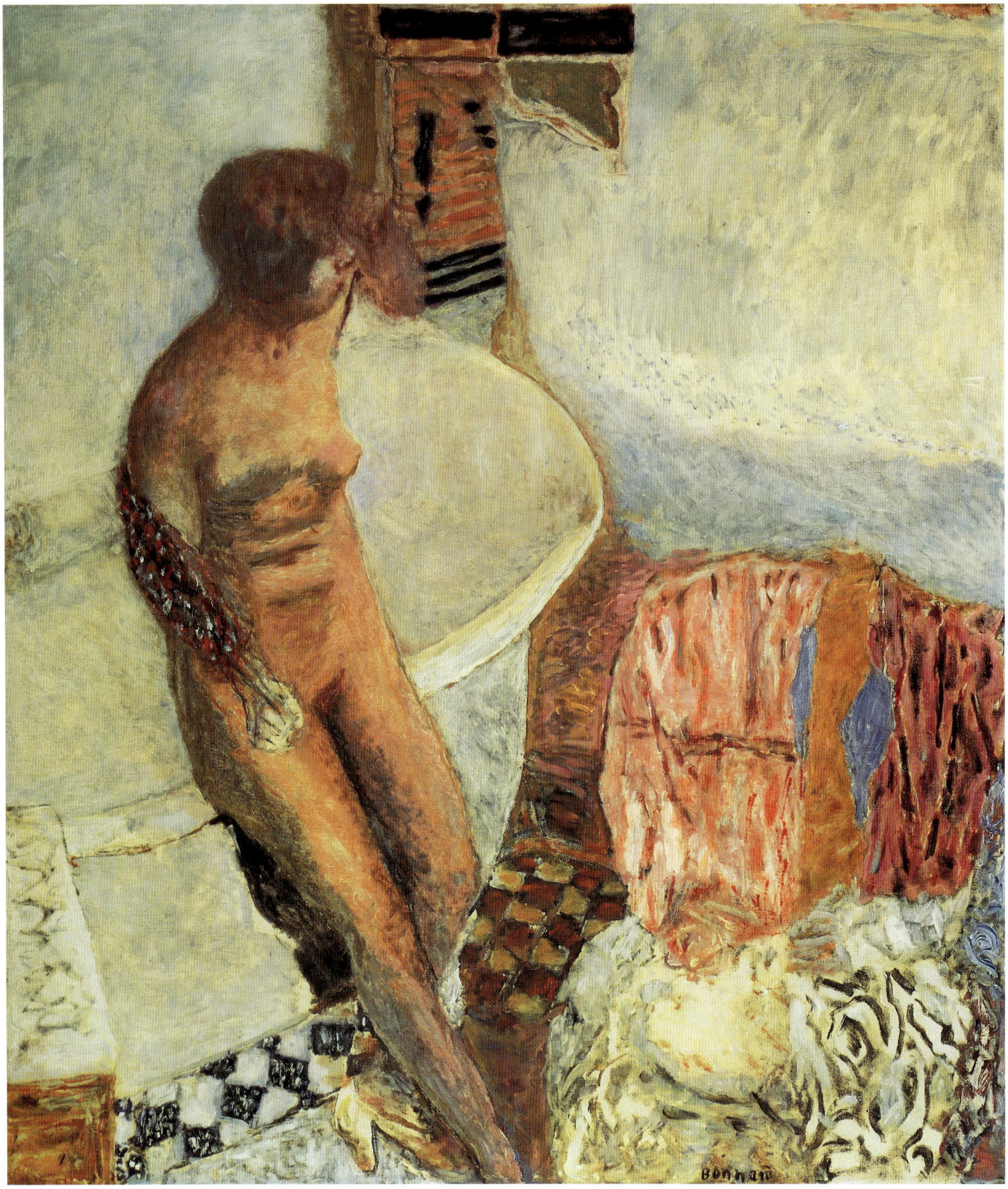

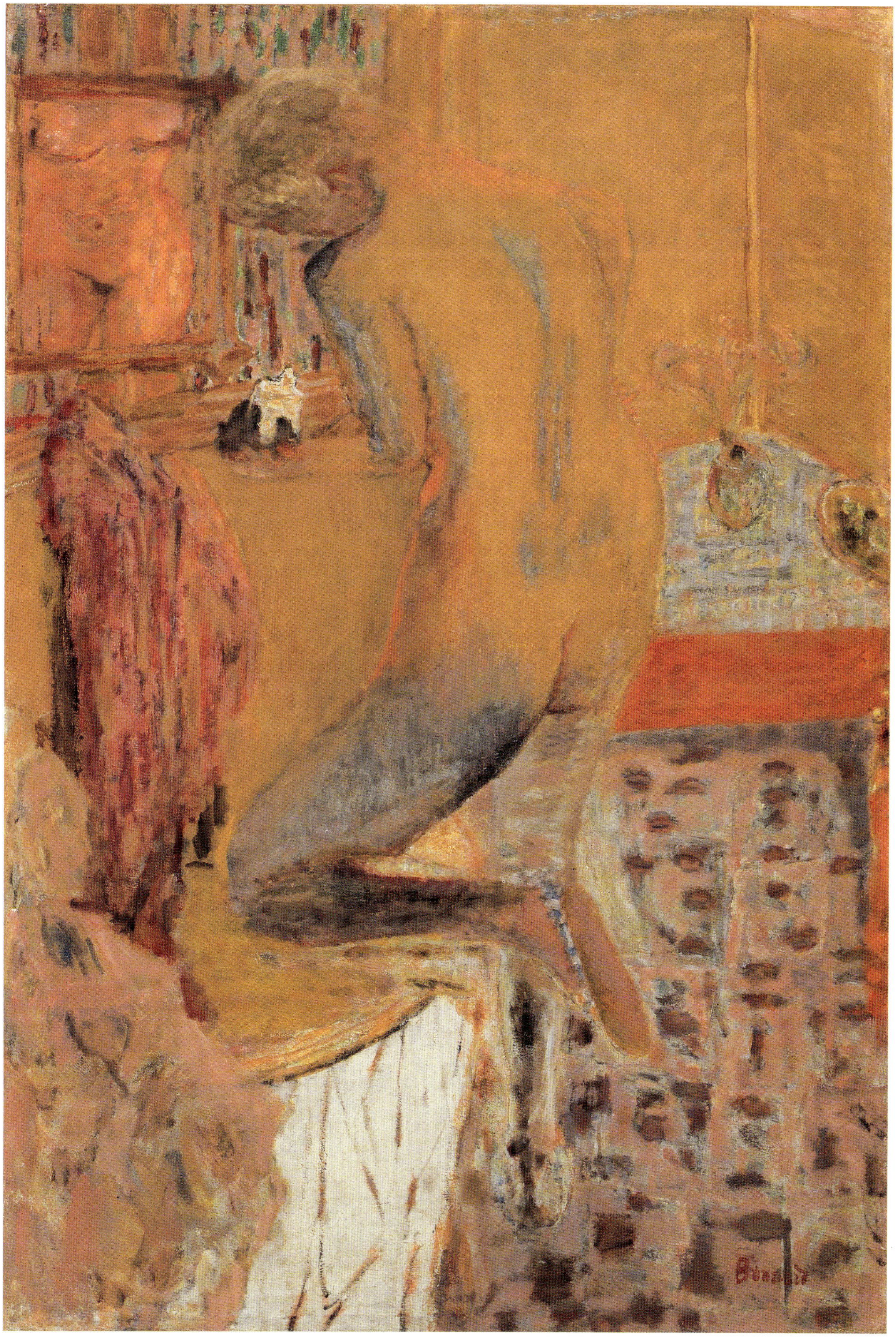
Bonnard

is juxtaposed on one side with the reflection of vegetation in the open French window and on the other with the mirror view of the interior. White is played against colour in an unfolding sequence from the radiator on the left to the door on the extreme right.

Two sides of the small sitting room are flattened across the surface of the more ambitious *Intérieur blanc* to include both the bathroom door and the mantlepiece with flowers arranged in the jug, and the dialogue between this still life in the top left-hand corner and the landscape of Le Cannet on the extreme right constitutes a major theme. A new hierarchy is instituted in which the scale of objects is dictated by their importance in the picture. Bonnard's presence is suggested by the dominant orange back to the chair on the left, and Marthe's head is bent over on the right to form part of the structural plane defining the floor. Our normal expectations are reversed: the interior is light and the landscape outside dark. The darkness of the exterior flows in across the floor, its mottled red, black and deep blue colouring reaching a conclusion in the fireplace.

The power of light to take possession of and transform an interior was extended to the treatment of the human figure. Like Daphne arrested in the process of being turned into a laurel, the model in *Nu de dos à la toilette*, 1934 (Plate 153), has almost been absorbed in the golden light of the background. The raised pink foot registers the lingering humanity of the nude whose life blood has been drained into the reddened reflection of her torso in the mirror behind. The metamorphosis of form through light

154
Nature morte au bouquet de fleurs. 1930.
Oil on canvas, 60×130.5cm.
Kunstmuseum, Basle

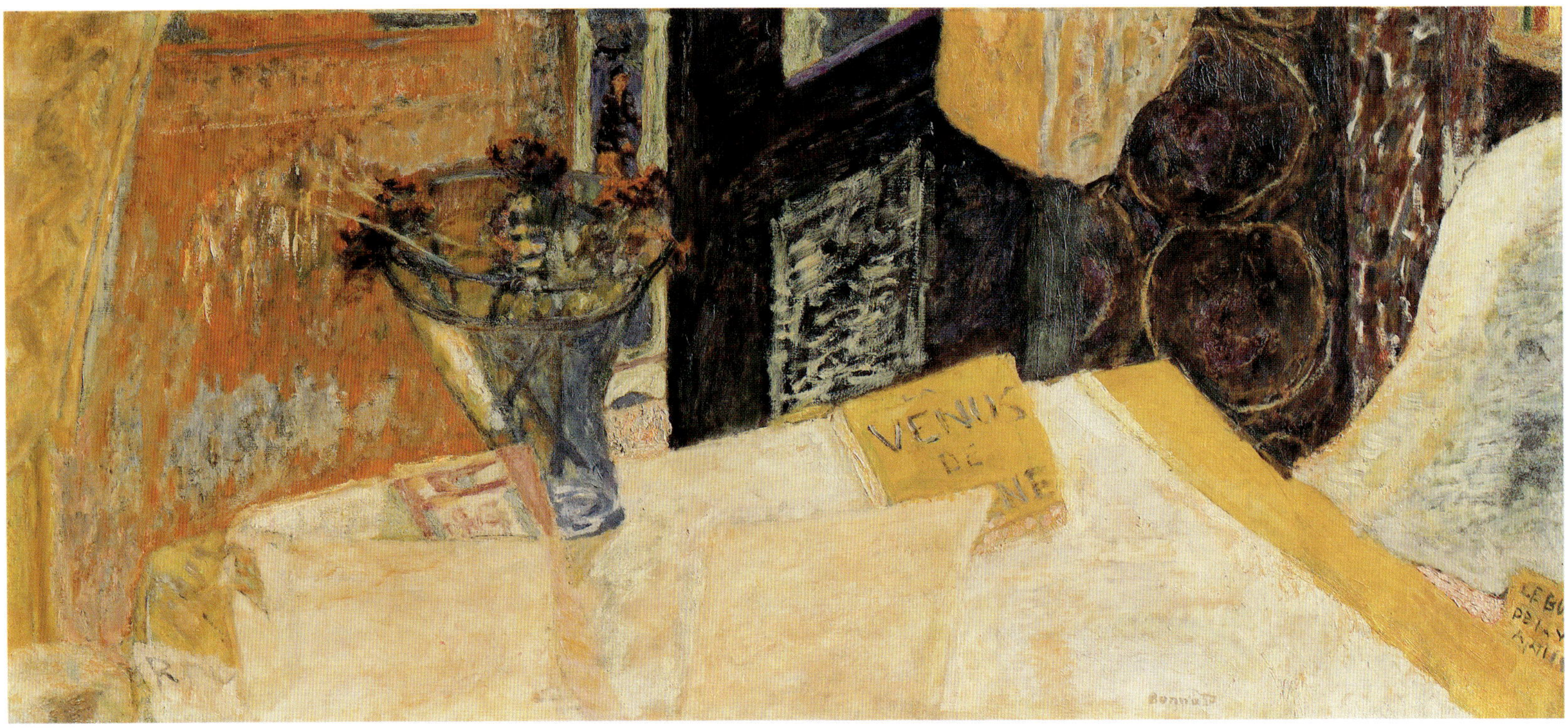

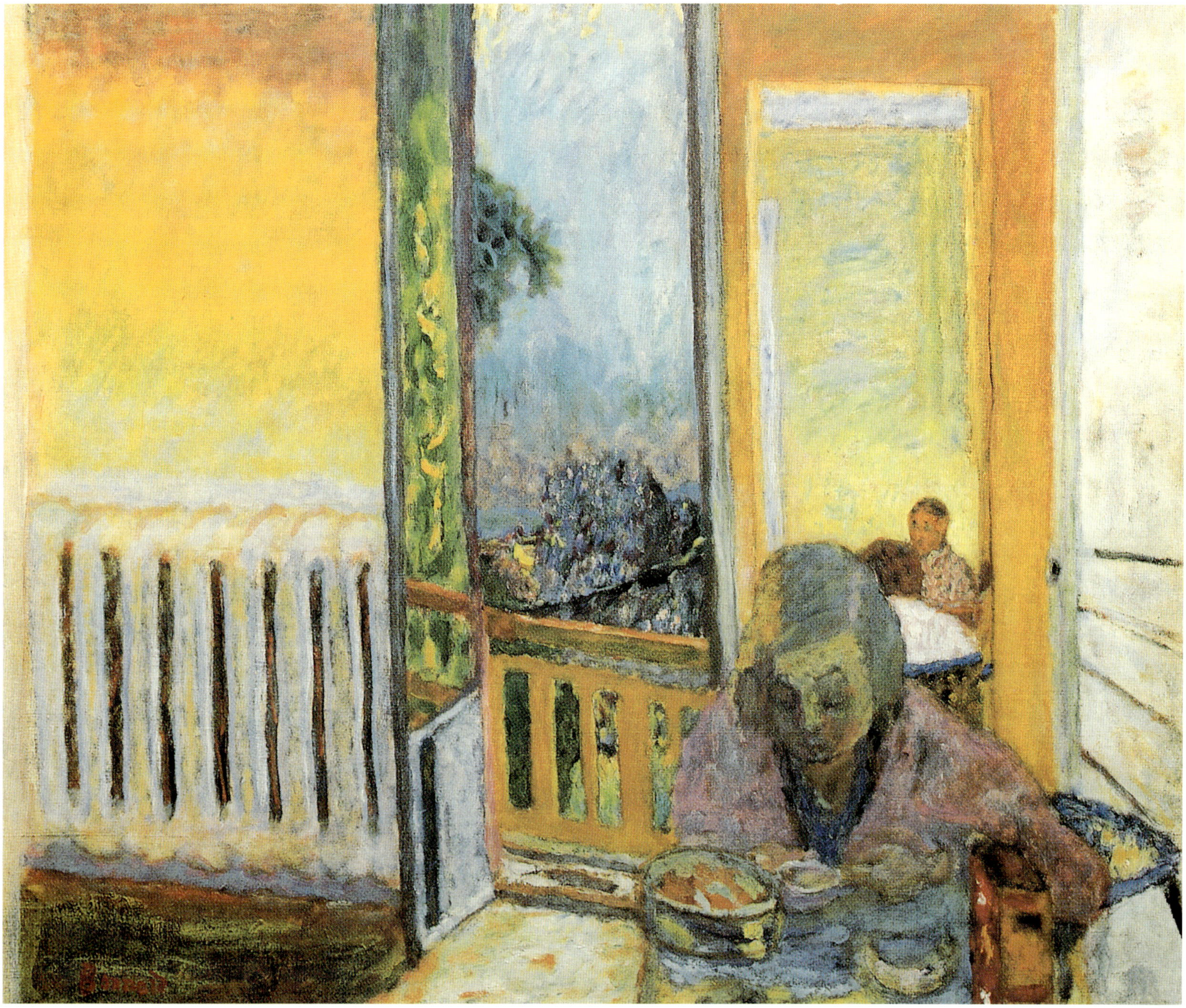

155
Le Petit Déjeuner au radiateur. *c*.1930.
Oil on canvas, 74×84cm.
Private collection

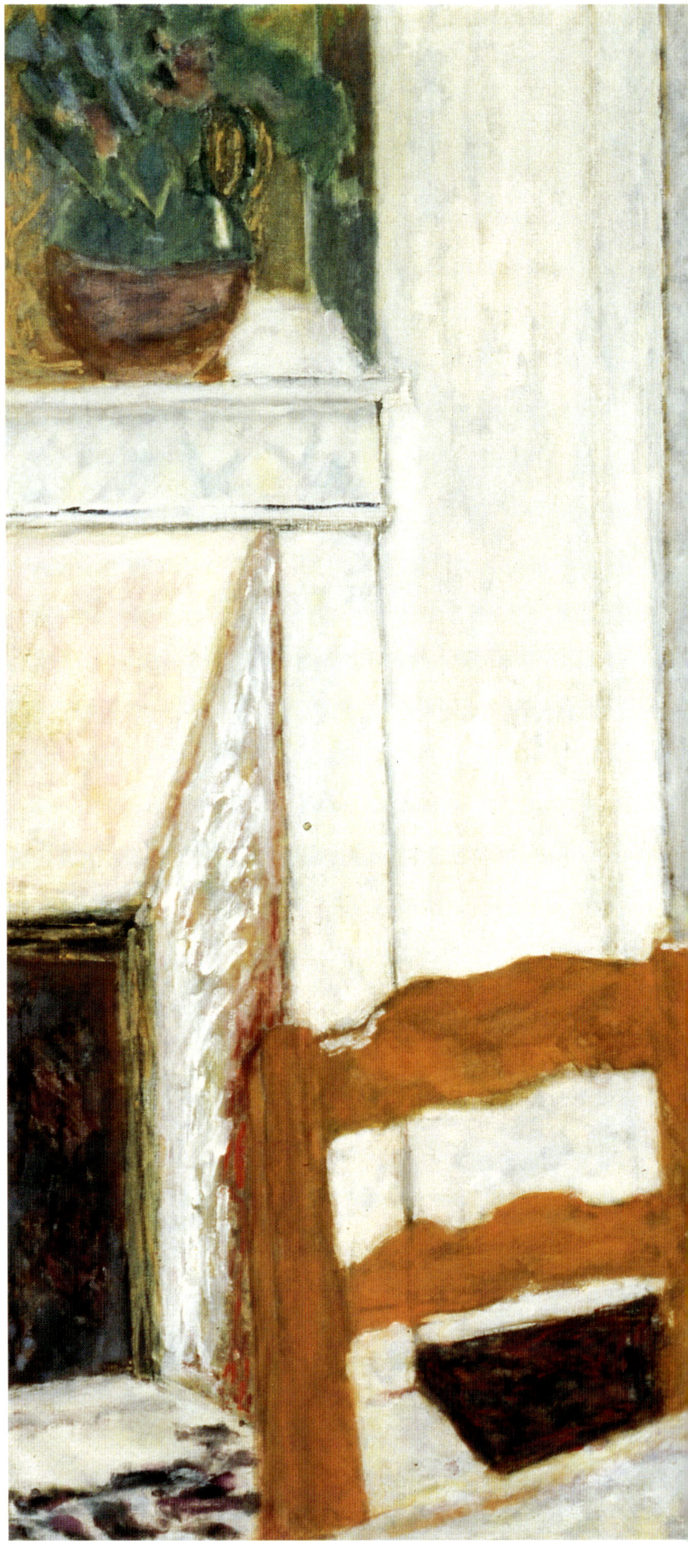

156
Intérieur blanc. 1932.
Oil on canvas, 109×156.5cm.
Musée de Grenoble

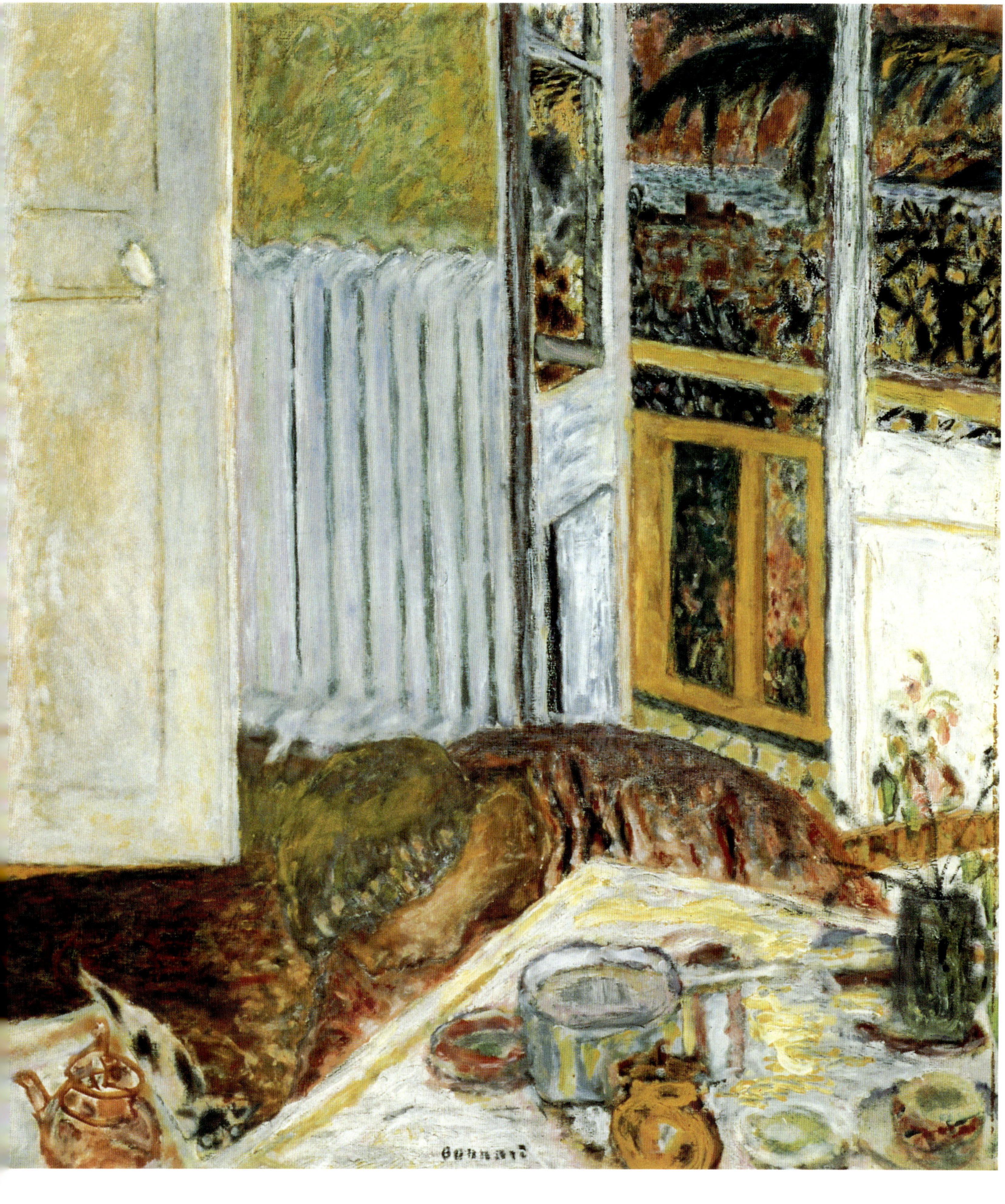
Bonnard

157
Le Pot provençal. 1930.
Oil on canvas, 75.5×62cm.
Private collection, Switzerland

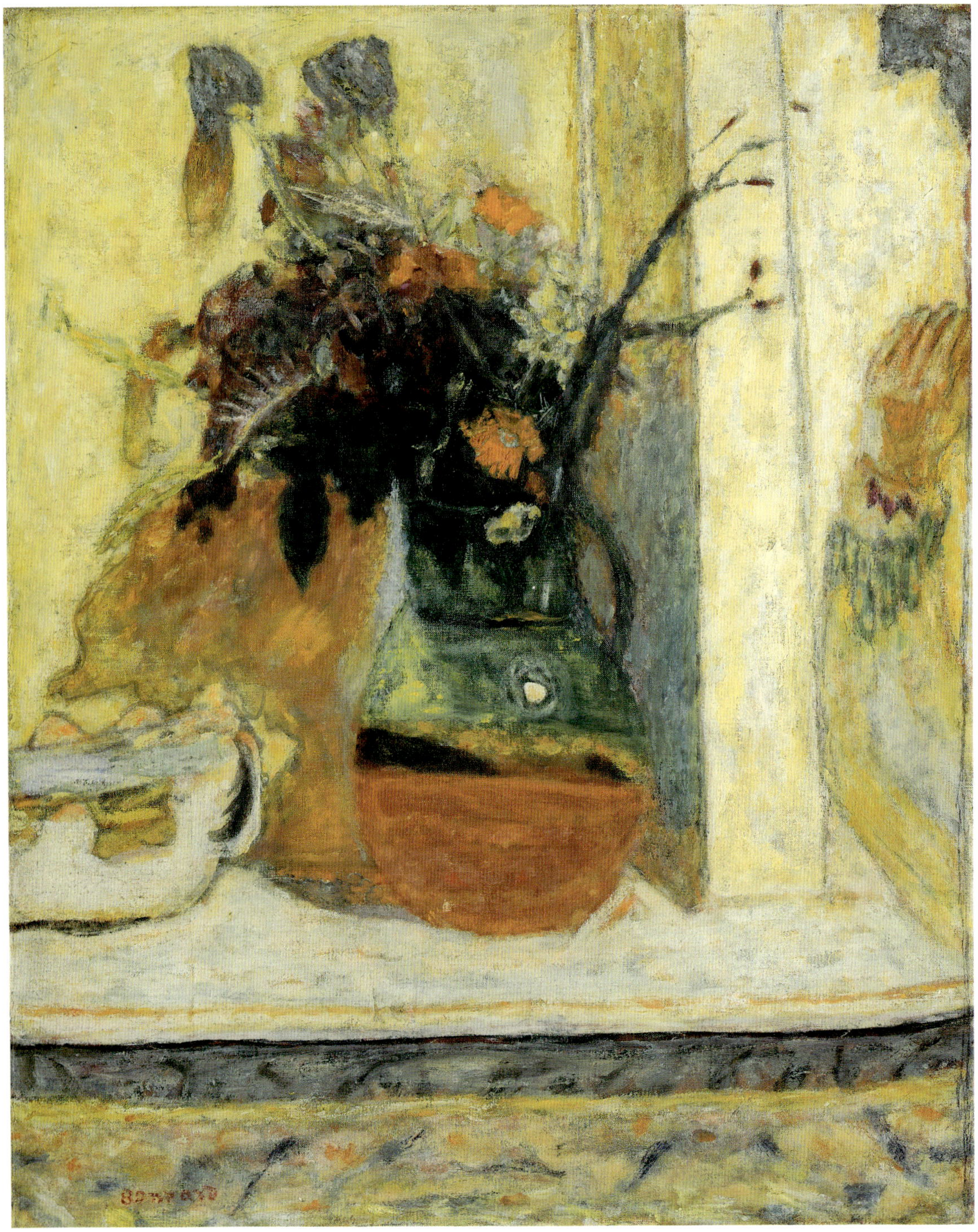

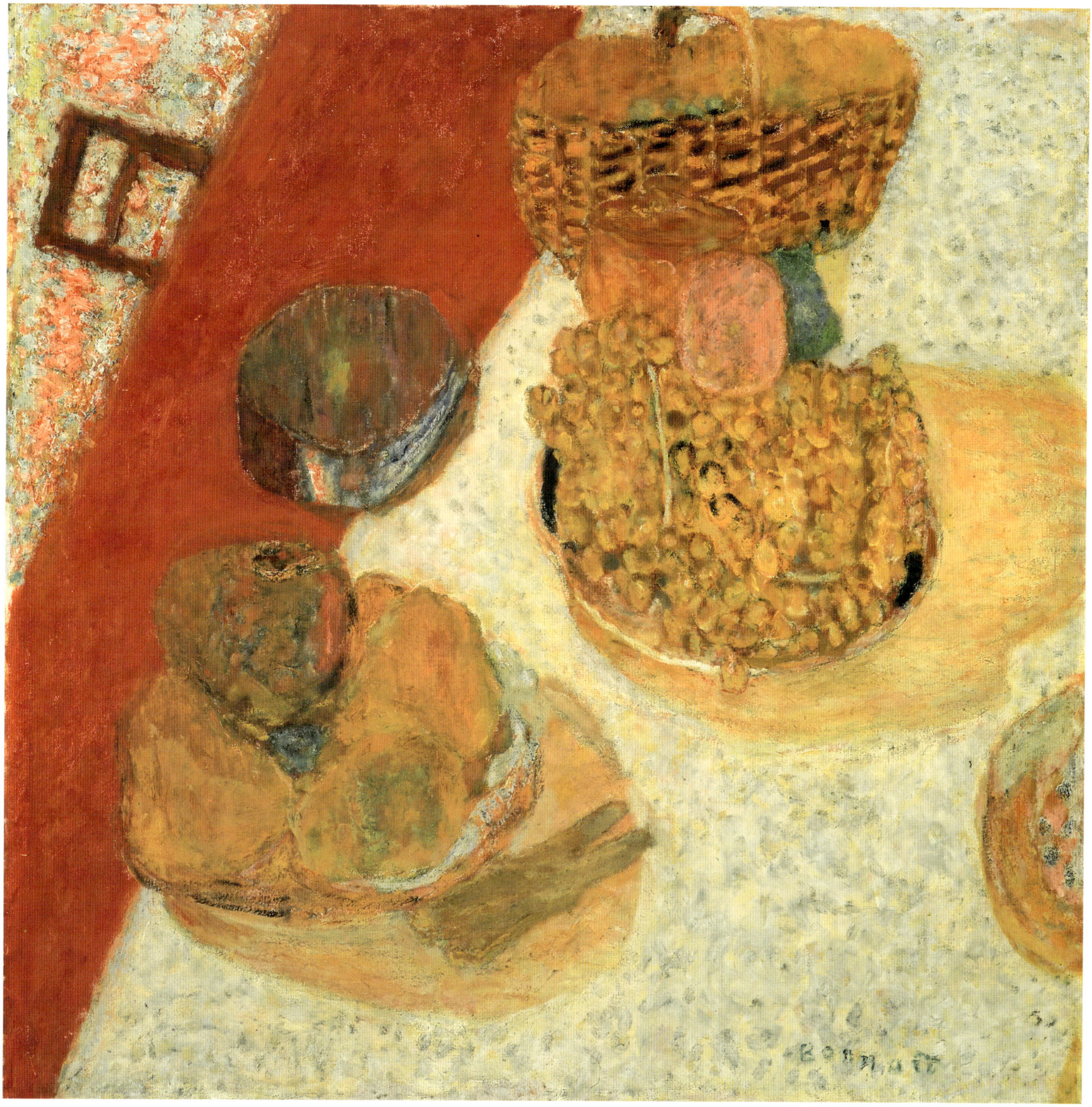

158
Coin de table. 1935.
Oil on canvas, 67×63.5cm.
Musée National d'Art Moderne, Centre Georges
Pompidou, Paris

became Bonnard's consuming passion and the ultimate subject in what he regarded as his most challenging motif: the nude stretched out in the bath. In *Nu à la baignoire* 1936 (Plate 148), the bath is twisted, and expanded at one end, to form part of a surface pattern of reflected colours in a sequence of rectangular mirror-shapes structuring the background. The nude, rather than the window, is the principal light source. Light from her body bathes the back wall and spills like water on to the blue-tiled floor, gelling into solidified blobs of gold.

Yet again Bonnard was not isolated in this concern for metamorphosis, which became a key concept in modernist art in Paris in the 1930s. While there are few overt formal links between Bonnard and Surrealism, which after all shared his origins in the Symbolist poetry of the 1890s, the comparison with Braque is more pertinent. In the 1930s Braque materialized space into a musical accord between surfaces, and, like Bonnard, he came to identify his practice as a painter with metamorphosis. 'Everything', Braque stated towards the end of his life, 'is subject to metamorphosis; everything changes according to circumstance. So when you ask me whether a particular form in one of my paintings depicts a woman's head, a fish, a vase, a bird or all four at once, I can't give you a categorical answer, for this 'metamorphic' confusion is fundamental to what I am out to express.'[44]

Only the physical substance of paint itself possessed any semblance of reality, the rest was illusion. Bonnard agreed with Matisse, in a letter dated 1 February 1935, that 'the only solid ground for a painter is the palette and the tones',[45] but the moment pigment becomes colour the problems began. In the process of metamorphosis colour became light and light colour. Colour, he told Charles Terrasse 'has the power to abstract',[46] and the drive towards abstraction lay behind much of his art in the 1930s. His theme of balancing colour with white received its most abstract formulation in *Coin de table*, 1935 (Plate 158). The objects on the white cloth and red felt covering the dining-room table at Le Bosquet are metamorphosed into rafts of colour on a frothy sea of white, balanced by the strident diagonal plane of red. A chair-back sticks out of the red plane like a geometric ear. Visual equilibrium is all. The logic is internal. In *Corbeille et assiette de fruits sur la nappe à carreaux rouges*, *c.*1939 (Plate 159), a similar theme is transposed into the key of red: red fruit, pink reflection on the plate, red checks on the white cloth and red felt, all flattened against the picture plane. His art had come full circle in the 1920s and 1930s: the patterned analysis of form typical of his Nabis decorative style was finally reconciled with the light and colour of Impressionism.

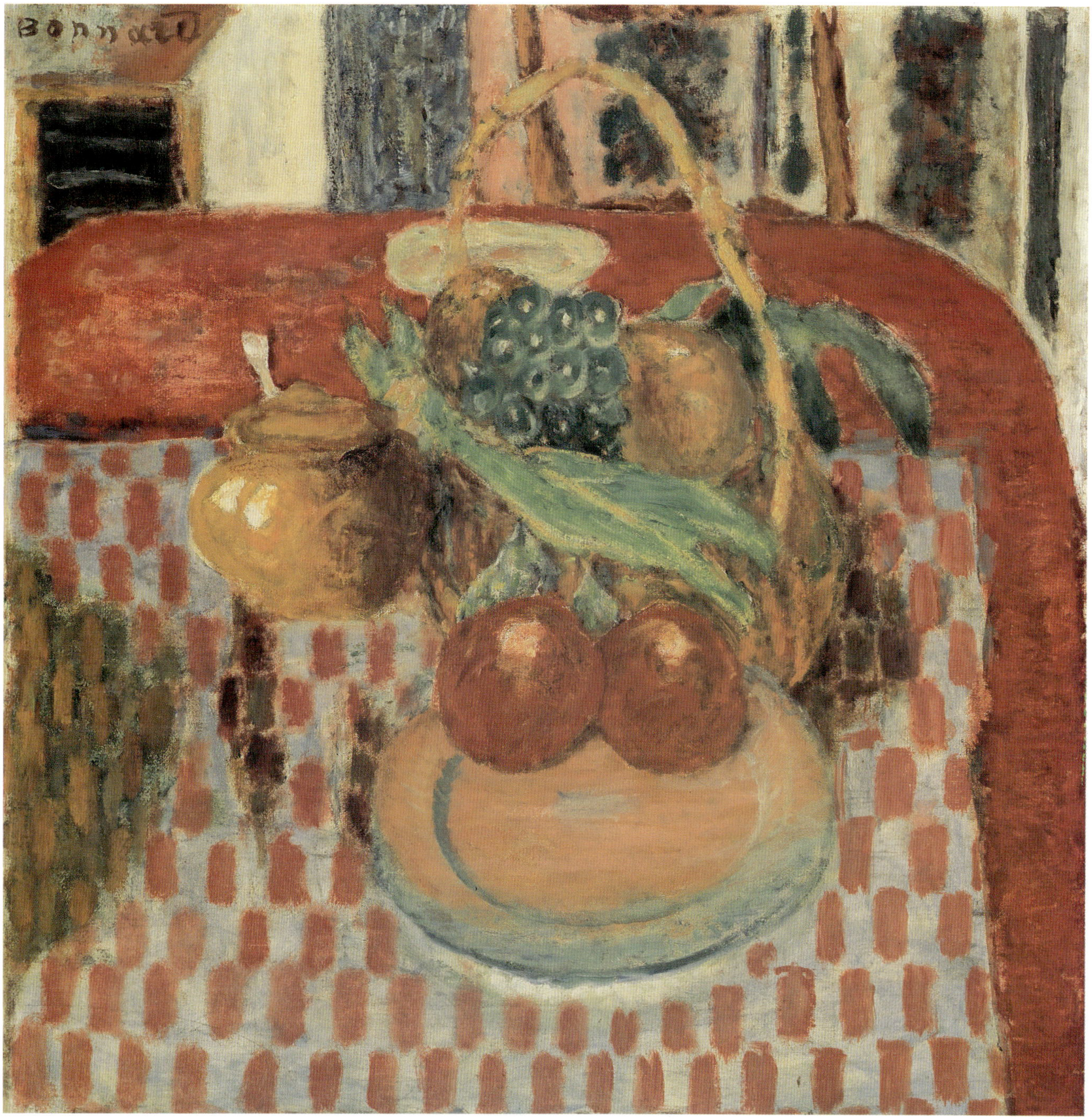

159
*Corbeille et assiette de fruits sur la nappe à carreaux rouges. c.*1939.
Oil on canvas, 58.4×58.4cm.
The Art Institute of Chicago, gift of Mary and Leigh Block

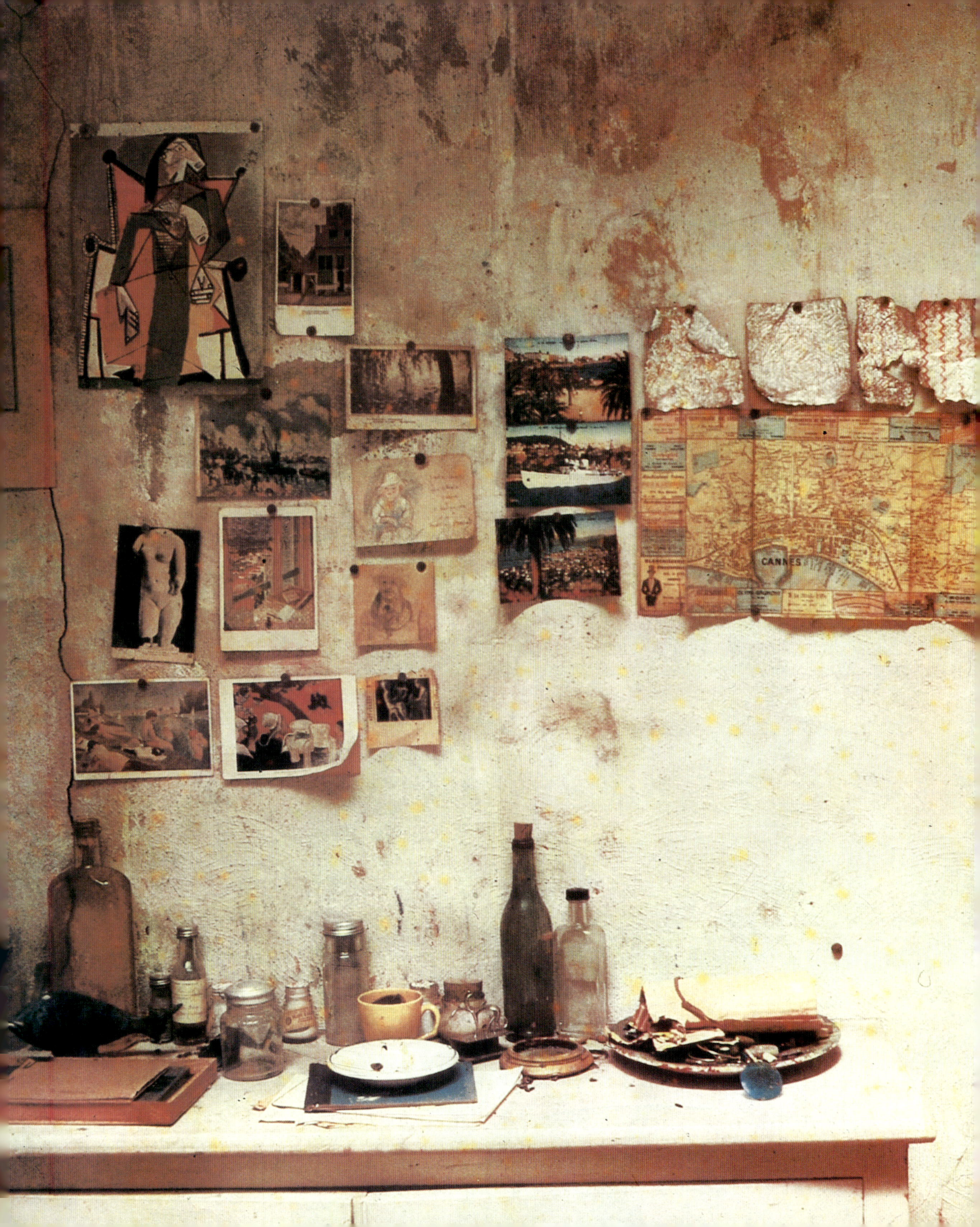
CANNES

Chapter 5

The final years

Bonnard spent the war years at Le Cannet, shut away in the rooms of Le Bosquet. His remaining links with Normandy were severed by the German occupation. He had sold Ma Roulotte, his house at Vernonnet, in 1938. Two week-long trips to Trouville in July and August 1939 were to be his last. He was deeply affected by the destruction of the region in the battle of 1944, writing to Charles Terrasse about 'the impassivity of despair'.[1]

His terrible sense of isolation was compounded by the deaths of those closest to him. Matisse and Bonnard came together in adversity, two old campaigners, cut off in the south by petrol rationing, personal loss, loneliness and poor health, corresponding to maintain their morale and their art. On 4 March 1941 Bonnard informed Matisse of the death of his brother Charles in Algeria: '... a large part of my life went with him'.[2] On 31 March Matisse reported the death of their dealer Josse Bernheim.[3] Vuillard died on 21 June. Bonnard was deeply affected and never allowed his name to be mentioned again.[4] Vuillard's face was resurrected in Bonnard's *Saint François de Sales*, 1942–5, painted for the church at Assy, which in a sense served as a memorial to his friend. Worse was to come. On 26 January 1942 Marthe died. Bonnard was shattered. 'Life is wrecked,' he told two younger artists, André Giverny and Jean Matisse, Matisse's son, who saw him two weeks after the event.[5] His companion had gone. The loss was too painful for him to come to terms with, let alone talk about, and he symbolically kept her bedroom door locked. Maurice Denis died on 2 November 1943, and the deaths of two other companions from his early Nabis days followed in quick succession: Ker-Xavier Roussel on 6 June 1944 and Aristide Maillol on 24 September.

There is an element of total self-absorption in old people, particularly in artists. Health is a consuming topic running through the correspondence between Bonnard and Matisse, aggravated by the difficulty of getting essential supplies such as coal during the cold winter months. Visitors to Le Bosquet found Bonnard distracted, as though his mind was elsewhere. Work was the only thing that kept him going. Asked by Giverny if he was disturbed by the visit, Bonnard replied: 'Not with you, while I am talking I'm looking; often a solution comes which perhaps I would not have found if I had been alone.'[6] He was evidently worried by the lack of sales for he even considered doing a commissioned portrait, something he usually preferred to avoid, of Marshal Pétain. Nothing came of it, because his wish to reserve the right to destroy the painting if it did not work out proved unacceptable.[7]

160
The studio, Le Bosquet. *c.*1946.
Photograph

Several canvases remained unfinished in his studio and were continuously reworked. *Le Cheval de cirque*, 1936–46 (Plate 161), was started in Deauville in August 1936 and finally completed at Charles Terrasse's house at Fontainebleau in 1946, shortly before Bonnard's death in 1947.[8] Nearing the end of his life, Bonnard retreated into memories of his childhood and formative years, which he published in 1943 in the form of a series of illustrated letters, titled *Correspondances*, recalling incidents at Le Clos, life in the Parisian streets, his frequent vists to the Cirque Medrano, and so on.[9] *Le Cheval de cirque* combines two ideas sketched out in his diary entries in 1934 and 1936, the old cab horse and its attendant, and the looming portrait head of a horse filling the format. The final setting shows the stalls of a well-equipped, old-fashioned stable like Chantilly. The fact that this haunting image pursued Bonnard to the very end of his life led Jean Clair to suggest that it may represent a mythical beast, the *Psychopompos*, that comes to those approaching death to carry their souls to the hereafter.[10]

Marthe lived on in his paintings after her death in 1942. The final bath scene *Nu dans le bain au petit chien* (Plate 162), begun in 1941, and *L'Atelier au mimosa* (Plate 164), begun in 1939, with her ghostly presence barely registerd in the bottom left-hand corner, were both finished only in 1946. The bath scene was exclusively Marthe's preserve. Dina Vierny, a favourite model of Maillol, posed for Bonnard's last nude, *Nu sombre*, 1942–6 (Plate 163), in the studio at Le Bosquet. By contrast with other artists for whom she had posed, notably Matisse, Dina Vierny recalled how Bonnard liked her to stay silent but not still, letting her find a pose natural to her.[11] The point of departure for *Nu sombre* is to be found in the Renoir nude hanging on Bonnard's studio wall. However, in comparison with the classical equanimity of the Renoir, Bonnard's nude is bowed within the format, consumed with melancholy.

A fascinating aspect of Bonnard's art in the 1940s is the way in which he and Matisse were preoccupied with similar concerns. Both artists wanted to convey the corporeal solidity and expressive significance of Giotto's figures in colour. In a letter to Bonnard of 7 May 1946, Matisse saw his ultimate ambition to achieve a modern equivalent of Giotto as too difficult for a single lifetime.[12] Bonnard, on the other hand, in addition to realizing the model solidly in colour, wished to dissolve form in light. *Nu sombre* is partially consumed by reds bursting into strokes of yellow. In *Nu dans le bain au petit chien* the bath is almost completely dissolved and the disembodied nude floats in a pool of pale blue which merges with the wall and floor to form changing patterns of colour within light, from the yellow, violet and green squares on the right to the predominantly blue squares on the left. Only the dog, secured to a patch of white on the floor, has the substance of reality.

Marthe had for so long formed part of the atmosphere of his life and art that with her death he himself was left alone as his principal subject, confronting her loss and his own destiny in a deeply moving series of self-portraits, which came to a conclusion with *Portrait de l'artiste dans la glace*, 1945 (Plate 166; see also Plate 7), a harrowing Belsen-like head, with sad sunken eyes and emaciated body, glowing red as though caught by the setting sun.

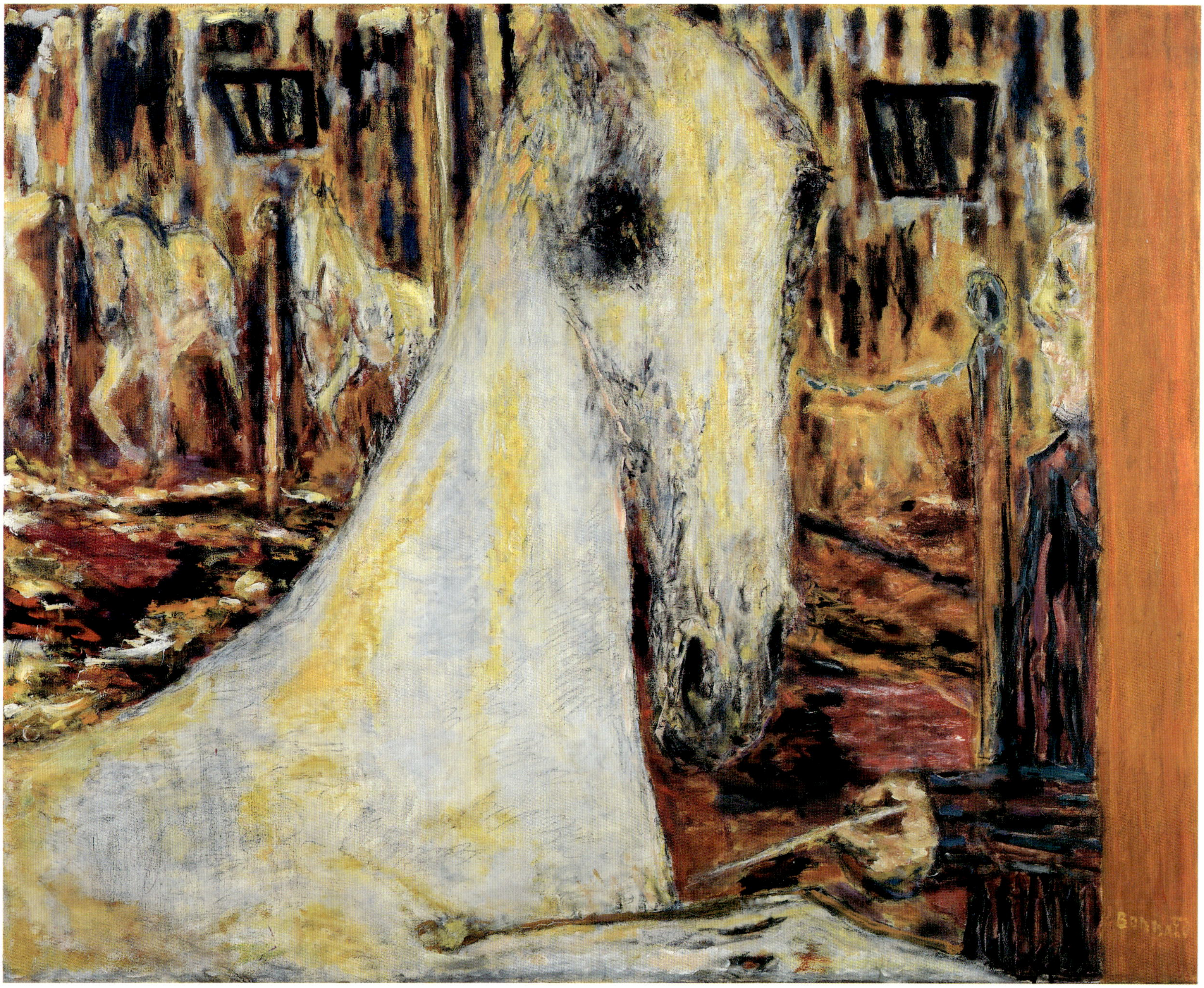

161
Le Cheval de cirque. 1936–46.
Oil on canvas, 94×118cm.
Private collection, Fontainebleau

162
Nu dans le bain au petit chien. 1941–6.
Oil on canvas, 123×152cm.
Carnegie Institute, Pittsburgh, acquired through the generosity of the Sarah Mellon Scaife family

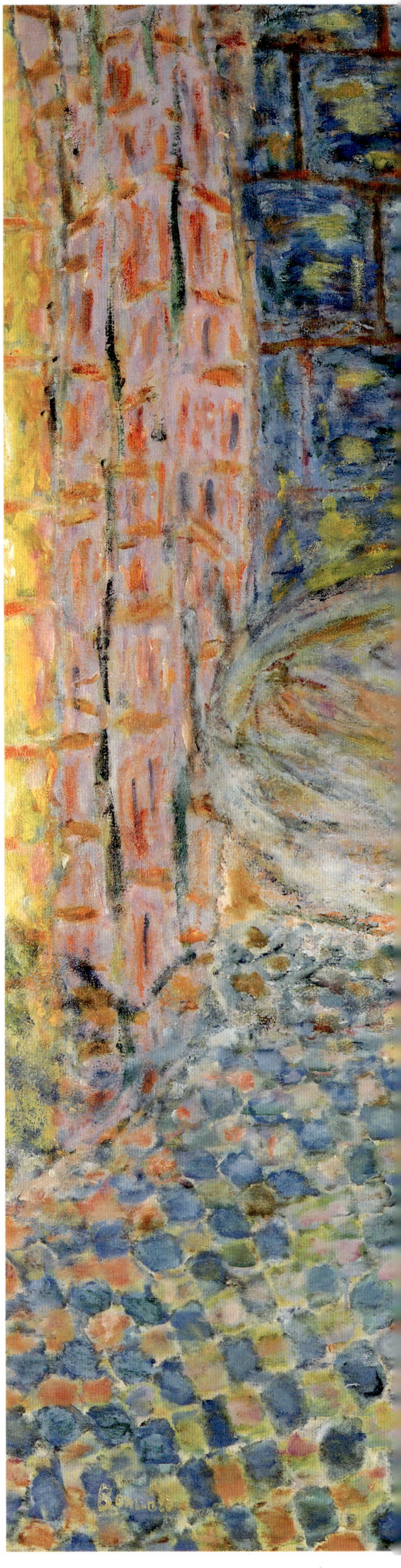

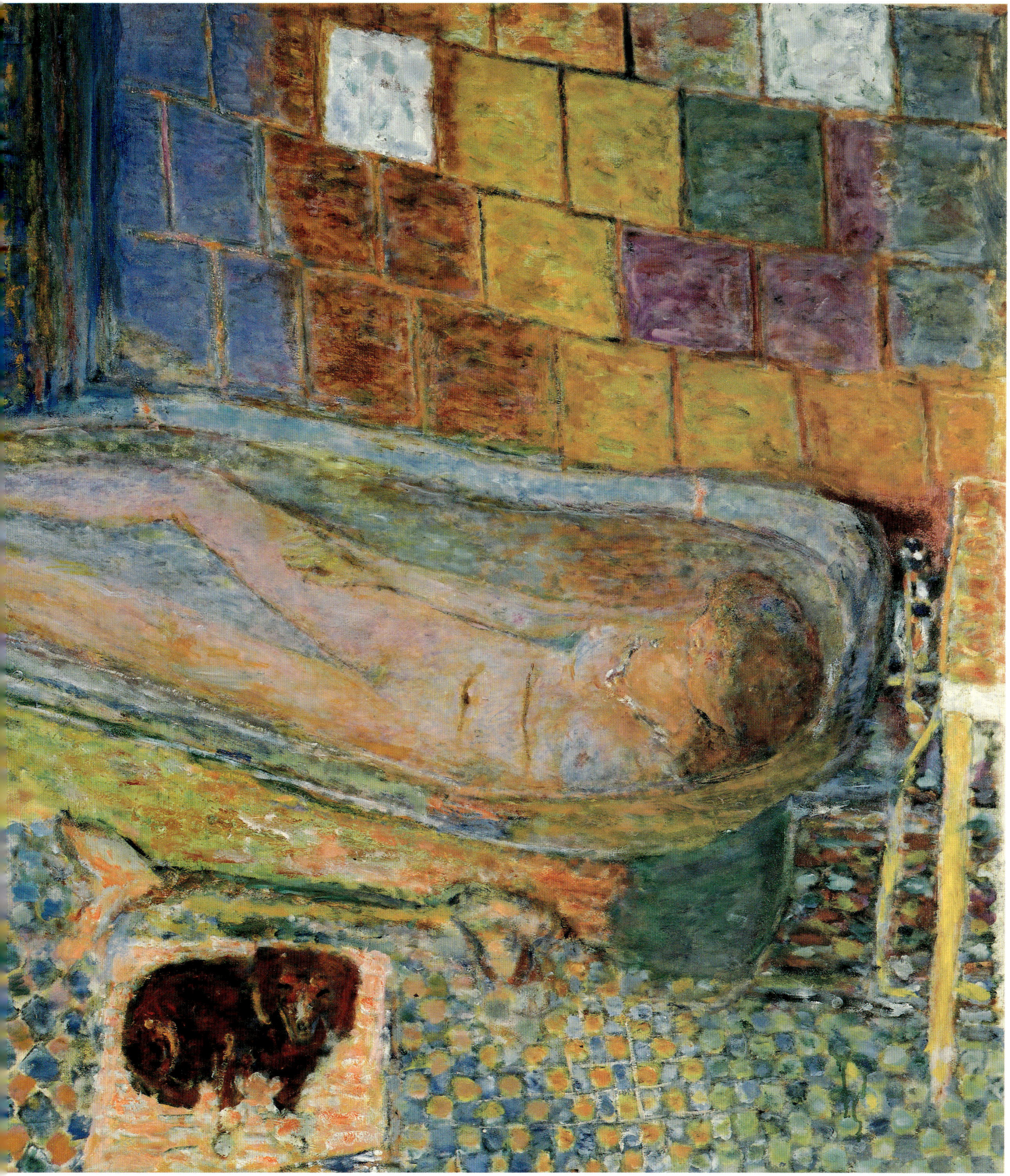

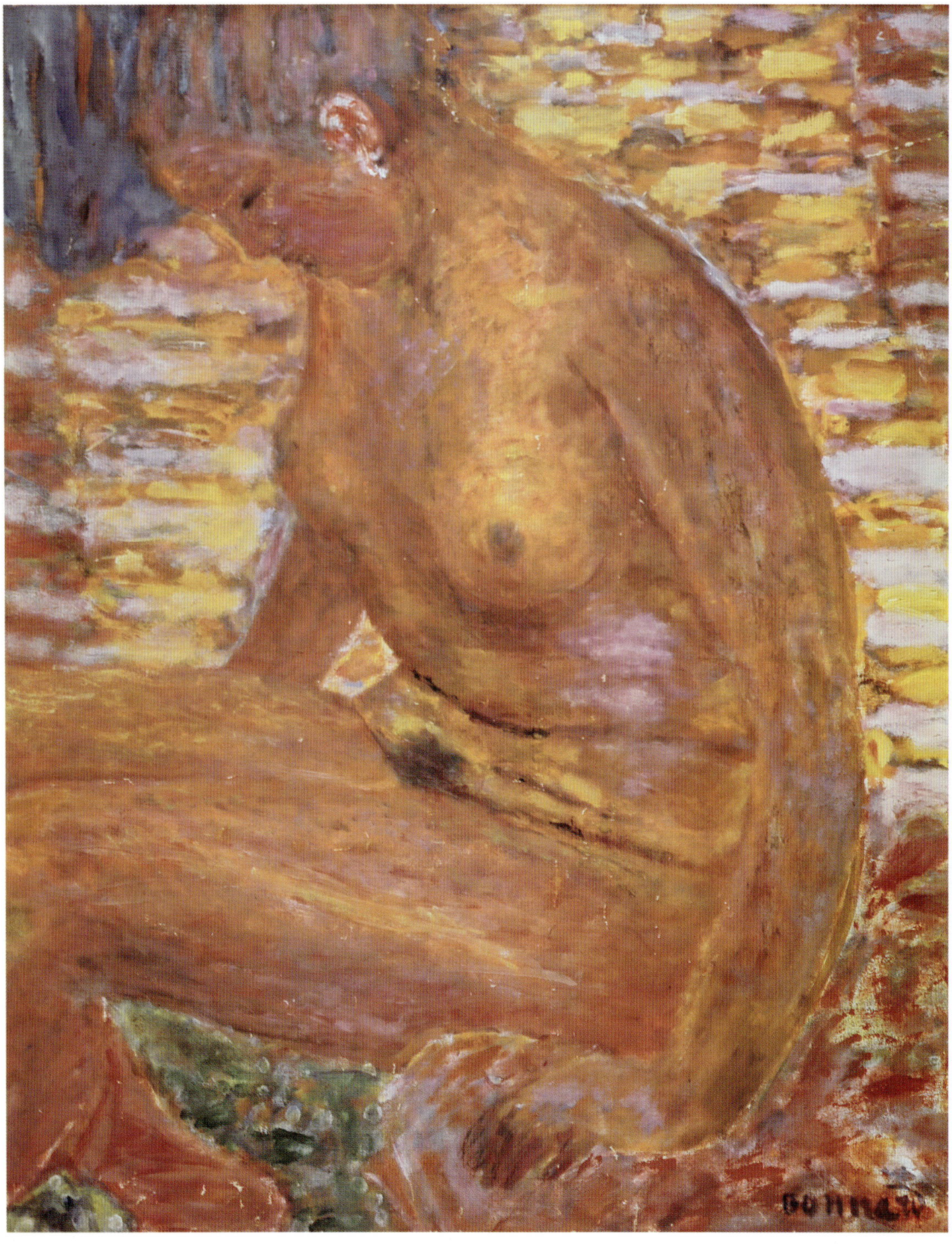

163
Nu sombre. 1942–6.
Oil on canvas, 81×55cm.
Private collection, Paris

A concomitant of Bonnard's life-long celebration of the transient was an ever-present consciousness of mortality, but to over-emphasize this aspect of his art would be to distort his achievement. The pain and desolation of the final self-portraits were vanquished by the radiant vision of his late style. Light assumed symbolic significance and became the key factor in his art. Light was the prime substance of vision, the energy of life itself. Human existence, in fact all life, was for him a process of metamorphosis in light. Form existed within, and was subject to, light. Light was love, hope and warmth. To merge with light was to acquiesce in fate. Death ultimately was but obliteration within light. 'Our God is light,' Bonnard told a young painter. 'A day will come when you will understand what that means.'[13]

A golden light suffuses the late paintings in a nostalgic glow. Bonnard's palette became hotter and richer. Paintings that began in the memory of the first impression – which he aimed to preserve – were transformed through colour into glorious light-filled tapestries. The view across the mouth of the Touque to Trouville from his rented villa at Deauville became the subject of *Le Port de Trouville* (Plate 167), which he began in 1936 and completed a decade later in 1946. An everyday scene is endowed with the sumptuous warmth of a Venetian pageant painted by Turner. 'Yes, isn't it a beautiful view?', Bonnard asked rhetorically in his interview with Ingrid Rydbeck at Deauville in 1937. 'But you should see it at high tide when the water reaches up and mirrors the houses and the boats ...'[14] He then took the idea of water as a mirror and turned the sea into a surface of silver, shot through with the golden threads of the setting sun and framed at the bottom by double bands of deep blue and claret red.

Nature for Bonnard continued to be both a balm and a source of inspiration. His correspondence, diaries and published statements are full of references to changes in atmosphere, light and colour. 'Nature', he wrote to Charles Terrasse on 28 December 1939, 'is the only consolation at this time.'[15] But rather than repeat trusted formulas as a form of therapy, Bonnard approached landscape in a spirit of exploration, feeling that he was breaking new ground. 'I am very interested in landscape,' he informed Vuillard in a letter written in April or May 1940, 'and my walks are filled with reflections on the subject.'[16] In his diary entries for 8 and 9 February 1940 he had drafted out four landscape categories: 'Spatial landscape with interesting foreground/ Intimate landscape with expressive objects/ Landscape with light effect predominating/ Decorative landscape little sky and furnished',[17] which he encapsulated in a letter to Matisse, adding the rider that he saw 'different things each day, the sky, the objects, all change continually, one can drown in it.'[18] His difficulty in maintaining a coherent vision in front of an ever-changing nature remained a problem and a stimulus to the very end.

While there is little of the programmatic about Bonnard's late landscapes, they are generally bolder, broader in execution, more colourful and decorative. Forms tend to merge with colour in a soft-focused, pulpy iridescent glow, as though the whole canvas surface has been fingered into life. *Paysage du Cannet, vue des toits*, 1941–2 (Plate 168), could be described in Bonnard's terms as a 'spatial landscape with interesting fore-

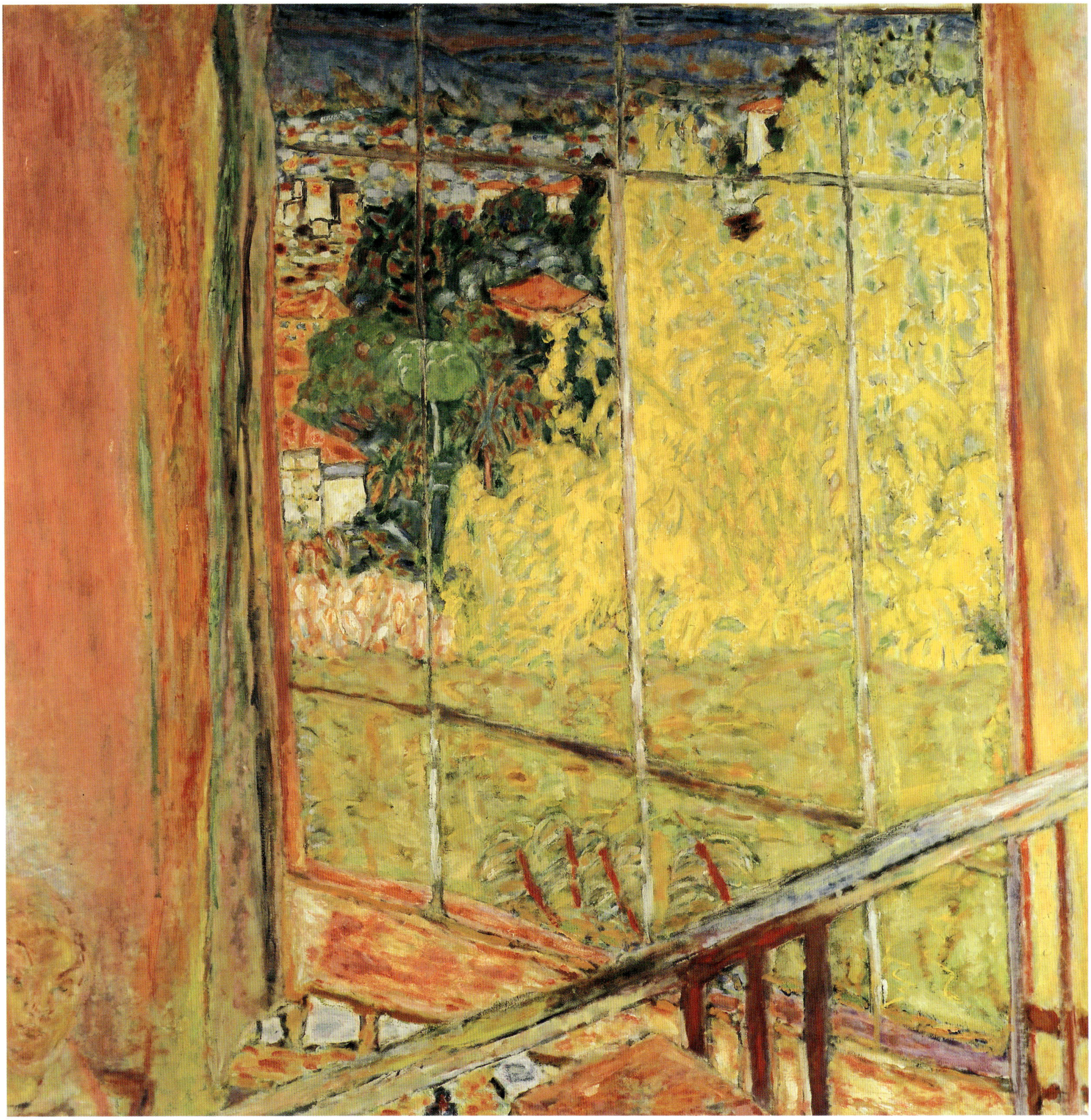

164
L'Atelier au mimosa. 1939–46.
Oil on canvas, 127×127cm.
Musée National d'Art Moderne, Centre Georges
Pompidou, Paris

ground'. To give the vast panorama from just behind Le Bosquet the necessary spatial breadth, Bonnard composed the painting in broad horizontal bands banked up the surface, from the tilled field broken into red blobs and roof-tiles glowing red against the green and yellow vegetation in the foreground to the distant mountains of the Esterel, topped by a dark green strip of cloud.

The creation of space and mood through colour remained one of Bonnard's constant preoccupations in the 1940s and ideas developed in one genre were transferred to another. *La Descente au Cannet*, 1940 (Plate 169), combines the theme in *Coin de table*, 1935 (Plate 158), of balancing a concentrated note of colour with an expanded area of white, with the idea in *Le Jardin*, *c.*1936 (Plate 124), of a path of colour leading through a vegetal tapestry. In *Grand paysage du Midi*, 1945 (Plate 170), the path changes from green to yellow and leads uphill. The marks making up the surface change in intensity from the energetic strokes of the foreground to the gentle, marbelized effect of the background. In both cases Bonnard probably began with the path of colour and then balanced it, if necessary enlarging the format with more canvas. He could never decide beforehand precisely what format he wanted and therefore preferred to work on unstretched canvas. 'If one just has a colour to start out from,' he told Ingrid Rydbeck, 'then one builds the whole painting round it. Colour has just as

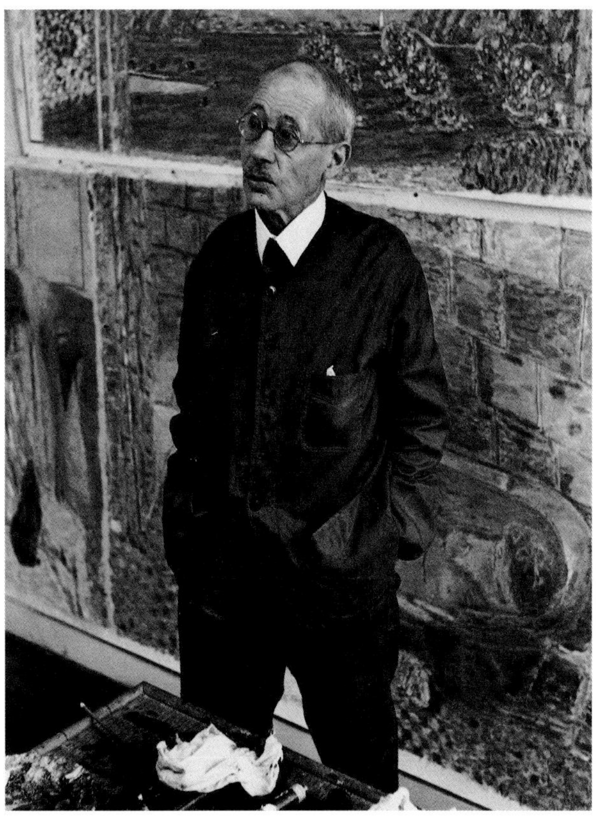

165
Pierre Bonnard. 1945–6.
Photograph by André Ostier

strong a logic as form. It's a matter of never giving up before one has managed to re-create the first impression ...'[19]

Bonnard's highly flexible technique and working methods in his last years have been well documented. Michel Terrasse described him as 'constantly active', moving from canvas to canvas 'like a bee'.[20] Oil paint was his preferred medium: '... I work so slowly', Bonnard explained, 'that I must have a material which I can keep on reworking. I want to keep on changing things and adding new things. It actually comes to me with difficulty.'[21] André Giverny noticed that Bonnard kept a separate plate, his palette, for each painting. Not only was a plate easier to clean, and showed up the colours better, but the actual colour scheme for a painting could evolve on this improvised palette. 'Why destroy a series of ideas which could be useful?', Bonnard observed.[22] The name Bonnard became synonymous with retouching; his paintings were never really finished, rather he stopped working on them. He had already signed his very last painting, *L'Amandier en fleur*, 1947 (Plate 172), the tree outside his bedroom window which he had painted on several occasions, when he noticed that the 'green on that bit of ground on the bottom on the left is not as it should be. It needs yellow ...', and too weak to do anything about it himself he got Charles Terrasse to help him touch it over in a golden yellow.[23]

To talk about Bonnard's colour is really to talk about his art as a whole. André Lhote saw Bonnard's colour as based on the transition from orange, forming the highlights in the foreground, to blue, the shadows in the background, via yellow and green or red-violet and blue-violet, and he established two groups of painters, those like Van Gogh who favoured the red, yellow and blue triangle and those like Bonnard who favoured the violet, green and orange triangle.[24] The preference for violet is frequently pointed out as unique to Bonnard. Jean Clair, on the other hand, read this system in reverse, suggesting that Bonnard gave the blue prominence in the foreground and positioned the orange furthest from the centre of vision.[25]

Such attempts to define Bonnard's colour in terms of a single system afford valuable insights, but fail to acknowledge that his art was made up of antitheses and contrasting conventions. In an interview in *Comoedia* of 10 April 1943, Bonnard made a distinction between the decorative painter and the 'painter of feeling'.[26] While it would be convenient to place Matisse in the former category and Bonnard in the latter, the truth is that both artists were working towards an expressive language of colour in the 1940s but by different routes: Matisse by flat colour and line and Bonnard by close-toned changes of colour within light. However, even here the distinction is by no means clear-cut, for they learned from each other. On a visit to Matisse at Vence in 1946 Bonnard noticed two paintings, *L'Asie* and *La Dame à la robe blanche*, and was struck by his own inability to handle flat colour; Matisse dispatched the paintings to Le Bosquet, where they hung for several weeks.[27] In a letter to Matisse Bonnard typically reported how the colours in *L'Asie* changed appearance with the light: 'the red is magnificent in the evening. By the day it's the blue that plays the main role.'[28]

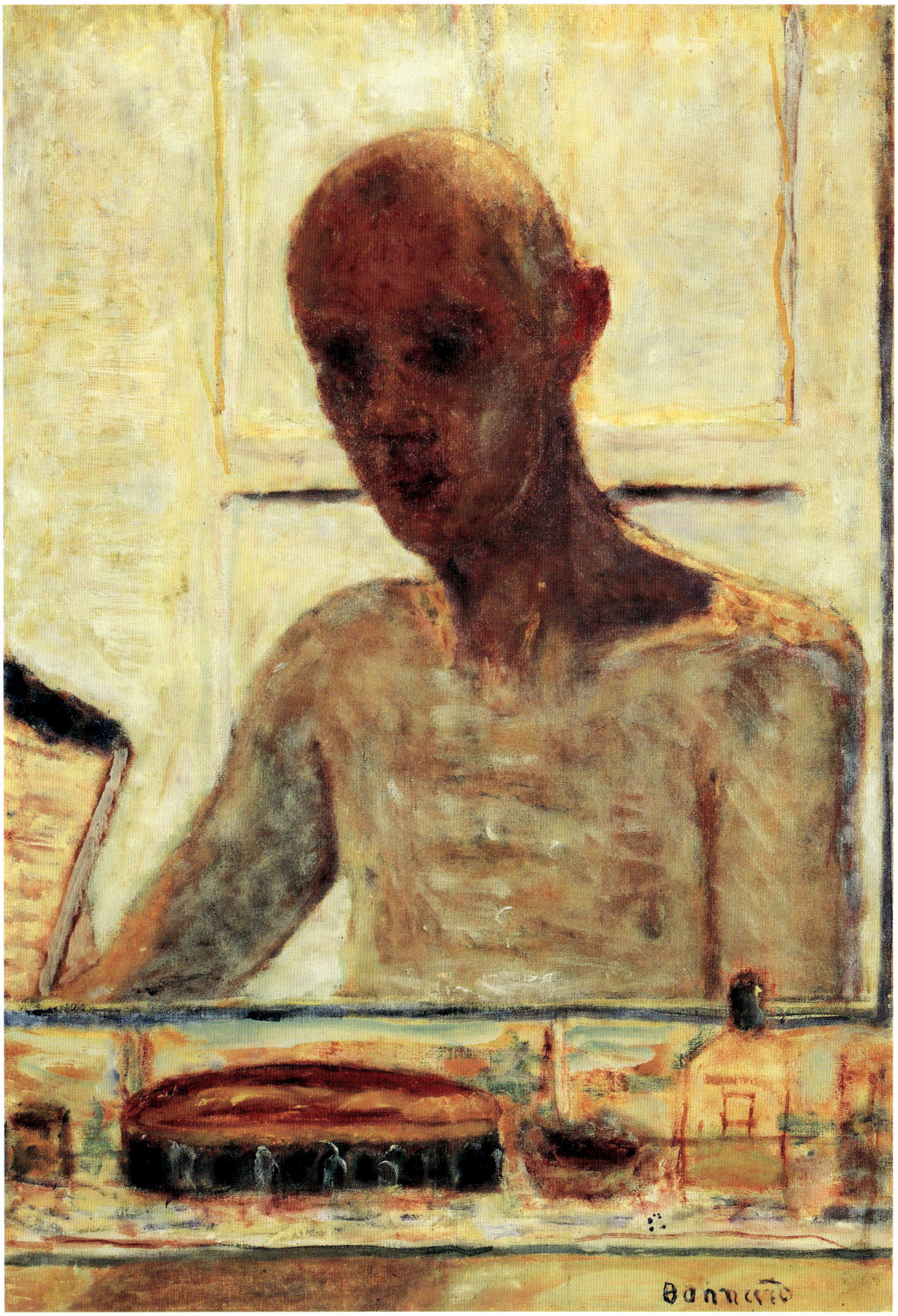

166
Portrait de l'artiste dans la glace. 1945.
Oil on canvas, 73×51cm.
Musée National d'Art Moderne, Centre Georges Pompidou, Paris

The polarity persisted in Bonnard's art between flat colour and luminosity, symbolized by the reproduction of Gauguin's *Vision after the Sermon*, 1888 (Plate 13), and the old silver paper sweet wrappers, used to gauge the scatter of reflected light, which he kept on his studio wall at Le Bosquet (see Plate 160). During his career he had evolved a completely novel way of thinking about colour, in which the emphasis was placed on brilliance and light, on rippling, rich surfaces made up of a myriad of little touches, rather than on large areas of unbroken, flat colour. This approach, although obviously indebted to the Impressionists, had much in common with Byzantine mosaics, which he may have looked at on his trip to Venice with Vuillard and Roussel in 1899.[29] André Lhote hailed this 'resurrection of the nuance' and Bonnard's 'prodigious chromatic subtlety'.[30]

Bonnard's final interiors are among his most successful and challenging paintings, because the rooms provided the architectural structure, enabling him to deal with flooding colour in abstract form, without losing touch with reality. The mirror, reflecting the basket of fruit on the sideboard, provides the framework in *Corbeille de fruits se reflétant dans une glace de buffet*, 1944–6 (Plate 171). In *L'Atelier au mimosa*, 1939–46 (Plate 164), Bonnard's last masterpiece, the window structures the landscape in a grid of squares, and the balcony acts as a see-saw balancing the movement between interior and exterior. The expansive yellow of the mimosa permeating the reddened warmth of the interior is balanced by the relatively small areas of deep blue and green in the landscape outside. Intimism is combined with decoration. The painting stands as Bonnard's final paean to the transforming power of light.

Pierre Bonnard died at Le Cannet on 23 January 1947. His reputation, which had declined between the wars, along with that of the Impressionists and their successors, picked up in the 1940s, as his art was once again seen as a fitting antidote to the times. Pierre Courthion, in his book on Bonnard published in 1945, placed him alongside Renoir in the Impressionist school.[31] Depending on the critic's stance, to be linked with the Impressionists was a sign either of approval or weakness, even failure. According to Bonnard's supporter, Claude Roger-Marx, 'he was reproached, like them [the Impressionists], with what one may term his lack of construction, the inconsistency of his surface [matière], the fragility of his drawing.'[32] Zervos went much further in his extremely hostile article in *Cahiers d'Art* of 1947, written in response to the Bonnard retrospective exhibition at the Orangerie. The short answer to the question of his title, 'Pierre Bonnard est-il un grand peintre?' was definitely no. Bonnard for him was a minor talent. He could think of nothing more decisive to clarify the nature and degree of his objection to Bonnard than 'to indicate his position between the end of Impressionism and the new generation'.[33]

Bonnard's dealers and the authors of his *catalogue raisonné*, Jean and Henry Dauberville, the sons of Josse Bernheim, have pointed out that Picasso and Matisse enjoyed global reputations when Bonnard was only appreciated in Europe.[34] This was partly Bonnard's own fault. Although pleased to receive recognition abroad, he

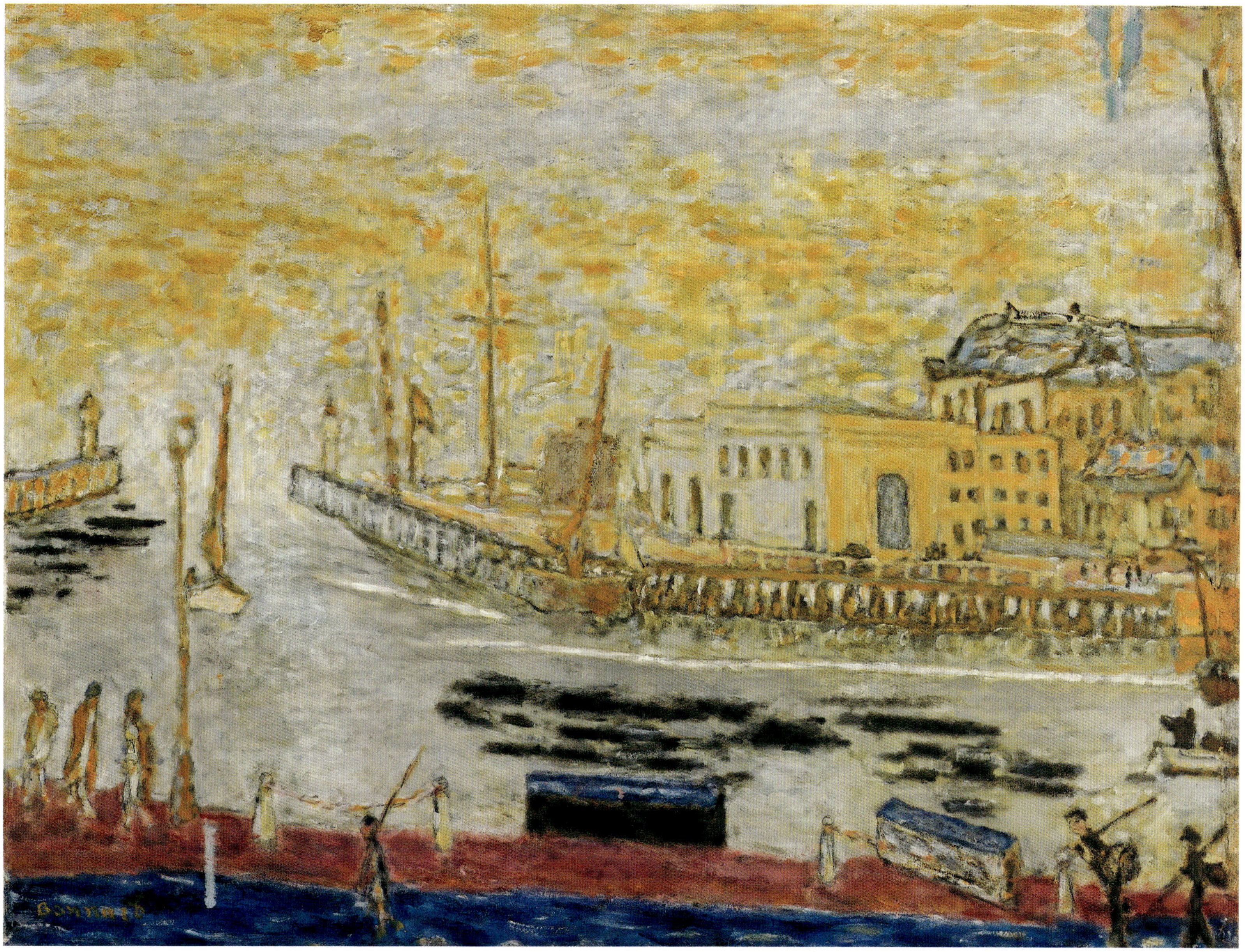

167
Le Port de Trouville. 1936–46.
Oil on canvas, 77×103cm.
Musée National d'Art Moderne, Centre Georges Pompidou, Paris

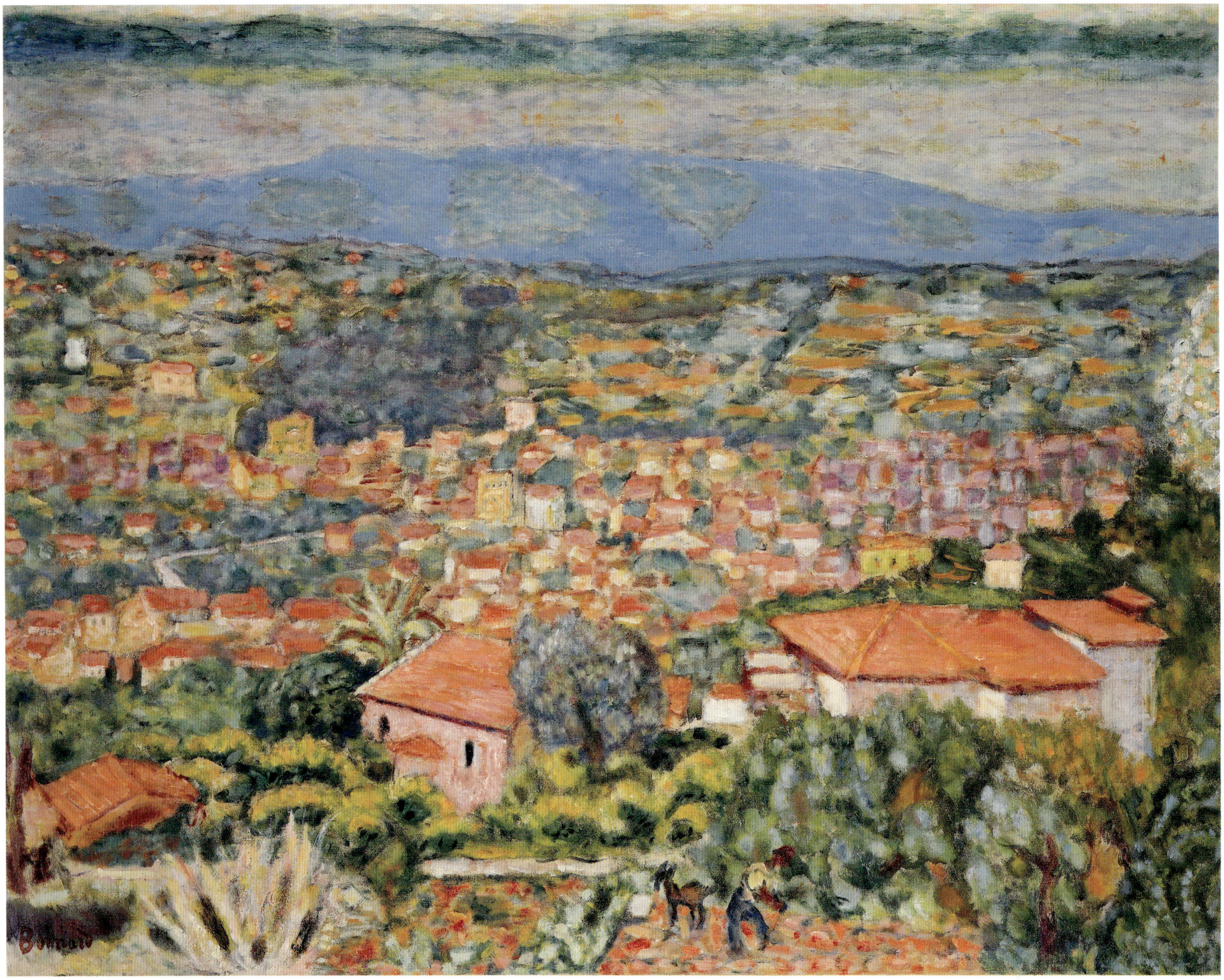

168
Paysage du Cannet, vue des toits. 1941–2.
Oil on canvas, 80×104cm.
Private collection

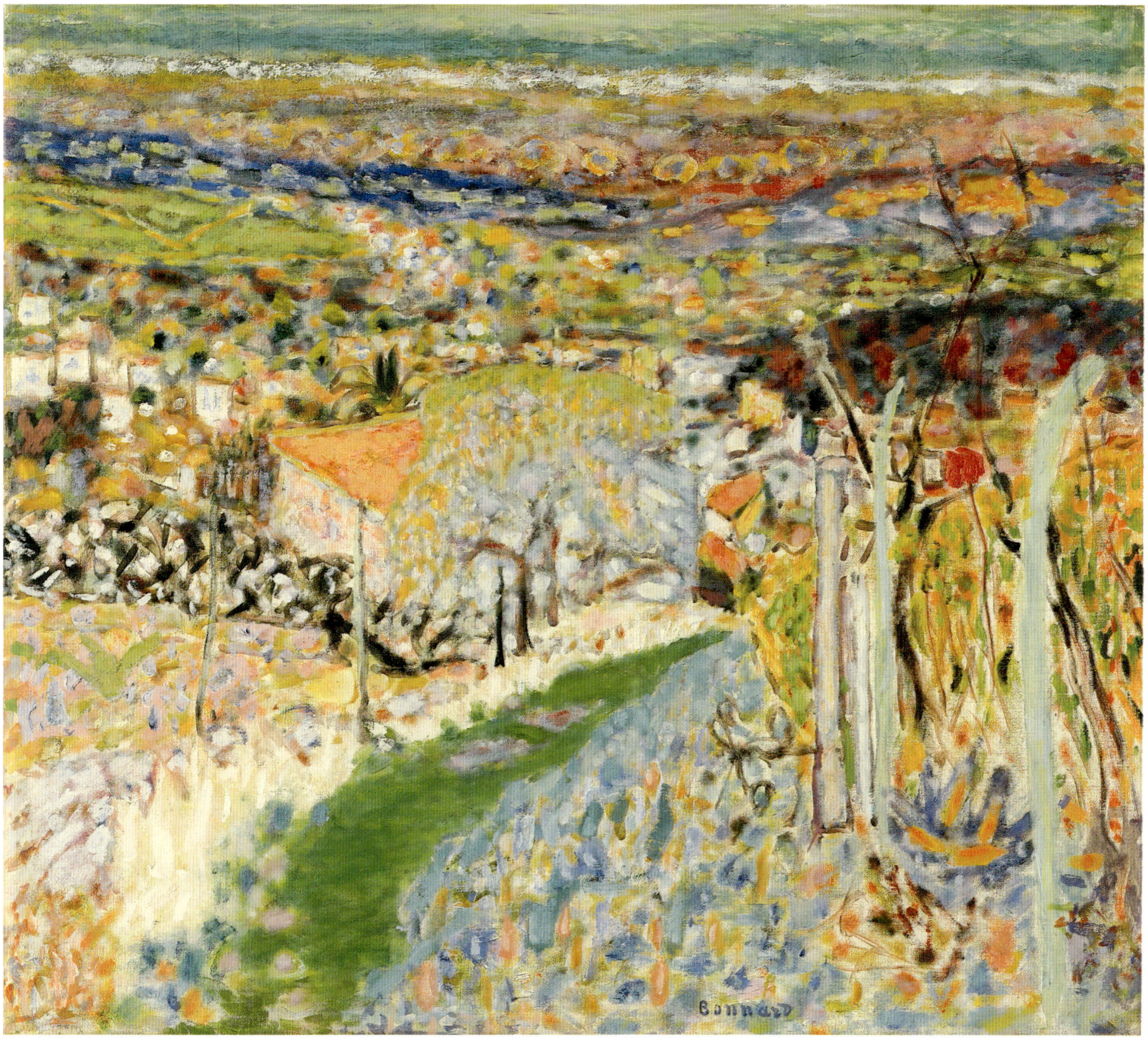

169
La Descente au Cannet. 1940.
Oil on canvas, 65×72cm.
Metropolitan Museum of Art, New York,
Robert Lehman Collection, 1975

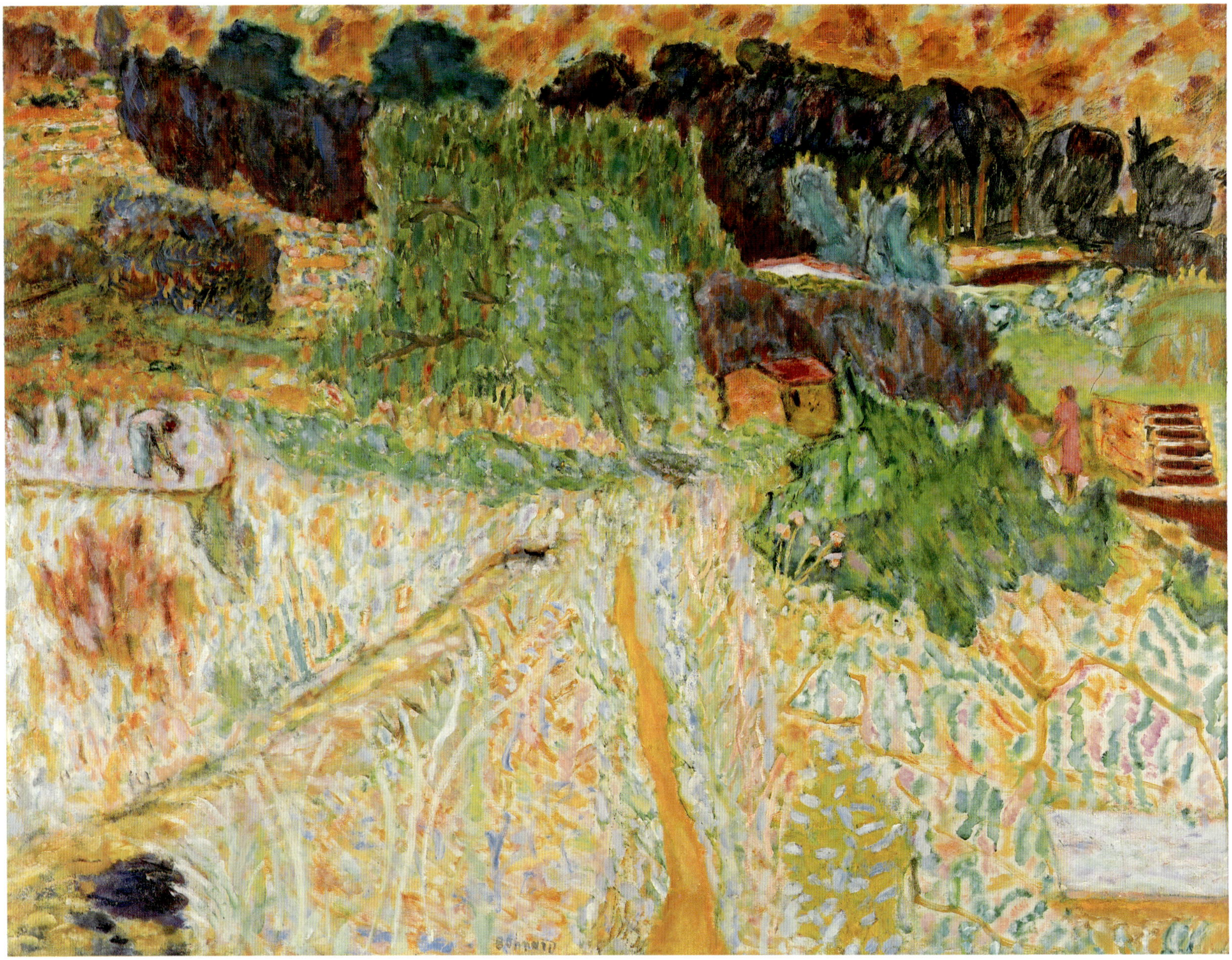

170
Grand paysage du Midi. 1945.
Oil on canvas, 95×125cm.
Milwaukee Art Museum, gift of Mr and Mrs Harry
Lynde Bradley

remained chauvinistically French. In the autumn of 1946, he asked the Daubervilles not to push his sales in the United States.[35]

Bonnard became better known abroad through the retrospective exhibitions held after his death. His status as a latter-day Impressionist went largely unchallenged. Writing in the introduction to the catalogue of the Bonnard–Vuillard exhibition, held at the Royal Scottish Academy during the Edinburgh Festival of 1948, Clive Bell thought that historians of the twenty-first century would probably end up by classifying the two young Nabis of the 1890s as the last of the Impressionists, and he compared Bonnard with Renoir 'in his appetite for beauty and power of making us share that enjoyment'.[36] In the catalogue to the Bonnard memorial exhibition organized by The Museum of Modern Art, New York, in collaboration with The Cleveland Museum of Art, in 1948, John Rewald concluded: 'The successor and last survivor of Impressionism, Bonnard carried on a glorious tradition, revitalized through the harmonious interplay of acute observation, happy imagination and innate lyricism. His ultimate message was the apotheosis of color, as if he felt that in these troubled times it would bring salvation.'[37]

Some sixteen years later this perception of Bonnard's position had hardly changed. Ostensibly without what Lawrence Gowing described as 'a single innovation of style',[38] his art continued to be discussed within the framework of Impressionism. James Thrall Soby began his catalogue introduction to the exhibition *Bonnard and His Environment*, organized in 1964 by the The Museum of Modern Art, New York, in collaboration with the Los Angeles County Museum of Art and the Art Institute of Chicago, by saying: 'It is a paradox of Pierre Bonnard's long and most distinguished career that in the United States, where the French Impressionists found a number of early and fervent champions, their spiritual heir, Bonnard, has only lately come to great fame ... Possibly our taste for visual revolution, once aroused, found Bonnard belated in aim. At any rate his following and patronage remained predominantly European until after the war.'[39]

It has been largely left to Bonnard's close supporters and fellow artists to give more complex readings of his art. Claude Roger-Marx saw him as having abandoned to his dear friend Vuillard 'the habitual mysteries and greys of silence, he followed Odilon Redon into the imaginary, into earthly paradises where the simplest object – tub or basket – and the most familiar nudes are endowed with a supernatural irradiation.'[40] After the Second World War Bonnard's message was one of hope, of faith in the infinite human capacity to see life afresh, without cynicism. Floating between intimism and decoration, his art appealed to both figurative and abstract artists. The painter and critic, Patrick Heron, wanting 'to assist the reader to become more conscious of the palpable realities of painting and sculpture', wrote a seminal essay on Bonnard in 1947, which was published in 1955.[41] Picasso was the yardstick by which Bonnard was often judged and found wanting, but Heron interestingly saw Picasso's influence on the wane and the young French painters turning more to Matisse and Bonnard: 'So, when we regard Bonnard solely in the context of twentieth-century painting; even, that is, if we study him with eyes accustomed to the lens that is Picasso, we shall not make the mistake of assigning him to the Past: we shall not look upon him as an intruder into the Present from the Impressionist Nineties; as the final ambassador of an anachronism. He is nothing of the kind.'[42] Bonnard for Heron was a painter of the highest imaginative order. Neither decorative, nor imitative, he combined 'the abstract music of interacting form-colour' with subject-matter drawn across the surface in an all-over pattern.[43]

One could argue that the very fact that there has been little agreement as to Bonnard's achievement has meant that he has remained open for succeeding generations of artists to discover on their own terms as a vital source of inspiration. It is also a supreme testament to his strength and depth as an artist that they have continued to do so. Bonnard is above all a painter's painter whose radiant vision gives profound pleasure to us all.

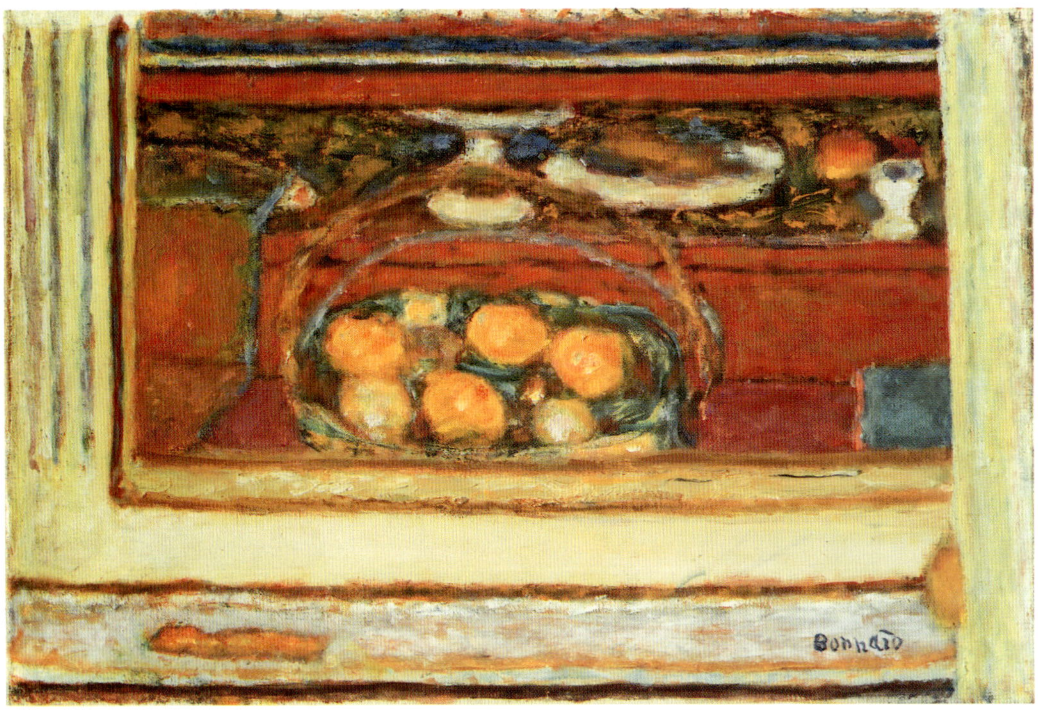

171
Corbeille de fruits se reflétant dans une glace de buffet. 1944–6.
Oil on canvas, 47.3×71.4cm.
Museum of Modern Art, New York, gift of Mr and Mrs David Rockefeller

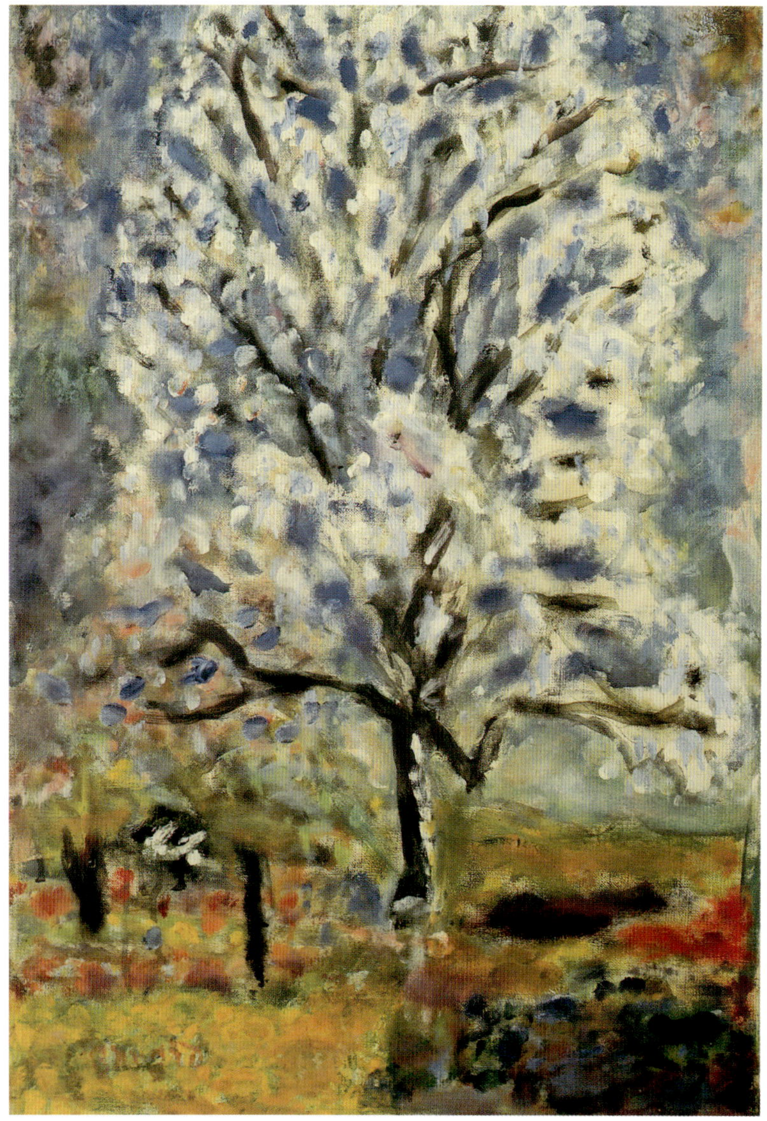

172
L'Amandier en fleur. 1947.
Oil on canvas, 55×37.5cm.
Musée National d'Art Moderne, Centre Georges Pompidou, Paris

Notes to chapter 1

1. Courthion, 1945, pp. 23.
2. Roger-Marx, 1950, unpaginated.
3. Charles Terrasse, 1944, p. 27.
4. For the most complete discussion to date of Bonnard's background and education, see Giambruni, 1983, pp. 1–13.
5. Charles Terrasse, 1927, p. 27.
6. Cogniat, 1968, p. 16.
7. Bonnard, 1944, pp. 7–77.
8. Giambruni, 1983, p. 16.
9. Frèches-Thory and Terrasse, 1990, p. 13.
10. Denis, 1903.
11. Marlais, 1993, p. 123.
12. Boyer, 1988, p. 4.
13. Frèches-Thory and Terrasse, 1990, p. 87.
14. Weisberg, 1991, pp. 14, 13.
15. Diehl, 1943.
16. Perucchi-Petri, 1976, p. 50.
17. Diehl, 1943.
18. Bouvet, 1981, pp. 5, 6.
19. Mauner, 1978, p. 70.
20. Lugné-Poe, 1930, pp. 189–92.
21. Huret, 1891, p. 869.
22. Robichez, 1957, p. 53.
23. Frèches-Thory and Terrasse, 1990, p. 94.
24. Perucchi-Petri, 1976, p. 43.
25. Halperin, 1988, p. 226.
26. Boyer, 1988, p. 38.
27. Bernier, 1983, pp. 7–9.
28. For details of Misia's life see Gold and Fizdale, 1980.
29. Vaillant, 1966, p. 77.
30. Rearick, 1983, pp. 27–74.
31. Sasha M. Newman, 'Nudes and Landscapes', in Ives, Giambruni and Newman, 1989, p. 152.
32. Helen Giambruni, 'Domestic Scenes', in Ives, Giambruni and Newman, 1989, p. 46.
33. Antoine Terrasse, 1988/9, p. 22.
34. Antoine Terrasse, 1988/9, p. 312.
35. Roger Marx, 'Les Indépendants', *Le Voltaire*, 28 March 1893, quoted in Giambruni, 1983, pp. 148–9.
36. Vollard, 1978, p. 16.
37. Rearick, 1983, p. 176.
38. Ives, 1988 (B), p. 38.
39. Cogniat, 1968, p. 30.
40. Natanson, 1951, p. 28.
41. Nicholas Watkins in *Bonnard*, Tokyo, 1991, p. 143.
42. Makarius, 1984, p. 110.
43. Quoted by Fumet, 1944, p. 18.

Notes to chapter 2

1. Pissarro, 1950, p. 398.
2. Rydbeck, 1937.
3. Bouvet, New York and London, 1981, p. 106.
4. Sasha Newman, 'Nudes and Landscapes', in Ives, Giambruni and Newman, 1989, p. 162.
5. Carter, 1969, p. vii.
6. Hilley, 1988, p. 28.
7. Perman, 1963, p. 11.
8. Heilbrun and Néagu, 1987, p. 7.
9. Bernier, 1983, p. 23.
10. Arne Eggum, 'Munch tente de conquérir Paris (1896–1900)', in *Munch et la France*, 1992, pp. 188–203.
11. Longus, 1968, p. 17.
12. Bouvier, 1943.
13. Frèches-Thory and Terrasse, 1990, p. 70.
14. Heilbrun and Néagu, 1987, pp. 127–30.
15. Proust, 1983, p. 903.
16. Barber, 1989, p. 68.
17. Vaillant, 1966, p. 94.
18. Henry Dauberville, 'Bonnard vivant', in Dauberville, 1965–74, vol. 1, p. 41.
19. Watkins, 1984, p. 70.
20. Richardson, 1991, p. 424.
21. Cocteau, 1926, pp. 98–9.
22. *Bonnard/Matisse Correspondance*, 1991, p. 63.
23. Cogeval, 1993, p. 86.
24. Gabriel P. Weisberg, 'Premier printemps', in *Bonnard*, Tokyo, 1991, pp. 148–9.
25. Havard, 1892, p. 130.
26. Ives, Giambruni and Newman, 1989, p. 133.
27. Pierre Courthion, 'Impromptus, Pierre Bonnard', *Les Nouvelles littéraires*, 24 June 1933, quoted in Ives, Giambruni and Newman, 1989, p. 142.
28. Cogeval, 1993, p. 94.
29. Henry Dauberville, 'Bonnard vivant', in Dauberville, 1965–74, vol. 1, pp. 19–20.
30. Vaillant, 1966, p. 110.
31. Vaillant, 1966, p. 128.
32. Henry Dauberville, 'Bonnard vivant', in Dauberville, 1965–74, vol. 1, pp. 13 and 23.
33. Dauberville, 1965–74.
34. Sert, 1952, p. 94.
35. Bothe, 1989, p. 314.
36. Vollard, 1978, p. 223.
37. Dauberville, 1965–74, vol. 1, pp. 40 and 59.
38. Vaillant, 1966, p. 103.
39. Vaillant, 1966, p. 110.
40. Vaillant, 1966, pp. 182–3.
41. For a full account of the sources and genesis of the painting see Margit Hahnloser-Ingold, 'La Promenade en mer, image et portrait', in *Bonnard*, Paris, 1984, pp. 207–17.
42. *Renoir*, 1985, p. 241.
43. Vollard, 1978, p. 90.
44. Antoine Terrasse, 1988, p. 86.
45. Richard Thomson, 1988, p. 223.
46. Antoine Terrasse in conversation with the author, Fontainebleau, March 1991.

Notes to chapter 3

1. Fry, 1912, quoted in Bullen, 1988, pp. 87–8.
2. Dyer, 1978, pp. 29–36; Bernard, 1975, pp. 108–10.
3. Fridenson, 1992, p. 1.
4. Silver, 1989, p. 9.
5. Silver, 1989, pp. 43–50.
6. Cowling and Mundy, 1990, p. 11.
7. Vaillant, 1966, p. 113.
8. Vauxcelles, 1903.
9. Kostenevich and Semyonova, 1993, p. 14.
10. Bullen, 1988, p. 380. It is unclear which of the two versions of the painting the critic is referring to.
11. Sophie Fourny-Dargère, 'Promenade de long de la Seine', in *Scènes de la Seine*, 1986, p. 160.
12. William H. Gerdts, 'American Art and the French Experience', in *Lasting Impressions, American Painters in France 1865–1915*, 1992, pp. 11 and 43.
13. Levine, 1976, p. 297.
14. Spate, 1992, p. 238.
15. Levine, 1976, p. 393.
16. Frèches-Thory and Terrasse, 1990, pp. 131 and 134.
17. Spate, 1992, p. 164.
18. Charles Terrasse, 1927, p. 141.
19. Cogeval, 1993, p. 100.
20. Published in Newman, 1984 (A), p. 132.
21. Charles Terrasse, 1927, pp. 128–9.
22. Antoine Terrasse, 1967, p. 122.
23. Mann, 1984, p. 10.
24. Michel Terrasse, 1988, p. 9.
25. Mann, 1991, p. 49.
26. Natanson, 1951, p. 79.
27. Antoine Terrasse in conversation with the author, Fontainebleau, March 1991.
28. Brassaï, 1982, p. 11.
29. Charles Terrasse, 1927, p. 120.
30. Jean Clair, 'The Adventures of the Optic Nerve', in Newman, 1984 (A), pp. 29–30.
31. Mann, 1991, pp. 126–7.
32. Cogeval, 1993, p. 108.
33. Bonnard's link with tapestries was a subject of frequent comment, from the first monographs. See Fosca, 1919, p. 14.
34. Newman, 1984 (A), p. 170.
35. Newman, 1984 (A), p. 182.
36. Sargy Mann in conversation with the author, March 1991.
37. Dauberville, 1965–74, nos. 1123–8.
38. Antoine Terrasse in conversation with the author, Fontainebleau, March 1991.
39. Cogeval, 1993, p. 124.
40. Ibid.

Notes to chapter 4

1. Fosca, 1919, p. 7.
2. Roger-Marx, 1924, p. 3.
3. Fosca, 1919, p. 61.
4. For the most complete chronology to date of Bonnard's life and art, see Antoine Terrasse, 1988, pp. 240–302.
5. Dauberville, 1965–74, vol. 1, p. 13.
6. Courthion, 1945, p. 30.
7. Heron, 1955, p. 118.
8. Clair, 1975, p. 18.
9. Bryson, 1990, pp. 60–95.
10. Quoted Rookmaaker, 1972, p. 71.
11. Quoted in Antoine Terrasse, 1988, p. 166.
12. Published in Newman, 1984 (A), p. 69.
13. Antoine Terrasse in conversation with the author, Fontainebleau, March 1991.
14. 'Les Notes de Bonnard', published in *Bonnard*, Paris, 1984, p. 191.
15. Roger-Marx, 1950, unpaginated.
16. Newman, 1984 (A), p. 51.
17. Jean Clair, 'The Adventures of the Optic Nerve', in Newman, 1984 (A), pp. 37–40.
18. Jean Clair, 'The Adventures of the Optic Nerve', in Newman, 1984 (A), p. 39.
19. Newman, 1984 (A), p. 69.
20. Rudenstine, 1976, pp. 39–41.
21. Charles Terrasse, 1927, p. 152.
22. Mme Marthe Lebasque-Reymond interviewed by Donia Appoline, Nice, 1983, in Banner and Fairbanks, 1986, p. 72.
23. Newman, 1984 (A), pp. 16 and 128.
24. Antoine Terrasse in conversation with the author, Fontainebleau, March 1991.
25. Bouvet, 1981, pp. 240–1.
26. Mann, 1991, p. 92.
27. Wollheim, 1991, p. 14.
28. Newman, 1984 (A), p. 148.
29. Natanson, 1951, p. 94.
30. Quoted in Antoine Terrasse, 1988, p. 296.
31. *Bonnard*, Paris, 1984, p. 186.
32. Michel Terrasse, 1988, p. 12.
33. Vaillant, 1966, p. 142.
34. I am deeply indebted to Mme Michel Terrasse for expertly guiding me round Le Bosquet.
35. Michel Terrasse, 1988, p. 121.
36. I am grateful to my colleague Professor Anthony Sutcliffe, Department of Economic and Social History, University of Leicester, for information on the economic history of the mirror in Paris.
37. Rydbeck, 1957.
38. 'Les Notes de Bonnard', in *Bonnard*, Paris, 1984, p. 183.
39. Watkins, 1984, pp. 174–5.
40. *Bonnard/Matisse Correspondance*, 1991, pp. 34–5.
41. 'Les Notes de Bonnard', in *Bonnard*, Paris, 1984, p. 182.
42. 'Notes by Hans R. Hahnloser', in Vaillant, 1966, p. 184.
43. Vaillant, 1966, p. 184.
44. Quoted in Richardson, 1959, p. 26.
45. *Bonnard/Matisse Correspondance*, 1991, p. 58.
46. Charles Terrasse, 1927, p. 180.

Notes to chapter 5

1. Letter to Charles Terrasse, 20 June 1944, in Antoine Terrasse, 1988, p. 217.
2. *Bonnard/Matisse Correspondance*, 1991, p. 90.
3. *Bonnard/Matisse Correspondance*, 1991, p. 91.
4. Vaillant, 1966, p. 137.
5. Giverny, 1945, p. 59.
6. Ibid.
7. Ibid.
8. Newman, 1984 (A), p. 234.
9. Bonnard, 1944.
10. Clair, 1975, unpaginated.
11. Pérez, 1984, pp. 12–3.
12. *Bonnard/Matisse Correspondance*, 1991, p. 127.
13. Rewald, 1948, p. 57.
14. Rydbeck, 1957, p. 3.
15. Letter to Charles Terrasse in Antoine Terrasse, 1988, p. 293.
16. Letter to Vuillard, in Antoine Terrasse, 1988, p. 293.
17. Published in Newman, 1984 (A), p. 64.
18. *Bonnard/Matisse Correspondance*, 1991, p. 68.
19. Rydbeck, 1957.
20. Michel Terrasse, 1988, p. 21.
21. Rydbeck, 1957.
22. Giverny, 1945, p. 59.
23. Charles Terrasse, 1964, p. 144.
24. Clair, 1975, p. 46.
25. Clair, 1975, pp. 44–5.
26. Bonnard, *Comoedia*, 10 April 1943.
27. *Bonnard/Matisse Correspondance*, 1991, p. 126.
28. Ibid.
29. Dr Elizabeth James, 'Painting with Light. Colour in Byzantine art', meeting of The Colour Group of Great Britain, The National Gallery, London, 4 November 1992.
30. Lhote, 1948, p. 3.
31. Courthion, 1945, p. 86.
32. Roger-Marx, 1950, unpaginated.
33. Zervos, 1947, pp. 1 and 4.
34. Dauberville, 1965–74, vol. 1, p. 43.
35. Dauberville, 1965–74, vol. 1.
36. Bell, 1948, pp. 3, 6, 7.
37. Rewald, 1948, p. 56.
38. Gowing, 1989/90, p. 21.
39. Soby, 1964, p. 9.
40. Roger Marx, 1950, unpaginated
41. Heron, 1955, p. ix.
42. Heron, 1955, p. 116.
43. Heron, 1955, p. 119.

Bibliography

Adriani, G., *Toulouse-Lautrec. The Complete Graphic Works. A Catalogue Raisonné*. Exhibition catalogue (Royal Academy of Arts, London, 1988).

Aurier, G.-A.,'Les Symbolistes', *La Revue encyclopédique*, 2, no. 32 (1 April 1892), pp. 475–86.

Alley, Ronald, *Tate Gallery. Foreign Paintings, Drawings and Sculpture* (Tate Gallery, London, 1959).

Alley, Ronald, 'Bonnard's "Le Bol de lait", c.1920 (Tate Gallery)',*The Burlington Magazine*, 110 (April 1968), p. 216.

Banner, Lisa A., and Fairbanks, Peter M., *Lebasque 1865–1937* (San Francisco, 1986).

Barber, Giles, *Daphnis and Chloe: the Markets and Metamorphoses of an Unknown Bestseller* (British Library, London, 1989).

Basler, Adolphe, and Kunstler, Charles, *La Peinture indépendante en France* (Paris,1929).

Bazin, Germain, *Impressionist Paintings in the Louvre* (London, 1958).

Beer, F.-J., *Pierre Bonnard* (Marseilles, 1947).

Bell, Clive, *Art* (London, 1914).

Bell, Clive, *Bonnard-Vuillard*. Exhibition catalogue (Royal Scottish Academy, Edinburgh, 1948).

Bernard, Philippe, *La Fin d'un monde 1914–1929* (Paris, 1975).

Bernier,G., *La Revue Blanche. Paris in the Days of Post-Impressionism and Symbolism* (Wildenstein & Co., New York, 1983).

Besson, G., *Bonnard* (Paris, 1934; revised edn., Paris, 1947).

Bonnard, Pierre, 'Souvenirs sur Renoir', *Comoedia* (18 October 1941).

'Pierre Bonnard nous écrit', *Comoedia* (10 April 1943).

Correspondances (Paris, 1944).

Bonnard. Exhibition catalogue (Centre Georges Pompidou, Musée National d'Art Moderne, Paris, 1984).

Bonnard. Exhibition catalogue (Kunsthaus, Zürich, 1984).

Bonnard. Exhibition catalogue (Palazzo Reale, Milan, 1988).

Bonnard. Exhibition catalogue (Fondation de l'Hermitage, Lausanne, 1991).

Bonnard/Matisse Correspondance. Presented by Jean Clair and Antoine Terrasse (Paris, 1991).

Pierre Bonnard. Exhibition catalogue (Tokyo, 1991).

Pierre Bonnard. Das Gluck zu malen. Exhibition catalogue (Kunstsammlung Nordrhein-Westfalen, Dusseldorf, 1993).

Bothe, Rolf (ed.), *Curt Herrmann* (Berlin, 1989).

Bouvet, Francis, *Bonnard. L'Oeuvre gravé* (Paris, 1981); English Edition, *Bonnard. The Complete Graphic Work*, translated by Jane Brenton (New York and London, 1981).

Bouvier, Marguerite, 'Pierre Bonnard revient à la litho ...', *Comoedia* (23 January 1943).

Boyer, Patricia Eckert (ed.), *The Nabis and the Parisian Avant-Garde* (New Brunswick and London, 1988).

Brassaï, *The Artists of My Life* (London, 1982).

Bryson, Norman, *Looking at the Overlooked. Four Essays on Still Life Painting* (London, 1990).

Bullen, J.B. (ed.), *Post-Impressionists in England* (London and New York, 1988).

Cachin, Françoise, *Paul Signac* (Milan, 1970).

Callen, Anthea, *Techniques of the Impressionists* (London, 1982).

Carco, Francis, *L'Ami des peintres* (Geneva, 1944).

Carter, A.E., *Verlaine. A Study in Parallels* (Toronto, 1969).

Cassou, Jean, 'The Lyricism of Bonnard', *Formes*, no. 9 (Paris and New York, November 1930), pp. 4–5.

Clair, Jean, 'Bonnard ou l'espace du miroir', *La Nouvelle Revue française*, no. 176 (March 1967), pp. 510–15.

Clair, Jean, 'Correspondance Matisse-Bonnard', *La Nouvelle Revue française*, no. 211 (July 1970), pp. 82–100; no. 212 (August 1970), pp. 53–70.

Clair, Jean, *Bonnard* (Paris, 1975).

Cocteau, Jean, *Le Rappel à l'ordre* (Paris, 1926).

Cogeval, Guy, *Bonnard* (Paris, 1993).

Cogniat, Raymond, *Bonnard*, (Paris, 1968; English edition, New York, 1968).

Cooper, Douglas, *The Courtauld Collection* (London, 1954).

Coquiot, Gustave, *Les Indépendants, 1884–1920* (Paris, 1920).

Coquiot, Gustave, *Bonnard* (Paris,1922).

'Couleur de Bonnard', *Verve*, 5, nos. 17–18 (Paris, August 1947).

Courthion, Pierre, *Bonnard. Peintre du merveilleux* (Lausanne, 1945).

Cowling, Elizabeth, and Mundy, Jennifer, *On Classic Ground. Picasso, Léger, de Chirico and the New Classicism 1910–1930*. Exhibition catalogue (Tate Gallery, London, 1990).

Dauberville, Jean and Henry, *Bonnard: Catalogue raisonné de l'oeuvre peint*, 4 vols. (Paris, 1965–74).

Daurelle, Jacques, 'Chez les jeunes peintres: M. Pierre Bonnard', *L'Echo de Paris* (28 December 1891).

Denis, Maurice, 'L'Influence de Paul Gauguin', *L'Occident* (October 1903).

Denis, Maurice, *Théories, 1890–1910, du Symbolisme et de Gauguin vers un nouvel ordre classique*, 3rd edition (Paris, 1913).

Derain, André, *Lettres à Vlaminck* (Paris, 1955).

Diehl, Gaston, 'Pierre Bonnard dans son univers enchanté', *Comoedia* (10 July 1943).

Diehl, Gaston, *Les Fauves* (Paris, 1971).

Diehl, Gaston, *The Fauves* (New York, 1975).

Doener, M., *The Materials of the Artist* (London, 1976).

Dorival, Bernard, *Twentieth Century Painters. Nabis, Fauves, Cubists* (New York, 1958).

Dubief, H., *Le Déclin de la troisième République 1929–1938* (Paris, 1976).

Dunlop, I., *The Shock of the New* (London, 1972).

Duthuit, Georges, *Les Fauves* (Geneva, 1949); English edition, *The Fauvist Painters* (New York, 1950).

Dyer, Colin, *Population and Society in Twentieth-Century France* (London, 1978).

Earp, T.-W., 'Modern French Painting at the Tate Gallery', *Apollo*, 4 (August 1926), p. 64.

Easton, Elizabeth W., exhibition review, 'Pierre Bonnard: The Graphic Art, Metropolitan Museum of Art, New York, 1989', *The Burlington Magazine* (April 1990), pp. 293–5.

Elderfield, John, *The 'Wild Beasts': Fauvism and its Affinities* (New York, 1976).

Escholier, Raymond, 'Le Salon des Indépendants', *Art et décoration*, 37 (March 1920), pp. 73–80.

Escholier, Raymond, *Matisse, ce vivant* (Paris, 1956); English edition, *Matisse from the Life* (London, 1960).

Estienne, Charles, 'Les Grandes Expositions de Paris: au Musée de l'Orangerie: Pierre Bonnard', *Arts*, no. 136 (17 October 1947), p. 8.

Fels, Florent, *L'Art vivant de 1900 à nos jours* (Geneva, 1950).

Fénéon, Félix, 'Sur les murs', *Chat noir*, 10 (6 June 1891).

Fénéon, Félix, 'Quelques peintres idéistes', *Chat noir*, 10 (19 September 1891).

Fénéon, Félix, *Au delà de l'impressionisme*, ed. Françoise Cachin (Paris, 1966).

Fermigier, André, *Pierre Bonnard* (Paris, 1969; English edition, New York, 1969, London, 1970).

Flam, Jack, *Matisse. The Man and His Art, 1869–1918* (New York, 1986).

Flam, Jack, ed., *Matisse. A Retrospective* (New York, 1988).

Fontainas, André, *Bonnard* (Paris, 1928).

Formes et couleurs, 6, no. 2 (1944), special issue devoted to Bonnard.

Fortunesco, Irina, *Bonnard* (Bucharest, 1980)

Fosca, François, *Bonnard* (Geneva, 1919).

Frèches-Thory, Claire, and Terrasse, Antoine, *The Nabis* (Paris, 1990).

Fridenson, Patrick, *The French Home Front, 1914–1918* (Providence and Oxford, 1992).

Fry, Roger, 'The International Society at the Grafton Gallery', *The Nation* (20 April 1912).

Fry, Roger, 'La Peinture moderne en France', *L'Amour de l'art*, 5, no. 5 (May 1924), pp. 141–60.

Fumet, Stanislas, 'Bonnard comme expression française de la peinture', *Formes et couleurs*, 6, no. 2 (1944).

Gauville, Hervé, 'Bonnard en pleine couleur', *Cahiers du Musée National d'Art Moderne*, 13 (1984), pp. 107–9.

Geffroy, Gustave, 'Bonnard', *La Vie artistique* (1894).

Geffroy, Gustave, 'Pierre Bonnard', *Le Journal* (8 January 1892).

George, Waldemar, 'Le Salon des Indépendants', *L'Amour de l'art*, 4, no. 2 (February 1923), pp. 460–6.

Giambruni, Helen Emery, *Early Bonnard, 1885–1900*, PhD dissertation (University of California, Berkeley, 1983).

Gide, André, 'Promenade au Salon d'Automne', *Gazette des beaux-arts*, 34 (1 December 1905), pp. 475–85.

Giry, Marcel, *Le Fauvisme: ses origines, son évolution* (Fribourg, 1981; English edition, New York, 1982).

Giverny, André, 'Bonnard', *La France libre*, 6, no. 31 (15 May 1943), pp. 57–61.

Gold, Arthur, and Fizdale, Robert, *Misia* (New York, 1980).

Golding, John, *Cubism. A History and an Analysis* (London, 1968).

Goodman, N., *Languages of Art* (Indianapolis, 1978).

Gordon, D.E., *Modern Art Exhibitions 1900–1916* (Munich, 1974).

Gowing, Lawrence, 'Bonnard and the School of Paris in the Gelman Collection', in *Twentieth-Century Modern Masters. The Jacques and Natasha Gelman Collection*. Exhibition catalogue (New York, 1989, and London, 1990), pp. 18–23.

Green, Christopher, *Cubism and its Enemies* (New Haven and London, 1987).

Greenberg, Clement, ('Pierre Bonnard'), *The Nation*, 164, no. 2 (11 January 1947), p. 53.

Grenier, Jean, 'Bonnard: peintre de la couleur pure', *La Galerie des arts*, no. 41 (February 1967), pp. 8–13.

Guéguen, Pierre, 'Bonnard l'enchanteur', *XXe siècle*, no. 2 (May–June 1938), pp. 3–8.

Haftmann, Werner, *Painting in the Twentieth Century*, 2 vols. (New York, 1960).

Hahnloser-Buhler, Hédy, *Félix Vallotton et ses amis* (Paris, 1936).

Halperin, Joan Ungersma, *Félix Fénéon, Aesthete and Anarchist in Fin-de-Siècle Paris* (New Haven, 1988).
Hamilton, G.H., *Painting and Sculpture in Europe, 1880–1940* (London, 1967).
Havard, H., *La Décoration*, 2nd edition (Paris, 1892).
Heilbrun, F., and Néagu, P., *Pierre Bonnard Photographe* (Paris, 1987).
Herbert, R.L. (ed.), *Neo-Impressionists and Nabis in the Collection of Arthur G. Altschul* (New Haven, 1965).
Herbert, R.L. (ed.), *Neo-Impressionism* (New York, 1968).
Hermann, Fritz, *Die Revue blanche und die Nabis*, 2 vols. (Munich, 1959).
Heron, Patrick, *The Changing Forms of Art* (London, 1955).
Hiepe, Richard, *Pierre Bonnard* (Leipzig, 1971).
Hilley, David, *Verlaine. Fixing an Image* (Durham, 1988).
Hobbs, R., *Odilon Redon* (London, 1977).
Holten, R., *L'Art fantastique de Gustave Moreau* (Paris, 1960).
'Hommage à Bonnard', *Arts* (8 August 1947), p. 3.
'Hommage à Pierre Bonnard', *Art et industrie*, no. 7 (Paris, 1947), p. 37.
House, John, *Monet. Nature into Art* (London, 1986).
Humbert, Agnès, *Les Nabis et leur époque* (Geneva, 1954).
Huret, Jules, 'Enquête sur l'evolution litteraire', *Echo de Paris* (3–5 March 1891); reprinted in Stephane Mallarmé, *Oeuvres complètes* (Paris, 1945), p. 869.
Huyghe, R., 'Colour and the Expression of Interior Time in Western Art', in Portmann, A., et al., *Colour Symbolism* (Eranos Excerpts, Zürich, 1977), pp. 129–65.
Hyslop, F.E. (ed), *Henri Evenepoel à Paris lettres choisies, 1892–1899* (Brussels, 1971).
Ives, Colta, 'Pierre Bonnard: Place Clichy', in *The Metropolitan Museum of Art Recent Acquisitions: A Selection, 1987–1988* (New York, 1988), p. 41 (A).
Ives, Colta, 'The Little Laundress', *The Metropolitan Museum of Art Bulletin* (Summer 1988) (B).
Ives, Colta, Giambruni, Helen, and Newman, Sasha M., *Pierre Bonnard: The Graphic Art*. Exhibition catalogue (The Metropolitan Museum of Art, New York, 1989).
Jakowski, Anatole, 'Interviews et opinions: Bonnard', *Arts de France*, 11–12 (1947), pp. 27–31.
Jamot, Paul, 'Le Salon d'Automne', *Gazette des beaux-arts*, 36 (December 1906), pp. 456–84.
Januszczak, Waldemar (ed.), *Techniques of the World's Great Painters* (Oxford, 1980).
Jarry, Alfred, 'Paul Verlaine Parallèlement, illustré par Pierre Bonnard', *La Revue Blanche*, 24 (15 February 1901), p. 317.
Jedlicka, Gotthard, *Pierre Bonnard. Ein Besuch* (Erlenbach-Zurich, 1949).
Jirat-Wasiulynski, V., *Gauguin in the Context of Symbolism*, PhD dissertation (Princeton University, 1975).
Josipovici, Gabriel, *Contre-Jour* (London, 1986).
Jourdain, Francis, *Bonnard ou Les Vertus de la liberté* (Geneva, 1946).
Joyes, C., et al., *Monet at Giverny* (London, 1975).
Kaposy, Véronique, 'Une Feuille de croquis de Pierre Bonnard', *Bulletin du Musée Hongrois des Beaux-Arts*, 44 (1975), pp. 123ff.
Kearns, James, 'Bonnard/Matisse Correspondance 1925–1946', *French Studies*, 47, no. 2 (April 1993), p. 236.
Klingsor, Tristan, 'Pierre Bonnard', *L'Amour de l'art*, 2, no. 8 (August 1921), pp. 241–6.
Kober, Jacques, 'Hommage', in *Derrière le miroir*. Exhibition catalogue (Galerie Maeght, Paris, February–March 1947).
Kochno, B., *Diaghilev and the Ballets Russes* (New York, 1970).
Komanecky, Michael, and Butera, Virginia Fabbri, *The Folding Image: Screens by Western Artists of the Nineteenth and Twentieth Centuries*. Exhibition catalogue (Yale University Art Gallery, New Haven, 1984).
Kono, T., and Okada, T., *Bonnard* (Tokyo, 1978).
Kostenevich, Albert, and Semyonova, Natalia, *Collecting Matisse*, translated by Andrew Bromfield (Paris, 1993).
Laprade, Pierre, 'Bonnard', *Les Marges*, 50 (17 June 1914).
Laprade, Jacques de, *Bonnard* (Paris, 1946).
Laprade, Jacques de, 'Gravures, illustrations, dessins de Pierre Bonnard', *Formes et couleurs*, 6 (1944), pp. 50–62.
Lasting Impressions. American Painters in France 1865–1915. Exhibition catalogue (Musée Américain, Giverny, 1992).
Leach, Eleanor Winsor, *Vergil's Eclogues. Landscapes of Experience* (Ithaca and London, 1974).
Lehman, A., *The Symbolist Aesthetic in France 1885–1895* (Oxford, 1950).
Lethève, J., *Daily Life of French Artists in the Nineteenth Century* (London, 1972).
Levine, Stephen Z., *Monet and His Critics* (New York and London, 1976).
Leymarie, Jean, 'Présence de Bonnard', *L'Amour de l'art*, 26, no. 9 (1946), pp. 264–6.
Lhote, André, *Bonnard. Seize peintures 1894–1946* (Paris, 1948).
Loeb, Pierre, 'Pierre Bonnard, peintre français', *L'Age nouveau*, 19 (1947), pp. 29–32.
Loevgren, S., *The Genesis of Modernism* (Indiana, 1971).
Liberman, Alexander, 'Bonnard', *Vogue*, 128 (1 October 1956), pp. 136–9.
Liberman, Alexander, *The Artist in his Studio* (New York, 1960).
Longus, *Daphnis et Chloé*, illustrated by Bonnard (Paris, 1902).
Longus, *Daphnis and Chloe*, translated and introduced by Paul Turner (unexpurgated version, London, 1968).
Lugné-Poe, *La Parade: Le Sot du tremplin. Souvenirs et impressions de théâtre* (Paris, 1930).
Lugné-Poe, *La Parade: Acrobates. Souvenirs et impressions de théâtre (1894–1902)* (Paris, 1932).
Lynton, Norbert, 'Bonnard: The Act of Re-Creation', *Studio International*, 172 (July 1966), pp. 34–6.
Lynton, Norbert, *The Story of Modern Art* (Oxford, 1980).
Makarius, Michel, 'Bonnard et Proust. Les Couleurs du temps retrouvé', *Cahiers d'art moderne* (Paris, 1984), pp.110–13.
Mallarmé, Stephane, *Oeuvres complètes* (Paris, 1945).
Mann, Sargy, *Drawings by Bonnard*. Exhibition catalogue (Nottingham, 1984).
Mann, Sargy, *Bonnard Drawings* (London, 1991).
Marlais, Michael, 'Conservative Style/Conservative Politics: Maurice Denis in Le Vesinet', *Art History*, 16, no. 1 (March 1993).
Martini, Alberto, 'Gli inizi difficili di Pierre Bonnard', *Arte antica e moderna*, 1 (1958), pp. 255–79.
Marx, Roger, 'L'Art décoratif et les "Symbolistes"', *Le Voltaire* (23 August 1892).
Masuda, Y., *Bonnard* (Tokyo, 1932).
Masuda, Y., 'Les Indépendants', *Le Voltaire* (28 March 1893).
Mauner, George L., *The Nabis. Their History and Their Art, 1888–1896* (London, 1978).
Meier-Graefe, Julius, 'Bonnard', *Art News*, 37 (31 December 1938), pp. 8–9.
Mellerio, André, 'Exposition: les éditions Vollard', *L'Estampe et l'affiche*, 3 (1899), pp. 98–9.
Milner, John, *The Studios of Paris* (New Haven and London, 1988).
Munch et la France. Exhibition catalogue (Musée d'Orsay, Paris, and Musée Munch, Oslo, 1992).
Nansen, Peter, *Marie* (Paris, 1898).
Natanson, Thadée, 'IXe exposition de la Société des Artistes Indépendants', *La Revue Blanche*, 4 (April 1893), pp. 139–46.
Natanson, Thadée, 'Pierre Bonnard', *La Revue Blanche*, 10 (15 January 1896), pp. 71–4.
Natanson, Thadée, *Le Bonnard que je propose 1867–1947* (Geneva, 1951).
Negri, Renata, *Bonnard e i Nabis* (Milan, 1970).
Newman, Sasha M. (ed.), *Bonnard* (New York and London, 1984) (A).
Newman, Sasha M. (ed.), 'Bonnard 1900–1920', *Cahiers du Musée National d'Art Moderne*, 13 (1984), pp. 96–105 (B).
Olivier, Fernande, *Picasso et ses amis* (Paris, 1933).
Oppler, E.C., *Fauvism Re-examined*, PhD dissertation (Columbia University, New York, 1979).
Pérez, Annie, 'Entretiens avec Diana Verny', in *Pierre Bonnard*, Les Grandes Expositions, Beaux-Arts Magazine (Paris, 1984).
Perman, R.C.D. (ed.), *Verlaine. Selected Poems* (Oxford, 1965).
Perucchi-Petri, Ursula, *Die Nabis und Japan. Das Fruhwerk von Bonnard, Vuillard und Denis* (Munich, 1976).
Phillips, Duncan, *A Collection in the Making* (New York, 1926).
Phillips, Duncan, *A 'Pierre Bonnard', The Kenyon Review*, 11 (autumn 1949), pp. 561–6.
Phillips, Marjorie, *Duncan Phillips and his Collection* (Boston and Toronto, 1970).
Pissarro, Camille, *Lettres à son fils Lucien* (Paris, 1950).
Proust, Marcel, *Remembrance of Things Past*, translated by C.K. Scott Moncrieff and Terence Kilmartin (London, 1983).
Puy, Michel, *L'Effort des peintres modernes* (Paris, 1933).
Rearick, Charles, *Pleasures of the Belle Epoque. Entertainment and Festivity in Turn-of-the Century France* (New Haven and London, 1985).
Renoir. Exhibition catalogue (Arts Council of Great Britain, Hayward Gallery, London, 1985).
Rewald, John, *Pierre Bonnard*. Exhibition catalogue (The Museum of Modern Art, New York, in collaboration with The Cleveland Museum of Art, 1948).
Richardson, John, *Georges Braques* (London, 1959).
Richardson, John, *A Life of Picasso*, vol. 1, *1881–1906* (London, 1991).
Robichez, Jacques, *Le Symbolisme au théâtre. Lugné-Poe et les débuts de l'Oeuvre* (Paris, 1957).
Roger-Marx, Claude, 'Bonnard: Illustrateur et lithographe', *Art et décoration*, 43 (1923).
Roger-Marx, Claude, *Pierre Bonnard* (Paris, 1924).
Roger-Marx, Claude, *Bonnard* (Paris, 1950).
Roger-Marx, Claude, *Bonnard lithographe* (Monte Carlo, 1952).
Rookmaaker, H.R., *Gauguin and 19th Century Art Theory* (Amsterdam, 1972).
Rudenstine, Angelica Zander, *The Guggenheim Museum Collection: Paintings 1880–1945*, vol. 1 (New York, 1976).

Rumpel, Heinrich, *Bonnard* (Bern, 1952).
Russell, John, *The Meanings of Modern Art* (New York, 1981).
Rydbeck, Ingrid, 'Hos Bonnard i Deauville', *Konstrevy*, 13, no. 4 (Stockholm, 1937).
Scènes de la Seine. Exhibition catalogue (Rouen, 1986).
Sert, Misia, *Misia* (Paris, 1952).
Sérusier, Paul, *ABC de la Peinture* (Paris, 1942).
Shattuck, R., *The Banquet Years* (London, 1969).
Shiff, R.A., *Impressionist Criticism, Impressionist Color and Cézanne*, PhD dissertation (Yale University, New Haven, 1973).
Signac, Paul, *D'Eugène Delacroix au Néo-Impressionisme* (Paris, 1899, reprinted, Françoise Cachin, ed., Paris, 1964).
Silver, Kenneth E., *Esprit de Corps. The Art of the Parisian Avant-Garde and the First World War, 1914–1925* (London, 1989).
Soby, James Thrall, 'Last of the Impressionists: Pierre Bonnard', *Town and Country*, 102 (19 May 1948).
Soby, James Thrall, et al., *Bonnard and His Environment*. Exhibition catalogue (The Museum of Modern Art, New York, 1964).
Spalding, F., *Roger Fry. Art and Life* (London, 1980).
Spate, Virginia, *The Colour of Time. Claude Monet* (London, 1992).
Stein, Gertrude, *The Autobiography of Alice B. Toklas* (New York, 1933).
Stein, Leo, *Appreciation. Painting, Poetry and Prose* (New York, 1947).
Sterling, Charles, 'Bonnard', *L'Amour de l'art*, 14, no. 4 (April 1933).
Sutton, Denys, *Bonnard, 1867–1947*, (London, 1957).
Sutton, Denys, *Pierre Bonnard, 1867–1947*. Exhibition catalogue (Royal Academy, London, 1966).
Terrasse, Antoine, *Pierre Bonnard* (Paris, 1967 and 1988).
Terrasse, Antoine, 'Le Dessin de Bonnard', *L'Oeil*, no. 167 (November 1968), pp. 10–17.
Terrasse, Antoine, *Bonnard Posters and Lithographs* (New York, 1970).
Terrasse, Antoine, *Pierre Bonnard* (revised edition, Paris, 1988).
Terrasse, Antoine, *Pierre Bonnard Illustrateur* (Paris, 1988); English edition, *Pierre Bonnard Illustrator. A Catalogue raisonné*, translated from the French by Jean-Marie Clarke (London, 1989).
Terrasse, Charles, *Bonnard* (Paris, 1927).
Terrasse, Charles, 'Maisons de campagne de Bonnard', *Formes et couleurs*, 6, no. 2 (1944), pp. 27–38.
Terrasse, Charles, 'La Vie des musées: nouvelles acquisitions du Musée National d'Art Moderne, "L'Amandier en fleur" de Bonnard', *La Revue du Louvre et des musées de France*, 14, no. 3 (1964).
Terrasse, Charles, 'Recollections of Bonnard', *Apollo*, 83 (January 1966), pp. 62–7.
Terrasse, Michel, *Bonnard at Le Cannet* (London, 1988).
Thomson, Belinda, *The Post-Impressionists* (Oxford, 1983).
Thomson, Belinda, *Vuillard* (Oxford, 1988).
Thomson, Richard, *Degas and Nudes* (London, 1988).
Toulouse-Lautrec. Exhibition catalogue (Hayward Gallery, London, 1991, and Galerie Nationale du Grand Palais, Paris, 1992).
Twentieth-Century Modern Masters. The Jacques and Natasha Gelman Collection. Exhibition catalogue (The Metropolitan Museum of Art, New York, and The Royal Academy of Arts, London, 1989–90).
Vaillant, Annette, *Bonnard* (Neuchâtel,1965; English edition, London, 1966).
Vauxcelles, Louis, 'Le Salon d'Automne', *Gils Blas* (17 October 1905).
Vauxcelles, Louis, 'La Vie artistique: Le Salon d'Automne: peintres et sculpteurs', *L'Amour de l'art*, 1, no. 6 (October 1920), pp. 205–13.
Verkade, Dom Willibrod, *Le Tourment de Dieu* (Paris, 1923).
Verlaine, Paul, *Sagesse* (Paris, 1881).
Verlaine, Paul, *Parallèlement* (Paris, 1889); illustrated by Bonnard, Paris, (1900).
Verlaine, Paul, *Oeuvres poétiques complètes* (Paris, 1962).
Verlaine, Paul, *Sagesse, Parallèlement* (Paris, 1977).
Vollard, Ambroise, *Recollections of a Picture Dealer*, translated from the French by Violet M. MacDonald (Boston, 1936; New York, 1978).
Vollard, Ambroise, 'Mes portraits', *Arts et métiers graphiques*, 64 (15 September 1938), pp. 39–44.
Watkins, Nicholas, *Matisse* (Oxford, 1984).
Werth, Leon, *Bonnard* (Paris, 1923).
Whitfield, Sarah, 'Bonnard at the Royal Academy', *The Burlington Magazine*, 108 (February 1966), pp. 105–7.
Weisberg, Gabriel P., 'Pierre Bonnard and Japan', in *Bonnard*. Exhibition catalogue (Tokyo, 1991), pp. 14–16.
Wollheim, Bruno, 'Pierre Bonnard: The Obscure Object of Desire', *Modern Painters*, 4, no. 3 (autumn 1991), pp. 12–15.
Zeldin, T., *France 1848–1945*, 2 vols. (Oxford, 1973 and 1977).
Zervos, Christian, 'Pierre Bonnard est-il un grand peintre?', *Cahiers d'art*, 22 (1947), pp. 1–6.

Photographic acknowledgements

Aberdeen Art Gallery: 141
ARTEPHOT, Paris/Private Collection: 19, 180
ARTEPHOT, Paris/Bibliothèque Nationale: 32, 42
BAL/The Minneapolis Institute of Arts: 137
BAL/Private Collection: 72, 107
BAL/Victoria & Albert Museum, London: 35
The Barnes Foundation © 1995, All Rights Reserved: 84
Museum of Fine Arts: Berne,: 33, 126
Musées Royaux des Beaux-Arts de Belgique, Brussels/photo Speltdoorn: 100, 112
Musée des Beaux-Arts et d'Archéologie, Bésançon: 97
Bibliothèque Nationale, Paris: 39, 47, 92
Musée des Beaux-Arts de Brest: 143
Carnegie Museum of Art, Pittsburgh. Acquired through the generosity of the Sarah Mellon Scaife family, 70.50: 214/215
© 1995 The Art Institute of Chicago. All rights reserved: 110 (Potter Palmer Collection), 209
Sterling and Francine Clark Art Institute, Williamstown, Massachusetts: 26
Giraudon, Paris/Private Collection: 14 (Collection of Mr and Mrs Donald Stralem, New York), 193, 213, 216
Gӧtesburg Kunstmuseum: 87
© Solomon R. Guggenheim Foundation, New York/photo Carmelo Guadagno: 178
Musée de Grenoble: 204/5
Colorphoto Hans Hinz/Öffentliche Kunstsammlung Basle, Kunstmuseum: 202
Hermitage, Lausanne/Photo Routhier: 94
Museum of Fine Arts, Houston. The John A. and Audrey Jones Beck Collection: 115
National Gallery of Ireland, Dublin: 55
Josefowitz Collection: 70
Los Angeles County Museum of Art, Gift of Mr and Mrs Sidney Brody: 95
Fondation Maeght, Saint-Paul-de-Vence/photo Claude Germain: 132/3
Galerie Maeght, Paris: 82, 158/9
© Manchester City Art Galleries: 152
Metropolitan Museum of Art, New York: 41 (The Jacques and Natasha Gelman Collection), 148/9, 223 (Robert Lehman Collection)
Milwaukee Art Museum, Gift of Mr and Mrs Harry Lynde Bradley: 226
Museum of Modern Art, New York: 48 (Gift of Mr and Mrs Allan D. Emil), 177, 228 (Gift of Mr and Mrs David Rockefeller)
Galerie Nathan, Zurich: 86
Niigata City Art Museum, Niigatashi: 110
Kunstsammlung Nordrhein-Westfalen, Düsseldorf: 146/7
The Phillips Collection, Washington DC: 88, 155 (photo Edward Owen), 157, 173
Musée Nationale d'Art Moderne, Centre Georges Pompidou, Paris: 200, 201, 207, 223, 218, 221, 229
Photothèque des Musées de la Ville de Paris: 161, 194
Musée départemental du Prieuré, Saint-Germain-en-Laye: 54, 81, 127
Private Collection: 10, 11 (photo H. Josse, Paris), 12, 13 top and bottom, 17, 20 left (photo Routhier) and right, 27 left (Courtesy of Christie's, London) and right, 37 left, 41, 50, 57, 78, 80, 94 (top), 98, 106, 108, 111, 114, 118, 120, 129, 131, 135, 138 left, 140 (Courtesy of Sotheby's, London), 141 bottom, 146 left, 154, 167, 169, 170, 174 (photo H. Josse, Paris) 179, 184, 185, 186, 187, 188, 190, 191, 196, 198, 203, 206 (photo Gerhard Howald, Switzerland), 224
Reuters Ltd, London: 160
RMN/Musée d'Orsay, Paris: 11 left, 19, 23, 24, 26, 30/31, 49, 51, 60, 64, 74 below, 76, 79, 105, 109 above, 138 right
RMN/Louvre, Paris: 139
By kind permission of the Duke of Roxburghe: 62;
By kind permission of Sir Robert and Lady Sainsbury: 46
SCALA, Milan/Hermitage, St Petersburg: 90, 96, 122/3, 136
SCALA/Pushkin Museum, Moscow: 117, 125
Tate Gallery, London: 163, 166, 175, 183, 197
Fundaçion Coleccion Thyssen-Bornemisza, Madrid: 101;
Musée d'Unterlinden, Colmar
Victoria & Albert Museum, London: 65, 66, 67, 68
National Gallery of Victoria, Melbourne: 71
National Museum of Wales, Cardiff: 124
National Gallery of Art, Washington: 113
Kunsthaus Zurich: 58, 103

The publishers would especially like to thank the following for their kind and invaluable help in the preparation of this publication:
Acquavella Galleries, New York
Christian Neffe and Kate Daniels at JPL Fine Arts, London
Browse & Derby, London
François Daulte; Antoine Terrasse
Wildenstein & Co, New York